# PAUL, *the* PASTORAL EPISTLES, *and the* EARLY CHURCH

# PAUL, *the* PASTORAL EPISTLES, *and the* EARLY CHURCH

James W. Aageson

LIBRARY OF PAULINE STUDIES

Stanley E. Porter, *General Editor*

HENDRICKSON PUBLISHERS

**Paul, the Pastoral Epistles, and the Early Church**

© 2008 by Hendrickson Publishers, Inc.
P. O. Box 3473
Peabody, Massachusetts 01961-3473

ISBN 978-1-59856-041-1

"2 Timothy and Its Theology: In Search of a Theological Pattern," Society of Biblical Literature Seminar Papers 36 (1997): 692–714. (Rearranged, modified, and included in part of chapter 2 in the book. Used with permission.)

"The Pastoral Epistles, Apostolic Authority, and the Development of the Pauline Scriptures," in *The Pauline Canon* (ed. Stanley E. Porter; vol. 1, Pauline Studies; Leiden and Boston: Brill, 2004), 5–26. (Rearranged, modified, and included in part of chapter 4 in the book. Used with permission.)

*Printed in the United States of America*

*First Printing — January 2008*

**Library of Congress Cataloging-in-Publication Data**

Aageson, James W., 1947–
    Paul, the Pastoral Epistles, and the early church / James W. Aageson.
        p. cm.—(Library of Pauline studies)
    Includes bibliographical references and indexes.
    ISBN-13: 978-1-59856-041-1 (alk. paper)
    1. Church history—Primitive and early church, ca. 30–600.  2. Paul, the Apostle, Saint.  3. Bible. N.T. Pastoral Epistles—Theology.  4. Bible. N.T. Epistles of Paul—Theology.  I. Title.
    BR162.3.A24 2007
    227′.830609015—dc22
                                    2007027570

With deep respect and appreciation, I dedicate this book to very important teachers in my life.

Paul J. Achtemeier
Terence E. Fretheim
Anthony E. Harvey
Philip A. Nordquist
Daniel J. Simundson
David L. Tiede
Geza Vermes

# TABLE OF CONTENTS

# Acknowledgments

EVERY AUTHOR of a scholarly book is indebted to a great many people, and that is especially true in my case. To all who have contributed to the body of literature on this topic, I deeply appreciate your effort, your insights, and your arguments. May this book be worthy of your contributions. To my colleagues at Concordia College in Moorhead, Minnesota, thank you for reading, critiquing, and assisting me with various sections of the manuscript. May this book be a credit to our collective work as a department. To my colleagues from other institutions who have heard my presentations and responded with questions and comments, thank you for stimulating my thinking and where necessary refocusing my arguments. But above all, this project has depended on the love and dedication of my wife, Julie, and our family. Thank you for your unwavering encouragement.

# ABBREVIATIONS

## GENERAL

C.E.          Common Era
gk. frg.      Greek fragments
SBL           Society of Biblical Literature

## BIBLE TEXTS AND VERSIONS

NRSV          New Revised Standard Version
NT            New Testament
OT            Old Testament

## APOSTOLIC FATHERS

*1 Clem.*        *1 Clement*
Ign. *Eph.*      Ignatius, *To the Ephesians*
Ign. *Magn.*     Ignatius, *To the Magnesians*
Ign. *Phld.*     Ignatius, *To the Philadelphians*
Ign. *Pol.*      Ignatius, *To Polycarp*
Ign. *Rom.*      Ignatius, *To the Romans*
Ign. *Smyrn.*    Ignatius, *To the Smyrnaeans*
Ign. *Trall.*    Ignatius, *To the Trallians*
Pol. *Phil.*     Polycarp, *To the Philippians*

## NEW TESTAMENT APOCRYPHA

*Acts Paul*      *Acts of Paul*

# PATRISTIC LITERATURE

Clement of Alexandria
| | |
|---|---|
| *Paed.* | *Paedagogus* |
| *Protrept.* | *Protrepticus* |
| *Strom.* | *Stromata* |

Cyprian
| | |
|---|---|
| *Dom. or.* | *De dominica oratione* |
| *Eleem.* | *De opere et eleemosynis* |
| *Fort.* | *Ad Fortunatum* |
| *Hab. virg.* | *De habitu virginum* |
| *[Idol.]* | *Quod idola dii non sint* |
| *Laps.* | *De lapsis* |
| *Mort.* | *De mortalitate* |
| *Pat.* | *De bono patientiae* |
| *Test.* | *Ad Quirinum testimonia adversus Judaeos* |
| *Unit. eccl.* | *De catholicae ecclesiae unitate* |

Eusebius
| | |
|---|---|
| *Hist. eccl.* | *Historia ecclesiastica* |
| *Virg.* | *De virginibus velandis* |

Irenaus
| | |
|---|---|
| *Haer.* | *Adversus haereses* |

Origen
| | |
|---|---|
| *Cels.* | *Contra Celsum* |
| *Princ.* | *De principiis* |

Tertullian
| | |
|---|---|
| *Bapt.* | *De baptismo* |
| *Carn. Chr.* | *De carne Christi* |
| *Praescr.* | *De praescriptione haereticorum* |
| *Prax.* | *Adversus Praxean* |
| *Pud.* | *De pudicitia* |
| *Res.* | *De reurrectione carnis* |

# SECONDARY SOURCES

| | |
|---|---|
| *ABD* | *Anchor Bible Dictionary* |
| *ABR* | *Australian Biblical Review* |
| AnBib | Analecta biblica |
| *AThR* | *Anglican Theological Review* |
| BBET | Beiträge zur biblischen Exegese und Theologie |
| BDAG | Bauer, W., F. W. Danker, W. F. Arndt, and F. W. Gingrich. *Greek-English Lexicon of the New Testament and Other Early Christian Literature.* 3d ed. Chicago, 2000 |
| BHT | Beiträge zur historischen Theologie |

| | |
|---|---|
| *CBQ* | *Catholic Biblical Quarterly* |
| *HBT* | *Horizons in Biblical Theology* |
| *JBL* | *Journal of Biblical Literature* |
| *JECS* | *Journal of Early Christian Studies* |
| *JETS* | *Journal of the Evangelical Theological Society* |
| *JSNT* | *Journal for the Study of the New Testament* |
| JSNTSup | Journal for the Study of the New Testament: Supplement Series |
| NovTSup | Supplements to Novum Testamentum |
| *NTS* | *New Testament Studies* |
| *PRSt* | *Perspectives in Religious Studies* |
| PTS | Patristische Texte und Studien |
| SBLDS | Society of Biblical Literature Dissertation Series |
| SBLMS | Society of Biblical Literature Monograph Series |
| SBLSymS | Society of Biblical Literature Symposium Series |
| *SecCent* | *Second Century* |
| *SJT* | *Scottish Journal of Theology* |
| SNTMS | Society for New Testament Studies Monograph Series |
| StPatr | Studia Patristica |
| *Them* | *Themelios* |
| *TynBul* | *Tyndale Bulletin* |
| *VC* | *Vigiliae christianae* |

# ◂ 1 ▸

# PAUL, THE PASTORAL EPISTLES, AND THE PAULINE LEGACY

## INTRODUCTION

PAUL'S INFLUENCE on the history of Christian life and theology is as profound as it is pervasive. A brief survey of almost twenty centuries of Christian thought and practice will confirm the enduring importance of Paul for the life of the church in the Roman and Protestant traditions of the West, as well as the Orthodox traditions of the East. Even as Christianity, at the dawn of its third millennium, has become increasingly global and traditions have come to develop and intersect in new and complex ways, Paul's place in the story of Christianity remains deeply rooted in the church's theology, worship, and pastoral life. In both past and present, Paul's influence on the Christian church can hardly be overestimated.

Among the many intriguing issues generated by the historical Paul, his New Testament letters, and early church history is the question, "What happened to Paul after Paul?" Whether we think in terms of the reception of Paul's theology, or the ongoing legacy of Paul, or early Christian reinterpretation of his letters, a number of important questions persist. What did the early church do with Paul's memory? How did it reshape his theology? What role did his letters come to play in the life of the church? This book focuses on how these issues played out in the early decades and centuries of Christianity, a time when the memory and legacy of Paul came to serve varied and often competing interests. It was a time when Paul's reputation and his importance to the church were reinforced and when his epistles gained the authority that would ensure their place among the sacred texts of Christianity. It was also the time when the burgeoning Jesus movement forged itself into Christianity. In this process Paul played a pivotal role and eventually also became an object of revision and transformation himself. What is virtually indisputable is that Paul and his letters, during his lifetime and after, played a critical role in making Christianity what it was to become.

If the image of Paul and the theology of his letters were thoroughly interwoven in the early church, as they undoubtedly were, the adaptation of Paul and his words by the early Christians was more than an issue of simple textual reinterpretation. It was also a matter of an evolving Pauline image merging with the developing concerns of the day, where the words and ideas of the apostle came to bear on the circumstances and conflicts of the church. Paul's personal authority continued to inform this process and his legacy endured through the ongoing reinterpretation of his letters. All the while, the Christian church continued to grow in size, develop as an institution, and mature theologically.

## THE PASTORALS AND PAUL'S LEGACY

The Pastoral Epistles and the images of Paul represented in them have an important place in the symbolic and ecclesiological matrix of early Pauline tradition. They also contributed in significant ways to the development of this tradition. Contrary to the position taken by some scholars, the developing mainstream of Christianity did not reject Paul.[1] Rather, the re-imaging of the apostle Paul and the echoes of his theology over the early decades and centuries of Christianity illustrate the church's complex, and most often conflicted, development as a diverse social and religious movement. From the early attempts to define Christian orthodoxy, to Marcionites and gnostics, and on to the countercultural movements of early Christian women and martyrs reflected in the *Acts of Paul and Thecla*, the apostle was valorized as an authority figure and wonder-worker. His letters were cited and alluded to, and his legacy often burst forth in new and unanticipated ways. The reception of Paul and his letters in the church was exceedingly complex, diverse, and uneven. There is rarely a straight-line to be drawn in this history. The Pastorals represent only one part of this complex Pauline tale, and it is this aspect of the story, to the middle of the third century when the church began to confront a new set of troubling issues, that is the focus of the discussion that follows.

In the case of the Pastoral Epistles, we are able to see how one part of the early church responded to the problem of *incorrect* belief and practice (heterodoxy and heteropraxy), to the church's relationship with Jews and the Jewish law, and to what some saw as a problematic form of Christian asceticism. Already in 1 Timothy and Titus we see an emerging sense of church order expressed in the writer's concern for the qualities appropriate for overseers, deacons, and elders, identified as leaders in the church. In 2 Timothy we can hear the call for Timothy to suffer as Paul has suffered, a

---

[1] Martinus C. DeBoer underscores the point that some scholars (e.g., Adolf Harnack and Walter Bauer) have found a striking Pauline silence, even a rejection of Paul, in early mainstream forms of Christianity, whereas others (e.g., Andreas Lindemann) think this is not the case, "Comment: Which Paul," in *Paul and the Legacies of Paul* (ed. William S. Babcock; Dallas: Southern Methodist University Press, 1990), 45–46.

message sure to resonate among those in the early church who would be called upon to suffer for their faith in Christ. Confronted with disunity that threatened to tear the church apart, the Pastorals reflect an effort to unite the church in the face of both internal and external threats.

Despite the absence of the Pastorals from $\mathfrak{P}^{46}$ and Codex Vaticanus in the manuscript tradition, we are able to detect in these three letters a sense of the Pauline writings as Scripture, perhaps even the early functioning of a Pauline canon.[2] Even more to the point, the plea to Timothy to guard the "good deposit" foreshadows the church's debates about the relationship between Scripture and tradition and also the role of the church, represented by its bishops and theologians, as the bearer and protector of the truth. In retrospect, we can see that the Pastorals reflect many of the issues that would confront the church in the early centuries: the character of the truth and true faith, the relationship of Christians to Jews and things Jewish, Christian asceticism, the threat of disunity, the formation and functioning of a canon, the balance between Scripture and tradition, the place of women, and the role of the church represented by episcopal hierarchy in preserving the faith and practice of the *true church*. As we look at the Pastoral letters in relation to this development of the church more broadly, we are able to see quite clearly how the figure of Paul served to confront crucial issues of the emerging church with the apostolic authority that had accrued to him and his teaching.

## SCHOLARSHIP: PAUL AND THE PASTORALS

It will be helpful to identify a number of the important areas of scholarship related to the Pastorals and the development of early Pauline tradition. The intent here is not to provide an exhaustive treatment of scholarship on the Pastorals but rather to provide a sketch of the scholarship important for the arguments developed later in the book.

### The Pastorals and Pauline Authorship

In addition to the large body of commentary literature on the Pastoral Epistles, there are numerous monographs that focus primarily on exegetical aspects of these three letters, their place in the scope of Pauline theology and

---

[2] Raymond F. Collins, *1 and 2 Timothy and Titus: A Commentary* (New Testament Library; Louisville: Westminster John Knox, 2002), 1; Luke Timothy Johnson, *The First and Second Letters to Timothy* (Anchor Bible 35A; New York: Doubleday, 2001), 16–18; and Jerome D. Quinn and William C. Wacker, *The First and Second Letters to Timothy* (Eerdmans Critical Commentary; Grand Rapids: Eerdmans, 2000), 3–4.

tradition, and their role as pseudepigraphic documents.[3] For example, Lewis Donelson has focused explicitly on the character of pseudepigraphy and ethical argument in the Pastoral Epistles.[4] Margaret Y. MacDonald has looked at the institutionalization of the Pauline writings from a socio-historical point of view,[5] whereas Frances Young has focused exclusively on the theology of the Pastoral Epistles.[6] James D. Miller has recently revived a version of the composite document theory of the Pastorals,[7] while Luke Timothy Johnson has challenged many of the traditional assumptions used to argue against Pauline authorship.[8] Still others have focused on letter writing and the rhetoric of the Pastorals.[9] More specifically, Gerhard Lohfink, Peter Trummer, and J. Christiaan Beker have examined Pauline theology and tradition in the Pastorals.[10]

The critical issue that runs, either directly or indirectly, through a number of these works as well as through the body of commentary literature, is the question of Pauline authorship. For most modern critical scholars, that question has been largely settled for some time. The linguistic and

---

[3] For a survey of recent scholarship on the Pastorals see Collins, *1 & 2 Timothy and Titus*, 2–5; Johnson, *First and Second Letters to Timothy*, 55–90; I. Howard Marshall, "Recent Study of the Pastoral Epistles," *Them* 23 (1997): 3–21; Quinn and Wacker, *First and Second Letters to Timothy*, 18–22.

[4] Lewis R. Donelson, *Pseudepigrapha and Ethical Argument in the Pastoral Epistles* (Tübingen: J. C. B. Mohr [Paul Siebeck], 1986).

[5] Margaret Y. MacDonald, *The Pauline Churches: A Socio-Historical Study of Institutionalization in Pauline and Deutero-Pauline Writings* (SNTSMS 60; Cambridge: Cambridge University Press, 1988).

[6] Frances Young, *The Theology of the Pastoral Letters* (New Testament Theology; Cambridge: University Press, 1994). Cf. also Jouette M. Bassler, "A Plethora of Epiphanies: Christology in the Pastoral Letters," *Princeton Seminary Bulletin* 17, no. 3 (1996): 310–25 and Lorenz Oberlinner, "Die 'Epiphaneia' des Heilswillens Gottes in Christus Jesus: Zur Grundstruktur der Christologie der Pastoralbriefe," *Zeitschrift für die neutestamentliche Wissenschaft und die Kunde der älteren Kirche* 71 (1980): 192–213.

[7] James D. Miller, *The Pastoral Letters as Composite Documents* (SNTSMS 93; Cambridge: Cambridge University Press, 1997).

[8] Johnson, *First and Second Letters to Timothy*, 78–97; and Luke Timothy Johnson, *Letters to Paul's Delegates: 1 Timothy, 2 Timothy, Titus* (The New Testament in Context; Valley Forge: Trinity, 1996), 19–32.

[9] See. e.g., Michael Prior, *Paul the Letter-Writer: And the Second Letter to Timothy* (JSNTSup, 23; Sheffield: JSOT Press, 1989).

[10] Gerhard Lohfink, "Paulinische Theologie in der Rezeption der Pastoralbriefe," in *Paulus in den Neutestamentlichen Spätschriften: zur Paulusrezeption im Neuen Testament* (Questiones disputatae 89; Freiburg: Herder, 1981), 70–121; Peter Trummer, *Die Paulustradition der Pastoralbriefe* (BBET 8; Frankfurt: Peter Lang, 1978); and J. Christiaan Beker, *Heirs of Paul: Paul's Legacy in the New Testament and in the Church Today* (Minneapolis: Fortress, 1991). Cf. also E. Earle Ellis "Traditions in the Pastoral Epistles" in *Early Jewish and Christian Exegesis: Studies in Memory of William Hugh Brownlee* (ed. Craig A. Evans and William F. Stinespring; Atlanta: Scholars Press, 1987), 237–53; Philip H. Towner, "Pauline Theology or Pauline Tradition in the Pastoral Epistles: The Question of Method," *TynBul* 46 (1995): 291–300; and B. Paul Wolfe, "Scripture in the Pastoral Epistles: Premarcion Marcionism," *PRSt* 16 (1989): 5–16.

theological dissimilarities with the seven undisputed Pauline letters, as well as the difficulty of situating these three letters in the chronology of Paul's ministry, raised for many scholars the prospect of the Pastoral's pseudepigraphic character. The new and seemingly more developed sense of church structure, authority, and leadership reflected in the Pastorals also appeared to confirm their dating after the death of Paul, perhaps as late as sometime in the second century. Likewise, the issues of Gentile inclusion and righteousness by faith, so important in Paul's epistles to the Galatians and the Romans, appeared to be much more subdued and to have lost much of their urgency in the Pastorals. Taken together, these considerations prompted most modern scholars to conclude that, despite the fact that Paul is the named author of these three epistles, it is most likely that they were written by someone other than Paul.[11] To be sure, not all subscribed to the majority view, but for many scholars the non-Pauline authorship of the Pastorals became virtually axiomatic.

For some who continued to maintain Pauline authorship, the question of authorship had theological implications, since the idea that someone other than Paul could have written these letters seemed to contradict what the letters themselves actually say. From a conservative theological perspective, this could be thought problematic. More recently, Luke Timothy Johnson and others, unpersuaded by the traditional arguments for non-Pauline authorship, have sought to challenge the seeming consensus and reopen the question. As a result, a group was formed in the Society of Biblical Literature in the 1990's to address this and other related issues. Even if this has not in the end altered the majority view, it is still healthy to have assumptions reconsidered and scholarly canons challenged. It is also a reminder not to presume too quickly that the critical issues related to the study of Paul are necessarily settled.

In the present investigation, the question of authorship will be neither the centerpiece of the discussion nor argued directly, but it will be considered more generally in terms of a comparison of literary and theological patterns. One of the interesting possibilities to come from this is the prospect that the author of 1 Timothy and Titus might not have been the person who wrote 2 Timothy. Furthermore, as we will argue, the epistle to the Philippians appears to be the linchpin in considering the relationship between 2 Timothy and the other two Pastoral letters. When all of this is considered it still seems that the evidence leans in the direction of the non-Pauline authorship of the Pastorals whether all three of them were written by the same author or not.

## Paul and the Early Church

William Schoedel, in his commentary on the letters of Ignatius, has explored the influence of the Pauline letters and their theology on the

---

[11] See the discussion of these issues and related bibliography below, especially pp. 86–89.

Bishop, and in this commentary, he pays particular attention to the influence of 1 and 2 Timothy and Titus.[12] Regarding Polycarp and the Pastorals, Hans von Campenhausen argued that Polycarp is the author of the Pastoral Epistles.[13] But while there can be no doubting the links between Polycarp's letter to the Philippians and the Pastorals, the claim of common authorship is not finally persuasive. Donald Hagner and James Carleton Paget have also examined the use of Pauline material in Clement of Rome and the *Epistle of Barnabas*.[14] More broadly, Andreas Lindemann has investigated the legacy of Paul, his letters, and theology in the early church to the time of Marcion, including the Pastorals.[15] Rolf Noormann in turn has written a major work focusing on the reception of the Pauline letters in Irenaeus.[16] Similarly, Richard Norris has addressed Irenaeus' use of Paul specifically in his debate with the gnostics.[17] Robert Sider has written on the figure of Paul in Tertullian,[18] and David Rankin has focused more narrowly on Tertullian's use of the Pastoral Epistles in his doctrine of ministry.[19]

With the exception of Rankin and Campenhausen, these authors all consider the full corpus of Pauline letters, and the influence of the Pastorals is only part of the reception of Paul's epistles more generally. Whereas the question of Pauline authorship of the Pastorals focuses attention back to the historical Paul, the issues addressed here center attention on the legacy of Paul and the reception of his letters in the post-Pauline period of the early church. This makes clear that the Pastoral Epistles are close to the balance

---

[12] William R. Schoedel, *Ignatius of Antioch: A Commentary on the Letters of Ignatius of Antioch* (Hermeneia; Philadelphia: Fortress, 1985), 9–10.

[13] Hans von Campenhausen, "Polykarp von Smyrna und die Pastoralbriefe," in *Aus der Frühzeit des Christentums: Studien zur Kirchengeschichte des ersten und zweiten Jahrhunderts* (Tübingen: J. C. B. Mohr [Paul Siebeck], 1963), 197–252.

[14] Donald A. Hagner, *The Use of the Old and New Testaments in Clement of Rome* (Supplements to Novum Testamentum 34; Leiden: E. J.: Brill, 1973) and James Carleton Paget, "Paul and the Epistle of Barnabas," *NovT* 38 (1996): 359–81.

[15] Andreas Lindemann, *Paulus im ältesten Christentum: Das Bild des Apostels und die Rezeption der paulinischen Theologie in der frühchristlichen Literatur bis Marcion* (BHT 58; Tübingen: J. C. B. Mohr (Paul Siebeck), 1979); and also Anthony J. Blasi, *Making Charisma: The Social Construction of Paul's Public Image* (New Brunswick: Transaction, 1991). Cf. Charles Merritt Nielson, "Polycarp, Paul, and the Scriptures," *AThR* 47 (1965): 199–216.

[16] Rolf Noormann, *Irenäus als Paulus interpret: Zur Rezeption und Wirkung der paulinischen und deuteropaulinischen Briefe im Werk des Irenäus von Lyon* (WUNT 2; Tübingen: J. C. B. Mohr [Paul Siebeck] 1994).

[17] Richard A. Norris, Jr. "Irenaeus' Use of Paul in His Polemics Against the Gnostics," in *Paul and the Legacies of Paul* (ed. William S. Babcock; Dallas: Southern Methodist University Press, 1990), 79–98.

[18] Robert D. Sider, "Literary Artifice and the Figure of Paul in the Writings of Tertullian," in *Paul and the Legacies of Paul* (ed. William S. Babcock; Dallas: Southern Methodist University Press, 1990), 99–120.

[19] David Rankin, "Tertullian's Use of the Pastoral Epistles in His Doctrine of Ministry," *ABR* 32 (1984): 18–37.

point between the historical Paul on the one hand and the Pauline legacy on the other, and the decision about authorship simply moves the Pastorals from one side of that balance point to the other. In either case, we must attend to their links to the historical Paul, to the undisputed letters, and to the Pauline legacy.

## The Pastorals and the Acts of Paul Debate

The arguments by Dennis MacDonald and Richard Bauckham set the categories for this scholarly debate.[20] According to MacDonald, the author of the Pastoral Epistles represented a socially conservative movement in the church that reacted against the more radical Paul reflected in certain folk traditions and attitudes toward women. We might characterize MacDonald's depiction of the relationship between the Pastoral Epistles and the *Acts of Paul* as a conflict model, where conservative forces contend against more popular and radical elements in the church, elements marked by openness to women and their central place in the church, as well as an ascetic and celibate way of life.

After acknowledging the close relationship between the *Acts of Paul* and the Pastoral Epistles, especially with 2 Timothy, Bauckham contends that the evidence is best explained by claiming that the *Acts of Paul* was intended as a sequel to the Acts of the Apostles. The author of the *Acts of Paul* sought to continue the story of Paul from the point where the Lukan account left off to the time of the apostle's eventual martyrdom in Rome. Because the author of the *Acts of Paul* assumed the events reflected in 2 Timothy and 1 and 2 Corinthians came from a time after the events reported in Acts he drew his characters from these letters (perhaps also from Titus) rather than Acts. Unlike MacDonald, who argues that both the *Acts of Paul* and the Pastoral Epistles were dependent on a common oral tradition, Bauckham claims that the author of the A*cts of Paul* worked with those Pauline letters thought to come from the end of Paul's first imprisonment in Rome to his martyrdom in the imperial capital. Thus, the *Acts of Paul* was an extension of the Pauline story whereby the author searched the texts thought to come from the time in Paul's life following the Acts of the Apostles.

In either case, the Pastoral Epistles are linked in some fashion to the *Acts of Paul* tradition, and the respective arguments affirm once again the importance of the Pastorals in shaping the Pauline tradition and the legacy of Paul. Perhaps most importantly, the two arguments also suggest different models for how to understand the important question of authority in the

---

[20] Dennis R. MacDonald, *The Legend and the Apostle: The Battle for Paul in Story and Canon* (Louisville: Westminster John Knox, 1983); and Richard Bauckham, "The Acts of Paul as a Sequel to Acts," in *The Book of Acts in Its Ancient Literary Setting* (ed. Bruce W. Winter and Andrew D. Clarke; vol. 1 of *The Book of Acts in Its First Century Setting,* ed. Bruce W. Winter; Grand Rapids: Eerdmans, 1993), 105–52.

early church: conflict (MacDonald) and extension (Bauckham). Moreover, in the particular episode in the *Acts of Paul* dealing with Paul and Thecla, we see Paul's legacy developing in terms of a countercultural movement in the church, a movement centering on issues associated with authority, women and sexual purity. To the extent that the Pastorals and their views of women are connected to the apocryphal tradition of Paul and Thecla, we can see that the lines between more and less normative notions of Pauline authority intersect in complex ways in the early church.

## Paul the Person, Paul the Personage

In terms of the construction of Paul's image in the early church, Anthony Blasi's argument about *charisma* is important. He argues that charisma is bigger than an individual and the person who has charisma is not only a "person" but a "personage."[21] The term "person," according to Blasi, refers to a historical individual, whereas the term "personage" refers to an individual's public and charismatic persona constructed in the minds of other people. For a person to maintain charisma and continue to be a personage, his or her charisma must be constructed anew for each generation. This, Blasi argues, is exactly what happened in the case of Paul.[22] As this process of construction moves from generation to generation, there is a renewed sense of why the person is important and is endowed with special power and authority. Hence, Paul's charisma was a matter of how the public perception of him was formed and invested with significance by those who honored his place in the social and theological world of the early church. The construction of this perception was a creative and imaginative effort by those who turned to Paul as man of authority and charisma.[23]

In short, Paul's various images in the early church were social constructions, and the Pastorals, especially if they were pseudepigraphic, represent but one of those constructions. In these epistles, Paul's persona is that of the protector of sound teaching and the guardian of the "good deposit," the exhorter to proper behavior, the imprisoned and suffering apostle who invites others to follow his example (2 Timothy), the founder of churches (Titus), the one who legitimates qualities of leadership as well as persons fit to be leaders in the church, the identifier of individuals with whom Christians should and should not associate, the bearer of apostolic memory, and the defender of the church's unity.[24] Hence, it is not just Paul's letters or his theology that are significant for the early church but also his personal legacy and the authority this brings to bear.

---

[21] Blasi, *Making Charisma*, 6.
[22] Ibid.
[23] Ibid., 9–10.
[24] Ibid., 103–6.

## The Pastorals and the Questions of Genre and Audience

Even though the Pastoral Epistles are ostensibly letters and have the character of letters, the identification of their genre needs to be done with more precision. According to Benjamin Fiore, the Pastorals belong under the heading *traditional instruction*, a form marked by hortatory material and exhortation recalling the authoritative foundation upon which the true teaching, taught in this case by the divinely appointed teacher, is based.[25] Among the most conspicuous features of this hortatory structure are contrast and personal example, in which the speakers or teachers are their own example of what is taught.[26] With great care, Fiore shows the way the Pastoral letters stand in a long line of hortatory literature.

Luke Timothy Johnson argues that 2 Timothy is an example of a personal paraenetic letter, whereas 1 Timothy and Titus are similar to the royal correspondence known as *mandata principis*, or commandments of the ruler.[27] He also notes that scholars often identify 2 Timothy as a farewell discourse, but to do so tends to prejudge the question of authorship because in this genre someone else normally recorded the words of the dying person.[28]

Regardless of who wrote these letters, it is constructive for the discussion here to note that contrast and personal example are important formal literary features of the Pastorals that clearly shape the pattern of their theological presentations. In addition to the literary axis in these letters between Paul (the stated author) and Timothy/Titus (the stated recipients), a larger audience, which would probably have heard these texts read aloud, can also be assumed to enter into the thought world of the letters.[29] This larger audience, whether it is thought of as the community's leaders or the community more broadly, becomes yet another dimension of the text's referential world and its theology. This larger implied audience also enters into the hortatory drama right alongside the stated recipients of the letters. What may be beyond our grasp at this point is the precise connection between the historical Timothy or Titus and the stated recipients of the letters, as well as the precise identification of the larger audience who may have read the epistles or heard them read.

---

[25] Benjamin Fiore, *The Function of Personal Example in the Socratic and Pastoral Epistles* (Analecta biblica 105; Rome: Biblical Institute Press, 1986), 6. See also Collins, *1 & 2 Timothy and Titus*, 6–9; Johnson, *First and Second Letters to Timothy*, 96–97; Johnson, *Paul's Delegates*, 32; and Robert J. Karris, *The Pastoral Epistles* (New Testament Message 17; Wilmington, Delaware: Michael Glazier, 1979), 8; Quinn and Wacker, *The First and Second Letters to Timothy*, 8–11.

[26] Fiore, *The Function of Personal Example*, 21, 36.

[27] Johnson, *First and Second Letters to Timothy*, 96–97.

[28] Ibid., 97.

[29] Ibid., 12; Arland J. Hultgren, *I, II Timothy, Titus* (Augsburg Commentaries on the New Testament; Minneapolis: Augsburg, 1984), 107; and Karris, *The Pastoral Epistles*, 7.

*History, Epistolary Text, and Context*

In his work on Philemon, now over two decades ago, Norman Petersen refocused the critical distinction between text and history—between the world of the text (literary construction) and contextual history (time of writing)—and applied it to the referential world of Paul and his epistles, especially Philemon.[30] In the course of his attempt to clarify the differences between narratives and epistles with regard to these historical and textual distinctions, Petersen wrote: "In letters, as well as in narratives, we have to move from the text to its referential, narrative world, and from its narrative world to history."[31] Petersen's argument is germane to the following discussion of the Pastorals in at least two ways: (1) epistles have referential worlds and (2) history must be constructed from the referential world of the document. What is not entirely clear in the case of the Pastorals, however, is the extent to which their referential worlds overlap their contextual worlds. If Paul actually wrote the Pastorals, presumably—though not certainly—the referential and contextual worlds overlap to a greater extent than if someone else wrote in the name of Paul at a later date. If, however, the letters were written pseudonymously at some date after Paul's death, the time in and for which they were written is clearly removed from the events and circumstances projected back onto the time of Paul, Timothy, and Titus. In any case, it would be a methodological fallacy to assume congruence between the two when there may in fact be little or none.

## The Argument and Approach

In this section, we will lay out the approach we will take in assessing the epistolary texts and their theologies, comparing their theological patterns, and discerning their place in the canon and the early church. We will also conclude with a brief statement about the contribution this book makes to the larger scholarly conversation about Paul and his legacy. In each case, the issues will be framed here only in general terms in order that they can be developed more fully later in terms of specific texts and arguments. We begin first with the question of the Pastorals and their theologies.

---

[30] Norman R. Petersen, *Rediscovering Paul: Philemon and the Sociology of Paul's Narrative World* (Philadelphia: Fortress, 1985), 1–42.

[31] Ibid., 8–9. In that same discussion Petersen also writes: "The only history *referred to* in a letter is its contextual history, which is the total history envisioned by the writer as relevant for the letter. However, as real as this difference between letter and narrative is, because letters refer to a world they have *referential worlds*, and these are the *narrative worlds*, from which any real-world history must be reconstructed."

## Text and Theology

The approach of this book is to begin in chapter 2 by assuming neither the authenticity nor pseudonymity of the Pastoral Epistles. In contrast to much scholarship on the Pastorals, the starting point for this discussion is the textual character and theological world of the respective letters.[32] Each of the three epistles will be examined carefully on their own terms to determine the character of their particular theology and thought world. Only then will we compare the respective letters and their theologies. Although the issue that drives this discussion is not the question of Pauline authorship, it will be necessary to think about the literary features of authorship. It will also be necessary to frame the issue of authorship in such a way that historical questions do not surreptitiously preempt our starting point or our focus on the theology represented in the literary worlds of the texts.

The theology of the Pastorals is understood broadly here as the pattern of convictions and behaviors related to God and to the activity of God represented in these texts. This is an intentionally broad definition in order not to screen out any of the elements of the thought world of these letters. If the theology of the Pastorals reflects a patterned, as distinct from a thoroughly systematic, view of reality with a single organizing center, it stands to reason that the initial goal of this project is to understand the relationship of the elements in that pattern. It is not necessarily an attempt to find the *key* that unlocks the theology of each letter or the *scarlet thread* that runs through it and ties it together. Instead, it is a matter of understanding the pattern of convictions and behaviors presented in each. A more appropriate metaphor may be an orchestrated collage, as opposed to a random and disconnected set of elements, where a pattern of images is constructed that shapes and defines the individual elements within the whole. In chapter 2, this is the pattern that we are looking for in each of the Pastorals.

The theology and thought of the Pastorals appears on many different levels. For the sake of this discussion, two of these levels need to be distinguished. On the first level, the form and shape of the epistles' theology is explicit. In other words, it is on the surface level of the texts that its pattern can be discerned most directly. On the second level, the epistles only hint at theological conceptions and patterns that are at most implicit in the literary worlds of the texts. They are part of the theological subtext. At various points in the following discussion, this distinction between explicit and implicit theology will become clearer. The presence of these two levels means that any attempt to identify the pattern of the Pastoral Epistles' respective theologies will necessarily have gaps and places where the patterns are less than clear.

---

[32] A survey of commentaries and books on the Pastoral Epistles illustrates that the argument about authorship, based on the standard criteria of theology, linguistic style, vocabulary, and Pauline chronology, is often one of the first issues to be addressed. From a conclusion about the issue of authorship, the interpretation of the epistles then proceeds.

Interpreters customarily deal with a text's implicit theology in two ways. First, they seek to draw a fuller picture of the thought world and theology of the Pastorals by appealing to the clues inherent in the texts themselves. In this way, interpreters seek to make explicit that which is only implicit. The second approach is more interesting for our purposes. It involves placing the letters in a broader literary and theological framework as a way of drawing the latent theology of the texts to the surface. Grouping 2 Timothy with 1 Timothy and Titus, as modern scholarship has done for the last two hundred years, or grouping 1 and 2 Timothy and Titus with the larger Pauline corpus on the basis of authorship is, from a textual point of view, really a matter of claiming how that larger referential world ought to be construed. Once the larger theological background is identified, it becomes a way of elaborating this second level of theology and of drawing it to the fore.

In modern historical critical scholarship, the method of choice for determining this broader framework is to argue comparatively for or against Pauline authorship on the basis of internal theological, stylistic, and linguistic evidence and to situate the Pastoral Epistles historically in the chronology of Paul's ministry. This approach is undoubtedly predicated on assumptions about the importance of historical context for determining theological meaning. It also assumes a high degree of correspondence between the context of the author, the thought of the author, and the text the author produces. Since we, in contrast, are concerned about the shaping of Paul's image and his thought as represented in the respective Pastoral texts, the next step will be to bring these patterns into comparison in chapter 3. We will compare them both with each other and with material from the undisputed Pauline Epistles through an analysis of the respective patterns of thought and theology. From this we can in turn make judgments about the relationships between and among the Pastoral Epistles and the undisputed Pauline material.

## Comparison of Patterns

Although we are thinking in this discussion not about the comparison of religious systems broadly conceived but of texts and the conceptual and theological matrices represented by those texts, it is still necessary to be mindful of the triadic character of comparison. Jonathan Z. Smith observes that "the statement of comparison is never dyadic, but always triadic; there is always an implicit 'more than', and there is always a 'with respect to.' In the case of an academic comparison, the 'with respect to' is most frequently the scholar's interest, be this expressed in a question, a theory, or a model. . . ."[33] In chapter 3, the "with respect to" is the question, how do 1 & 2 Timothy and Titus represent God, the activity of God, and the character and behavior appropriate for those in the church? More specifically, how do

---

[33] Jonathan Z. Smith, *Drudgery Divine: On the Comparison of Early Christianities and the Religions of Late Antiquity* (Chicago: The University of Chicago Press, 1990), 51.

these epistles represent God, God's redemptive activity in Christ, godliness, truth, knowledge, faith, exhortation, and instruction? For example, how do the epistles address the issue of God or Christ? How do the epistles express the redemptive activity of God? How do they represent godliness? How do they identify truth or knowledge and so on? This element, stated in the form of a question, identifies the substantive point of the comparison. These comparisons, each developed relative to a different element or question, when seen together allow us to understand more clearly the structural similarities and differences between and among the respective patterns and images in the developing Pauline tradition.

Further on in the process, the issue of "more than" will at certain points also become apparent. For example, we will be able to say that structurally 2 Timothy is more like Philippians than 1 Timothy or Titus with respect to the exhortation to suffer, or that Titus is more like Galatians than 1 Timothy with respect to the issue of works and grace. As the points of comparison accrue, we will be in a better position to see how the Pauline patterns and images correspond to one another in their canonical and historical contexts. We will also be in a better position to assess the issues of authorship and historical context. This approach, of course, will not result in certainty on these issues but rather relative probabilities. Furthermore, these comparisons will provide different lenses through which to view the Pastoral Epistles, as well as different frames of reference within which to see them, their effects on each other, and the ongoing process of representing Paul and his theology.

In these comparisons, points of dissimilarity will be of special importance. They are markers not merely of conceptual divergence; they may also suggest changes in context as well. Identifiable differences between texts, traditions, and images make points of similarity all the more striking and meaningful. From a semantic and conceptual point of view, difference and contrast are also ways that meaning is generated.[34] By attending to the differences among the texts, traditions, and images under comparison, we can begin to see the ways the authors sought to generate meaning, encourage action, appeal to sources of authority, and shape the behavior of the recipients of the epistles. For example, the more sharply the contrast is drawn between correct and incorrect belief in 1 Timothy and Titus, the more poignantly the author can appeal to the faithful to resist those who have gone astray. Likewise, the more sharply the author identifies the qualities necessary for a leader in the household of God, the clearer the qualities of those unfit for leadership become. Hence, dissimilarity will be of special importance in this process of comparison.

---

[34] See for example Eugene A. Nida, *Componential Analysis of Meaning: An Introduction to Semantic Structures* (The Hague: Mouton, 1975), 32; and Eugene A. Nida, *Exploring Semantic Structures* (International Library of General Linguistics 11; Munich: Wilhelm Fink, 1975), 14–15.

Throughout the comparisons in chapter 3 and subsequent chapters, identification of isolated and random similarities will be strictly limited. Such parallels in thought and theology may or may not be inherently meaningful or indicate a genetic relationship between the various texts and traditions. Even when the parallels are more than mere coincidence, the real significance of these parallels is often not apparent.[35] More to the point for our purposes is to compare the patterns and structures of thought, theology, literary character, and social organization that help us situate the Pastorals in their proper symbolic matrix and to find, their contributions, if any, to this matrix. Our purpose is not necessarily to try to determine strict literary and theological dependence. Furthermore, the relationships between texts and traditions cannot be limited to quotations or simple parallels in wording. Significant features of religious texts and traditions are frequently exposed by highlighting the structural characteristics of the tradition, such as the deep-seated impulses that prompt the writing of a text, assumptions about the audience's problems and how to respond to them, images of authoritative figures in the text, and the theological worldview that supports the concepts and claims of the text.

## Canon and Early Church

In chapter 4, we shall investigate the development of Pauline apostolic authority and the emergence of the Pauline writings as Scripture, perhaps even in a rudimentary sense as canon, in the Pastoral Epistles. Working from the conclusion based on the comparison of literary and theological patterns in chapter 3 that two different authors may be responsible for the three Pastorals, we will begin to see that the Pastorals display a perceptible sense of the Pauline writings as authoritative for the "good deposit" and the correct faith. In other words, there is a movement in these letters towards an established form of Christianity and an impulse to consolidate a notion of Christian truth ecclesiologically. This need not mean that the Pastoral Epistles are second-century documents. To draw such a conclusion depends more on one's theory of Christian development than it does on any one particular piece of concrete evidence. In chapter 4, we shall also extend the patterns of comparison to include other New Testament documents in addition to the undisputed Pauline letters: Acts and the deuteropaulines. The goal of this comparison is to differentiate the Pastorals from other New Testament images of Paul and other early strands of Pauline development. By seeing beneath the differences in genre, we shall be able to explore the structural similarities and differences in order to understand more clearly the Pauline framework for the Pastoral Epistles and their place in that framework.

---

[35] Samuel Sandmel many years ago warned of the dangers of "parallelomania" ("Parallelomania," *JBL* 81 [1962]: 1–13).

Continuing these comparisons into the period of the early church Fathers, and probably Mothers, in chapters 5 and 6 we will illustrate the contours of Paul's legacy as it passes through the Pastorals and into the developing Christian church. Once again, we will differentiate the traditions represented by the Pastorals and those displayed in other parts of the developing church through a process of comparing structural patterns. There will be no attempt to provide a comprehensive discussion of Paul's legacy in all of the various strands of the early church,[36] but rather to use these other lines of development to bring into bold relief the movement toward forms of so-called orthodox Christianity and the formation of a church drawn together in belief and practice. Since the thrust of this argument is comparative and diachronic, reference to the context of the Pastorals means primarily the way these letters are situated in the struggles of the early church to define the faith, to determine who is responsible for preserving the faith, to preserve the unity of the church, and to establish the authority of both Scripture and the apostolic witness to the gospel. Only secondarily does it refer to the historical situation of the Pastorals and the circumstances of their writing.

## *Argument and Contribution*

Because we are focusing on the Pastoral Epistles, the legacy of Paul represented by them, and their place in the formation of Christian traditions, it will be necessary to use these three letters as a two-way lens to look back to Paul and his undisputed letters and ahead to the development of the postapostolic church. The former is important in understanding the place of the Pastorals in the development of the Pauline tradition and the latter in seeing the role of these letters in the ongoing legacy of Paul in the church. In both directions, the three issues of chronological development, geographical area, and literary function are important for understanding the Pauline matrix of the early church and the place of the Pastorals in it. Our concern, however, is not primarily with the historical Paul or the character of his own personal theology but is with the image of Paul and his thought in the Pastorals and the shaping and transmission of the Pauline legacy through the line represented by these three letters. The argument is that the roots of early church tradition concerning ecclesiology, orthodoxy, Christology, and the transmission of tradition run deep into the New Testament period and grow out of concerns and issues that emerge in the church well before the end of the first century. The imaging of Paul in the Pastorals reflects this development and contributes to it in substantive ways.

With this in mind, we can state the argument as follows: A comparative analysis of theological patterns illustrates that even as the Pastoral

---

[36] Andreas Lindemann has already done an admirable job of surveying and examining the legacy of Paul in the broad sweep of early church history until the time of Marcion (*Paulus im ältesten Christentum*).

Epistles represent Paul and his theology in new contexts, they also reflect and foreshadow the significant issues confronting the church in the first two centuries. Among these issues are the nature of the true faith, the relationship of the church to Judaism, Christian asceticism, the prospect of church unity and the threat of disunity, the formation of the canon, the balance between Scripture and tradition, the place of women, and the role of authorized leaders in preserving the true faith and practice of the church. These are pressure points of early Christian debate, and the Pastoral Epistles mark all of them in varying degrees. In this sense, the Pastorals serve as a kind of sourcebook for identifying, and in some cases detailing, the points of contention that characterize the church in the first three centuries. Perhaps no other set of documents in the New Testament point to such a broad range of conflicted issues in the early church as do the epistles of 1 & 2 Timothy and Titus.

What then is the place of this book in the larger scholarly landscape? Its contribution is threefold. First, this discussion takes seriously the literary and conceptual world of each of the individual letters as discrete documents that have integrity in their own right. This is not the case in much scholarship on the Pastorals. They are often treated as a Pastoral corpus, which disguises the substantive differences between them, especially between 1 Timothy and Titus, on the one hand, and 2 Timothy, on the other. Viewing the Pastorals as a block also makes it difficult to situate these letters properly in the developing Pauline tradition. Moreover, there is rarely an effort to approach the thought and the Pauline images of these letters from the point of view of the literary thought world of the respective letters. The primary objective of this discussion is to establish the literary contours of the thought world of the Pastorals, their theology, and their representations of Paul and Pauline authority. In light of this, the approach in this discussion is fundamentally comparative—that is, comparative in terms of the structural patterns represented by the respective texts and traditions. Specifically, that means the conceptual and theological patterns, the patterns of ecclesiastical order, and the various images of the apostle Paul.

Second, this investigation focuses primarily on one part of the developing Pauline tradition, the lines of development represented by the Pastoral Epistles in the growth of the early church. Others have focused on the use of Paul in more marginal groups within early Christianity, for example Marcion and the gnostics. Or, in the case of Andreas Lindemann, who casts his sights more broadly, the focus of the investigation is on the earlier period of the post-New Testament church.[37] The primary concern here is with the representations of Paul, his authoritative presence, and his thought in what came to be for the most part mainstream church traditions. The goal in this discussion is not to write the history of the making of the early church, but to

---

[37] Lindemann, *Paulus im ältesten Christum;* see also Elaine Pagels, *The Gnostic Paul: Gnostic Exegesis of the Pauline Letters* (Philadelphia: Fortress, 1975).

situate the Pastoral Epistles in, and to trace their contribution to, that larger tradition. The lens through which to view this process is, as we have said above, that of the Pastoral Epistles, looking both back to the historical Paul and his letters and forward to the post-New Testament church. In this part of the discussion the thought world of the Pastorals is the interpretive lens, not a social theory or model of early church development. What this lens lacks in abstract explanatory power it makes up for in conformity with and proximity to the world being investigated.

Third, this approach takes seriously the developmental character of Paul's transformation from a Jew and an apostle of Christ into a saint of the church, as well as the transformation of his epistles from occasional letters into authoritative texts that continued to inform the life and theology of the early church. In that sense, we are concerned with what Anthony Blasi calls Paul's "charisma," which is closely related to the sacralizing and ultimately canonizing of his letters. For Paul to continue to be a figure of authority in the church, his charisma had to be reconstructed and renewed through the generations, and that is what happened. Paul, along with Peter, came to be considered one of the apostolic pillars of the church. It is virtually impossible to think about the rise of early Christianity without thinking about the transformation of Paul from a persecutor of the early church into a revered figure who continued to inform and shape the church through his letters and through his personal authority.

# ⌇ 2 ⌇

# THE PASTORAL EPISTLES AND THEIR THEOLOGICAL PATTERNS

EACH OF the Pastoral Epistles displays its own discrete set of literary and theological patterns. The immediate goal of this chapter is to identify those structural patterns and to see the individual theological elements in their respective literary contexts. The further goal is to begin to position these letters conceptually in the developing Pauline tradition by providing the baseline for later comparisons of Pastoral and Pauline material and for identifying the earliest signs of the Pauline writings as Scripture. This will also help us assess how the tradition of the Pastoral Epistles contributes to theological formation and consolidation in the early church. The method for identifying these structural patterns will be to examine the literary and textual characteristics of each of the Pastoral texts in turn.

## 1 TIMOTHY

The world of 1 Timothy turns on the literary axis that runs from Paul to Timothy, the named author and reader respectively of the epistle. In the world of this text, it is along this axis that the various instructions and exhortations, as well as the pattern of the epistle's theology, begin to come into view for the reader. On the face of it, quite apart from the literary question of genre, this epistle is a private correspondence between two people, Paul and Timothy. To that extent, 1 Timothy is much like 2 Timothy. What distinguishes 1 Timothy from 2 Timothy most dramatically is that in 1 Timothy the shape of the discussion is cast broadly in terms of οἰκονομία (divine training/order; 1:4) and εὐσέβεια (godliness) for those within the household of God (3:15). Along this Paul-Timothy axis, the ecclesial dimension of 1 Timothy shapes the context for the instructions, exhortations, and theology that emerge from the literary world of the epistle. In 2 Timothy, as we shall see, the Paul-Timothy axis turns more directly on the intimate relationship between the two, most especially on the appeal for Timothy to suffer as Paul has suffered. With this in mind, it is clear that the household of God, the church in Ephesus according to the text, also functions as an implied audience in 1 Timothy. On that level, the Paul-Timothy axis becomes also a Paul-household of God axis.

The function of the greeting in 1:1–2 is to establish this axis between Paul and Timothy. The author identifies himself as "an apostle of Christ Jesus according to the command of God our savior and Jesus Christ our hope." Paul portrays himself as being under a divine command, and as such becomes the authoritative voice in the text that addresses Timothy and the household of God.[1] But even more than that, God is identified as "our" savior and Christ as "our" hope. Already in this opening statement of the greeting, the common bond between the author and the reader in the household of God is established. They are united in God and in Christ. In turn, the text identifies Timothy as a true child in the faith as well as the recipient of the letter on whom grace, mercy, and peace are bestowed by God and Christ through the words of greeting from Paul. Timothy, the child, is addressed by Paul, the apostle.

Unlike the conclusion of 2 Timothy with its final testament, personal notes, and greetings, 1 Timothy ends abruptly with the words: "Grace be with you." Although the entire sequence of 1 Timothy is structured around the relationship between Paul and Timothy established at the beginning of the letter, the end of the text presents no corresponding discussion portraying the personal connection between the two. That relationship is presumed in the world of the text and the abrupt ending, rather than reiterating that bond between the author and the reader,[2] simply intrudes to bring the discussion to a close.

## From the Greco-Roman Household to the Household of God

In his study of Philemon and the sociology of Paul's narrative world, Norman Petersen wrote, over twenty years ago, concerning the transformation of literal references into metaphorical references:

> It is now apparent that Paul has borrowed the role names of master, slave, father, child, sons, brothers, and sisters from the kinship and master-slave institutions in the world outside the church. But because he transforms the literal reference of the role names taken from these worldly institutions into metaphorical reference to roles in the church, we can see that the world and the church are two separate domains within Paul's narrative world. . . . The believer's identity as a believer is represented by borrowed language, but the

---

[1]For a discussion of the authoritative image of Paul in the Pastorals see J. Christiaan Beker, *Heirs of Paul*, 37–39.

[2]The use of the plural pronoun ὑμῶν (you) in 6:21b reinforces the perception that the wider community was also thought of as part of the audience of 1 Timothy. The textual tradition indicates that this pronoun was changed to the singular in some manuscripts, presumably to convey the sense of the epistle being a private correspondence between two people.

believer is not governed by the institutions from which it was borrowed. The role names are the same in both domains, but in the domain of the world they refer to the literal relationship between actors, . . . all of whom are governed by institutional rules of behavior to be followed by the role players. In contrast, within the domain of the church the same role names are also used to refer to two different sets of actors, one set of which is superior to the other set, but with strikingly different significance.[3]

Similar to the shift identified by Petersen in Philemon, the rules and patterns governing relationships in the church, understood literally in 1 Timothy as the household of God, are not, strictly speaking, identical to those in the institution of the Greco-Roman household. Personal qualities and behaviors were obviously important to those concerned with the management of the Greco-Roman household, as they were to those concerned with the well-being of the church. However, the assembly of the living God represented in the text as the household of God in fact operates on a conceptual level with a somewhat different pattern of expectations, and this affects the sociological implications of the exhortations and instructions of the epistle. This discussion addresses how the transformation of images from the Greco-Roman household to the church takes place in the world of 1 Timothy. To put it another way, what happens when the social patterns and expectations governing the one (the church) shift, if not also transform, the patterns that pertain to the other (the Greco-Roman household), even though they are connected in the symbolic reference of the text by the image of the household of God?

In light of the extensive work already done on the background and context of the New Testament "household codes,"[4] three intersecting lines of that investigation are important for the present discussion: origin, function, and circumstance. Increasingly, the household management traditions in the Greco-Roman world have come to be understood as the originating context for the New Testament "household codes."[5] Their function in the New Testament turns on either the need to silence criticism of the community by outsiders and hence to avoid scandal and attract converts or to order the internal affairs of the community before the advent of more formal

---

[3] Norman R. Petersen, *Rediscovering Paul*, 25.

[4] See the following discussions of scholarship on the "household codes": David Balch, "Household Codes" in *Greco-Roman Literature and the New Testament: Selected Forms and Genres* (Atlanta: Scholars Press), 25–36; David Balch, *Let Wives Be Submissive: The Domestic Code in 1 Peter* (SBLMS; Chico, Calif: Scholars Press, 1981), 1–62; Clayton N. Jefford, "Household Codes and Conflict in the Early Church," StPatr 31 (1997): 121–27; Angela Standhartinger, "The Origin and Intention of the Household Code in the Letter to the Colossians," *JSNT* 79 (2000): 117–22. See also David C. Verner, *The Household of God: The Social World of the Pastoral Epistles* (SBLDS 71; Chico, Calif: Scholars Press, 1983), 83–125.

[5] See especially the work of David L. Balch, "Household Codes," 25–36; and *Let Wives Be Submissive*, 1–62; see also Andrew T. Lincoln, "The Household Code and Wisdom Mode of Colossians," JSNT 74 (1999): 100–102.

ecclesiastical structures.[6] Further, Clayton Jefford identifies the consistent circumstance of schism or theological conflict from the first appearance of "household codes" in the letter to the Colossians to their final appearance in the letter of Polycarp to the Philippians.[7] The common thread running through all of these is the maintenance of or quest for order, whether under the guise of managing a household (ordering a household), silencing critics (not threatening the order of society), structuring the life of the church (ordering the assembly of the living God), or dealing with conflict and division (reordering the community). In line with this common thread, the household becomes, both metaphorically and socially, a microcosm of the city, or the empire. In the case of 1 Timothy the household serves as a microcosm for the household of God, the church. Hence, as we shall argue below, οἰκονομίαν Θεοῦ τὴν ἐν πίστει in 1:4 is best translated "divine order to which members of the household ought to conform in faith," because it conveys both the sense of order that is underscored by divine purpose and the duty incumbent on Timothy to conform to that divine order. This is played out in the context of what Ramsay MacMullen has described as the key to understanding the social scale of the Roman empire, "verticality," and the responsibility of everyone through their behavior to maintain the prescribed order of Roman society.[8]

In light of all this, we must, however, be more precise about the use of the terms "household," "household of God," and "church." The terms "household" and "church" point to social phenomena, the one represented in discussions of the household in Greco-Roman literature and pertaining to the character and management of household life and the other projected in the text of 1 Timothy as the ecclesial community. What connects them is the term "household of God," a metaphor and linguistic link between the two social realities. As a linguistic link, it may not say much directly about the actual social realities of either the Greco-Roman household or the church, though the linkage presumes that the established social reality of the household is in some sense a model for the real life of the church. To make the metaphor work as a model, the author—in addition to what is said about the life of the church in the text—must also presume on the readers' own experience of household life. What the term "household of God" does relate to directly, however, are the instructions related to other household terms in the literary world of 1 Timothy: overseers, deacons, women, elders, older men, widows, and slaves. Once again, the extent to which these instructions are manifested or will be manifested in the actual communal life of the epistle's readers we are not able to know with precision.

---

[6]Jefford, "Household Codes," 121–23.
[7]Ibid., 122. See also Verner, *The Household of God,* 76–77.
[8]Ramsay MacMullen, *Roman Social Relations: 50 B.C. to A.D. 284* (New Haven: Yale University Press, 1974) , 94, 105; see also Verner, *The Household of God,* 80.

As literary realities, the image of the household of God in 1 Timothy and the instructions and exhortations pertaining to the management of the church are on one level largely consistent with what we think we know about the order and management of household life in the Greco-Roman world.[9] In 1 Timothy's frame of reference, various classes of people are identified and instructed concerning the appropriate qualities and behaviors for each. While the rough outlines of an ecclesial structure come into view, there is in 1 Timothy no concern to sketch the job descriptions for those positions identified as overseer, deacon, and elder. On the contrary, the concern in this text is with the characteristics and behaviors that ought to be exhibited by those people who have designated public roles in the household of God.[10] Relationships within the household are crucial, and the qualities and behaviors necessary to maintain those relationships are of paramount concern in the world of this text. If the church is to function as the household of God, it must function according to patterns that contribute to the proper network and ordering of relationships among people in the community. In short, this is the way to maintain the good order of the church.[11]

However, if we do not also consider the theology of 1 Timothy, we miss the full implication of the shift involved in borrowing the language of the household and applying it by means of a metaphorical link to the church. Here, we could argue, the prepositional phrase ἐν πίστει (in faith) in 1:4 and the genitive θεοῦ (God) in 3:15 function as qualifiers that require the household of God metaphor to be understood in relation to the full range of conceptual, theological patterns in the textual world of 1 Timothy and not simply in relation to the various individuals and groups explicitly identified in the epistle. To put it another way, both the instructions that pertain to the individuals and groups as well as the theological patterns represented in the epistle affect the way the household of God imagery applies to the church. It is on this level that the movement from the one domain to the other exhibits the most profound shift, a shift that would have had important social implications for the church as well. Hence, it is not adequate to divorce the theology of 1 Timothy from the issue of the household of God, as either an image or as a model for the church. The social character of the church and the qualities expected of those who exercise leadership roles in

---

[9] Johnson, *Letters to Paul's Delegates*, 144–45.

[10] Bassler, *1 Timothy, 2 Timothy, Titus*, 63–72; and Young, *Theology*, 17–20.

[11] We might conclude, depending precisely on what we determine the originating context for the household of God image to be, that the transition from the domain of household life to the household of God as a metaphor and model for the church exhibits a high degree of consistency and a low degree of social transformation. However, Verner writes: "The station code schema has influenced the shape of the material in 1 Tim 2:1ff. and Titus 2:1–10, 1:5ff., 3:1ff., although this influence is considerably greater at certain points than at others. At the same time the schema has been freely adapted, modified, and even ignored as concrete problems of the church have been addressed" (*The Household of God*, 106).

the church are circumscribed by 1 Timothy's theology and sense of piety. These put the household of God in a distinctive frame of reference when compared to the Greco-Roman household.

## *The Household of God*

In 3:14b–15, the author writes: "so that, if I am delayed you may know how it is necessary to behave in the household of God (οἴκῳ Θεοῦ), which is the assembly (ἐκκλησία) of the living God, the pillar and foundation of the truth." This image, presented midway in the discussion, sets the referential context for Paul's instructions and exhortations. The author's words are directed to Timothy and to the household of God; and in the sociology of this text, attention is directed inward to the assembly of the living God. Insiders are implicitly distinguished from outsiders, and the injunctions about proper behavior, personal characteristics, and patterns of life are intended for those who are inside this household. Modeled on the pattern of household life in the Greco-Roman world,[12] this text projects, in a literary way, the ideal pattern of life in the household of God. In short, the patterns seen in the real world are picked up in the literary world and shaped into a context for the instructions, injunctions, and theological claims of the epistle. The patterns of the household in the real world shape the ideal patterns of the household of God in the literary world, which in turn are intended to order the real life of the church.[13] This is the social and literary interplay that circumscribes this text, and it is the household of God concept in 3:15 that emerges as the crucial image for understanding the literary context of 1 Timothy's theology, as well as for understanding the instructions and exhortations that are directed to Timothy.

The household of God image may or may not be the center of 1 Timothy's theology,[14] but it is clearly framed by the theological statements in 3:16: "Without a doubt the mystery of godliness (εὐσεβείας) is great. Who was manifested in flesh, vindicated in spirit, seen by angels, preached to Gentiles, believed in throughout the world, taken up in glory."[15] As the pillar and foundation of the truth, the assembly of the living God rests upon the great mystery of godliness, which is cast in christological terms. The unmistakable implication is that the work of the living God and the mystery of godliness are

---

[12] See Jouette M. Bassler, *1 Timothy, 2 Timothy, Titus* (Abingdon New Testament Commentaries; Nashville: Abingdon, 1996), 73–74; Collins, *1 & 2 Timothy and Titus*, 102–6; and Frances Young, *Theology*, 17, 22.

[13] A fuller discussion of the relationship between the Greco-Roman household and the household of God in 1 Timothy will be presented in the conclusion to this section.

[14] Johnson, *First and Second Letters to Timothy*, 231; and Jerry L. Sumney, "'God Our Savior': The Fundamental Operational Theological Assertion of 1 Timothy," *HBT* 21 (1999): 109–10.

[15] Johnson, *Letters to Paul's Delegates*, 157.

to be understood in terms of Christ, and all of these are tied directly to life in the household of God. If the household of God image projects a context for theology in 3:15–16, the work of the living God expressed in Christ sustains that household in truth. In that sense, the church is the assembly of God.

The inward focus of attention in the literary world of 1 Timothy comes to the fore immediately following the opening greeting in 1:3. Timothy is urged once again to stay in Ephesus and to instruct certain people not to teach a different, presumably incorrect, doctrine. Those who occupy themselves with myths, endless genealogies, and speculations are to be corrected. Without any doubt, these are people within the household of God who are straying from the truth into false doctrine. The concern is not with outsiders at this point, and to the extent there is a concern with outsiders in 1 Timothy, it is primarily with the image the household of God projects to the outsiders.[16] The perceived threat is from false teachers within rather than the threat of persecutions from without. More specifically the threat comes from those who wish to be teachers of the law but have no understanding about the things of which they teach and end up in idle chatter (1:6–7).

The false doctrines of the false teachers—their myths, genealogies, and debates—are contrasted with the οἰκονομίαν Θεοῦ τὴν ἐν πίστει. The meaning of this phrase is critical for understanding life in the household of God and for the injunctions that shape much of 1 Timothy's textual world. A brief survey of English translations of 1 Tim 1:4 and of recent debates about the meaning of the term οἰκονομία indicate the diversity of renderings.[17] Lexicons themselves confirm this diversity of options.[18] There are two general schools of thought regarding the term οἰκονομία: the term has either the sense of divine order or it conveys the sense of cultivating the proper form of godliness.[19] In deciding between these two schools of thought, the first point to be observed is the adversative nature of the sentence structure. The false teachers occupy themselves with myths and genealogies which give rise to debates, instead of (μᾶλλον ἤ) the οἰκονομίαν Θεοῦ that is known or received in faith. Syntactically it appears that two forms of behavior on the part of people in the household have two different results, speculative debates or knowing in faith. If such parallelism is in the text, then it would seem to tilt the argument

---

[16] Cf. 6:1. See also Beker, *Paul's Heirs,* 45. MacDonald says we find no desire in the Pastoral Epistles for rejection of the world, *The Pauline Churches,* 164–70.

[17] See the article by Luke Timothy Johnson, "Oikonomia Theou: The Theological Voice of 1 Timothy from the Perspective of Pauline Authorship" and the response to it by Margaret M. Mitchell, "'Speaking of God as He Was Able': Three Accounts of the Theology of 1 Timothy Compared," *HBT* 21 2 (1999): see especially pages 95–103 and 130–34 in the article and the response. Also Collins, *1 & 2 Timothy and Titus,* 27; and Johnson, *First and Second Letters to Timothy,* 164.

[18] BDAG suggests that "training" best fits the context of 1 Timothy 1:4, whereas J. P. Louw and E. A. Nida, eds., *Greek-English Lexicon of the New Testament* (2d ed.; New York: United Bible Societies, 1988–1989), 1: 358, opt for the term "plan."

[19] See the discussion by Young, *Theology,* 54–55.

slightly in favor of the practice of godliness as the proper translation of the term. Although this does not rule out the sense of knowing in faith the divine order of things, it is stated directly in 1:5 that the goal of this instruction is "love that comes from a pure heart, a good conscience, and a genuine faith." On the face of it, this sounds very much like the language of piety and devotion. At least this much is clear in light of the parallelism identified: different forms of human activity have different results, debates or knowing in faith. What seems to be ruled out is the idea that divine order is merely a static concept apart from any human concern or activity.

If this term is understood to convey the idea of divine order, then the instructions and exhortations that alternate throughout the epistle ought to be understood as seeking to replicate the divine order of things in the household of God that is also found more generally in the Greco-Roman household. If on the other hand, the term encourages the practice of godliness, then the emphasis is on shaping piety and devotion in the household of God. When faced with this alternative, two things are important to observe. First, the translation decision ought not be made solely on the basis of 1:4–5 but must be made in light of the entire textual world of 1 Timothy. Second, these alternatives cannot be set in rigid contrast to each other, for there is evidence in 1 Timothy for both proper conduct leading to good order in the church and conduct that leads to godliness.[20] It would also be a mistake to try to understand the thought world of 1 Timothy by making a definitive decision about the translation of this term and then reading the entire text through that lens. A better approach is to identify the alternate emphases in light of 1:4–5 and then to examine the text's theological and rhetorical patterns to see how the text might nuance and shade the meaning of the term. Hence, this issue will be revisited after the pattern of 1 Timothy's thought world has been sketched and discussed.

What is clear to this point is that the household of God image provides the organizing structure within which the instructions, exhortations, and theological claims of the letter are made. This image, drawn from everyday life in the Greco-Roman world,[21] establishes the underlying symbolic network that gives the discussion in 1 Timothy intelligibility and poignancy. Moreover, within this concept of the household, the οἰκονομία, whatever its particular nuance in 1:4, is critical for understanding behavior, life, and thought in the assembly of the living God.

### God, Godliness, and Salvation

In 1 Timothy, God is identified as one (2:5), and Christ Jesus is the mediator between the one God and humanity. In this statement, the divide

---

[20] Εὐσέβεια, for example, appears in 2:2; 3:16; 4:7, 8; 6:3, 5, 6, 11; εὐσεβέω appears in 5:4.

[21] MacDonald, *Pauline Churches*, 200–201. See below, p. 35.

between God and humanity is clearly implied, and Christ serves as the mediating bridge between them. But more than this, God is also portrayed in the text as a "living God" (3:15; 4:10) and as a God who "gives life to all things" (6:13). God is the creator of everything that has life. In the literary world of 1 Timothy, God is, on the one hand, separated from humanity in terms of redemptive reality and works through a mediator, Christ. On the other hand, God is immanent in his direct involvement in the giving of life. In the pattern of 1 Timothy's theology, divine transcendence (mediated redemptively by Christ) and divine immanence (life given by God to all things) are both suggested by the framework that informs the discussion of the epistle.

In the thought world of 1 Timothy, the most conspicuous image associated with God is God as "savior."[22] Already in the greeting, God is identified as "our savior" (1:1), a claim that is repeated in 2:3–4: "This is good and acceptable before God our savior who desires all people to be saved and come to knowledge of (the) truth." God is both savior and the one who desires all people to be saved.[23] The saving and the desiring are both part of God's image. This is reinforced in 4:10 where God is identified as both a living God and a God who is the "savior of all people, especially of those who believe." This text confirms the image of God as savior but extends the implication. The saving activity of God is not disconnected from the human component, in this case from the faith of those whom God desires to be saved.[24]

This human dimension of salvation becomes even more pronounced in 4:16: "Attend to yourself and (your) teaching, continue in them, for by doing this you shall also save both yourself and those who hear you." In the exhortation to Timothy in 6:12 this human dimension is portrayed in yet another way: "Fight the good fight of faith, take hold of the eternal life to which you were called when you made the good confession before many witnesses."[25] In 2:15 there is the reference to women being "saved through childbearing if they remain in faith and love and holiness." This rather strange statement likely points to the need to mind one's place in the order of social expectations.[26] These statements do not negate or diminish the image of God as savior. God is still the one who saves. But in the textual world of 1 Timothy people apparently have a role to play in this process. In the redemptive nexus between God and humans, God is portrayed as savior and humans are projected as fully engaged in their own salvation as well, not as earning their salvation but as taking hold of it in faith, in correct

---

[22] Sumney, "God Our Savior," 108; and Young, *Theology*, 50.

[23] Johnson, *Paul's Delegates*, 131–32; Johnson, *First and Second Letters to Timothy*, 190–91; and Bassler, *1 Timothy, 2 Timothy, Titus*, 52.

[24] See below, pp. 30–31.

[25] Cf. 6:19 and 1:16

[26] As Bassler points out, this may be to encourage women to avoid the message of celibacy (*1 Timothy, 2 Timothy, Titus*, 61; see also S. E. Porter, "What Does It Mean to Be 'Saved by Childbirth' [1 Timothy 2:15]?" *JSNT* 49 [1993]: 87–102).

teaching, and in proper behavior. In other words, there are things that people can do or not do to jeopardize their own salvation, even though God desires that all should be saved.

By simple extrapolation, it is clear that Paul's instructions and exhortations to Timothy, and through him to the entire household of God, are set forth against the backdrop of soteriology. What people do and how they behave in the assembly of the living God make a difference for their salvation. The evidence suggests that the language of salvation refers to eternal life (especially 6:12), but there may also be a sense that salvation has a social and this-worldly dimension as well (e.g., 2:15). In that sense, salvation manifests itself also in the household of God.

The particularity of Christ's appearance in the flesh as the one who is proclaimed to the Gentiles and believed throughout the world becomes clear in 3:16. And Christ's reappearance in the future at a time when the "blessed, powerful one, king of kings, and lord of lords" shall choose is projected beyond the time frame of the text's temporal scope in 6:14–16 to an indeterminate future.[27] Christ appeared in the flesh and Christ will be manifested again in due time. The urgency implicit in Paul's instructions and exhortations is the theological conviction that ultimately salvation hangs in the balance.

As we already saw in 2:5, Christ is the mediator between God and human beings, and in that sense is a central figure in salvation. In that same context, Christ is also identified as the one who gave himself as a ransom (ἀντίλυτρον) for all (2:6). Moreover, Christ came into the world to save sinners (1:15), of whom the author identifies himself as foremost. This assertion is introduced as "true and worthy of all acceptance," which suggests that it is close to the heart of 1 Timothy's notion of redemption. In the greeting, Christ is also portrayed as "our" hope (1:1). In the literary contour of this epistle, Christ the ransom and Christ the forgiver stand close together and form a critical part of the divine work of salvation.

Arrayed around the image of God as savior in 1 Timothy is Paul's desire that people in the household of God live in godliness (εὐσέβεια).[28] In 2:2 the term stands in relationship to the call to pray for those in high places in order that "we" may live quietly in all godliness and modesty. Devotion and piety are the goals of life in the household of God, and the author urges that entreaties on behalf of the powerful for the solitude that makes this possible be made.[29] This leads in 2:3 directly to the claim that "this is good and acceptable before God our savior." It is not entirely clear what the antecedent to "this" is but it is reasonable to think that it is the godliness and modesty sought by the author. In this way, εὐσέβεια is clearly linked to God and salvation.

---

[27] In 6:14 the Greek form of the word for "epiphany," normally translated in English as "appearance" or "manifestation," appears referring to Christ's return. For a discussion of the "epiphany" Christology in the Pastorals see below, pp. 98–99.

[28] Ibid., 51.

[29] Collins, *1 & 2 Timothy and Titus,* 54–59.

The implications of εὐσέβεια become clearer still in 4:7–9: "Avoid profane and foolish myths. Train yourself in godliness. For physical training is of limited value, but godliness is of value in every way for it holds the promise of life now and in the future. This saying is sure and worthy of full acceptance." This statement is preceded in 4:1–5 by a rejection of those who forbid marriage and abstain from certain foods, and it is followed in 4:10 by a reiteration of the author's hope in God who is the "savior of all people." Once again, the injunction to godliness is closely connected to God and salvation. More than that, however, godliness is explicitly set in opposition to certain forms of behavior. It is contrasted with the actions of those who turn from the faith and follow deceitful spirits and demonic teachings through the hypocrisy of liars (4:1–2). Likewise, the godly are not to reject that which is created and "made holy through the word of God and prayer," namely marriage and food (4:3–5). If Timothy follows these instructions, he will be a good minister of Christ Jesus (4:6). Godliness, portrayed according to the model of physical training (4:7–8), implies that it is to be exercised and trained. The shape of that training gradually comes into view as the discussion unfolds in the rest of the epistle. [30]

The implications of godliness are brought into still clearer focus in 6:3–6 where it is closely connected to correct teaching and the sound words of "our" Lord Jesus Christ. Εὐσέβεια is not simply a matter of behavior but is also an issue of adhering to the proper teaching. Following false teachers and teachings is, of course, a matter of behavior because it leads to debates and quarrels that threaten the order of God's household, as is implied in 6:5. There are even those who think godliness is a form of gain. It is clear in the pattern of 1 Timothy's theology, then, that right thinking and right behavior are intimately connected,[31] and that they are urgent issues in the world of the text precisely because salvation is at stake. Godliness is clearly concerned with piety and devotion to God, but it is also linked to the proper ordering of life in the church. God, the giver of life and savior, orders the expectation that people in the assembly are to exhibit lives of εὐσέβεια (godliness). This is summed up nicely in the charge in 6:11: "But you, O man of God, flee these things, pursue righteousness, godliness, faith, love, steadfastness, gentleness." These are the virtues to be sought by the person of God.

## Truth, Sound Teaching, and Faith

The concept of truth is critical for understanding the nature of correct doctrine in 1 Timothy. In the household of God, knowledge of the truth is a

---

[30] Cf. 5:4. In this text, a verbal form of εὐσέβεια is used and pertains to the household of widows with children or grandchildren who are to honor their religious duty to their own family.

[31] See the discussion of the close connection between theology and ethics in Young, *Theology*, 27–28.

virtue. In 2:4, for example, knowledge of the truth is coordinate with God's desire that all people be saved. Salvation and knowledge of the truth are linked in the desire of God, and it may be that salvation is in fact dependent upon knowledge of the truth. Knowledge of the truth is linked in 4:3 with faith for those who eat with thanksgiving the food created by God.[32] The concepts of knowledge and faith are approached from the opposite direction in 6:20–21: "O Timothy, guard the deposit that has been entrusted to you and turn away from profane chatter and contradictions of what is falsely called knowledge which some have confessed and have deviated from the faith."[33] Paul identifies himself as a teacher of the Gentiles in faith and truth (2:7). Here Paul establishes his own credentials as one who is on the side of truth and faith. And in 3:15, the church of the living God is the pillar and foundation of the truth.

When we look at the concept of truth in 1 Timothy, we see that it is associated with a complex of other terms (especially "faith") that are intended to designate the idea of correct belief and teaching. While the content of this correct doctrine is not made explicit in all its various forms, one senses that it is only slightly submerged beneath the surface of the text. It is part of the underlying theological world of 1 Timothy, and, as such, it comes to the surface only occasionally in the course of the discussion. As a feature of this literary world, the concept of correct doctrine clearly functions to distinguish those who possess the truth from those who do not. It also serves to provide a context for the instructions and exhortations that run through the epistle.

Genuine faith is either explicit or assumed in a series of references in 1 Timothy: 1:4–5 (faith is associated with "a pure heart and a good conscience), 1:14 (grace of our Lord overflowed to me with the faith and love that are in Christ Jesus), 1:16 (believe in him to eternal life), 1:19 (have faith and a good conscience), 4:3 (those who believe and know the truth), 4:6 (nourished on the words of faith and sound teaching), 4:10 (the living God, who is the savior of all people, especially those who believe), and 6:12 (fight the good fight of faith). Faith, along with truth, is part of a complex of terms and images that characterize the godly life in the household of God. In these references, faith is identified with a series of vivid affective images—"pure heart," "good conscience," "love," "nourished"—but the term also suggests that a certain content is in view. It is associated with the "words of faith" and "sound teaching." Moreover, in 1:13 Paul refers to his former life when he acted ignorantly in unbelief. By implication, he did not live in truth and knowledge. He acted ignorantly according to truth and knowledge. And in 4:1 and 6:10, it is asserted that some shall turn or have already turned from the faith. Presumably this turning from faith involves more than abandoning the affective dimensions of faith. It means turning from truth and knowledge, which implies turning from the true doctrine and teaching that is to be

---

[32] Cf. 1:6–7.
[33] See the discussion of the "good deposit" below, pp. 37, 95–96, 100–101.

represented in the household of God. In the thought world of 1 Timothy, the term "faith" conveys both the theological and the personal dimensions of godliness; there is no suggestion that these can be separated.

Another dimension of faith in 1 Timothy has to do with instruction and the example of those who serve the church. The author identifies himself in 2:7 as a preacher, an apostle, and a teacher of the Gentiles in faith. The character of faith is also associated with various categories of people in the church: deacons (3:9), women (3:11), those who serve well (3:13), the pastor (4:12), and whoever does not care for relatives (5:8). In this list, faith is linked with Paul's expectations for those who have particular roles in the church. Faith is critical for defining life and behavior in the community. Consequently people who conduct themselves improperly are considered to have departed from the faith.

A further aspect of this language complex is the idea of teaching. Part of this concept pertains to the content of teaching. The opponents and problem individuals are promoting a different teaching through myths, genealogies, speculations, wives' tales, and meaningless talk that are opposed to sound teaching and proper behavior (1:3–4, 6–10; 4:7; 6:2–5). Correspondingly, Paul exhorts and instructs Timothy and the household with regard to the activity of teaching. In 4:11 Timothy is exhorted to teach, and in 4:13 he is instructed to occupy himself with reading, exhortation, and teaching. Toward the end of the epistle in 6:2–3, Timothy is called upon to teach and exhort slaves to give due honor to their masters, and he is reminded that anyone who teaches otherwise is, to put it mildly, ignorant (6:4–5).

Particular categories of people are instructed with regard to teaching. Women are not permitted to teach (2:12), whereas the ἐπίσκοποι (overseers) are to be skillful teachers (3:2). The πρεσβύτεροι (elders) who work in the word and teaching are worthy of double honor (5:17), and slaves are instructed to give honor to their masters in order that the name of the Lord and the teaching might not be blasphemed. Some of those who have deviated from true doctrine have desired to be teachers of the law but have been ignorant of the law (1:7–9). They simply have not known anything about the law and the things of which they claim to teach. If there is a focal point for the opposition to the faith, truth, and sound teaching in 1 Timothy, it is to be found here. From the perspective of 1 Timothy, the teaching of the law is a bone of contention, and it is around this ignorant teaching that the opposition is singled out for special mention in the text.[34] The law is not set forth for the innocent but for the disobedient. It may also be that the errors related to other issues also stem ultimately from a misunderstanding of the law: those who forbid marriage and certain foods (4:1–3); those who teach things that are contrary to the teachings of Paul and do not agree with the

---

[34] For references to the opposition (e.g., false teachers, misguided ascetics, and divisive people) see Bassler, *1 Timothy, 2 Timothy, Titus*, 38–42; and Johnson, *Paul's Delegates*, 108–9.

words of our Lord Jesus Christ (6:3–6); those who engage in profane and idle talk and in contradictions (6:20). In 1 Timothy these could descriptions could be pointing to those who claim to be teachers of the law yet have no understanding of the law.

As we plot the theological pattern of 1 Timothy, we see that the terms "truth," "faith," and "teaching" are all part of a semantic field that points to an activity as well as to a framework of conviction that helps us map the symbolic world of this text. In this world, thought and action are closely linked. There is no hint that theology and behavior can be wedged apart. In fact, the theology of 1 Timothy does not emerge through the discourse of theological argumentation but rather through the ebb and flow of instruction and exhortation to Timothy and to the household of God. While these terms seem to represent content—the correct doctrine that stands behind them—the character of this content often remains only implicit in the text. It is only explicitly identified here and there on the surface level of the discourse. The distribution of this terminology in the text also gives the impression that the discourse is linked together by a complex interweaving of terms and ideas that provides a kind of rhetorical coherence for a text that otherwise often appears quite random.[35] To distill this interconnectedness, one must discern the web of terms and ideas that identify the symbolic world of the text. From the image of God and the household of God extending on to the interlocking concepts of truth, faith, and teaching, one can begin to detect the pattern, if not the order, in the thought world of 1 Timothy. And it is in the ordered pattern of this world (with its emphasis on the household of God; God, godliness, and salvation; and truth, sound teaching, faith) that the instructions regarding the ecclesial concerns of 1 Timothy are anchored.

## Qualities and Instructions Appropriate for Members of the Household of God

In 1 Timothy's frame of reference, various classes of people are identified and instructed concerning the appropriate qualities and behaviors for each. While the rough outlines of an ecclesial structure come into view, there is in 1 Timothy no concern to sketch the job descriptions for those positions identified as overseer, deacon, and elder. On the contrary, the concern in this text is with the characteristics and behaviors that ought to be exhibited by those people who have designated public roles in the household of God.[36] Relationships within the household are crucial and the qualities and behaviors necessary to maintain those relationships are of paramount

---

[35] Here we echo the observation by Luke Timothy Johnson regarding the non-systematic, even haphazard, nature of the presentation in 1 Timothy (*Paul's Delegates*, 106).

[36] Bassler, *1 Timothy, 2 Timothy, Titus*, 63–72; Collins, *1 & 2 Timothy and Titus*, 78–93; Johnson, *First and Second Letters to Timothy*, 212–25; and Young, *Theology*,

concern in the world of this text. Once again, the household of God is modeled on the Greco-Roman household of the wider culture, and the characteristics appropriate for that wider household are also appropriate for the managers of the household of God.[37] If the church is to function as the household of God, it must function according to patterns that contribute to proper relationships between people in the community. In short, this is the way to maintain the good order of the church.

The ἐπίσκοπος (overseer) is to be "beyond reproach: husband of one wife, temperate, self-controlled, honorable, hospitable, able to teach, not a drunkard, not aggressive but gentle, peaceable, not greedy" (3:2–3). Listed both positively and negatively, we find the qualities that are desirable for an overseer. They sum up what the irreproachable life is thought to be like. In each case, the desired qualities are those that should contribute to the proper order and functioning of the community. Further on in the discussion, the concern for the household is made explicit: "He must be able to manage his household well and keep his children in submission. For if someone does not know how to manage his own household, how can he care for the assembly of God?" (3:4–5). The connection between the Greco-Roman household and household of God is made as direct as it can possibly be in these verses. Management of one's own house is evidence of one's fitness to manage the church, and apparently the qualities necessary for the one are necessary for the other. In the literary world of 1 Timothy, the expectations and characteristics of household management outside the church are projected onto the assembly of God, and the congruence between the two is very close. The discussion of overseers concludes with the further qualifications indicating that they must not be a recent convert and must also be well thought of by outsiders (3:6–7). Those in positions of responsibility on the inside should provide no affront to those on the outside. While the point of view of the text is clearly directed to those inside the community, the responsibility of the community's overseers extends beyond the boundaries of the community, at least to the extent of not bringing themselves and the community into disrepute. In this way, the world inside and the world outside are connected.

Similarly, the διάκονος (deacon) must be "dignified, not deceitful, not partaking of much wine, not fond of dishonest gain, and must hold to the mystery of faith with a clear conscience" (3:8–9). If when tested they prove themselves to be above reproach, they are permitted to serve. As with the overseers, they are to be husbands of one wife and are to manage their children and own households well. Once again the emphasis is on the personal qualities that are to mark those who minister in the church. In so doing they

---

17–20. See also the discussion of ministry in the Pastorals by Joseph A. Fitzmyer, "The Structured Ministry of the Church in the Pastoral Epistles," *CBQ* 66 (2004): 582–96.

[37]Johnson, *Paul's Delegates*, 144–45; Fitzmyer, *Structured Ministry*, 584–87.

achieve "good standing" in the community and "much confidence in the faith that is in Christ Jesus" (3:13). As in the case of the overseer, a role in the life of the community is identified but a well defined and fully institutionalized office structure is still not yet clearly in view. This is indicated by the emphasis on personal characteristics necessary for the various roles rather than the formal requirements and functions associated with an office.[38]

In 5:17–20 the πρεσβύτεροι (elders) are singled out for consideration. Elders, especially those who labor in word and teaching, are worthy of double honor. In this case the tone of the discussion tends toward the procedural. Charges should not be leveled against an elder except on the evidence of two witnesses, and where elders persist in sin they are to be reproved. As is the case with deacons, the epistle lauds those elders who are involved in managing and directing the affairs of the community.

First Timothy fully expects that different roles will be assumed in the life of the community and seeks to order those roles and activities in accord with a perception of how the household of God is to function based on the model of the family.[39] It is quite a different matter to claim that by the time of 1 Timothy distinct offices with formally differentiated expectations had already developed. We might expect that at this time there was still some overlap between the roles attributed, for example, to overseers and elders. Furthermore, the development of roles and expectations during the New Testament and early post-New Testament period may also have occurred independently in different locations.

Instructions for other groups are also woven into the discourse of the epistle. Women are singled out and instructed to dress modestly, clothing themselves with good works, learning in silence and all submission (2:9–11). Women are not to teach or have authority over a man but to keep silence (2:12).[40] The justification for this is that Adam was born before Eve and was not deceived as Eve was (2:13–14). The underlying assumption for these instructions is that there is a structural order of things, presumably in nature and society, that ought to be observed and that holds true for the household of God as well.[41] Imprinted on the literary world of the text is a perception of how reality is structured, and the social order in this structure is understood to be part of the nature of reality. Conforming to this structure in life and behavior is tantamount to godliness.

---

[38] Embedded in the middle of the discussion about deacons is the comment that women are to be "serious, temperate, and faithful in all things and not to engage in slander" (3:11). This remark also emphasizes the personal behavior and character dimension of the discussion, in contrast to a focus on the roles and expectations somehow inherent in the office described.

[39] Cf. 5:1–2.

[40] MacDonald argues that false teaching was linked with the activity of women (*Pauline Churches*, 187–89).

[41] Bassler, *1 Timothy, 2 Timothy, Titus*, 59–60.

Widows are also instructed; in this case there is apparently a group of widows who are enlisted for service in the community. Those sixty years of age and over who have been the wife of one man, attested for their good works and child rearing, known for their hospitality, washing the feet of the saints, and helping the afflicted are to be put on the list (5:9–10). Younger widows are not to be enrolled for they are preoccupied with sensual desires and wish to marry. Moreover, they are generally idle gadabouts who gossip (5:11–13). What is especially interesting about this group of widows is that they are not to have a public role in the household of God but to devote themselves to their tasks in the domestic household by marrying, bearing children, and managing their own homes (5:14). Once again, the domestic household and the household of God are both in view. In this case, the instruction to the younger widows, unlike the older widows, is to fulfill their godliness by confining their involvement to the domestic spheres of household life.

Slaves and those desiring to be rich are also given instruction. Slaves are advised to honor their masters "in order that the name of God and the teaching may not be blasphemed" (6:1). An extra measure of service is instructed for those slaves who have believing masters on the ground that their service redounds to the benefit of other believers (6:2). Even in these instructions to slaves, the familiar distinction between those in the household of God and those outside is drawn. The actions of slaves are in some measure affected by the kind of master to whom they are enslaved, whether an insider or an outsider.

In 6:9–10 those who desire to be rich are warned that the love of money is the root of all evil. In their desire for money, some have also wondered away from the faith. In contrast, the "man of God" should avoid this and "pursue righteousness, godliness, faith, love, steadfastness, and gentleness" (6:11). The love of money is apparently contrary to the life of godliness and can draw people away from the faith, which of course threatens their very salvation.

Woven through these various instructions to groups in the household of God are instructions that are directed quite specifically to Timothy. In 1:18–20 Paul instructs Timothy so that he might fight the good fight, have faith and a good conscience, and not blaspheme. Immediately following this statement Timothy is encouraged to make supplications, prayers, petitions, and thanksgivings for all people (2:1). And in 4:6–16 Timothy is instructed and exhorted regarding his own manner of life. Referring to the previous discussion, Paul advises Timothy that if he gives these instructions to the people in the church he will be a good minister of Christ Jesus (4:6). Following this introduction, Timothy is instructed to have nothing to do with myths and idle tales but is to train himself in godliness (4:7); to set an example in word and deed (4:12); to attend to reading, exhorting, and teaching (4:13); to honor the gift that was given through prophecy with the laying on of hands (4:14); and to practice and persevere in these things (4:15). Further on in the discussion, he is called upon not to rebuke an older man but speak to him as a father (5:1); to show honor to widows (5:3); to keep Paul's instructions regarding elders without prejudice and partiality (5:21); and he is not "to lay hands on anyone "hastily (5:22). He is also to take a little wine for his stomach ailments (5:23). Finally, in 6:20–21 he is commanded to guard that which has been entrusted to him and to avoid that which is falsely called knowledge. In the literary construct of this text, the author addresses the stated reader (Timothy) and an implied audience (the household of God in Ephesus). It is around this double axis that Paul's instructions are organized and directed, and it is not always easy to distinguish them from each other.

## Divine Order and Conformity in Faith

In the literary world of 1 Timothy divine order, natural and social, stands alongside the expectation that people in the household of God should pursue godliness. The proper manner of life—the godly life—is a matter of bringing one's character and behavior into conformity with the perceived order of reality and one's place in that reality. Training in the way of godliness is important in the church, and it is patterned on the model of physical training in 4:7–8. Both of these are part of the structure of 1 Timothy's literary world, and they pertain to the way we ought to think about the οἰκονομίαν Θεοῦ in 1:4. This expression conveys a sense of divine order but it also communicates an expectation that in faith this order is observed by the godly. Those who pursue godliness build up the household of God into conformity with God's purposes and plans. This is important for both the present life and the life to come. Hence, we propose that οἰκονομίαν Θεοῦ τὴν ἐν πίστει ought to be translated: "divine order to which members of the household ought to conform in faith." This conveys the sense of divine order, but also implies the sense of actively conforming one's life in faith to εὐσέβεια (godliness). Deeply embedded in the thought world of 1 Timothy is the image of a natural order to which people in the household of God ought to conform, the result of which is a tendency towards consolidation and conformity, rather than novelty and innovation.

# 2 TIMOTHY

The literary axis of 2 Timothy is established immediately in the first two verses of the text, the greeting. Paul, the named sender of the epistle, is identified as an apostle of Christ Jesus διὰ θελήματος Θεοῦ (through the will of God), κατ' ἐπαγγελίαν ζωῆς (in accordance with the promise of life), and ἐν Χριστῷ Ἰησοῦ (in Christ Jesus). The objects of the prepositions identify different aspects of Paul's apostleship: "the will of God," "promise of life," and "Christ Jesus." Each of these has theological implications for the identity and authority of the stated author of the letter. The authority of the apostle is by the will of God, it is in accordance with the promise of life, and its source is in Christ Jesus.[42] Timothy, the recipient of the epistle, is identified on the other hand as the "beloved child." Clearly implied in this description is an ongoing and intimate relationship with Paul that precedes the immediate time frame of the text. Just as Paul the apostle confers the grace, mercy, and peace that comes from God the Father and Christ Jesus "our" Lord, the "beloved child" Timothy is also linked to the will of God, the promise of life, and Christ Jesus through the apostleship of Paul.

While the literary axis that runs from Paul to Timothy is established already in the greeting, it is this axis that shapes the exhortations, personal examples, ethical patterns, and theological claims that run through the epistle. Though these may in fact alternate in the sequence of the epistle, they all turn on the relationship between Paul and Timothy which is set out at the very beginning of the letter. Eavesdropping on this epistolary monologue is the presumed audience that would also have entered into the exhortations, personal examples, ethical patterns, and theological claims of the epistle as it was read and heard. This audience, too, is expected to heed the apostle's warnings and exhortations to Timothy. Once again, the authority behind these apostolic exhortations and personal examples for this presumed audience is the divine will. The purpose for heeding them is the promise of life, life that extends beyond the present circumstances and comes to fulfillment with the reappearance of Christ.

## The Pattern of Faith

In 1:3–5 Paul shapes his thanksgiving around remarks focused primarily on Timothy. In other words, with the exception of the reference to the God whom Paul worships καθαρᾷ συνειδήσει (with a clear conscience), as did his ancestors, and the remembrance of Timothy in prayer night and day,[43] this epistolary thanksgiving is organized around things that are worthy of thanksgiving in Timothy's life: σου τῶν δακρύων, ὑπόμνησιν . . . ἐν σοὶ ἀνυποκρίτου πίστεως . . . πρῶτον ἐν τῇ μάμμῃ σου . . . καὶ τῇ μητρί σου . . . ὅτι καὶ ἐν σοί (your tears . . . reminded of your sincere faith . . . that lived first in your grandmother . . . and your mother . . . that lives also in you). By juxtaposing the God whom Paul and his ancestors worshiped and the genuine faith of Timothy and his ancestors, there is a presumed connection between the God of Paul and the faith of Timothy. This connection is encompassed retrospectively by the literary world of the letter, even though

---

[42] Following the suggestion regarding ἐν Χριστῷ Ἰησοῦ by Bassler (*1 Timothy, 2 Timothy, Titus*, 126).

[43] Hultgren asserts that "clear conscience" here means "without reservations," (*I, II Timothy, Titus*, 109).

it precedes the immediate time frame of the text. At this point, however, the link between God and Timothy's faith is only implicit.

Although the formal content of faith is rarely made explicit in the letter, πίστις (faith) does appear in 1:5, 13; 2:18, 22; 3:8, 10, 15; 4:7. In 1:13, Timothy is exhorted to hold to the "standard of sound teaching" (ὑγιαινόντων λόγων), which he heard "in the faith and love that are in Christ Jesus." Once again, the description of the content of this faith is not the point of 1:13. While it is clear that "sound teaching" is not simply identified with faith—the "sound teaching" was heard in the faith—the text may imply the character of Timothy's reception in Christ of the teaching that Paul presented to him. If this inference is appropriate, there is at least an implicit connection between the "sound teaching" and the faith in Christ with which Timothy received that teaching. The alternate interpretation is that Paul presented the "sound teaching" in the faith and love that are in Christ. In which case, the connection is between Paul's faith, which has its source in Christ, and the "sound teaching." In both interpretations faith, either on the part of Paul or Timothy, is connected with "sound teaching." Furthermore, Timothy is exhorted to hold to this teaching. In whatever way we read this text, it is clear that the character of this faith is not spelled out, except for the claim that it is related to Christ Jesus and in some general way to "sound teaching."

The reference to "sound teaching" in 1:13 is bracketed by references to guarding παραθήκη in 1:12 and 14.[44] While the translation problems, especially of 1:12, are well known,[45] it is clear that παραθήκη implies some substance, if not content, to that which has been deposited. Whether the deposit is entrusted to God or to the apostle, Paul knows in whom he has believed (πεπίστευκα) and is persuaded there is something to be guarded. Furthermore, God has a role in protecting it διὰ πνεύματος ἁγίου τοῦ ἐνοικοῦντος ἐν ἡμῖν (through the Holy Spirit which dwells in us, 1:14) and ὅτι δυνατός ἐστιν τὴν παραθήκην μου φυλάξαι εἰς ἐκείνην τὴν ἡμέραν (that he is able to guard my good deposit until that day, 1:12). While Paul exhorts Timothy to guard the good deposit with the help of the Holy Spirit, in 2:2 he also instructs him to pass on to faithful (πιστοῖς) people what he has heard from Paul through many witnesses. They will in turn teach it to others. The tradition is to be passed on, and it will be guarded. In the theological world of this text, there is a close connection between the divine and human roles in protecting that tradition as it is passed on.[46]

---

[44] Louw and Nida, *Lexicon,* 1:464, define παραθήκη as "that which has been entrusted to the care of someone. . . ." BDAG defines it as "deposit, property entrusted to another."

[45] Louw and Nida, *Lexicon,* 1:464, assert that the most likely translation of 1:12 is "because he is able to keep what he has entrusted to me," but that ". . . 'what I have entrusted to him,'" is a possible translation. See also Quinn, *First and Second Letters to Timothy,* 604–5.

[46] Karris argues that what has been entrusted is not a fixed and unchanging package of truth but is rather quite dynamic (*The Pastoral Epistles,* 14–15). Bassler

In 2:18 πίστις (faith) appears again, and in this context it is asserted that those who have deviated from the truth and claimed that the resurrection has already taken place are upsetting the faith of some people. While there may not be a direct link in the world of the text between the faith that is being unsettled and the deviating claim that the resurrection has already taken place, the implication is unmistakable. Faith has a particular expectation about the resurrection, and when it is contradicted it is unsettled. For genuine faith, the resurrection is a future expectation.[47]

In 2:22, Timothy is exhorted to flee "youthful passions" and pursue righteousness, faith, love, and peace.[48] Here, faith and its parallel terms are set opposite the passions of youth, and in the immediate context it is clear that "youthful passions" refers to inappropriate behavior. The virtuous qualities, faith among them, represent good behavior as opposed to bad. The very mention of this contrast sets the context for Paul's exhortation to flee "youthful passions." Do this and not that. The more sharply the contrast is drawn, the more pointed the exhortation becomes.

In 3:10, Paul turns to his own autobiography, where faith is included in a list of attributes and activities that mark his personal narrative: my teaching, conduct, aim, faith, patience, love, steadfastness, persecutions, and suffering the sorts of things that happened to him in Antioch. An entire domain of terms is formed that causes the individual terms to shade into one another as the personal story and authority of the author is conjured up for Timothy and for the audience. In this linguistic pattern, Paul's faith is listed alongside his teaching, as well as a series of other terms that designate his conduct and personal circumstance (patience, steadfastness, persecution, and suffering). Hence, in 2 Timothy, Paul's faith is not simply the act of teaching (faithfully teaching as an apostle) or the content of his teaching (teaching in accord with the true faith). It is both, and it is also closely linked to conduct, persecution, suffering—in short, the circumstances of the stated author's own life. An autobiographical appeal is made again in 4:7: "I have fought the good fight, I have finished the race, I have kept the faith."

The implications of faith are extended still further in 3:8, where the corruption of mind, opposition to the truth, and inappropriate behavior are all closely linked. As Jannes and Jambres opposed Moses in the past, there are those who oppose the truth, are corrupt of mind, and have an unfit faith. A genuine faith would presumably correspond to the truth and a healthy mind. The precise character of this truth, healthy mind, and genuine faith is not made completely clear, but the things of the mind and faith are closely connected with behavior and conduct in the thought world of the text. What

---

also notes that careful transmission is an aspect of guarding and is a common element in testamentary literature (*1 Timothy, 2 Timothy, Titus,* 139).

[47] See also 1:12; 2:10; 4:8.

[48] See 3:14, where ἐπιστώθης is used in a hortatory context: "But as for you, remain in what you have learned and believed. . . ." Cf. also πιστοῖς (faithful) in 2:2.

stands out most conspicuously in these references, however, is contrast. Even though we only get glimpses of the content of faith in the referential world of 2 Timothy, the fact that unfit faith is contrasted with genuine faith makes clear that faith has theological substance, if not content, as well as ethical form. What that theological substance and ethical form may be in 2 Timothy is not always clear, but the fact of the contrast itself signals that it is there. Without that implicit theological substance and ethical form, there would be no basis for the contrast.

In 3:15, the text reads: ". . . from childhood you have known the sacred writings that are able to instruct you for salvation through faith in Christ Jesus." Scripture instructs for salvation, but more than that it instructs for salvation *through faith which is in Christ Jesus.* Salvation and faith are here linked explicitly. Scripture instructs for salvation, and faith in Christ is the means to salvation. Hence, the sacred writings may well be important for instruction in faith, as the means to salvation.[49] Similarly, Paul's faith (πεπίστευκα)—apparently faith in Christ—is connected in 1:12 with his own suffering, lack of shame, and with the expectation of "that day" (ἐκείνην τὴν ἡμέραν). Here, too, belief or faith is apparently connected with salvation.

Though the full character of faith is not made explicit in the theology of 2 Timothy, several of its features come into view when we begin to see the theological pattern of this textual world. Genuine faith is linked to both God and Christ,[50] and there is also an implicit connection between faith and the concept of "sound teaching." Even though the precise content of faith may be unclear to us, the fact that faith has theological substance and ethical form is not to be doubted. For example, the deviant claim that the resurrection has already occurred (2:18) is contrary to faith, at least genuine faith. Moreover, the implication of the contrast is that it is possible to differentiate true faith from untrue faith. Faith is also tied to appropriate forms of behavior and becomes in that way part of the context for the paraenesis. Faith is one of the markers of appropriate behavior. Paul has remained steadfast in this faith, and Timothy is exhorted to hold firmly to it as well. Finally, faith in Christ is also linked to Scripture and salvation. Scripture instructs for salvation, and salvation is through faith in Christ Jesus.

## The Word of Truth

Ἀλήθεια (truth) appears in 2:15, 18, 25; 3:7, 8; 4:4 and is closely linked to the pattern of faith in 2 Timothy. The content of this truth, whatever it may be, only comes to the surface of the text incidentally. In 2:15 Timothy is exhorted to explain the "word of truth," and in 2:18 Hymenaeus and Philetus are said to have deviated from the truth by claiming the resurrection has

---

[49] Collins, *1 & 2 Timothy and Titus*, 261–63; and Johnson, *First and Second Letters to Timothy*, 419–21.

[50] See the reference to God's faithfulness in 2:13 and the discussion below.

already come. In the first example, the emphasis is on the exhortation to an activity (explaining the word of truth); whereas in the second, it is on the deviation of those who have made claims about the resurrection (which they say has already occurred).

In 2:25 Paul counsels Timothy to correct opponents with gentleness, for it may be that God will grant them repentance that leads to knowledge of (the) truth (ἐπίγνωσιν ἀληθείας). In this case, knowledge of the truth is said to follow repentance. Whatever the content of this truth, it is dependent on Timothy's correction and God's granting of repentance. The women in 3:6–7, who are overcome by their sins and are always being instructed, are never able to come to knowledge of (the) truth. Apparently, knowledge of the truth does not result from teaching alone. It follows from repentance that God grants as well (2:25).[51] Moreover, according to 3:8, those who have an unfit faith and a corrupt mind oppose the truth. Corruption of mind and inauthenticity of faith go hand in hand with resistance to the truth. There will also come a time when people will turn from listening to the truth and turn to myths (4:4). A notion of truth, closely connected to faith, stands in the background of 2 Timothy's theological world and comes into the foreground on certain occasions, primarily to contrast the opponents and their faith from Paul and Timothy and their faith. Linked closely to truth in 2 Timothy is the manner of life to which Paul exhorts Timothy and his church.

## *The Gifts and Power of God*

Paul's thanksgiving for Timothy's faith turns into exhortation in 1:6–8. Timothy is called upon to rekindle the gift of God that is within him through the laying on of "my" hands. God did not give Timothy a "spirit of cowardice but a spirit of power, love, and self-control." It seems that the gift to be rekindled is the spirit of power, love, and self-control.[52] Hence, the gift of God and the exhortation to Timothy stand side by side in this text. The exhortation to Timothy continues in 1:8 with the plea not to be ashamed of the μαρτύρον τοῦ κυρίου ἡμῶν (testimony of our Lord) or of ἐμὲ τόν δέσμιον αὐτοῦ (me his prisoner). He is also exhorted to join with Paul in suffering for the gospel κατὰ δύναμιν θεοῦ, according to the power that comes from God.[53] From the perspective of the epistle's place in literary time, Paul's imprisonment and suffering precede the exhortation to Timothy, whereas the fulfillment of the exhortation necessarily comes after it. Along this temporal axis that runs between the past and the present and on to an expected future

---

[51] Dibelius and Conzelmann claim that in the Pastorals μετάνοια is "the return to the truth," *The Pastoral Epistles: A Commentary on the Pastoral Epistles* (trans. Philip Buttolph and Adela Yarbro; Hermeneia; Philadelphia: Fortress, 1972), 113.

[52] Bassler, *1 Timothy, 2 Timothy, Titus*, 130.

[53] See the references to suffering in 1:12; 2:3, 9; 3:11–12; 4:5.

where Timothy displays confidence and not shame, the theology of divine power and activity emerges from the text.

God is the one who saved and called "us" to a holy calling. This saving and calling was not according to "our" works but according to "his own" plan and grace, which was given to "us" in Christ Jesus before the ages (1:9). These have already been accomplished. Moreover, it is clear that this God is both a saving and calling God who does these things according to divine grace and purpose, not as a result of human deeds and effort. While these were given before the ages began, they have now become manifest through the epiphany of "our" savior Christ Jesus who abolished death and brought life and immortality to light through the gospel (1:10).[54] In the temporal "now," what have already become realities—the saving, calling, divine purpose, and grace—have come to light. They represent the gifts and power of God, and these are the reasons that Timothy need not be ashamed of the testimony of the Lord and can suffer for the gospel with confidence. They are also the reasons that Paul says he has been appointed a preacher, apostle, and teacher, and for which he suffers without shame (1:1–12).

These theological realities, which are portrayed as being manifestations of divine power and as having objective reality, are situated in a context framed by Paul's exhortation and personal example. This exhortation to confidence and suffering for the gospel is intended to have added persuasive power because it is driven by the reality of divine power which *now* is manifest. Although this exhortation turns on the axis that extends from Paul to Timothy, it is expected that the audience overhearing these instructions is also being called to suffering and confidence within the context of divine power and activity. But what is especially striking about this is that divine gift and power are in no way set against the exhortation to a particular manner of life. The theology and the ethical pattern to which Timothy is exhorted are inextricably linked.[55] In fact, the power of God is portrayed as the reason why Timothy ought to heed the exhortation not to be ashamed of the testimony of the Lord and why he ought to join Paul in suffering for the gospel.

In 2:1–3 Timothy, "my" child, is exhorted to be strong in the grace which is in Christ Jesus and to entrust to the faithful what has been heard through many witnesses, who in turn will be able to teach others. Once again, Timothy is called upon to share suffering, in this case as a good soldier. Following the three analogies in 2:4–6, Timothy is also called upon to remember Christ Jesus, who was raised from the dead and is identified as a descendant of David. This is the gospel for which Paul is said to suffer even to the point of being chained like a criminal. Though the word of God is not

---

[54] For the "epiphany" Christology of 2 Timothy, see 1:10; 4:1, 8. See also Collins, *1 & 2 Timothy and Titus*, 202–3.

[55] Hultgren, *I, II Timothy, Titus*, 137.

bound, he endures these chains on account of the elect, in order that they may gain the salvation that is in Christ Jesus (2:8–10).

In this text, Timothy is exhorted to be strong in grace. In Christ, this is what Timothy possesses. Whereas in chapter one Timothy is exhorted to suffer for the gospel relying on the power that comes from God, here he is to find strength in grace. What is significant at this point is the theological pattern that develops. The power of God and the grace that is in Christ Jesus are both sources of confidence and strength for the suffering to which Timothy is called. In 1:9 it is clear that salvation and the call are not by "our" works but are according to his plan and the gift of his grace, and in 2:1 it is equally clear that Timothy is called upon to be strong in this gift. Once again, the divine gift is not contrary to the implications of the exhortation but rather sustains the one who heeds the call to suffer. Hence, the call to suffering has important theological dimensions. Not only is the gospel that for which Paul himself suffers, but it is the theological reality of the gospel that sustains and gives confidence in the face of this suffering. And that is why Timothy ought to heed Paul's exhortation.

Because these sufferings are endured for the sake of the elect and their salvation, it is obviously the case in the theological world of this text that election does not automatically confer salvation. To put it more directly, election and the ultimate realization of the promise of life are not only tied closely to the gift of God's power and grace but also to faith, a proper manner of life, and the work of the apostle, a part of which is apparently to endure suffering as required for the sake of the elect. These elements cannot be wedged apart, and together they form a complex theological pattern that shapes the paraenesis. Furthermore, the use of personal example in the paraenesis is also bound up with the theological reality represented in the text. What is theologically the case for Paul is also the case for Timothy: God saves and calls, he bestows a spirit of power and love and self-control, there is grace in Christ Jesus, Christ has abolished death, and so there is a promise of life for those who live in genuine faith. Since these theological realities pertain to both Paul and Timothy, the example of one (Paul) can serve as a model for the other (Timothy, and also the audience).

In 2:11–14 the preceding exhortation is reinforced yet again by a set of four theological assertions. In parallel fashion, the first three assertions are designed to relate a future theological consequence to a present action. Living with Christ presupposes having died (with him).[56] Reigning with him presumes enduring (with him). Denying (him) will result in his denying "us." And finally, being faithless to him does *not* result in divine faithlessness. The fourth member of the saying breaks the expected literary pattern that was established in the preceding line: if we are faithless, God will also be faith-

---

[56] Despite the omission of the pronoun, we follow most English translations and assume that the reference is to dying with Christ. See the discussion by Bassler, *1 Timothy, 2 Timothy, Titus,* 144–47.

less. The words, "he is not able to deny himself," intrude into the pattern of the text and explain why the expected pattern cannot be so. To be God is to be faithful. By breaking the pattern, divine faithfulness stands in bold relief. But even more than that, the previous exhortations depend for their force on the reliability of God. If God is not inherently faithful (πιστός), then God cannot be trusted; and if God cannot be trusted, Paul's appeal to Timothy to be steadfast in suffering, upright in behavior, and without shame at the testimony of the Lord is eviscerated.[57]

## *The Pattern of Behavior*

In 2:14, Paul calls upon Timothy to remind the people in his care of "these things;" that is, the things that have just been said in 2:11–13 about dying, enduring, denying, and faithlessness. Coordinate with this are the warnings (before God) and exhortations that follow in 2:14–18. As this discussion proceeds, the warnings to the people and the exhortations to Timothy seem to shade into one another. Timothy is to warn people against disputes over words for they are of no use and are ruinous to those who listen (2:14). But in 2:15 Timothy is called upon to make every effort to present himself approved by God, a worker who is not ashamed and one who rightly expounds the word of truth. In this verse, the command to warn others has become a command directly to Timothy. In 2:16 the plea to avoid godless chatter, because it leads to more and more ἀσέβεια (ungodliness), is apparently directed to Timothy, but may be directed to those faithful people under his care as well. As examples to reinforce the nature of the problem, Hymenaeus and Philetus are said to have deviated from the truth by claiming the resurrection has already occurred (2:17–18).[58]

These warnings and exhortations culminate in yet another theological assertion, enhanced in this case by allusions to Scripture. In the face of these deviations from the truth, God's solid foundation nonetheless stands bearing this inscription: "'the Lord knows those who are his,' and 'let those who name the name of the Lord turn from unrighteousness (2:19).'"[59] As we have seen before, a theological claim, in this case God's knowledge of those who belong to him, is combined with an exhortation, in this context to turn from unrighteousness. Theological claims and exhortations are two sides of the same coin in the textual world of 2 Timothy.[60] Moreover, the theological claims that run through the text add power and substance to the exhortations. The personal

---

[57] Bassler (*1 Timothy, 2 Timothy, Titus*, 146–47) discusses the full range of interpretive issues for this statement.

[58] See 2:25 where Timothy is told that the servant of the Lord must not be quarrelsome but ought to correct the opponents with gentleness that God may grant that they repent and come to knowledge of the truth.

[59] Cf. Num 16:5 and Isa 26:13.

[60] Dibelius and Conzelmann, *The Pastoral Epistles*, 113. They argue that paraenesis draws its motivation from the awareness of election in the theology of the text.

example of the author certainly gives credibility and authority to the paraenesis of 2 Timothy. But it is the theology generated in the first two chapters of the text that serves as the foundation for the exhortations and makes the desired pattern of behavior compelling. The analogy of the vessels in 2:20–21 is not about the divine prerogative in creating some vessels for special use and others for ordinary use.[61] It is about cleansing oneself of the inappropriate behaviors that have been mentioned previously in the discussion. Those who do so will be useful to the δεσπότης (owner of the house) and prepared for every good work. Presuming that the lesson of the analogy is clear, the discussion is driven forward as Paul launches into a virtual list of appropriate and inappropriate behaviors: shun youthful passions; pursue righteousness, faith, love, peace (with those who call upon the Lord with a pure heart); avoid foolish and stupid controversies that breed quarrels; it is necessary that the Lord's servant not quarrel but be gentle to everyone, able to teach, patient, in kindness correcting opponents that God may bring them to repentance that leads to the knowledge of the truth and that they may escape from the devil's snare (2:22–26). To be sure, exhortation drives this discussion, but now the behavior appropriate (and inappropriate) for those who have cleansed themselves and are prepared for every good work is being laid out. Moral and ethical content is now being injected into the paraenesis in a more deliberate way than earlier in the discussion.

In contrast to the list in 2:22–26, which has in the main a positive cast, the list in 3:1–5 is a catalog of vices. And among those people who engage in these condemned activities, one finds those who make their way into houses and mislead women who are overwhelmed by sins.[62] The temporal presumption of the text in 3:1–9 is that "now," in the present moment of the text, the distressing times of the "last days" (ἐσχάταις ἡμέραις) have come to pass (or are just about to come to pass). This is reinforced at the end of the catalog in 3:5 when Paul instructs Timothy to "turn away" from the people who do these things. In the theological world of 2 Timothy, the "last days" are on the horizon and accordingly people who exhibit these reprehensible behaviors are to be avoided. A sense of urgency and impending judgment is also being interjected into the exhortation. The time is short.[63] Set about the work at hand, and avoid these behaviors and those who do them. This entire exhortation, of course, is framed by Paul's impending departure and his desire that Timothy remain steadfast in his absence (4:6–8).

In 3:10–15, the author drives home yet again his appeal to live according to the proper manner of life. The exhortations in 2:14–19 are underwritten by appeal to theology and Scripture (Num 16:5, perhaps also allusions

---

[61] Cf. Rom 9:21.

[62] 3:6–9. See also the discussion above, pp. 38–39.

[63] Bassler downplays the apocalyptic outlook of this text preferring to connect "that day" with the end of Paul's suffering rather than the end of the world (*1 Timothy, 2 Timothy, Titus*, 158–59).

to Job 36:10 and Isa 26:13). In 2:20–26, they are illustrated by analogy and the negative consequences that follow from senseless quarrels. In 3:1–9, the exhortations are framed by the "last days" and allusion to scriptural imagery (Exod 7:11, 22, reference to Pharaoh's magicians). But in 3:10–15, appeal is made once again to Paul's own personal example, especially to his persecutions and sufferings, which are to be expected by all those who wish to live a godly life. Not only does Paul's example lend authority to the epistle's general hortatory tenor, but it gives form to the manner of life that is expected. Paul's prior conduct, as well as that which Timothy has learned and from whom he has learned it,[64] reinforce the bond between the author and recipient, the teacher and student, the parent and child. Paul is Timothy's authority figure and role model. This is a message presumably not lost on the audience that hears this text read and reread.

Conjuring up the image of eschatological judgment and the impending arrival of the kingdom in order to lend authority and urgency to the exhortations, Paul appeals to Timothy yet again (4:1), and commands him to "Preach the word, be persistent whether the time is favorable or unfavorable, convince, reprimand, and encourage in all patience and teaching" (4:2). In 4:5 the exhortation to Timothy is carried still further: "Be sober in everything, suffer hardship, do the work of an evangelist, fulfill your ministry." In the presence of God and Christ Jesus who judges both the living and the dead (4:1), Timothy is called upon to remain steadfast in his ministry. Though the time is coming when people will seek teachers to suit their own desires (4:3), Timothy is not to waver. The pattern of behavior set before him is clear and direct. And once again theology (or Christology), in this case Christ's reappearance and his judgment of both the living and the dead, frames the exhortations.

One of the most striking features of 2 Timothy's pattern of behavior is the theme of suffering. In 1:12; 2:9; and 3:11, the references are to Paul's suffering; whereas in 1:8; 2:3; and 4:5 the exhortation is for Timothy to suffer. The appeal to Timothy is not to suffer with Christ—with the possible exception of 2:11—but with Paul.[65] Since Paul has already suffered, the exhortation to Timothy is to join him in suffering (συγκακοπάθησον, 1:8; 2:3). The past reality of Paul's suffering is linked to the future expectation of Timothy's suffering. In the world of the text, suffering holds the prospect that the two might be united on yet another level. Not only are Paul and Timothy united by the bond between teacher and pupil, but they ought to be united as fellow sufferers for the sake of the gospel as well.

## A Theological Conclusion

The literary progression of 2 Timothy culminates in 4:6–8 with what seems like the author's final testament. Following this, the epistle concludes

---

[64] See Bassler's suggestion (ibid., 166).
[65] Ibid., 131.

with rather detailed instructions to Timothy. Although the testamentary material in 4:6–8 functions as the conclusion to the body of the epistle, it is unlikely that it defines the genre of the text. As already indicated,[66] 2 Timothy is more accurately described as a paraenetic letter.

One of the noteworthy conclusions of the preceding discussion is that the paraenesis does not rest on Paul's personal example and authority alone. The theology of the text, especially in the first two chapters, is thoroughly interwoven with the various exhortations and appeals to follow Paul's example. The reason why Timothy ought to suffer with confidence, not be ashamed, and behave appropriately has as much to do with God and the activity of God as it does with Paul's own example. To put it another way, it is the reality of what God has done and will do that makes Paul's example compelling and authoritative. In that regard, Paul lives and teaches the things of God. If 2 Timothy is in fact driven by paraenesis, it is paraenesis thoroughly informed and shaped by a view of God and the activity of God.

## Titus

Like 1 and 2 Timothy, the epistle to Titus is organized around a literary axis that runs from an author (Paul) to a reader (Titus in this epistle). As in those earlier epistles, the instructions, exhortations, and theological claims turn on this literary axis. With few exceptions, the discussion in Titus is not marked in the main by theological argumentation. Rather the theology in the text serves as a framework and foundation for the instructions and exhortations that Paul gives to Titus. This means that the theology of the text often remains embedded in the literary world that forms the backdrop to the discussion. As a result, the theology of this text usually comes to the fore only in relation to other kinds of issues.

In the beginning of the epistle, Paul, the stated author, identifies himself as δοῦλος Θεοῦ (slave of God) and an ἀπόστολος Ἰησοῦ Χριστοῦ (apostle of Jesus Christ). In these words, Paul establishes his credentials. Unlike 1 Timothy, however, this greeting is extended to indicate the purpose for which he is a slave and an apostle: "the faith of the elect and knowledge of the truth that is in accord with godliness" (εὐσέβειαν). In contrast to 2 Timothy, where Paul indicates that his apostleship is by the will of God and for the promise of life, the author in Titus identifies faith and knowledge as the operative concepts associated with his being a slave and an apostle. To this point, the temporal sense implied in the greeting to Titus is the present time, but this is extended into the past and the future in 1:2: ". . . for the hope of life eternal, which the God who does not lie promised before time began, in the proper time he revealed his word in preaching with which I

---

[66] See above, p. 9.

was entrusted by the command of God our savior." Paul's work as a slave and an apostle is for the sake of the faith of the elect and knowledge of truth, but it is also done in the hope of eternal life that was promised even before time began. In the proper time, presumably with the appearance of Christ, his word was manifested in preaching, and it is this word that Paul has been given by the God who saves. The activity of Paul, the apostle, is carried out in the face of a soteriological hope, that is, life eternal. It is also interesting to note that the greeting connects σωτῆρος (savior) with both God and Christ.[67] With this greeting, the author of the text and his work are firmly situated within the larger scope of divine activity, and in that sense the greeting is highly theological. Apostolic activity and divine purpose are thoroughly overlaid in establishing the authority and Pauline legacy of the stated author. Paul's bond with Titus is made explicit in 1:4. They share a common faith; and because of that, Paul and Titus are united in a common theological reality.

The text of Titus ends with a conclusion (3:12–15) that is somewhat closer to 2 Timothy with its personal greetings and instructions, than it is to 1 Timothy, with its virtual lack of personal comments and greetings. In 3:15 Paul sends greetings to Titus from all those who are with him and requests that Titus greet those who love "us" in the faith. The final blessing is the same as 1 Timothy except for the inclusion of πάντων (all). As in 1 and 2 Timothy, however, the author here uses the plural form of the pronoun, ὑμῶν (you), which indicates that within the text itself there are markers that point to a larger implied audience in the literary world of the epistle. Grace is bestowed not only on Titus but also on this wider community in Crete.

## God, Godliness, and Salvation in Christ

As we have already seen in the greeting of the epistle, God is a God who elects and this election is linked to the reason for Paul's apostleship. Moreover, God is explicitly identified in the greeting as one who is trustworthy, has made promises before the beginning of time, and has now entrusted his word to Paul (1:2–3). In 2:13 the blessed hope and manifestation of the glory of our great God is awaited along with "our" savior Jesus Christ. The temporal point of view of the text is shaped by the future eschatological expectation, when God's glory and salvation will be made known. This future is shaped by "Jesus Christ, our savior, who gave himself on our behalf in order that he might redeem us from lawlessness and cleanse for himself a chosen people, zealous for good works." In this highly condensed soteriological statement, God, Christ, and salvation are drawn together and linked

---

[67] God is identified as savior, or the one who saves, in 1:3; 2:10. Cf. 2:11; 3:4, 5, whereas in 1:4; 2:13; and 3:6 Christ is identified as the savior. Contrast the use of savior (σωτήρ) and save (σώζω) in 1 Timothy. See the excursus in Dibelius and Conzelmann, *The Pastoral Epistles*, 100–104.

in this future eschatological hope that marks the literary text's sense of time, in this case life eternal. Moreover, Titus is instructed to speak these things, exhort and correct with all commanding power (2:15). The summoning of these terms adds rhetorical weight to the preceding statements and signals their importance in the world of this text. These are anything but idle claims in Titus. They are to be proclaimed among the elect of God in Crete, and the elect are to be conformed to and reproved by these words of blessed hope. This soteriological statement is close to the heart of the epistle's understanding of God and salvation.[68]

Theology and Christology are once again thoroughly interwoven in 3:4–7. The temporal dimension of the text's thought world is injected into the discussion by the word ὅτε (when), but the first real theological assertion in this text is the claim that "the goodness and lovingkindness of God our savior" were made known (3:4). Not only is God identified as savior but the qualities of goodness and lovingkindness are also attributed to God. This interest in divine qualities echoes, for example, the claim in 1:2 that God is trustworthy. While the line between the character and the activity of God cannot be drawn sharply, 3:4 clearly attributes to divine character the virtues of goodness and kindness. In 3:5a this view of divine character is extended. God's activity of saving "us" was not because of our righteous works but because of God's mercy. In the world of this text, saving is an act of divine mercy rather than the result of righteous human deeds. The means to this salvation is through "the washing of regeneration" perhaps referring to baptism, and "renewal in the spirit" (3:5b). In the imagery of the text, one moves into the realm of salvation through washing, which also links up with the image of cleansing in 2:13, and renewal in the Holy Spirit which he poured out on "us" abundantly through Jesus Christ our savior. The ideas of purification and restoration are closely linked with salvation in the theological world of Titus. Moreover, in 3:4–7 both God and Christ are identified as savior. This identification seems to be used interchangeably in Titus without the slightest pause.[69] According to 3:7–8, the pouring out of the richness of the spirit through Christ is "so that we might be made righteous by his grace and become heirs of the hope of eternal life." Righteousness and inheritance in Titus clearly follow from God's actions, including the pouring out of the Holy Spirit, in Christ the savior.

This highly charged theological statement in 3:4–7 is concluded in 3:8a with an exclamation point: "This saying is sure." Rhetorically, this underscores the certainty and significance of the theological claims made in the preceding condensed kerygmatic statement,[70] but it also sets the stage for the call to Titus to insist on these things ". . . so that those who believe in

---

[68] For the OT allusions and echoes which anchor the argument in the authority of Scripture see Bassler, *1 Timothy, 2 Timothy, Titus*, 201.

[69] Young, *Theology*, 50–59.

[70] Johnson, *Paul's Delegates*, 246.

God might devote themselves to good works (3:8)." Far from putting forth this statement in 3:4–7 as an isolated matter of theological argumentation, the text indicates that it is to inform the behavior of the addressees. Presumably, the goodness and kindness of God are to be expressed, if not replicated, among those who believe in God. God's mercy, not our deeds, has resulted in our righteousness, but rather than suggesting that good works are unimportant, the opposite claim is made. Titus is instructed to hold fast to these claims so that as a result the believers might attend to good works that are profitable for everyone. The clear implication is that the theology of salvation is expected to shape the life of the believers; and if the implications of 2:11–12 carry over into 3:4–8, the renewal poured out in the abundance of the Holy Spirit may in fact enable a life of profitable good works and avoidance of controversy.[71] These are the righteous deeds that are to mark the community of believers, and they are linked in the text to the theology of salvation that unfolds in the discourse of the epistle, especially in 2:11–15 and 3:4–8. The narrative of salvation as rehearsed in these two texts represents the pattern, justification, and the empowering quality that is to govern the communal relations of the faithful in Crete.

Εὐσέβεια (godliness) and εὐσεβῶς (in a godly manner) each appear once in Titus (1:1 and 2:12). In addition, the term ἀσέβεια (ungodliness) also occurs in 2:12. As we saw above in the greeting,[72] the faith of the elect and knowledge of the truth for which Paul is an apostle are qualified as being in accord with godliness. The only further connection with godliness identified in this greeting is the link with the hope of eternal life that was promised before time began. But the more interesting text in this regard is 2:11–12: "For the grace of God was made known (bringing) salvation to all people and training (παιδεύουσα) us to reject ungodliness and worldly desires and to live modest, righteous, and godly lives in the present age." The grace of God brings salvation and does the training. It is not a matter of training oneself according to the model of athletic competition in the gymnasium,[73] but of being trained by the divine grace that has now been made known. The contour of this godly life, both negatively and positively, means that worldly desires are to be rejected and that lives of modesty, righteous behavior, and εὐσέβεια (godliness) are to be lived. The godly life is now possible precisely because divine grace has been revealed and has become the παιδευτής (instructor, teacher). Not only are theology and the godly life interwoven in the literary world of Titus, but the story of redemption and the revelation of God's grace indicate that because of these the godly life is now possible. Since the revelation of God's grace has come to pass, the godly life is a real prospect for the community of faith under the training of God's grace, and this godly life is couched in the full expectation of eternal life.

---

[71] Ibid., 247.
[72] See above, pp. 27–28.
[73] Cf. 1 Tim 4:7 and the use there of the term γυμνάζω.

## *Truth, Sound Teaching, and Faith*

As we have seen, the notion of the truth is encountered already in the greeting (knowledge of the truth, 1:1). In the imagery of the text, this may also be linked to the expression in 1:16: "They profess *to know God* but by their deeds deny him." It is clear that knowing the truth and knowing God are closely positioned on the conceptual map that underlies this text. In 1:13–14, the pointed and derogatory quote from a certain prophet about the Cretans being liars, brutes, and lazy gluttons is followed by Paul's assertion that this is a true testimony. Because of this, Titus is instructed to rebuke them "so that they might become sound in the faith and not heed Jewish myths and commandments of people who turn from the truth" (1:13b–14). While the concept of divine truth implying some notion of doctrinal content is not pervasive in Titus, the references in 1:1 and 1:14 suggest it is not far beneath the surface of the text.

This is also confirmed in 1:9 and especially 3:8. Though the terminology of truth changes from the language of "truth" to that of "faithfulness" (πιστός) in these references, the notion of dependability is clearly associated with the word that is in accordance with this teaching and right theology. The overseer, according to 1:9, is to cling to the trustworthy word (πιστοῦ λόγου) that is in accord with the teaching so that he might be able to exhort with sound teaching. And in 3:8, as we have seen, the tightly condensed theological statement in 3:4–7 is declared to be sure and trustworthy (πιστὸς ὁ λόγος). Each of these references, in its own way, suggests a concept of theological truth in Titus that has a doctrinal character to it. In the case of 3:8, this is expressed in terms of the narrative of salvation.

As we see in 1:9, sound teaching is closely associated with the truth and the true word, and this word is necessary for both preaching and refuting those who teach something other than the truth. In the discussion that follows in 1:10–11, the characterization of certain rebellious people, especially of a group identified as the "circumcision," perhaps referring simply to those who require adherence to Jewish practices such as circumcision, are said to teach for sordid gain things that are not right to teach. The reference to the opponents being associated with some type of Jewish heresy is reiterated in 1:14, as we have seen above. Rather than attending to the sound faith, they are giving heed to "Jewish myths and commandments of people who reject the truth." Moreover, the minds and consciences of those who have turned from the truth are defiled (1:15).

In 2:1 Titus is instructed to speak what is fitting for sound teaching, and in 2:6–7 he is to show himself as a model of good works, sound in the teaching, dignified, and above reproach. In 2:10 slaves are instructed to show all good faith so that they might "adorn the teaching of God our savior in everything." And this leads in 2:11–12 to the pedagogical role of God's grace as we have already discussed above.[74] Direct hints at what this teaching involves are given throughout the epistle, especially in the two kerygmatic passages, 2:11–15 and 3:4–7. But even where this is not made explicit the specter of correct doctrine hangs over the theological world that informs the discussion in Titus. In their adherence to "Jewish myths" (1:14), "commandments" (1:14), "genealogies" (3:9), "disputes about the law" (3:9), and perhaps even circumcision (1:10), the opponents are corrupt of mind and conscience. They are "rebellious" (1:10), "idle talkers" (1:10), "deceivers" (1:10), "upsetting whole houses with inappropriate teaching" (1:11), "liars" (1:12), "defiled" (1:15), and "professing to know God" while their actions show otherwise (1:16). In short, they have followed false doctrine and exhibited reprehensible behavior. They are to be "silenced" (1:11) and "rebuked" (1:13).[75]

Closely associated with the truth and the teaching in Titus are the references to "the word." In 1:3 the reference is to God's word of preaching, and in 1:9 it is to the instruction that the overseer must "hold fast to the reliable word that is in accord with the teaching." The word of God is linked here with both preaching and teaching. Women are charged in 2:5 with conforming to a list of behaviors that must be observed so that the word of God might not be brought into disrepute. The clear implication is that the word of God is a possession that is subject to being discredited by inappropriate behavior. Those who have this word must act accordingly and appropriate actions are clearly specified. Titus is to tell older women to be neither "slanderous" nor "enslaved to wine" (2:3). He should also tell them to "teach what is good" and to encourage younger women to love their husbands and their children, and to be thoughtful and chaste people who do work at home and are subject to their husbands. Conformity to the word of God might also be implied by the instruction to the young men in 2:8 to engage in "sound speech." Once again, the theological statement in 3:4–7 is referred to as the sure and certain word. The discussion to this point makes clear that the truth, the teaching, and the word of God point to a semantic complex that is deeply embedded in the literary world that underlies this text. It refers implicitly to a notion of correct doctrine and behavior.

The final terms in this semantic complex are the noun "faith" and the verb "to believe." In Titus faith appears to have primarily a doctrinal quality but conveys a more personal sense of piety as well. The use of the term in 1:1 (faith of the elect) , 1:4 (the common faith), 1:13 (that they may be sound in the faith), and 2:2 (steadfast in the faith),[76] suggests that faith is something

---

[74] See above, p. 49; see also Bassler, *1 Timothy, 2 Timothy, Titus*, 204.

[75] Johnson suggests the opponents may be outsiders (*Paul's Delegates*, 213), but Bassler sees the threat clearly coming from within (*1 Timothy, 2 Timothy, Titus*, 188). See also Jerry L. Sumney, *'Servants of Satan,' 'False Brothers,' and Other Opponents of Paul* (JSNTSup Series 188; Sheffield: Sheffield Academic Press, 1999), 290–96, 301–2.

[76] Cf. also 1:9.

exterior to the person, namely, a set of convictions that define what the believers believe or ought to believe. This, of course, is thoroughly consistent with and coordinate to the implications of the terms "truth" and "teaching" discussed above. There is an implicit sense in the text that there is a correct belief (or faith) to which those in the community adhere or ought to adhere, and this is expressed by a cluster of terms that on this point overlap semantically.

But there are also subtle hints that something more personal is conveyed by this term in this text. For example, in the conclusion to the epistle in 3:15 Paul asks that greetings be given to those "who love us faithfully." This paraphrase captures the sense that something more than sharing a common doctrine is being suggested here. Similarly, in 3:8 Paul instructs Titus to insist on the things that have been rehearsed in 3:4–7 "so that those who have come to believe in God might be careful to devote themselves to good works . . . (3:8)." While one could interpret this statement to imply some notion of doctrinal content, it seems clear that a sense of devotion to God is also indicated. This less than fully doctrinal sense of "faith" might also be implied in 1:15 when it is said that "to the corrupt and unbelieving (ἀπίστοις) nothing is clean." In Titus, faith cannot be reduced simply to an issue of correct doctrine, although that is by far the strongest implication of the term in this text.

### Qualities and Instructions Appropriate for Members of the Household

In 1:5 Paul reminds Titus why he has left him behind in Crete, namely, to set things in order and to appoint elders in every town as Paul has directed him. By calling to the fore in the discussion the prior circumstance of their work in Crete, the author reminds Titus why he is there and what he is to do. The temporal character of the literary text precedes the actual time frame of the discussion as presented in the text. This illustrates once again that the world that stands behind the text is periodically drawn to the fore in the discussion of the epistle. In this case, Titus is to appoint πρεσβύτεροι (elders) in every town, and the qualities necessary for these appointees are listed in 1:6. They are to be above reproach, husband of one wife, have children who are believers, not accused of debauchery or rebelliousness. Rather than instructing Titus concerning an existing group of elders in the community,[77] Paul is explicitly reminding him of the task he has been charged with fulfilling, and in the process of fulfilling that task these are the necessary qualities for the individuals appointed. As in 1 Timothy, this is not a description of the job of a πρεσβύτερος but of the character qualities of the person who is to do the job.

---

[77] Contrast 1 Tim 5:17–20.

Following on immediately in the epistle, Paul in 1:7 takes up the issue of the ἐπίσκοπος (overseer). As the θεοῦ οἰκονόμον (God's steward), the overseer is to be above reproach. Louw and Nida list the term for steward (οἰκονόμον) under the domain entitled "household activities" and indicate that it refers to "one who is in charge of running a household." Quite correctly, they point out that the emphasis is on management of the household, and the οἰκονόμος is the one who manages that household.[78] As in 1 Timothy, the household codes of the Greco-Roman world are close at hand in the imagery of this text. In the structure of this household, God stands as the paterfamilias, while the ἐπίσκοπος is God's agent in managing the duties of the house.[79]

According to 1:7b, the overseer "must not be arrogant, quick tempered, addicted to wine, violent, or greedy for sordid gain." These are the negative and inappropriate qualities that should disqualify a person from being an overseer. On the other hand, the positive qualities are stated in 1:8–9: "but he must be hospitable, love what is good, self-controlled, upright, devout, disciplined and he must cling to the true word that is in accord with the teaching in order that he might be able to exhort with the sound teaching and refute those who speak against it." This list of positive qualifications trails off into an assertion that he must hold fast to the sound teaching so he can exhort and refute. The ἐπίσκοπος (overseer) needs the moral authority represented by the sound teaching of the community for both exhortation and refutation, apparently of those within the community identified in 1:10–16 who have gone astray.[80] In this way, the qualifications appropriate for an overseer lead into and contribute to the execution of two of the overseers' duties, exhorting and refuting. At this point in the text, the concern for correct doctrine and episcopal duty intersect. The managers of the household can only manage properly if they hold fast to the true teaching, which is obviously the standard against which correct behavior is measured. In this way, the correct theology, the appropriate behavior in the community, and the duties of an overseer are intimately linked in the thought world of Titus.

In 2:1–8 Paul identifies the qualities appropriate for men and women, both young and old. Older men are to exhibit the virtues of temperance, seriousness, prudence, and soundness in faith, love, and endurance (2:2). The older women, on the other hand, are to be reverent in behavior, neither slanderous nor enslaved to wine, and teachers of that which is good. They are to encourage younger women to be chaste, prudent, as well as to love their husbands and children, be subject to their husbands, and be good managers of their domestic lives (οἰκουργός). All of this is so that the word

---

[78] Louw and Nida, *Lexicon,* 1:521.

[79] MacDonald, *Pauline Churches,* 210–12; and Fitzmyer, "Structured Ministry," 587–89.

[80] Bassler, *1 Timothy, 2 Timothy, Titus,* 187–88.

of God might not be brought into disrepute (2:3–5). Titus is to exhort the young men to be self-controlled, models of good works with integrity in the teaching, dignity, and sound speech (2:6–8). This is so that the opponents may be put to shame and have nothing evil to say of "us." What is clear from this listing of qualities is that there is a serious concern in the world of this text for the proper ordering of the community's life. The order of things is important and is deeply rooted in the nature of reality. Conformity to that order is critical in adopting the proper manner of life and the proper network of relationships in the community. When the community is in conformity with this proper ordering of things, there is no opportunity for the word of God to be discredited or for the community to be slandered. In the world of this text, the behavior appropriate for the community is not merely a matter of individual choice or determination. It is a matter of discerning the nature of reality and encouraging the community to conform its life and action to it.

The other large institution in the Greco-Roman world that impinged on the life and good order of the household was, of course, slavery. This issue is taken up in 2:9–10. Here Titus is reminded that slaves are to be "subject to their masters in everything." They are to "give satisfaction, not talk back, and be faithful." Once again, a justification is given: "so that the teaching of God our savior might be adorned in everything." And in 3:1, Titus is instructed to remind "them" that they are to be subject to the ruling authorities. The emphasis on conformity to the good order considered natural is, in these examples, so that that which the community stands for might be enhanced (the positive reason) and might not be discredited (the negative reason). While the point of view of the discussion in Titus is inward, the results of the behavior within the community are also implicitly being projected outward to a larger world that is thought to be watching.[81] More than that, however, it is very clear that these instructions are cast directly to the opponents who are being combatted. Not to conform to the proper expectations is thought to undermine the position of Titus and the faithful in this struggle to maintain sound doctrine.

Throughout this epistle, Titus is urged to instruct and exhort the community in Crete. In that sense, he is to be Paul's mouthpiece and presence in the community. But Titus is also instructed in how to behave himself. This subtle interaction is perhaps evident in 3:8–11 if we see the δέ (but) in 3:9 as adversative and see the instruction in 3:4–8 to be instruction about a theology that Titus is to uphold in the community ("I desire you to insist on these things . . ." [3:8]). The ensuing exhortation regarding the appropriate behavior in 3:9–11 is understood to be directed to Titus personally: "But (δέ) avoid foolish controversies and genealogies and strife and dissension about the law for they are useless and in vain. Refuse to have anything to do with

---

[81] Collins, *1 & 2 Timothy and Titus*, 345–48.

the factious individual after the first or second admonition because you know that such a person is perverted and sinful, being self condemned." The discussion moves from the statements of what Titus is to insist upon to a more specific set of assertions about how he is to behave in the face of the opposition in Crete.

It may not be too much of a stretch to suggest that Paul the apostle (1:1–3), Titus his delegate (1:4), and the grace of God now made known (2:11–12), are all part of the process of instruction and exhortation that is to shape the community's pattern of belief and behavior. As the authoritative δοῦλος (slave) of God, Paul instructs his devoted child and agent, Titus, who along with the Holy Spirit and grace of God is to train the people in correct doctrine and to exhort them to behave according to established good order. Thus, authority and training descend vertically from God to Paul to Titus and ultimately to the community. In the world of Titus, and consistent with social patterns in the Greco-Roman world, authority and power move downward in what is perceived to be a hierarchical structure of divine and social reality. In fact, the divine order and the social order are treated as virtually continuous with one another in the instructions given by Paul to Titus. They are not understood to be disconnected realms of reality.

## A Theological Conclusion

In the theological world of Titus, it is made explicit that the believers are not saved by righteous deeds but by the mercy of God through the water of rebirth and the renewal of the Holy Spirit (3:5). In the epistle to Titus, this claim is not a matter for argumentation or something that needs to be debated and defended, even though the opposition appears to have judaizing tendencies. It is simply declared as a proposition that is true; and in that sense, it is part of the theological world that is assumed in the epistle. Good deeds earn neither righteousness nor eternal life. There is no sense in this text, however, that in doing good works one might confuse the issue and slip into the trap of works righteousness. Behavior befitting the faithful community and the good order of the church are to be instructed and exhorted. Where there is reference to the judaizing behavior of the opponents, the problem does not appear to be a matter of Gentile inclusion into a mixed community of Christ, but of belief and behavior inconsistent with correct doctrine and life. The opponents are simply wrongheaded and their behavior threatens the proper order of things in the community.

Having established the basic contours of the discrete theological patterns in the three Pastoral letters, we will now subject these patterns in the next chapter to a comparative analysis, drawing the patterns from the three Pastorals into a comparative juxtaposition and in turn comparing that material with material from the undisputed Pauline epistles. Once again, our purpose is to place the images of Paul and the theological patterns displayed in the Pastorals in their rightful place in the developing Pauline tradition and in the emergence of the Christian church. As before, our focus will be on the structural patterns of the respective texts and traditions rather than on simple linguistic and theological parallels or on stylistic considerations. To that task we now turn.

# ~ 3 ~

# THE PASTORAL EPISTLES AND PAUL:
# A COMPARISON OF PATTERNS

## THE PASTORAL EPISTLES: PATTERNS IN COMPARISON

AS LITERARY texts, 1 and 2 Timothy and Titus represent discrete theological patterns. Each text has its own particular configuration of theological concepts, claims, instructions, and exhortations. There was no attempt in the previous chapter to compare or to account for these differences, but it is ultimately insufficient simply to identify the theological patterns of the respective texts. It is now necessary to bring these theological patterns into comparison in order to highlight, differentiate, and compare the respective materials. In this way, we can identify both the structural similarities and differences. In subsequent chapters, we will probe further the theological conceptions represented in these epistles by placing them in larger Pauline, canonical, and postcanonical frames of reference.

The primary objective of the discussion in this chapter is to begin the process of positioning the Pastorals more precisely in the symbolic and theological context of early Pauline tradition through comparative analysis. As a result of this discussion, we can frame a way of thinking about the authorship of the Pastoral Epistles; and though we will conclude that in all likelihood Paul is not the author of these letters, it is important for our purposes to see the result of this investigation in the wider framework of Pauline tradition and development. Modern scholarship on the Pastorals rightly takes the issue of authorship seriously, but in this book that question is important primarily as it relates to the issue of how these letters connect to the broader Pauline tradition. So the way we frame the issue of the authorship of the Pastorals and their relationship to the undisputed Pauline letters is virtually as important as our conclusion about the issue of authorship itself.

Methodologically that means that comparison of the respective Pastoral theological patterns produces in turn a deeper sense of the how each of these three letters is structured theologically as well as how they relate individually to each other. This analysis also sets the stage for the comparison of material from the Pastorals with material from the undisputed Pauline letters. In both sets of comparisons, the approach will be to identify and compare literary and theological patterns rather than isolated correspondences. We begin these comparisons with the images of God and Christ in the Pastoral Epistles following in turn with comparisons of godliness in the household; truth, knowledge, and faith; opponents and their opposition; and qualifications for leadership.

## Images of God and Christ in Comparison

Perhaps the most conspicuous image of God in the Pastoral Epistles is that of "savior" or the "one who saves." While the term σωτήρ (savior) occurs only once each in Ephesians and Philippians (in both cases referring to Christ, Phil 3:20 and Eph 5:23), it appears nowhere else in the Pauline tradition outside of its multiple attestation in the Pastorals.[1] The verbal form σῴζω (save) is attested frequently in Paul, especially in Romans and 1 Corinthians.[2] It is also commonly used in the Pastorals as well.[3] Σωτήρ as a divine descriptor is without doubt a special feature of the Pastoral Epistles relative to the rest of the New Testament Pauline tradition. But a closer look at the Pastorals also indicates some differences among these three epistles.

In 1 Timothy, God alone is referred to as savior, whereas in Titus the designation alternates between God and Christ. The single appearance of the term in 2 Timothy (1:10) is also used in connection with Christ. In 1 Tim 1:1 and 2:3 God is simply referred to as "our savior," and in 4:10 God is identified as a living God who is "savior of all people." The verbal form of the word in 1 Tim 2:4 has God as the subject, whereas in 1:15 Christ is clearly the subject of the infinitive verb: "Christ Jesus came into the world to save sinners." In Titus 1:3; 2:10; and 3:4, as in 1 Tim 1:1 and 2:3, God is designated "our savior," and in Titus 1:4; 2:13; and 3:6 Christ carries this appellation. In Titus 3:5 the subject of the verb "to save," referring back to 3:4, also has God as the subject. In 2 Tim 1:9 and 4:18 the verb "to save" is used. In the first case God is the subject, and in the second the "Lord," apparently referring to God, functions in that capacity. With regard to the identification of the "savior," the Pastoral Epistles consistently apply that designation to God or Christ, unlike the remainder of the New Testament Pauline tradition where the nominal form of the term rarely appears.[4] However, among the three Pastoral Epistles, there are also some noticeable differences in usage. Titus is the epistle most

---

[1] 1 Tim 1:1; 2:3; 4:10; 2 Tim 1:10; Titus 1:3, 4; 2:10, 13; 3:4, 6. Σωτήριος (salvation) also occurs in Titus 2:11 in the expression ἐπεφάνη γὰρ ἡ χάρις τοῦ Θεοῦ σωτήριος πᾶσιν ἀνθρωποις (For the grace of God has appeared bringing salvation to all people).

[2] Eight times in both Rom and 1 Cor, twice in Eph, and once each in 2 Cor, 1 Thess, and 2 Thess (Rom 5:9, 10; 8:24; 9:27; 10:9, 13; 11:14, 26; 1 Cor 1:18, 21; 3:15; 5:5; 7:16; 9:22; 10:33; 15:2; 2 Cor 2:15; Eph 2:5, 8; 1 Thess 2:16; 2 Thess 2:10.

[3] 1 Tim 1:15; 2:4, 15; 4:16; 2 Tim 1:9; 4:18; Titus 3:5.

[4] The only other New Testament document outside the Pastorals where σωτήρ occurs with some regularity is 2 Peter (five times, 1:1, 11, 2:20, 3:2, 18), and in that

ready to apply σωτήρ (savior) to Christ (three times for God and three times for Christ), whereas 1 Timothy uses "savior" only to refer to God (three times). Second Timothy, on the other hand, is noteworthy for the fact that the term "savior" appears only once (1:10), referring to Christ.

Against the backdrop of a future eschatological expectation, namely Christ's return, the image of God as savior in the Pastorals is set. In this regard, God is understood to be cosmic and universal.[5] Even though the focus of much of the attention in the Pastorals is inward, having to do with the parochial concerns of the community of faith—the household of God—the perception of God in these epistles clearly transcends those limits. This universality is emphasized most directly in 1 Tim 4:10, where God is identified as "the savior of all people." While the universality of this saving God is unmistakable, especially in 1 Timothy (cf. also Titus 2:11), the expectation that all will in fact be saved is not. God is savior of all but not all will be saved.[6] Designated as savior, God is without limits; but from the side of human disposition only those who believe and are within the circle of belief will be saved (cf. 4:10). Although the social realm may be divided between believers and unbelievers, God and God's intention for salvation are universal and undivided. It is this divine universality that gives credibility to the instructions and exhortations to remain steadfast in the truth, while it is the possibility of failure that gives them a sense of urgency. By standing firm in faith, the community establishes its bond with this universal God, and together they form the point and counterpoint of salvation, the savior and the saved. This dialectic of salvation is not argued or debated in the Pastorals, it is simply assumed as part of the theological structure of reality, especially evident in 1 Timothy and Titus.

The oneness of God is made explicit in 1 Tim 2:5, as is the oneness of the mediator between God and humanity, Christ Jesus.[7] This is the only place where this precise formulation of God and Christ ("There is one God, There is also one mediator between God and humankind") appears in the Pastorals, but the monotheistic image clearly echoes the references to the oneness of God in Rom 3:30, Gal 3:20, and 1 Cor 8:4. It is an image deeply rooted in Jewish religious experience and consequently in the prevailing theological perception of the early church. Indeed 2:5–6 may well represent a tradition prior to 1 Timothy. Though this monotheistic formulation only comes to the fore in 1 Timothy, there is no reason to think it is not also assumed in the theological worlds of 2 Timothy and Titus. In summary fashion, we might say that this one God gives life (1 Tim 4:10, 6:13) and is the

---

epistle the term is used consistently of Christ. In that series of occurrences the only ambiguous reference is 3:2, but even here it is most assuredly a reference to Christ as well. This might suggest some connection between the Pauline tradition of the Pastorals and 2 Peter.

[5] Young, *Theology*, 52–53. Cf. also 1 Tim 6:15–16.

[6] Cf. 1 Tim 4:16; 6:12.

[7] Cf. 2 Tim 1:10; 2:8.

foundation of the truth (1 Tim 3:15) and also acts in the world to call (2 Tim 1:8–9) and to bring eternal life to the elect (Titus 1:1–3). This God promised his grace before the ages began (2 Tim 1:9–10) and is trustworthy in the face of those promises (Titus 1:1–3). This God is also powerful and that power extends from God to God's faithful people (2 Tim 1:8).

But as 1 Tim 2:5 makes clear it is the mediator, Christ Jesus, who is the connecting link between the divine and human realities. In the dialectic of salvation, Christ is identified as singular, as savior (Titus 1:4; 2:13; 3:6), and as the agent who does the work of salvation. As savior, Christ is of God, and as redeemer, Christ engages in the work of saving sinners. While 1 Timothy reserves the designation "savior" for God, Titus alternates back and forth between applying the term to God and Christ. It is tempting to suggest that a subtle theological shift has taken place from divine being and intention in 1 Timothy to redemptive purpose and activity in Titus,[8] with 2 Timothy making only scant use of the designation. This, of course, is possible, but it may also be the case that in Titus God and Christ have come to be so identified that the appellation used of God naturally applies also to Christ. This is clearly suggested in Titus 2:13: "While we await the blessed hope and the manifestation of the glory of our great God and savior, Jesus Christ."

The Pastoral Epistles exhibit a high Christology, where to a significant extent Christ himself exhibits the attributes and activity of God at work for the redemption and salvation of sinners. Christ came into the world to save sinners, leading to their eternal life (1 Tim 1:15). As the mediator between God and humankind, he gave himself as a ransom for all people (1 Tim 2:5–6; Titus 2:14). Christ was made known in the flesh (1 Tim 3:16), and he will be manifested once again in the proper time (1 Tim 6:14–15). According to the text of Titus, God also poured out the spirit on "us" through Jesus Christ, "our savior" (Titus 3:6). In Christ, grace is present, and it is grace that can sustain Timothy in the face of suffering (2 Tim 2:1). The power of God and the grace that Timothy has in Christ are to support him in the suffering to which he is exhorted by Paul in the second epistle.[9] In Christ the very power of God is active. The obvious but unstated assumption throughout the Pastorals is, of course, that humanity stands in need of redemption. Human beings need that which Christ accomplishes.

In the identification of God as savior, the Pastoral Epistles—especially 1 Timothy and Titus—come from virtually the same theological frame of reference. Each epistle configures the presentation of God as savior in its own particular way, but there is no reason to think that they represent widely divergent, and certainly not incompatible, theological perspectives with respect to their images of God. It is therefore difficult to attribute too much significance to the variations between these two epistles. The identification of God as savior, however, is at substantial variance with the rest of

---

[8] Young, *Theology*, 53.
[9] See also 2 Tim 2:11–13.

the Pauline tradition. This is not terminology that has a natural home in the undisputed Pauline epistles. Furthermore, the common Pauline designation of Christ as κύριος (Lord) is not used at all in Titus, though it is found in 1 and 2 Timothy.[10]

With regard to the redemptive work of God in Christ, the terminology and images employed in these three epistles display variations, but in some cases these may be explainable in terms of the prior tradition used by the author. The most notable example is in 1 Tim 2:5 where Christ is identified as the mediator between God and humankind.[11] In the Pauline tradition, the term μεσίτης (mediator) appears only here and in Gal 3:19–20, where it is used with reference to the law, not Christ. The idea of Christ as mediator is not common in the New Testament—the only other NT author to use the term mediator of Christ is the author of the letter to the Hebrews (Heb 8:6; 9:15; 12:24). The claim that Christ gave himself as a ransom that he might redeem "us" (1 Tim 2:6; Titus 2:14; cf. Gal 1:4 and Eph 5:2),[12] was revealed in the flesh (1 Tim 3:16; cf. Rom 1:3, 2 Cor 5:16, ), died and lives again (2 Tim 2:8–11; cf. Rom 6:12–21, Gal 5:24), and will return to bring salvation and life eternal to the faithful (1 Tim 6:14–15; 2 Tim 4:1; Titus 1:2; 2:13; cf., e.g., 2 Thess 1:10; 2:8) are all ideas quite consistent with larger Pauline christological themes.[13]

## Godliness in the Household of God

As we saw in chapter 2, one of the conspicuous features of 1 Timothy is the emphasis on godliness as the proper disposition for those in the household of God. Within the context of the ordered household, εὐσέβεια (godliness) and its derivatives are the chief terms used to describe the manner of life that conforms in faith to the divine order of things (1:4).[14] In 1 Timothy, it is this frame of reference and the language that represents it that shapes the theology of the text (see 1 Tim 2:2; 3:16; 4:7, 8; 5:4; 6:3, 5, 6, 11). Even more than that, it shapes the theological world generated by the text. The same cannot be said of 2 Timothy and Titus.

But here we must be clear. Forms of εὐσέβεια do appear in 2 Tim 3:5, 12 (adverb); Titus 1:1; and 2:12 (adverb, cf. also ἀσέβεια [ungodliness] in 2 Tim 2:16 and Titus 2:12). But not only is this terminology much less frequent in 2 Timothy and Titus, it is incidental to the shape of the texts and

---

[10] 1 Tim 1:2, 12, 14; 5:5; 6:3, 14, 15; 2 Tim 1:2, 8, 16, 18; 2:7, 14, 19; 2:19, 22, 24; 3:11; 4:8, 14, 17, 18, 22. See also Young, *Theology*, 59–60.

[11] For a discussion of the emperor cult and its relation to the Christology of the Pastorals, see Young, *Theology*, 64–65.

[12] The term ἀντίλυτρον (ransom), however, appears only in 1 Tim 2:6 in the New Testament, but the idea of giving is certainly found in the Pauline tradition.

[13] For a fuller discussion of Christology in the Pastoral Epistles, see Young, *Theology*, 59–68.

[14] See above, pp. 23–25.

their theologies. In the case of 2 Timothy, this may in part be the result of the more personal nature of the epistle, but that would not be the case for Titus. In 2 Timothy, the plea for Timothy to suffer as Paul has suffered not only recurs thematically throughout the text but gives a distinctive form to the discussion. Neither the language nor the concept of εὐσέβεια, however, is foreign to the literary world of 2 Timothy or Titus with their concern for the well being and godliness of the community. The appearance of this terminology in these two epistles, terminology that is found infrequently elsewhere in the New Testament, suggests that in the case of "godliness" all three Pastoral Epistles have a similar underlying theological worldview, but only in 1 Timothy does it emerge full force to the surface level of the text and shape the presentation. To put it another way, all three Pastoral letters are drawing from the same theological well, but only in 1 Timothy does this language bubble to the surface in significant ways.

Though using different terminology, 1 Timothy and Titus both convey the idea of "training in godliness." In 1 Tim 4:7 the author writes: "Train (γύμναζε) yourself for godliness." Similarly, the author of Titus writes in 2:11: ". . . training (παιδεύσα) us to reject godlessness. . . ." While the vocabulary is different, the implication of both texts is that embracing godliness— or resisting its opposite—is a matter of conditioning and training. According to Titus, the grace of God is the agent of the training, whereas in 1 Timothy the exhortation to Timothy is to train oneself. In the example from Titus, the training is closely linked with the theology of divine grace, with correspondingly less emphasis on the exhortation to make oneself godly as appears to be the case in 1 Timothy. The difference between the two images is clear, but the idea of training or being trained is common to both texts. Second Timothy, on the other hand, does not reflect this idea, and appears not to be shaped explicitly or extensively by the imagery of godliness.

On the contrary, woven through the paraenesis of 2 Timothy is the exhortation to suffer, and that theme is one of the recurring features of the epistle.[15] Training in godliness has given way in 2 Timothy to following in Paul's path of suffering. Furthermore, there seems to be little concern in 2 Timothy to conform in faith to the divine order of things within the household of God. This is not one of the controlling features in the theology of 2 Timothy. This is a substantive difference in the theological worlds of 1 Timothy and Titus and the world of 2 Timothy. While we cannot say that these theological worlds are incompatible, they clearly reflect different experiences of the real world and how the community of faith should live in that world. They may also indicate that the reality confronting the community of faith is different: the threat of persecution (2 Timothy) rather than the prospect of living rather serenely in the larger social world in accord with the divinely established order of things (1 Timothy, Titus). This does not mean

---

[15] See above, pp. 45–46.

that both sets of images could not have arisen from the same underlying theological worldview once the circumstances facing the community changed, but it does seem that, whatever precipitated this difference of perspective, a fundamental orientation toward the larger social world also shifted substantially. The way the larger world outside the community is perceived affects the way that community and individuals within it organize their theological maps, and when that perception changes those maps likewise are reconfigured. Does this necessarily mean that the same person did not write 1 Timothy, Titus, and 2 Timothy? Not necessarily. Individuals and communities often readjust their worldview in response to changed circumstances. The more subtle question is, how much of a change is it reasonable to expect that a single author or single community could undergo in these circumstances and still maintained some psychological balance and coherent theological sense of God and the world? However this question is answered, 2 Timothy clearly seems to represent a departure from the underlying worldview of 1 Timothy and Titus at this point. The author of 2 Timothy expects trial, tribulation, and suffering. The author of 1 Timothy and Titus emphasizes the need for good order and structure in an institutional community that he expects to survive, if not thrive, for the foreseeable future.

## Truth, Knowledge, and Faith in Comparison

The theological worlds of 1 and 2 Timothy and Titus overlap almost perfectly in their conceptions of knowledge and truth. In 1 Tim 2:4 (cf. 4:3); 2 Tim 2:25; 3:7; and Titus 1:1, the expression ἐπίγνωσιν ἀληθείας appears and designates knowledge of the true doctrine represented by Paul to Timothy, Titus, and the respective communities. Similarly, in 1 Tim 4:3 the text makes reference to "knowing the truth," in 1 Tim 3:15 to the "foundation of truth," and in 2 Tim 2:15 to the "word of truth." In many examples, however, ἀλήθεια (truth) is simply used absolutely as in 1 Tim 2:7; 2 Tim 2:18; 3:8; 4:4; and Titus 1:14. Represented across these three texts is a concept of truth that is clearly identified and distinguished from untruth, yet the precise content of this truth is normally inferred only from the comments that identify the opponents and their heresies.[16]

As we have already seen, faith is closely linked in the Pastorals with knowledge and truth. In that sense, faith implies doctrinal content as we see in 1 Tim 1:4–5, 16; 4:3, 6, 10; 6:10 (cf. 1:13; 4:1); 2 Tim 1:13; 3:10, 15; Titus 1:4, 9, 11, 13; and 2:2. In this regard, we do not find substantial differences among the three epistles. Faith implies correct doctrine and sound teaching. In contrast to Romans and Galatians, however, faith in the Pastorals does not play itself out in a context shaped by the issues of Gentile inclusion or the defense of the Gentile mission. On this level, faith is simply linked with that which is perceived to be correct belief and the doctrine that is implied by it.

---

[16] See below, pp. 64–66.

But faith in the Pastorals implies more than doctrinal orthodoxy. At many points, it also suggests affective and religious sentiments, as when the author of 1 Timothy writes: ". . . and the grace of our Lord overflowed for me with the faith and love that are in Christ Jesus" (1:14). Or a few lines further on when he writes: ". . . having faith and a good conscience." (1:19). Or when he instructs that deacons must have the "mystery of faith in a clear conscience" (3:9). While 1 Timothy displays these dimensions of faith most clearly, they are found in the other two epistles as well. Paul, describing his own past in 2 Tim 3:10–11, also conveys similar sentiments when he says: "You have observed my teaching, my conduct, my purpose, my faith, my patience, my love, my steadfastness, my persecutions." The author of the letter to Titus concludes with the words: "Greet those who love us in the faith" (3:15). The portrayal of faith in the texts of the Pastoral Epistles cannot be reduced to a matter of correct doctrine, though that is a significant dimension of this imagery. In this regard, the theological representations of the three epistles are very closely related.

A similar convergence appears also in the case of "sound teaching." All three Pastoral Epistles make direct reference to "sound teaching" in some places (1 Tim 1:10 [cf. 4:6; 6:3]; 2 Tim 4:3; Titus 1:9; and 2:1; [cf. 2:8]) and clearly imply it in others (1 Tim 1:3–4; 4:7, 11, 13; 6:2–3; 2 Tim 3:16; 4:4; and Titus 1:11). Throughout these epistles, teaching is obviously considered to be an important activity in the community of faith,[17] but the content of teaching is also critical. "Sound teaching" corresponds to the "truth" and to "genuine faith." Once again, the concern for doctrinal correctness pervades these texts. The teaching function ascribed in 1 Timothy and Titus to those who have the qualities necessary for leadership in the community—except for women who are expressly prohibited from teaching in 1 Timothy—also corresponds to this theological perspective. Hence, teaching is both an important activity in the life of the communities reflected in these texts and an important concern in maintaining the doctrinal correctness of these communities. Those who deviate from the "sound teaching" and behave accordingly are the opposition and need to be combatted with exhortation and instruction.

## The Opponents and Their Opposition

The opposition in the Pastorals is accused of many things and condemned in no uncertain terms. That is not in itself particularly unusual. But who are the opponents and what is the nature of their opposition as repre-

---

[17] Martinus C. deBoer observes that the Pastoral Epistles represent the furthest development of Paul as the teacher of the church ("Images of Paul in the Post-Apostolic Period," *CBQ* 42 [1980]: 378). However, not only is Paul portrayed as the teacher of the church, but teaching is presented as an important feature of the church itself.

sented in the literary constructions reflected in the three epistles?[18] In 1 Tim 1:6–7, those who desire to be teachers of the law but do not understand the law are accused of engaging in meaningless chatter. In the process they have turned away from genuine faith and conformity with the divine order of things.[19] This is followed in 1:8–9 with the bold assertion that the law—presumably the Jewish law—is good, which is then qualified by the claim that it is good if it is used properly. Apparently some people are improperly teaching and apply-ing the law. What this means in the world of 1 Timothy is that the focus is not finally on the essence of the law and its goodness (which is affirmed), but on those people who misuse it. The proper understanding of the law turns on the notion that the law is laid down not for the innocent but the lawless and dis-obedient. According to 1 Timothy, some people have confused this.

First Timothy 4:1–5 illustrates further the nature of the opposition. As the spirit explicitly says, in the last times some will turn from the faith follow-ing false teachings and deceitful spirits. The error of these people's ways is that they forbid marriage and insist on abstinence from certain foods. While many have argued that this is evidence of the gnostic or proto-gnostic charac-ter of the opposition, the more likely explanation is that, at least on the textual level, it has to do with the misapplication of the Jewish law.[20] That is most consistent with the discussion in 1:6–7, and of course does not rule out an as-cetic character to the opposition. The rejection of this heresy is based on the goodness of God's creation and on the idea that nothing God has created should be rejected as long as it is received with thanksgiving. In strictly Jewish terms, the goodness of creation is pitted against abstinence from marriage and food and is argued for as the proper attitude of those who exhibit genuine faith and appropriate behavior. To be sure, 1 Timothy portrays the deceitfulness of those who have gone astray and their craving for idle talk and controversy as part of the opposition, but it is their misunderstanding and misapplication of the law that appears to be at the core of the problem.

As regards the character of the opposition, Titus is very much like 1 Timothy. In Titus 1:10 and 1:14 the Jewish character of this opposition is explicit.[21] The implication is that the "circumcision" is especially problem-atic, though the difficulty in Crete is not limited to this group. Moreover, in Titus as in 1 Timothy, the problem is related to what the opposition teaches (1:11). The reference to "Jewish myths" in 1:14 simply reinforces the Jewish nature of the opposition in Titus. However, the reference to purity in 1:15 may also link up with a similar concern for purity in 1 Timothy regarding abstinence from marriage and food (4:3–4), if the concern in here is at its core a purity issue. That disputes about the law are a point of contention in

---

[18] For a full treatment of the opponents in the Pastoral Epistles, see Sumney, *Opponents of Paul*, 253–302.

[19] Ibid., 257–58.

[20] Ibid., 260–62; and Sumney, "God Our Savior," 107.

[21] Sumney, *Opponents of Paul*, 291–301.

Crete is confirmed once again in Titus 3:9, as Paul warns Titus to avoid senseless controversies about the law. Finally, in 3:5 it is made clear that salvation does not result from doing works of righteousness but is according to the mercy of God. Whether this is a simple theological assertion or is in fact directed against a particular position held by the opposition to Paul in Crete is not clear.[22] In any case, on the literary level of the text it is clear that the core of the opposition revolves around Jewish issues and disputes about the Jewish law. One of the ironies of this is that 1 Timothy and Titus, the two epistles most closely related in terms of the opposition being combatted, are ostensibly written to two different communities, Ephesus and Crete. If these textual representations are congruent with the actual circumstances being addressed, then we must assume that these quite distinct and separate communities are both plagued by controversies over matters of behavior and application of the Jewish law.

Second Timothy, on the other hand, is quite distinct from the other two epistles. In addition to the general issues of controversy, wicked passions, and persecutions leading to suffering, there are those who disrupt some people by claiming that the resurrection has already taken place.[23] There is no explicit reference to the Jewish character of the opposition in 2 Timothy. The personal nature of the epistle and the concern for Timothy to follow Paul's example of suffering clearly present a different view of the opponents and the perceived threat. Instead of attempting to live in harmony with the divine order, both in heaven and on earth, 2 Timothy presumes that suffering is to be expected and embraced. Timothy ought to take up the mantle of suffering and follow in the footsteps of Paul. This is a different personal and theological agenda from that represented by 1 Timothy and Titus. Moreover, opposition as a "problem" in 2 Timothy differs from that portrayed in 1 Timothy and Titus, perhaps because it is generated by a different sense of the relationship between the church and the larger world.[24]

## *1 Timothy, Titus, and the Qualifications for Leadership*

On the matter of qualifications for leadership, 2 Timothy is once again at variance with 1 Timothy and Titus. Second Timothy makes no reference to the qualities or qualifications for leadership in the community of faith. Especially in the case of 1 Timothy, the concern for leadership qualities seems to be linked to the text's concern for conformity to the divine structure of reality. That is not a prominent feature of 2 Timothy, and correspondingly there is little concern in this text for the qualities appropriate for various roles and categories of people in the community. The emphasis on suffering in 2 Timothy and the text's corresponding orientation to the world reflect a

---

[22] Ibid., 300.
[23] Ibid., 289–90.
[24] Ibid., 289–90.

different concern from the structural—perhaps institutional—character of the community found in 1 Timothy and Titus. In the theological worlds of the respective texts, many of the issues that have already been discussed interlock and give rise to different literary expressions. This is one such example. If, as in 2 Timothy, the exhortation on the part of the author for Timothy to suffer as he himself has suffered is a controlling feature of the text, then it is not surprising to find little concern for matters of institutional leadership. At this point, too, the textual orientation of 2 Timothy seems to be substantively different from that found in 1 Timothy and Titus.

Both 1 Timothy and Titus address the qualities appropriate for overseers (ἐπίσκοποι), and a comparison of the texts illustrates some underlying similarities. In both there is a concern for self-control, hospitality, teaching, bullying, and excessive drink.

### 1 Timothy 3:1–7

3:1 The saying is sure: whoever aspires to the office of **bishop** desires a noble task.

3:2 Now a **bishop** must be ***above reproach,*** married only once, temperate, sensible, respectable, *hospitable,* an apt teacher,

3:3 not a drunkard, not violent but gentle, **not quarrelsome**, and not a LOVER OF MONEY.

    3:4 He must manage his own household well, keeping his children submissive and respectful in every way—

    3:5 for if someone does not know how to manage his own household, how can he take care of God's church?

    3:6 He must not be a recent convert, or he may be puffed up with conceit and fall into the condemnation of the devil.

    3:7 Moreover, he must be well thought of by outsiders, so that he may not fall into disgrace and the snare of the devil. (NRSV)

### Titus 1:7–9

1:7 For a **bishop**, as God's steward, must be ***blameless;*** he must not be arrogant or quick-tempered or addicted to wine or violent or GREEDY FOR GAIN;

1:8 but he must be *hospitable,* a lover of goodness, prudent, upright, devout, and **self-controlled**.

    1:9 He must have a firm grasp of the word that is trustworthy in accordance with the teaching, so that he may be able both to preach with sound doctrine and to refute those who contradict it. (NRSV)

The paired English words in each of the texts suggest similar ideas even though many of the words in the Greek text are not the same in the corresponding passages. The indented material is largely unique to the respective texts.

At each of the points identified above, the implications of the texts overlap, and the underlying sense of the qualities appropriate for an overseer converge. But as we see, 1 Timothy also emphasizes other issues, for example, the overseer's ability to manage his own household (especially his children). While this emphasis does not appear in Titus, it is certainly consistent with 1 Timothy's concern for the household of God. Management of the domestic household is thought to indicate the ability to manage the household of God. First Timothy is also concerned that an overseer not be a new convert, lest he be overcome with conceit, and that the overseer to be well thought of by the outside world. On this last point, it is clear that 1 Timothy reflects a desire that the overseer of the community be able to project an image to the larger world that will engender respect. What the people outside of the community think about those inside the community is important according to 1 Timothy, a concern consistent with the text's view of divine order in the household of God as it parallels the divine order enshrined in the larger social world. At this point, the theological world of 1 Timothy is structurally and textually consistent.

First Timothy also identifies the qualities for deacons, which Titus does not do. As with the overseer, there is a primary concern for the personal characteristics of the individual who assumes this role. Both 1 Timothy and Titus address matters related to elders (πρεσβύτεροι). In the case of 1 Timothy, the emphasis is on the double honor to be given to the elders who preach and teach (5:17), the nature of evidence against elders (5:19), and the problem of elders who persist in sin (5:20). In Titus, on the other hand, the instruction is for Titus to appoint elders in every town followed by a list of qualifications for these people: blameless, married only once, parent of believing children, not accused of debauchery, or rebellious (1:5–6). Here again 1 Timothy displays more than does Titus a concern for community order, in this case matters of procedure.

First Timothy and Titus each address the issue of slaves and their relationship with their masters. The counsel given to Timothy and Titus is quite consistent even though the vocabulary is somewhat different. First Timothy says that masters are worthy of honor so that the name of God and the "teaching" may not be blasphemed—presumably before those outside the community. To masters who are believers, slaves ought to show respect, indeed serve them all the more, because they are members of the church (6:2). Here, too, 1 Timothy is concerned about order within the community, as well as about the way outsiders will view the community. Similarly, Titus advises slaves to be submissive toward their masters, showing respect and faithfulness on the grounds that they are to be an ornament to the teaching of God (2:9–10). In both cases, conformity with the established order is advised and a concern for how the behavior will affect other people is used to justify the action.

First Timothy instructs three groups of people that do not appear in Titus: women (2:9–15), widows (5:3–16), and the rich (6:9–11). It is the widows who are of special concern and occupy most attention in the epistle. They occupy a special place in the text and apparently in the community to which the epistle is addressed. The elaborateness of the instructions would suggest that something specific in the church at Ephesus is at stake and needs attention, and so the author seeks to provide guidance on how to deal with the matter. Widows who are over sixty, not married more than once, and have the proper qualities are to be inscribed on the list. The issue appears to be which widows are to be given assistance by the community and which are not. Already the issue of entitlements had raised its head and was affecting the good order of the community. Into the breach, the words of 1 Timothy came seeking to bring the household into line with God's ordering of reality.

## Conclusion

In terms of theology and literary pattern there are conspicuous differences between 1 Timothy and 2 Timothy. Titus also displays a number of differences from 2 Timothy and to a lesser extent from 1 Timothy as well. At the heart of the differences between 1 and 2 Timothy is the divine ordering of reality to which the household of God is to conform on the one hand, and the perception of how the community of faith will, or ought, to engage the larger society on the other. This difference is illustrated most prominently in the distinction between the plea to conform to the divine order and the appeal to suffer. From these fundamental differences in outlook flow differences in the respective discussions, e.g., qualifications for various categories of leadership in the church. With its repeated appeals to suffer, it is not surprising that 2 Timothy represents a different view of how the faithful ought to engage the world than does 1 Timothy: suffering as opposed to building up the household of God.

In the matter of doctrinal correctness and the true faith, the three epistles are very similar. Doctrinal correctness is presumed in each and those who deviate from it in belief and practice are roundly condemned. Throughout these texts, theology and behavior are intimately connected and represent two sides of the same coin. At various points in the respective texts, the nature of correct belief comes to the surface and can be identified, but for the most part it remains submerged in the subtext. It is implicit and can only be inferred from the document. In 1 Timothy and Titus, the opposition centers generally on Jewish-related matters, but that does not appear to be the case in 2 Timothy.

Does this comparison of patterns suggest that 1 Timothy and Titus came from the hand of a different author than that of 2 Timothy? An answer to this question turns on two fundamental considerations. First, how much does a change in historical circumstances in Ephesus (or to whomever 1 & 2 Timothy were written) or in the situation of the author account for the differences in the literary and theological worlds of the epistles? And second, how much of a shift of attitude, worldview, theology, and language are we prepared to allow a single author? Most Pauline scholars would probably agree that a change in the circumstances of the addressees is likely to precipitate a substantial change in the character of an author's response. We certainly know that epistles written by Paul to different churches with different circumstances yielded quite different texts, if not different theological outlooks (compare Galatians and 1 Corinthians). Yet at the level of thought world and basic perspective, there should still be some coherence and some ability on our part to see how differences in theological and pastoral responses could arise from the same underlying theological orientation. If not, the author would simply be fragmented and incoherent. But the question persists: how much latitude are we inclined to allow a single author at this point?

On one level, the reality of doctrinal correctness is assumed in all three Pastorals, and those who deviate from it are thought to jeopardize the faith. In this regard, the three epistles clearly represent the same theological world of thought and the differences between them are negligible. On the level of their orientations to the larger world and their perception of divine order, 1 Timothy and Titus most assuredly come from the same frame of reference. But 2 Timothy is another matter. Either 2 Timothy was written by a different author or the circumstances in Ephesus and the author's own life had changed quite dramatically. Neither of these can be ruled out. At this point in the discussion, we can only say that there is a distinct possibility that a different author wrote 2 Timothy, an author whose experience of the larger social world was different from that of the author of 1 Timothy and Titus. In the next section, we will need to consider this question further in order to move our answer from the realm of possibility to probability.[25]

## THE PASTORAL EPISTLES AND PAUL

### Introduction

One of the most persistent issues in the scholarly study of the Pauline tradition has been the relationship of the Pastoral Epistles to Paul and the

---

[25] See the discussion below regarding 2 Timothy and Philippians, pp. 73–78.

undisputed Pauline letters.[26] In modern scholarship, the most common view has been that the Pastoral Epistles are in fact pseudonymous, written after Paul's death by someone in the Pauline tradition. To be sure, the pseudonymity of these epistles has not been accepted by all Pauline scholars,[27] but it has often functioned as a starting point, frequently with little argumentation, for much modern investigation of these texts. The purpose of this section is to expand the scope of our comparison of theological patterns in 1 and 2 Timothy and Titus. Having moved out concentrically from the discrete patterns of the respective epistles to a comparison of the three Pastorals in the previous section, we now bring these patterns into comparison with material from the indisputably authentic Pauline letters. Once again, the goal is to compare textual and structural patterns with an eye toward positioning the Pastorals in the developing Pauline tradition.

The observation that each of the Pastorals relates most closely to a different authentic Pauline epistle (1 Timothy to 1 Corinthians; 2 Timothy to Philippians; and Titus to Galatians) suggests a methodological way of proceeding that can perhaps help maintain the literary integrity of the respective texts.[28] In keeping with the concern here for literary and theological patterns, it seems appropriate procedurally to focus primarily, though by no means exclusively, on the respective Pastoral Epistles and selected patterns from their most immediate Pauline counterparts. In this way, the likelihood that the integrity of both sets of texts will be maintained in the comparison can be enhanced. Hence, comparison on this level requires that we stand back and look at the larger structural picture of the respective patterns and the concepts and images that represent them. It is these larger patterns that make the details of vocabulary, style, and theology especially meaningful. In this way, we will also be focusing on texts and the theological patterns of texts rather than on what may have been in the mind of a given author. This is consistent with the approach that has been taken throughout this discussion. Furthermore, this approach can help us resist creating a synthesis of

---

[26] For recent discussions of the Pauline authorship of the Pastoral Epistles, see Jouette Bassler, *1 Timothy, 2 Timothy, Titus,* 17–30; Lewis R. Donelson, *Pseudepigraphy and Ethical Argument,* 7–66; Luke Timothy Johnson, *Letters to Paul's Delegates,* 1–36; George Knight III, *The Pastoral Epistles: A Commentary on the Greek Text* (New International Greek Testament Commentary; Grand Rapids: Eerdmans, 1992), 3–54; I. Howard Marshall, "Recent Study of the Pastoral Epistles," *Them* 23 (1997): 3–21; and Philip H. Towner, "Pauline Theology or Pauline Tradition in the Pastoral Epistles: The Question of Method," *TynBul* 46 (1995): 291–300. See also James D. Miller's variation on the composite theory of the Pastoral Epistles (*The Pastoral Letters as Composite Documents* [SNTMS 93; Cambridge: Cambridge University Press, 1997], 1–33).

[27] See for example the commentary by Gordon D. Fee, *1 and 2 Timothy, Titus* (rev. ed; New International Biblical Commentary; Peabody, Mass.: Hendrickson, 1988). More recently James D. Miller has revived the argument that these three epistles are composite documents (*The Pastoral Letters as Composite Documents.*)

[28] See Johnson, *Paul's Delegates,* 37, 214; and "Oikonomia Theou," 93–95.

Paul's theology drawn from quite different texts and then using that as a point of comparison with the Pastorals. Theology here means the theology represented in specific texts and that requires careful attention to individual literary and theological contexts.

Since the centerpiece of this book is the positioning of the Pastoral Epistles and their theological patterns in the developing Pauline tradition in the early decades and centuries of the church, and not the question of the authorship of the Pastorals, it seems appropriate to concentrate on the most conspicuous images, ideas, debates, and claims that make up these theological patterns and to use these as points of comparison. As this relates to the question of the authorship of the Pastoral Epistles, these comparisons present a limited, though hopefully valuable, contribution to those larger discussions. To suggest that our focus ought to be on the larger theological patterns and literary constructions rather than on the peculiar stylistic and linguistic configurations is not to suggest that these latter considerations are unimportant. It is to say that these theological patterns and constructions are necessarily important for positioning the Pastorals in the developing Pauline tradition. In the present discussion, the question of Pauline or non-Pauline authorship of the Pastorals is important, but as stated at the beginning of this chapter, it is important primarily as it relates to the way these letters connect to the broader Pauline tradition. Against this larger backdrop, the Pastoral Epistles are strategically placed at or near the balance point between Pauline and post-Pauline tradition, and the decision about their Pauline authorship simply places the Pastorals on one side of the balance point or the other.

In the 1980's and early 1990's a group of prominent Pauline scholars gathered under the auspices of the Society of Biblical Literature to investigate the theology of the Pauline Epistles. One of the working assumptions of that group was that they would consider each of the letters as discrete texts with their own contexts, circumstances, and, in some sense, self-contained theologies. The reason for that decision was to prevent conflating the theologies of texts that in some cases have quite different contexts. The wisdom of that decision resulted in a series of essays producing important insights into the respective Pauline letters and their theologies. Although a comparative analysis such as that employed here necessarily involves bringing different texts into conversation, the impulse to place certain limits on the comparative investigation would seem to be as important for us as it was for the SBL working group. In this case, that means comparing each of the Pastoral Epistles with its most closely corresponding undisputed Pauline letter as they are identified above. While the focus in each comparison may be primarily on one of the Pastoral Epistles, it will not be limited only to that epistle. By circumscribing the comparisons in this way we can honor the respective theological patterns of the epistles and perhaps enhance the meaningfulness of our observations. There is no claim here that this approach exhausts the possibilities for the question of the Pastorals and Pauline authorship, but it does produce a different perspective with different insights. It also helps facilitate our primary goal of placing the Pastorals in the larger sweep of Pauline tradition.

To advance this goal, we will begin each comparison by using arguments and conclusions drawn from the SBL working group members on the respective Pauline letters as a kind of template for comparison with the Pastoral letters. Because the literature on Pauline theology is so vast, not providing limits on our comparisons could easily divert us from our primary goal and could diffuse the comparative insights with unnecessary detail and complexity.[29] This approach also gives us a range of perspectives from a variety of scholarly points of view. It does not lead to a comprehensive discussion about the Pauline or non-Pauline authorship of the Pastorals. That is for another time and place. The value of trying to identify a kind of template for the theologies of 1 Corinthians, Philippians, and Galatians is that it provides us with a frame of reference for the epistles that will facilitate comparison with the Pastorals. As a final procedural point, we will begin these comparisons with Philippians and the Pastorals, especially 2 Timothy, because this may well be one of the most important textual links for determining the conceptual relationship between the Pauline and Pastoral theological patterns. If our argument is correct, the relationship between Philippians and 2 Timothy is the linchpin in thinking about 2 Timothy's link with 1 Timothy and Titus as well as in thinking about the larger question of the Pauline authorship of the Pastorals.

## Philippians and the Pastorals

Stanley K. Stowers argues for the connection between theology in Philippians and ancient friendship letters.[30] For our purposes, it is important to summarize portions of this argument. Friendship in the ancient world was understood in terms of a wide-ranging set of interconnected relationships and institutions.[31] One of the expectations of friendship was that friends would spend time together; they would actually be in each other's presence. The letter of friendship functioned as a substitute for that presence when friends were absent. As a result, expressions of affection and longing for one's friends are commonly part of these letters.[32] Friendship was thought to involve sharing, oneness, giving and receiving, mutual assistance, and

---

[29] For the volume of material and the complexity of the arguments, see James D. G. Dunn, *The Theology of Paul the Apostle* (Grand Rapids: Eerdmans, 1998).

[30] Stanley K. Stowers, "Friends and Enemies in the Politics of Heaven: Reading Theology In Philippians," in *Pauline Theology* 1 (ed. Jouette M. Bassler; SBLSymS 4; Minneapolis: Fortress, 1991), 105–21. As Stowers points out, scholars of ancient letter writing for a long time have made the connection between Philippians and letters of friendship, but in this essay he brings this to bear on his reading of the theology of Philippians.

[31] Ibid., 108.

[32] Ibid., 109. See Phil 1:7–8; 2:17–18; 4:1, 14.

partnership. Paul urges the Philippians to stand firm in one spirit and with one mind struggle together for the faith of the gospel (1:27), to find consolation in love and fellowship in the spirit (2:1), to have the same mind (2:2), to agree in the Lord and become friends (Paul's advice to Euodia and Syntyche, 4:2), and "live as citizens (πολιτεύεσθαι) in a way that is worthy of the gospel of Christ" (1:27).[33]

Fundamental to the ancient friendship letter, according to Stowers, is the language of opposition. References to a person's enemies are common in friendship letters, and a basic feature of Philippians is, of course, the contrast between the behavior of Paul and that of his enemies.[34] Paul urges his friends in Philippi to stand firm against their opponents when he writes: ". . . I know that you are standing firm . . . and are in no way frightened by those who oppose you, which is to them evidence of destruction but of your salvation" (1:27–28).[35] Running through the epistle, but especially direct in 2:1–11, is the parallelism between Paul's relationship with the Philippians and the relationship the Philippians are to have with Christ and one another. As Stowers persuasively shows, Philippians is best seen as a hortatory letter of friendship addressed to a community of friends, calling upon them to become a particular type of people (1:9–10). Paul presents himself as a model of one who along with his friends at Philippi is struggling toward this goal himself.

The Pastorals, especially 2 Timothy, exhibit some of the same epistolary characteristics as those identified by Stowers in Philippians: a retrospective look (2 Tim 1:3–7; Phil 1:3–5); autobiographical elements (2 Tim 3:10–11; 4:6–8; Phil 3:4–16); opponents (1 Tim 1:8–10; 4:1–3; 6:11–19; 2 Tim 1:15; 2:22–26; 3:1–13; 4:1–16; Titus 1:10–16; Phil 3:2–11, 17–19); a sense of partnership (2 Tim 2:1–2:26; 1 Tim 1:3–7, 18–20; Titus 1:5–9; Phil 1:12–30; 3:17–21; 4:10–20); affection (2 Tim 1:3–7; Titus 1:4; Phil 1:3–11); a feeling of reciprocity (2 Tim 4:9–11; Phil 4:15–20); and suffering and imprisonment (2 Tim 1:8, 12; 2:3, 9; 3:11; 4:5; Phil 1:7, 12–14, 22–23; 2:17; 3:8).[36] As epistolary texts, 2 Timothy and Philippians have many of these features of friendship letters in common, but other elements do not correspond so clearly. Second Timothy is ostensibly written to an individual while Philippians is written to a community.[37] The character of the opposition in 2 Timothy seems to be related more directly to doctrinal issues and

---

[33] Ibid., 112.

[34] Ibid., 114–15. See Phil 1:15–17, 19–26.

[35] See also 1:15–17; 2:14–18.

[36] For the possible connections between 2 Timothy and Philippians, see David Cook, "2 Timothy 4:6–8 and the Epistle to the Philippians," *Journal of Theological Studies* 33 (1982): 168–71; and Johnson, *First and Second Letters to Timothy*, 368–69.

[37] As Stowers points out, Seneca's friendship letters, too, were written to individuals rather than communities ("Friends and Enemies," 108). As we have already noted, even though 2 Timothy is a very personal letter and clearly written as a private correspondence between Paul and Timothy, a larger audience is in view.

the preservation of correct doctrine than it does in Philippians (2 Tim 2:18). Second Timothy alternates more conspicuously between instruction and paraenesis than is obviously the case in Philippians. Finally, we do not find in Philippians the catalog of vices that mark 2 Tim 3:1–5. When Philippians is compared to 1 Timothy and Titus the differences are even more pronounced. The personal and affectionate tone so clear in Philippians is not nearly as apparent in these epistles. First Timothy and Titus are highly instructive, often focusing on the mandates of church order and the qualities of those who are to lead the community. Both in terms of genre and tone, 1 Timothy and Titus are distinct from Philippians. Second Timothy is the closest match, but here, too, there are substantial differences.[38] The paraenetic quality of 2 Timothy seems to be more pronounced than in Philippians, as is the concern for adherence to correct belief and resistance to heresy. As important as friendship motifs are in 2 Timothy, then, it is not evident that the friendship letter model suggests any kind of organic link between 2 Timothy and Philippians, and certainly not between 1 Timothy and Titus and the letter to the Philippians.

First Timothy and Philippians do, however, present interesting theological images for the church and the faithful person's place in the world, and these require comment at this point. As we have seen,[39] in 1 Tim 3:15 the household of God is identified as the "church of the living God," and in 1:4 the author appeals to Timothy to conform to the divine order in faith. Paul writes in Phil 3:20 that "our place of citizenship (πολίτευμα) is in heaven,"[40] and in 1:27 he urges the Philippians to "live as citizens (πολιτεύσθε) in a way that is worthy of the gospel." In these examples, a cultural or social image is projected onto the church and the people in the church. At their root, 1 Timothy and Philippians represent quite different images. In 1 Timothy, the structural images are the household and the social order based on the pattern of the Greco-Romans household, whereas in Philippians the place of one's citizenship is projected into heaven.[41] The governing metaphors of the two texts, both brought to bear on the theological character of

---

[38] See Fiore, *The Function of Personal Example in the Socratic and Pastoral Epistles* (AnBib 105; Rome: Biblical Institute Press, 1986), 1–9; and Johnson, *Paul's Delegates*, 32.

[39] See above, pp. 19–23.

[40] Louw and Nida define the term πολίτευμα as "the place or location in which one has the right to be a citizen—'state, commonwealth, place of citizenship,'" (1:132 [entry 11.71]).

[41] Pheme Perkins writes: "Though Paul's own difficulties might suggest that Christians ought to seek to establish a secure place for themselves within the diverse communities of the city, Paul's response denies them that option. They cannot invoke the links between Christianity and Judaism to establish their claim to a place within the city. Instead, this section summons Christians to see themselves as members of a heavenly *politeuma*, awaiting the arrival of their Lord and σωτήρ, much as members of the earthly city anticipated imperial visitations. Both the *politeuma* and the body, which is marked as belonging to the Christian community, are 'from

the church and the people in the church, arise from different though clearly linked experiences in the Greco-Roman world: the "divinely ordered" household and citizenship in the imperial realm. What unites the images in 1 Timothy and Philippians is that both are familiar cultural images that have been invested with a heavenly or theological meaning that is in turn projected onto the church. To be sure, this is a common Pauline, indeed New Testament, procedure,[42] and there is no suggestion that these images are inherently incompatible. In fact, imperial citizenship and good order may in some sense be an extension of the domestic household and its sense of proper order. But these two images do not, on the other hand, suggest strict congruity of thought between 1 Timothy and Philippians either. The penchant for conformity to the divine order of things displayed in 1 Timothy is not similarly reflected in Philippians.[43]

God is called "father" in Philippians (1:2; 2:11; 4:20), but only Christ is called "savior" (3:20). This is in contrast to the portrayal of God as savior in the Pastorals,[44] even though salvation is clearly said in Philippians to come from God (1:28, cf. 2:12–13). Both Philippians and 1 Timothy, however, also reflect a human element in the process of salvation (Phil 2:12 and 1 Tim 4:16). Because of 2 Timothy's relatively infrequent use of "savior" and "to save" with reference to God, it is perhaps closest to the theology of Philippians. Here, too, however, 2 Timothy and Philippians are in step with the other undisputed Pauline Letters and this cannot be used as evidence for some genetic connection between them.

The pervasive concern for correct belief in the Pastoral Epistles is not matched in the letter to the Philippians.[45] The terms "true" and "truth" appear only in Phil 1:18 and 4:8, and the concept of "sound teaching" does not appear at all in the Philippian text. While "faith" (1:25, 27; 2:17; 3:9) and "to believe" (1:29) appear with some regularity in Philippians, the terms do not imply a notion of correct doctrine to be preserved, which is, as we have seen,[46] commonly the case in the Pastorals.[47] To this extent, and in light of the obvious friendship concerns in Philippians, the two sets of epistles seem

---

heaven.' They cannot be attained by earthly means" (Pheme Perkins, "Philippians: Theology for the Heavenly Politeuma," in *Pauline Theology* 1 [ed. Jouette M. Bassler; SBLSymS 4; Minneapolis: Fortress, 1991], 102).

[42] See, e.g., my article on Romans 6, "'Control' in Pauline Language and Culture: A Study of Rom 6," *NTS* 42 (1996): 75–89.

[43] Εὐσέβεια, so important to the structure of 1 Timothy, does not appear in Philippians.

[44] See above, pp. 58–61.

[45] Lohfink claims that the Pastorals are the "very expression and concretizing of Phil 4:9a . . . the Pastorals are written thoroughly in the spirit of Phil 4:9a" ("Paulinische Theologie in der Rezeption," 85). If this is the case with respect to 1 Timothy and Titus, it would appear to be even more true of 2 Timothy and the plea to suffer.

[46] See above, pp. 63–64.

[47] The term γνῶσις (knowledge) does occur in Philippians, but only in 3:8.

to represent different literary and social worlds. Even 2 Timothy which is most like Philippians in terms of friendship motifs has a decided bent toward matters of correct doctrine and true knowledge, a concern not shared explicitly by Philippians. Apparently different issues are at stake in the two communities.

The most conspicuous similarity between 2 Timothy and Philippians is the common theme of suffering. In both epistles, Paul—the stated author—is in travail and the suffering of the apostle comes to the fore again and again in both texts. In 2 Timothy the references to Paul's suffering (1:12; 2:9; 3:11) are matched by a plea for Timothy to suffer as Paul has suffered (1:8; 2:3; 4:5). Only in 2:11 is it possible that the text suggests suffering with Christ, along the lines found in Rom 6:1–11. The structural paradigm of 2 Timothy goes something like this: I have suffered, I am your example, now follow my example and suffer as I have suffered.[48] All of these elements are present in Philippians, but there are also some subtle differences as well. Paul's suffering is expressly identified as an imprisonment in 1:7 and 1:17, and the things that have happened to him have served to aid the spread of the gospel according to 1:12. The Philippians are reminded that they have been granted the opportunity to suffer for Christ in 1:29 and they are urged to be imitators of Paul in 3:17. The author in 2 Timothy would seem to reflect a more general pattern of suffering over time (". . . my persecutions and suffering the things that happened to me in Antioch, Iconium, and Lystra," 3:17), unlike Philippians where the immediate situation of imprisonment governs the suffering and symbolizes the separation of Paul from his friends in the community at Philippi, a separation that the letter itself seeks to address.

It is clear from this discussion that 1 Timothy and Titus represent theological patterns that are substantially different from those found in Philippians. The genre of these epistles is strikingly different from that of Philippians, and they address theological and pastoral issues that are significantly removed from those of Paul's letter. The world of friendship and deep affection so evident in Philippians is only hinted at in the instruction of 1 Timothy and Titus. In short the tone is more distant and the personal relationships more muted than we encounter in Philippians. In almost every respect these texts appear to come from different contexts, indeed from different literary frames of reference. 2 Timothy as we have seen is a different matter, and its connection with Philippians is more intimate and subtle. The friendship motifs are strikingly similar though not identical and the concern for suffering is a feature common to both. In these respects the two texts represent closely related theological and structural patterns—even though the substantial differences identified above cannot be minimized.

---

[48] In both Phil 2:17 and 2 Tim 4:6, the term σπένδομαι (poured out, offered up) has sacrificial connotations relating to Paul's suffering. The term appears nowhere else in the New Testament.

For example, the concern for doctrinal correctness, shared by all three Pastoral Epistles, is not a mark of Philippian's textual world. *The upshot of this is that where 2 Timothy is most like 1 Timothy and Titus it is least like Philippians, and at the points where 2 Timothy is least like them it is most like Philippians.*

## Galatians and the Pastorals

In her essay on the theology of Galatians entitled, "The Singularity of the Gospel: A Reading of Galatians," Beverly Gaventa writes:

> Indeed, analyses of Galatians almost universally identify chaps. 3–4 as the theological center of the letter. Since the first two chapters are regarded as a defense of Paul's apostleship, they do not enter the discussion of "theology." Similarly, the last two chapters are frequently bracketed off as paraenesis, which, by virtue of its traditional character, is not regarded as shedding light on Paul's theology. The result of this analysis of the letter is that discussions about the theology of Galatians take chaps. 3–4 as their starting point and then move backward to chaps. 1–2 and forward to chaps. 5–6.
>
> If we attend not simply to chaps. 3–4 but to the whole of the letter, an alternative possibility emerges, namely, that although the letter arises out of the issue of law, the underlying theological convictions that shape Paul's response to the problem derive not from his interpretation of the law but from his christology. The theology reflected in Galatians is first of all about Jesus Christ and the new creation God has begun in him (1:1–4; 6:14–15), and only in the light of that christocentrism can Paul's remarks concerning the law be understood. The word "christocentrism" is the right word, in that Paul presupposes from the beginning to the end that there is only one gospel (1:6–9), the singularity of which consists of the revelation of Jesus Christ as God's son whose crucifixion inaugurates the new age. . . . The position to be argued here, then, is that the governing theological antithesis in Galatians is between Christ or the new creation and the cosmos; the antithesis between Christ and the law and between the cross and circumcision are not the equivalent of this central premise but follow from it.[49]

Gaventa's position is clear, the debates over the law are the precipitating cause for the letter to the Galatians while Christology is the operating premise for Paul's response to his opponents in Galatia. Paul's position is that the new creation inaugurated in Christ's crucifixion permits no supplementation by the law. To be more specific, she thinks the problem in Galatia is that the Galatians are wishing to have certainty that they indeed have a place in the church and know what is required of them by God. It is this certainty that Paul rejects with his appeal to the centrality of Christ and the singularity of the gospel.[50] Even if Gaventa has not correctly identified the nature of the opposition in Galatia, she has made a compelling case for plac-

---

[49] Beverly Roberts Gaventa, "The Singularity of the Gospel: A Reading of Galatians," in *Pauline Theology* 1 (ed. Jouette M. Bassler; SBLSymS 4; Minneapolis: Fortress, 1991), 148–49.

[50] Ibid., 159.

ing Christology at the center of the theological world of Galatians.[51] Christology is a central feature of Galatians' structure, and must be considered as such in our comparison with Titus and 1 Timothy.

Unlike Gaventa, James D. G. Dunn uses the more traditional starting point of works of law and faith in Christ and argues that Galatians is the first sustained attempt to deal with the issue of "covenantal nomism."[52] According to Dunn, Paul's argument has basically three aspects: 1) the outworking of God's saving power is consistent with its initial expression, 2) the initial expression of the covenant was in terms of promise and faith and it always had the Gentiles in view, and 3) law, understood in a way that conflicts with that initial expression, has a distorted role.[53] Paul drives a wedge between faith in Christ and works of law, at least law understood in exclusivistic terms. As Dunn states: "This outworking may be conceived in terms of the law, but not the law focused in such Jewish distinctives as circumcision, but focused rather in love of neighbor (5:6, 13–14) as exemplified by Christ (6:1–4)."[54] The basic issue in Galatians, according to Dunn, is whether the Gentiles who had come to faith in the Jewish messiah and claimed a share in God's covenant need to follow the law in order to maintain that claim.[55] In summary Dunn writes:

> In short, Paul's attitude to the law in Galatians has regularly been misperceived as more unyieldingly negative than it is. . . . But once the point has been grasped that Paul's chief target is a covenantal nomism understood in restrictively nationalistic terms—"works of the law" as maintaining Jewish identity, "the curse of the law" as falling on the lawless so as to exclude Gentiles as such from the covenant promise—then it becomes clear that Paul's negative remarks had a more limited thrust and that so long as the law is not similarly misunderstood as defining and defending the prerogatives of a particular group, it still has a positive role to play in the expression of God's purpose and will.[56]

In Titus 1:10–16, the Jewish character of the opposition in Crete is identified in general terms. The author writes that there are "many rebellious people, idle talkers and deceivers" (v. 10). These problem people come

---

[51] J. Louis Martyn reacts positively to Gaventa's emphasis on Christology and the singularity of the gospel as central to the theology of Galatians in his article in the same volume entitled, "Events in Galatia: Modified Covenantal Nomism versus God's Invasion of the Cosmos in the Singular Gospel: A Response to J. D. G. Dunn and B. R. Gaventa," in *Pauline Theology*, SBLSymS 4/1 (ed. Jouette M. Bassler; Minneapolis: Fortress, 1991), 164.

[52] James D. G. Dunn, "The Theology of Galatians: The Issue of Covenantal Nomism," in *Pauline Theology* 1 (ed. Jouette M. Bassler; SBLSymS 4; Minneapolis: Fortress, 1991), 125.

[53] Ibid., 125.

[54] Ibid., 129.

[55] Ibid., 130.

[56] Ibid., 137.

especially from the "circumcision," though apparently not exclusively so. They teach that which is improper to teach for shameful gain. The text goes on in 1:14 to say that those grounded in the true testimony should pay no attention to the "Jewish myths and commandments of the people who reject the truth." For the author of Titus, the problem of the commandments apparently turns on the issue of purity, associated with refraining from certain practices and from eating certain foods (cf. 1 Tim 4:3–5). According to the text of Titus, the nature of the opposition is limited to these problems. We may perhaps surmise that more is at stake in Titus' community than this, but such is not made explicit in the text.[57]

In this regard, the theological structures of Galatians and Titus have one thing in common. There is a problem with the Jewish law in both. But is the problem of the same variety, intensity, and pervasiveness? It does not appear to be so on any of these counts. Two entire chapters are devoted exclusively in Galatians to the issue of "covenantal nomism," whereas three verses at most address the issue of the commandments in Titus. While parts of Galatians seem to have a polemical quality—precipitated by the problem of "covenantal nomism"—Titus contains instructions given by Paul to Titus about a whole series of issues, many of which center on the proper ordering of the community.[58]

Moreover, the place of the Gentiles in the covenant, so central in the Galatians debate, is nowhere to be found in Titus. "Faith in Christ" is not juxtaposed opposite "works of law" in the theological world of Titus, and the problem of Jewish distinctiveness does not seem to be at issue either. For Titus, faith has more to do with correct doctrinal assent than it does with the promises of God as distinct from works of law, though the author makes clear without arguing the case that people are saved by the mercy of God and not works of righteousness (3:5).[59] The problem of purity and proper behavior in the community at Crete does not seem to be related to table fellowship and who will eat with whom (cf. Gal 2:11–14). Furthermore, Christology certainly runs deep in the theological and literary world of Titus, but it does not come to the surface of the text in any particularly striking ways that would link up with Galatians. In short, Titus and Galatians come from contextually and structurally quite separate worlds. The burning issues associated with the opposition— "covenantal nomism"— in Galatia are not the same as those found among the opposition in Crete, either in specific variety or intensity. Titus reflects a world in which the battles of Galatia, if they ever

---

[57] Sumney, *Opponents of Paul,* 290–301.

[58] See above, pp. 50–55.

[59] Abraham Malherbe argues that δικαιοσύνη (righteousness) in Titus 3:5 is not used in the sense of being in right relationship with God as Paul uses it, but in a moral sense, "a just life by virtue of Christ's grace." See Abraham J. Malherbe, "Response to Raymond Collins, Donald Hagner, Bonnie Thurston" (paper presented at the annual meeting of the Society of Biblical Literature, Orlando, Fla., November 22, 1998), 14.

were raging in Crete, have settled down, and there is only a nagging judaizing tendency on the part of some people in the churches there. Proper order and behavior in the church, so that the word of God might not be discredited (1:5–9; 2:1–3:2), is more critical in Titus.

As we have seen above,[60] 1 Timothy deals with an opposition in Ephesus that is identified with "myths," "genealogies," and "speculations" (1:4). More specifically, the author writes against teachers who teach about things of which they have little understanding (1:7). As in Titus, the law is the point at issue. In response, the writer says the law is good if it is used legitimately, that is if one understands that the law is set forth for the lawless and not the innocent (1:8–10). Galatians 3:19, read on its own terms in the context of Galatians, appears to suggest a view of the law that is structurally similar: "Why therefore the law? It was given because of transgressions. . . ."[61] In both texts, the function of the law is to deal with lawlessness and transgressions. In the text of 1 Timothy this is, of course, related to the ascetic problem of forbidding marriage and not eating certain foods. The opponents are presumably trying to impose these requirements on those in the community who would be faithful. That is a misunderstanding and misuse of the law, according to the author. In 1 Timothy this is not a theoretical problem, and it does not pertain to the place of the Gentiles and the promises of God in salvation history. There is to be sure an emphasis on training oneself in godliness in 1 Timothy (4:7), but there is no correlation between the law and a παιδαγωγός, a mentor. While there is a structural connection in the way the law is understood in 1 Timothy and in Galatians—in both the law is given for transgressions and lawlessness—it should be noted that the law in Galatians is given *because of transgressions,* whereas in 1 Timothy it is *laid down for the lawless and disobedient.* In the first instance the focus is on the transgressions and in the second it is on the transgressors.

Here too, however, the question needs to be asked, how pervasive is this apparent structural similarity in 1 Timothy? Once again, this issue in no way dominates the discussion in 1 Timothy as it does in Galatians. It only comes to the fore of the discussion in two brief references and pales in comparison with the emphasis on godliness and order in the household of God. "Covenantal nomism" does not significantly mark the theological world of 1 Timothy,[62] even though it is clear that a peculiar judaizing tendency is at work in the community and that there is an impulse to see the law as something that is intended to deal with transgressions and lawlessness. Christology is important in 1 Timothy, but it is not conspicuous as the organizing

---

[60] See above, pp. 64–66.
[61] See the discussion regarding the interpretation of Gal 3:19 by David J. Lull, "'The Law Was Our Pedagogue': A Study in Galatians 3:19–25," *JBL* 105 (1986): 482–86.
[62] See the definition of "covenantal nomism" given by Dunn, "The Theology of Galatians," 126.

theological center of the text. First Timothy identifies God as savior, but unlike Titus does not apply that terminology to Christ.

The points of structural theological similarity between 1 Timothy/ Titus—especially 1 Timothy—and Galatians are real but very limited. In comparing these texts, a sense of proportionality is required. What drives the argument in Galatians theologically is substantially different from what drives the discussions in 1 Timothy and Titus. The points of contact are more likely to be incidental, drawing on some deep structural similarities regarding the law in the churches in the Gentile lands of the first century, than they are evidence of an organic connection between the two sets of texts. If 1 Timothy and Titus were consciously patterned after aspects of Galatians, the resultant overlap between them is in the end not very extensive. And this is the case no matter whether we follow the reconstruction of Galatians' theology proposed by Beverly Gaventa or by James Dunn.

## First Corinthians and the Pastorals

When looking at the so-called parallels between 1 Corinthians and 1 Timothy, identified by Luke Timothy Johnson,[63] the most striking thing about that list is how general the connections are. Cumulatively the list may have some suggestive power regarding a series of topical convergences in the two epistles: teaching; people upsetting the community; wealthy persons and worship; slaves, wisdom, and knowledge; lawsuits; women and marriage; women and worship; widows; disputes over food; and financial support for ministers. They do not necessarily, however, suggest deep structural similarities between the theologies of the two epistles. They are more apt to be incidental convergences borne of problems and issues that were common in the early churches of the Mediterranean world. For example, it is easy to imagine that the role of widows in the community, or arguments over appropriate food to eat, or concerns about marriage would have arisen in many different communities and consequently would have been addressed in epistles dealing with pastoral issues. In that general sense, the common issues emerge out of a common milieu of problems and issues confronting the early church. To develop a more meaningful juxtaposition of 1 Corinthians and 1 Timothy we need to move the discussion to a comparison of some prominent theological patterns.

We need not rehearse our discussion of the "household of God" imagery in 1 Timothy here,[64] except to say that it is the fundamental metaphor for understanding the community of faith and is crucial to the theological pattern of the epistle. The most conspicuous counterpart in 1 Corinthians is,

---

[63] Johnson, "Oikonomia Theou," 94–95.
[64] See above, pp. 19–25.

of course, the "body of Christ" imagery in 12:12–31.[65] In his discussion of the discourse in 12:4–13:13, Victor Paul Furnish identifies three main points in this argument:

1. Those who confess Jesus as Lord have been graced with different kinds of gifts, although one and the same Spirit has bestowed them all; and further, these diverse manifestations of the Spirit have been granted "for the common good" (πρὸς τὸ συμφέρον, v. 7), 12:4–11.

2. Because of their diverse gifts, the members of this believing community, like the different parts of the human body, are totally interdependent and, as a consequence, necessary to one another (12:12–30). The analogy is introduced in vv. 12–13 . . . and is then is spelled out in vv. 14–26. Its applicability to the church is summarized in v. 27 . . . and is then concretely illustrated in vv. 28–30.

3. What is definitive for the life of this community, and is indeed the *sine qua non* of its existence, is nothing else but love (ἀγάπη), 12:31–13:13. Paul reflects, in turn, on the necessity of love (vv. 1–3), its qualities (vv. 4–7), and its distinctive permanence (vv. 8–13).[66]

In Paul's use of body language to describe the church, two things are in play: unity in the Spirit and diversity in the face of that unity.[67] These are the two central structural features of this text. In 1 Tim 3:15 and 1:4, however, the underlying concept is divine order and godliness among the members of the community that conforms to that divine order in faith. These metaphors, both applied to the church, appear to emerge from quite distinct patterns of life. The imagery in 1 Corinthians is from the domain of the body where features of the personal body are applied to the social body,[68] here focusing on the different kinds of gifts, the interdependence of the members of the body, and the necessity of love. The imagery in 1 Timothy on the contrary comes from the social reality of the household in Greco-Roman culture that is then overlaid onto the social reality of the church. The emphasis in this case is on conformity to divine order in faith, godliness, sound teaching, qualified leadership, and the exhortation to bring these about in the life of the church. The use of metaphorical language to say something about the church is common to both, but the character and representation of the two metaphors are distinctly different. Moreover, the purposes to which the respective metaphors are put do not seem to have much in common: understanding the varieties of spiritual gifts in the one church

---

[65] Cf. also the temple and body imagery in 3:16–17 and 6:19.

[66] Victor Paul Furnish, "Theology in 1 Corinthians," *Pauline Theology* 2 (ed. David M. Hay; SBLSymS 4; Minneapolis: Fortress, 1993), 70–71.

[67] Gordon D. Fee, "Toward a Theology of 1 Corinthians," in *Pauline Theology* 2 (ed. David M. Hay; SBLSymS 4; Minneapolis: Fortress, 1993), 54–55.

[68] See the discussion by Jerome H. Neyrey, *Paul in Other Words: A Cultural Reading of His Letters*, (Louisville: Westminster John Knox, 1990), 102–46.

according to 1 Corinthians, and divine training and proper behavior among the faithful in the church according to 1 Timothy. We cannot say these metaphors are incompatible or could not have come from the same theological mind, but they represent structurally, conceptually, and metaphorically quite distinct patterns to describe the church.

God in 1 Timothy and Titus is identified directly as savior, as is Christ in Titus.[69] Although σωτήρ (savior) and σωτηρία (salvation) do not appear in 1 Corinthians, Gordon Fee argues: "The gospel ultimately has to do with God, who alone stands at the beginning and the end of all things. Salvation is wholly the result of God's own initiative and activity; God foreordained it and effected it—through Christ."[70] Furthermore, according to Fee, Paul in this letter sees Christ in terms of God and his interest in Christ is soteriological.[71] He writes: ". . . Christ the Lord functions as savior, who effects the saving work of God in human history."[72] First Corinthians stands apart from the Pastorals in terms of the language that is used to describe God as savior but not in its intent. The lack of "savior" language to describe God and Christ may be a telltale sign that different authors are at work in the epistles; but at the level of underlying theological imagery, there is considerable agreement.

While eschatology is clearly part of the theological structure of the Pastorals (1 Tim 4:8; 6:14–15, 17, 19; 2 Tim 1:10, 18; 2:8–12, 18; 4:1, 8; Titus 2:13–14; 3:7), only in 2 Tim 2:18 is it clear that there is a problem concerning the resurrection. Hymenaeus and Philetus, among others, have claimed that the resurrection has already taken place. They have apparently claimed that the resurrection has already taken place and that they are presently living the postresurrection life. The author of 2 Timothy roundly rejects this idea. On the other hand, 1 Corinthians devotes the better part of a chapter to the issue of the resurrection. As 1 Cor 15:12 makes clear, the problem in Corinth is that some have denied that there will be a resurrection of the dead. According to Victor Furnish, the premise of Paul's argument about the resurrection is found in v. 20: "But in fact Christ has been raised from the dead, the first fruits of those who have died."[73] Furnish thinks that Paul is dealing with people who believe themselves to be spiritual and in that way as already living with Christ in glory.[74] To be sure, Paul views the resurrection of Christ as a matter of enormous eschatological significance. As an act of God, it is a manifestation of the life-giving power of the divine and of hope for both those who have died and those who are still alive.[75]

---

[69] See above, pp. 58–61.
[70] Fee, "Toward a Theology of 1 Corinthians," 40.
[71] Ibid., 43–45.
[72] Ibid., 45.
[73] Furnish, "Theology in 1 Corinthians," 75.
[74] Ibid., 74.
[75] See the discussion by Fee, "Toward a Theology of 1 Corinthians," 56–58.

Compared to the elaborate discussion in 1 Corinthians, the comment in 2 Tim 2:18 is made only in passing. There is no direct indication in the text that an over-spiritualized eschatology is the problem, though this perhaps could be inferred from the text. The point of the reference seems to be that some people are leading members of the community astray and as an example of this the problem of the resurrection is cited. There is no effort to refute the misconception theologically. It is simply evidence of the opposition that threatens the community and the doctrinal errors that ought to be resisted. First Corinthians 15 also addresses incorrect belief regarding the resurrection, but does so by mounting a direct theological argument against it. Based on the explicit evidence of 1 Corinthians and on the implicit evidence of 2 Timothy, it can be suggested that an overly spiritualized, perhaps enthusiast, conception of the resurrection and eschatology is being addressed in both texts. We cannot be sure that the problematic attitude is identical in both communities, but there is some reason to think they may be closely related. From that point on, however, the theological patterns of the two texts bear little resemblance.

One of the features common to the Pastorals is the cluster of terms—"truth," "faith," "knowledge," "sound teaching"—that suggest a notion of correct doctrine, an idea that runs deeply through the three letters.[76] The emphasis on wisdom associated with the crucifixion of Christ is, of course, a central feature of 1 Cor 1:1–3:23, but the word ἀλήθεια (truth) appears only in 5:8 and 13:6 and the word ἀληθής (true) does not occur at all in 1 Corinthians. In the two cases where "truth" is used it does not appear to emphasize a notion of doctrinal correctness as such. Πίστις (faith) occurs in 2:5; 12:9; 13:2, 13; 15:14, 17; and 16:13. In none of these references does there seem to be an emphasis on the doctrinal content of faith. It is at most only hinted at in 2:5 ("your faith" should not be based on human wisdom) and 15:14 and 17 (if there is no resurrection "your faith" is in vain). The verb πιστυείν (believe) occurs in 1:21; 3:5; 9:17; 11:18; 13:7; 14:22; 15:2, and 11, and here, too, the term does not refer in the main to an implicit doctrinal orthodoxy (cf. once again "wisdom" in 1:21 and the resurrection in 15:2 and 15:11). Paul in 1 Corinthians is not dismissive of questions of correct belief, as chapter 15 indicates; but unlike the Pastorals, the specter of doctrinal orthodoxy and conformity to divine order—largely presumed—does do not predominate in his epistle to the Corinthians. The language of "truth," "faith," and "sound teaching" is not by and large used to convey the concept of doctrine in 1 Corinthians. Furthermore, the first three chapters of 1 Corinthians turn on a redefinition of wisdom, knowledge, and the cross of Christ, a redefinition that once again finds no clear counterpart in the Pastorals.[77] In fact, apart from

---

[76] See above, pp. 63–64.

[77] See my article, "A Theoretical Context for Understanding 1 Cor 1:18–2:16," *Teaching at Concordia* 19 (1996–97), 1–3; and Furnish, "Theology in 1 Corinthians," 64–68.

places where the Pastorals probably draw on earlier traditions, the cross as a central redemptive symbol does not appear to predominate, as it does in the early chapters of 1 Corinthians.

First Corinthians has no counterpart to the concern for qualities and qualifications of leadership so conspicuous in the textual worlds of 1 Timothy and Titus. Groups of people are sometimes identified in 1 Corinthians but not in terms of the qualities necessary for leadership or particular roles in the community.[78] In that regard, the text of 1 Corinthians comes out of a different theological world, and certainly draws on different metaphors to understand and describe the church. As we have seen, the "household of God" metaphor is quite distinct from the "body of Christ" metaphor. Where the Pastorals and 1 Corinthians do overlap structurally and conceptually, they do so at a very general level. The literary and theological affinity between them is neither marked nor extensive.

## A Conceptual Conclusion on the Question of Authorship

Regarding the question of authorship in light of these comparative observations, the logical issue runs as follows: if 2 Timothy, in terms of its theological pattern, is as close to Philippians as it is to 1 Timothy and Titus and if 2 Timothy was written by the same author as 1 Timothy and Titus, then why should we not think that 2 Timothy and Philippians have been written by the same author as well? And if so, Paul must be the author of all four epistles. This, of course, does not mean that they in fact are all from Paul himself, but it illustrates one of the logical problems in arguing against Pauline authorship. That same conclusion would also force us to see 1 Timothy/Titus and Philippians, epistles representing quite different theological worlds and representing different ends of the spectrum in the Pauline tradition, as coming from the same author, clearly a possibility but not an easy fit to make, as two centuries of scholarship have made clear. On the other hand, if 2 Timothy was not written by the same author as 1 Timothy and Titus, then there may be no compelling logical reason to think that 2 Timothy and Philippians were written by the same author either. In fact, we may have three different authors. And none of these observations can rule out the possibility that 2 Timothy was patterned after Philippians by someone in the later Pauline tradition.

As this discussion suggests, the case of 2 Timothy and Philippians represents the linchpin in the argument concerning Pauline authorship of the Pastorals. And the way we position 2 Timothy relative to 1 Timothy and Titus and 2 Timothy relative to Philippians is critical in this discussion. If 1 Timothy and Titus did not come from the same author as Philippians and if the substantial differences between 2 Timothy and the other two Pastorals

---

[78] Cf. the issue of women being silent in 1 Tim 2:11 and 1 Cor 14:34–35. See also Fitzmyer, "Structured Ministry," 582–93.

suggest different authors, the evidence indicates at least two, and possibly three, authors are responsible for the four epistles. Either Philippians and 2 Timothy were both written by Paul and 1 Timothy and Titus were written by someone else;[79] or Philippians was written by Paul, 1 Timothy and Titus were written by someone in the Pauline tradition, and 2 Timothy was written by yet a third author who patterned his epistle loosely after features from Philippians and perhaps even 1 Timothy. While there are some—though modest—theological and structural features linking Galatians, 1 Corinthians, and the Pastorals,[80] it is the relationship between Philippians and 2 Timothy that is crucial in any argument connecting the Pastorals to Paul. As stated previously, where 2 Timothy is structurally most like 1 Timothy and Titus, it is least like Philippians; and at the points where 2 Timothy is least like them, it is most like Philippians.[81] *Hence, we might conclude that there is a relatively low probability that Paul wrote all three of the Pastorals, a somewhat higher probability that Paul wrote 2 Timothy but not 1 Timothy and Titus, and a slightly higher probability still that Paul did not write any of the Pastorals; rather 2 Timothy was written by one author, and 1 Timothy and Titus were written by yet another.*

With this in mind, it is clear that Pauline imitation in 2 Timothy turns to a significant degree on the issue of suffering and following Paul's example.[82] Not only is correct doctrine to be observed but the proper manner of life, especially Paul's example of suffering, is to be followed.[83] In this way, the text of the epistle personifies the link representing and conveying the apostle, his theology, and suffering to the recipients of 2 Timothy in the hope that they will follow his example and be united with him in this act of suffering. If, as seems distinctly possible, the author of 2 Timothy is not Paul—or the writer of 1 Timothy or Titus for that matter—he has linked the

---

[79] Jerome Murphy-O'Connor concludes that 2 Timothy is written by Paul (*Paul: A Critical Life* [Oxford: Oxford University Press, 1997], 356–59).

[80] Towner ("Pauline Theology and Pauline Tradition," 291–300) summarizes four themes or benchmarks for assessing continuity and discontinuity between the Pastoral Epistles and Paul as (1) local community; (2) salvation-historical, eschatological context of ecclesiology; (3) relation of the church to the gospel; and (4) place and nature of church office/ministry/leadership.

[81] The point is that common authorship for the three Pastoral Epistles is not well-founded and thus the character of Pauline authority and the formation of a notion of Pauline Scripture, or even canon, may not be identical in all three epistles. See the claim by Michael Prior, *Paul the Letter-Writer*, 169.

[82] Dibelius and Conzelmann emphasize that the exhortation to suffer is based on the bond between teacher and disciple (*The Pastoral Epistles*, 98). This clearly forms the immediate circumstance for the plea to suffer.

[83] Lohfink asserts that the apostle is a "prototype," not only in the proclamation of the word but in his person and life, and that this constitutes the substructure of 2 Tim ("Paulinische in der Rezeption," 83). See 1 Tim 1:15–16; 4:12; and 2 Tim 3:10–14. Lohfink also claims that the immediacy of Paul's suffering is lost in the Pastorals and that suffering is now formalized, (ibid., 94).

example of Paul to a hoped for pattern of life (e.g., suffering) and correct belief that presumes an uneasy relationship between the recipients of the letter
and their wider social world. If Paul has already died by the time 2 Timothy
is written, the epistle keeps the example of the apostle alive in terms of his
paradigmatic and exhortative value,[84] and the author of the epistle serves to
bring that image of Paul and his audience into juxtaposition. In the case of
the exhortations to true faith, it is not entirely clear to what extent the teachings derive from the apostle and to what extent the character and image of
Paul is in fact used to validate the teachings of the author of 2 Timothy.[85]
Of course, these are not mutually exclusive.

Based on our work with 1 Timothy, Titus, and the undisputed letters,
the textual and theological evidence suggests that these two pastoral letters
represent an even more conservative and conformist social strand in the developing Pauline tradition than does 2 Timothy (with their concerns for
church order, qualifications for leadership, conformity with the household
of God, hierarchical notions of social structure, and their views of women's
roles). While the way of suffering—a countercultural image focused inter-
nally—is to be enjoined according to 2 Timothy, conformity with some
rather well prescribed imperial social expectations for the sake of the
church's image among outsiders is of concern in 1 Timothy and Titus. What
the larger world thinks about the church and the behavior of its members is
important. In particular, what distinguishes 1 Timothy from 2 Timothy most
dramatically is that in 1 Timothy the shape of the discussion is cast broadly
in terms of οἰκονομία (divine training/order) and εὐσέβεια (godliness) for
those within the household of God (3:15). In 2 Timothy, however, the Paul-
Timothy axis turns more directly on the intimate relationship between the
two, most especially on the appeal for Timothy to suffer as Paul has suffered.
Furthermore, the representation of the Lord as σωτήρ (savior), found only in
Phil 3:20 in the undisputed Paulines, comes to predominate in the christological language of 1 Timothy (1:1; 2:3; 4:10) and Titus (1:3, 4; 2:10, 13; 3:4,
6), and in 2 Timothy 1:10. This terminology is rooted in imperial language,
a designation regularly applied to the Roman emperor, that is incorporated
increasingly into the christological language of the Pauline tradition as represented by 1 Timothy and Titus. Here, too, 2 Timothy appears to be in a
category different from the other two Pastorals. This also suggests that
within the tradition that ensues from Paul there are impulses and forces that

---

[84] Beker, *Heirs of Paul,* 37. Fiore argues that the function of example is not
simply for better comprehension but for action. The example is a demonstration of
what is being taught. Fiore, *Personal Example,* 36–37. See also Donelson, *Pseudepigraphy and Ethical Argument,* 93, 105–6.

[85] To the extent Paul's theology was received by the author(s) of the Pastorals,
Lohfink raises the question of whether it was transmitted through the Pauline letters
themselves or through the oral tradition ("Paulinische Theologie in der Rezeption,"
70). Given the character of the connections between the Pastorals and the undisputed Pauline letters this, of course, is a very difficult question to answer.

emphasize conformity with Roman society as well as those that presume a more countercultural posture (i.e., suffering) with respect to the world of the empire. The former is represented most vividly in 1 Timothy and Titus and the latter in 2 Timothy and Philippians. This is not meant to suggest, however, that these are entirely incompatible impulses, or that they could not reasonably be held together by Christian individuals or communities at the same time.

# ∽ 4 ∾

# APOSTOLIC AUTHORITY, IMAGES OF PAUL, AND THE DEVELOPMENT OF THE PAULINE SCRIPTURES

## PAUL, AUTHORITY, AND SCRIPTURE IN THE PASTORALS

### Introduction

IF THE Pastoral Epistles do not come directly from Paul but from someone else in the Pauline tradition, it raises a number of questions pertaining to the emergence of the Pauline writings as Scripture. How does the authority of Paul serve to validate the authority of the Pastoral texts? How does the attempt to emulate the authentic—and earlier—Pauline Epistles shape the Pastoral Epistles? Finally, can we see already in the Pastoral Epistles the beginnings of a movement toward the development of a body of Pauline Scriptures and ultimately a Pauline canon?[1] If, however, we were to conclude that the Pastorals are in fact from Paul himself, these questions undoubtedly shift, but not dramatically so in each case. The question of Pauline authority still pertains, and the issue of a developing concept of Pauline Scripture shifts only slightly. If the Pastoral Epistles are authentically Pauline, the issue of emulation changes significantly. Paul, of course, would not emulate himself, as would someone writing pseudepigraphically in the name of Paul. In either case, however, the issue of an emerging concept of Scripture is linked to the theological contour of the Pastoral Epistles, as well as to their relationship with one another and with the larger Pauline corpus.[2] The argument to be developed in this section of the chapter is that

---

[1] Here we observe the common distinction between the terms Scripture and canon. See Harry Y. Gamble, "Canon," *ABD*, 1:852–61.

[2] As indicated above (pp. 3–5, 86–89), it is most plausible to view the Pastorals as pseudepigraphic, but the argument developed about Pauline authority and the formation of the Pauline Scriptures in this section does not rest entirely on this issue. Hence, it is important to recognize the questions that have prompted this discussion and how those questions shift if a different conclusion is reached regarding the issue of authorship.

a Pauline concept of Scripture, the precursor to a full-fledged Pauline canon, can be detected already in the theological and literary patterns of the Pastoral Epistles.

## The Image and Authority of Paul in the Pastorals

Noting that the designation "apostle" appears in the Pastorals in only five places,[3] Gerhard Lohfink claims that this term, along with the terms "preacher" and "teacher,"[4] form a triadic picture of Paul and that the title "apostle" in the Pastoral Epistles has lost significance in comparison to the authentic letters.[5] No longer is he simply apostle to the Gentiles (Rom 11:13) but he is the teacher of the Gentiles (1 Tim 2:7).[6] In the Pastorals, Paul is the authoritative teacher, not just any teacher but the one true teacher.[7] As apostle, Paul is the proclaimer of the gospel and the teacher of the people. To that extent, the apostleship of Paul is described in a new way in the Pastoral Epistles, not a description apprently derived from the authentic Pauline letters.[8] Interpreting Titus 1:1, Lohfink argues that Paul is not apostle according to the norm of the faith of the church but on account of the faith to serve the elect of God and to make possible knowledge of the truth.[9] 2 Timothy 1:1–14 and Titus 1:1–3 establish the uniqueness of God's revelation in Paul's gospel, and this underwrites the uniqueness of his apostleship.[10]

Raymond Collins argues even further that "apostle" in the Pastorals is now an office of the church and as such Paul's authority must be recognized.[11] Unlike the image in the undisputed Paulines, the apostolate in the Pastorals is singular and the authority of Paul establishes the authority of the apostolic office. The fullness of the apostolate is present in him, and as

---

[3] 1 Tim 1:1; 2:7; 2 Tim 1:1, 11; Titus 1:1.

[4] Paul is identified as a preacher in 1 Tim 2:7 and 2 Tim 1:11. In each case, the author(s) make this identification in connection with his being an apostle. Paul is designated a teacher in 1 Tim 2:7; 2 Tim 1:11; and 4:3. In the undisputed Paulines, the designation "teacher" occurs only in Rom 2:20; 1 Cor 12:28, and 29, none of which refers specifically to Paul. See also Raymond F. Collins, "The Image of Paul in the Pastorals," *Laval théologique et philosophique* 31 (1975): 147–58.

[5] Lohfink, "Paulinische Theologie in der Rezeption," 71. See also the discussion of the title apostle in De Boer, "Images of Paul," 363–65.

[6] Ibid., 71.

[7] Collins remarks that the description of Paul as teacher is unusual in the NT as this is not a term normally used of Christian preachers, "Image of Paul," 153. Cf. De Boer, "Images of Paul," 378.

[8] Lohfink, "Paulinische Theologie in der Rezeption," 71–73.

[9] Ibid., 73.

[10] In the sequence, apostolic title, revelation, gospel, and commission of the apostle with the gospel, the connections with the authentic Paulines is clear, according to Lohfink (ibid., 75–78).

[11] Collins, "Image of Paul," 155.

the one in whom this authority resides he guarantees the soundness of the church's teaching.[12] Pushing the argument even further, Collins asserts that as the figure in whom this authority resides, Paul also functions as the one who decides who should be admitted to the circle of deacons, elders, and widows.[13] While this last claim by Collins may be stretching the argument too far, the singular and authoritative character of Paul is unmistakable: he is an authority figure now represented to the church by his image in the Pastoral Epistles.

In light of these claims by Lohfink and Collins, the appeal to correct doctrine in the Pastorals serves to present Paul as the representative of the true faith. He not only argues for it, but he represents it.[14] In 1 Timothy and to a lesser extent in Titus, as we have observed, this is framed in terms of the household of God, whereas in 2 Timothy it is linked with the appeal to follow Paul on the way of suffering. In all three texts, the true faith and the proper manner of life as proclaimed and represented by Paul are set against the opponents who threaten the truth and undermine the community. It is not merely that these epistles function in the apostle's stead in his absence or as his extension, but the epistles themselves come to define true doctrine and correct behavior. In that regard, the texts over time presumably come to have a presence of their own and hence must be reckoned with in their own right. In that sense, the epistles come to project both an apostolic presence and a textual presence. By itself this would not constitute the Pastoral Epistles as Scripture. However, to the extent that early church communities accept the apostolic preaching and teaching authority of Paul as divinely given and submit to the authority of the texts as representing the gospel and correct teaching, these epistles will come to be heard as sacred address.[15] Thus, the validity of these texts as Scripture depends in good measure on the authority invested in them by the communities to which they are addressed and in which they come to function.

In the case of 1 Timothy and Titus, the function of the letters, in addition to preserving the true faith of the recipients, is to conform life in the communities to the pattern of the household, which is now identified as the household of God. The social order of this household is patterned after the qualities and qualifications necessary in the Greco-Roman household. This perhaps also suggests a tendency in these two letters to accommodate the church in some sense to the prevailing order of the Greco-Roman household. In doing so, the author uses Paul to sanction a model for the church. Here

---

[12] Ibid., 156–61.

[13] Ibid., 161.

[14] Lewis R. Donelson writes: "Paul is not simply author. Paul inscribes himself in his own text. Or, in my opinion, an unknown author has Paul inscribe himself in his own text" ("Studying Paul: 2 Timothy as Remembrance," *Society of Biblical Literature Seminar Papers* 36 [1997]: 721).

[15] Cf. the discussion by Beker, *Heirs of Paul*, 36–39.

Paul is less the compelling example than he is the authoritative teacher instructing the church in the way to live and organize itself in the face of both internal and external requirements.[16] As in the case of 2 Timothy, the epistles of 1 Timothy and Titus resound with the voice of Paul but do so in different ways and for different purposes. In a real sense, all three epistles become the voice of Paul for their respective audiences,[17] and to the extent that his gospel and his apostleship are thought to be from God, that voice and the text that projects it are also thought to be from God, to be Scripture, and as such transcend Paul.[18] The following diagram illustrates these relationships:

| *God/Christ* | *Paul* | *Voice of Paul* | *Pastoral Texts* |
|---|---|---|---|
| Creator | Slave of God | Example | Transmitter |
| Redeemer | Apostle of Christ | Instruction | Amplifier |
| Savior | | Demonstration | Voice of Paul |
| | | Gospel | Voice of God |

## Scripture and the Beginnings of a Pauline Canon

As important as it is for the presentation of this argument to make distinctions between 1 Timothy/Titus and 2 Timothy and to position the Pastoral Epistles broadly in relation to the undisputed Paulines, it is not the question of Pauline authenticity or pseudepigraphy that finally gets to the heart of the matter. Brevard Childs first sharpened this in canonical terms when he wrote:

First of all, among those scholars who have recently attempted to interpret the Pastorals as an example of pseudepigraphical literature the model of strictly his-

---

[16]Johnson says that in 2 Timothy Paul presented his behavior as exemplary, whereas in 1 Tim 1:12–20 it is God's mercy that is exemplary. In the case of Titus, he says that the epistle takes the form of a *mandata principis* letter where Titus is to show himself as a model of good deeds (*Delegates*, 122, 212). See also the discussion of Paul the teacher by Gerhard Lohfink, "Paulinische Theologie in der Rezeption," 71 and also 97–113.

[17]Donelson asserts: "In order for the cosmological-ethical connections believed in by our author to gain a hearing in his church and thus acquire power and influence, this theology must be anchored in reliable roots. The ability of these teachings to persuade and thus to save reside in the believability of the fiction of Pauline origins." (*Pseudepigraphy and Ethical Argument*, 151).

[18]In a concise summary, Brevard Childs sets forth the proposals regarding the function of these epistles made by those who hold these epistles to be pseudepigraphic: written fifty years after Paul by a follower who tries to apply Paul's teaching to a new situation in the church; a personalizing of the tradition; development of a commissioning office that would project Pauline authority into the next generation of the church; and the projection of an apostolic presence into the period after the death of Paul. The problem, as Childs points out, is that clear exegetical support for these claims is difficult to find (Brevard S. Childs *The New Testament as Canon: An Introduction* [Philadelphia: Fortress, 1984], 381).

torical referentiality of meaning continues to remain dominant. The literary genre is continually interpreted in reference to its allegedly 'real' historical situation, namely, one some fifty years after the death of Paul. The effect of this move is that the literary genre is actually viewed as something 'pseudo,' whose true meaning only emerges when the genuine historical setting is reconstructed. A concomitant effect of this hermeneutical model is that the description of the Pastorals as pseudepigraphical usually functions to establish from the outset the referentiality of the letters to be derived from the creative imagination of the author. As a result, a rich variety of possible relationships, both simple and complex, between the literature and its referent is lost because the genre description simply decides the issue as if by reflex. . . . The kerygmatic witness of the text is, thereby, rendered mute, and its interpretation is made dependent on other external forces which are set in a causal relationship.[19]

To this we might add that a preoccupation with Pauline authenticity can, in some cases, also exhibit the same issue, an overriding concern with historical correspondences, which obscures the complex internal relationships of the Pastoral Epistles as literary texts that claim the authority of Paul and indirectly the authority of God. Whether written by Paul or someone else, the Pastoral Epistles exhibit a web of internal relationships that reflect, however altered, a Christology rooted in Paul and the early church,[20] preformed traditions,[21] quotations and echoes of the Scriptures of Israel,[22] and episodes from the life of Paul.[23] This does not mean that the author or authors of the Pastoral Epistles have not reshaped the traditions at their disposal and creatively addressed their own audiences, but it indicates that the texts display a kerygmatic and theological frame of reference that reaches back into the tradition and brings to the fore a remembrance of Paul and the traditions that are being passed on.[24] In doing so, all three Pastorals are linked to an authoritative tradition. It is that linkage, we would argue, that draws the Pastoral Epistles into the rudimentary yet substantive beginnings of a Pauline canon.[25]

---

[19] Ibid., 382–83.

[20] See, e.g., the "in Christ" language in 1 Tim 1:14; 3:13; 2 Tim 1:1, 9, 13; 2:1, 10; 3:12, 15.

[21] As candidates for preformed traditions, see 1 Tim 2:5–6; 3:16; 2 Tim 2:11–13; Titus 2:14; 3:5–7.

[22] See apparent echoes and quotations in 1 Tim 2:2, 8, 13–14; 5:5, 18–19; 6:7; 2 Tim 2:19; 3:8; 4:17; Titus 2:11, 14.

[23] See, e.g., 1 Tim 1:3, 20; 3:14; 4:13; 2 Tim 1:3–7, 15–18; 3:10–11; 4:6–22; Titus 1:5; 3:12–15.

[24] E. Earle Ellis has addressed this in "Traditions in the Pastoral Epistles" in *Early Jewish and Christian Exegesis: Studies in Memory of William Hugh Brownlee* (ed. Craig A. Evans and William F. Stinespring; Atlanta: Scholars Press, 1987), 237–53; and Peter Trummer in *Die Paulustradition der Pastoralbriefe*, (BBET, 8; Frankfurt: Peter Lang, 1978).

[25] In some measure, this issue turns on the dating of the Pastorals. If the Pastorals were written pseudepigraphically shortly after Paul's death, the early collection of the community letters would have had less time to develop a substantive shape and form than if they were written many decades following his death. Undoubtedly,

The notion of remembrance and passing on the tradition is most poignant in 2 Timothy. In some cases, the remembrance refers to Paul or Timothy and their past (1:3, 5; 3:15), but still other texts refer to the passing on of the tradition from Paul to Timothy (1:6, 13; 2:2; 3:10, 14; cf. 1:12, 14). This chain of tradition is not limited to the past and the present but is also carried by Timothy from the present into the future (2:2, 15; 4:1–2), as he is called upon to instruct others. Perhaps only in 1:6 (Timothy) and 1:11 (Paul) is there anything approaching an office implied in 2 Timothy. The epistle clearly portrays, however, a continuum of tradition from the past to the future that is to be remembered and preserved. This imagery culminates in 2 Tim 1:12 and 14, where the deposit (παραθήκην) is portrayed as being guarded. There are well-known translation problems associated with this term, especially in 1:12,[26] but at least in 1:14 Timothy is charged to guard the "good deposit" through the Holy Spirit. Regardless of whether this deposit is understood in 2 Timothy in static or dynamic terms,[27] it is clearly situated in this chain of tradition and presumably has some kerygmatic content.

Gerhard Lohfink argues that the "good deposit" is nothing other than the gospel itself. God's grace, having appeared in Christ, is now bestowed on human beings, and it is with the proclamation of this gospel that Paul and the church are entrusted until the epiphany of Christ.[28] Lohfink rejects the claim that the "good deposit" represents the totality of the "Paulus-'Gutes,'" arguing rather that this is in fact too broad and ought to be included under the concept of διδασκαλία (teaching, instruction).[29] He is surely correct to make a distinction between "gospel" and "teaching" in the Pastorals, but it is less clear what the precise relationship between them is and how the one affects the other. Presumably, Paul's instruction is influenced and affected by the gospel. Or, at least, it is thought to be consistent with the gospel. To that

---

the early selection and ordering of the community letters would have involved a process of shaping and framing. We might think that the result of this process was more malleable in the early period than it would become later. In our view it is most plausible that the Pastorals were written before the end of the first century and probably within twenty to twenty-five years of Paul's death. If 2 Timothy was written by Paul, it, of course, would be an exception to this. To be sure, with this dating range it is likely there would have already been a process of compiling and ordering Paul's letters before the Pastorals were written. We might presume, however, that whatever collection there was by this time it was still fairly fluid and subject to considerable refinement and reinterpretation. See also the proposal by B. Paul Wolfe, "Scripture in the Pastoral Epistles: Premarcion Marcionism," *PRSt* 16 (1989): 5–16.

[26] See the discussions by Bassler, *1 Timothy, 2 Timothy, Titus*, 133–34; and Johnson, *Delegates*, 55. We also note the distinction between παράδοσις (tradition), which appears in the undisputed Paulines but not in the Pastorals, and παραθήκη (handing down) which appears only in 1 & 2 Timothy.

[27] Compare Childs, *New Testament as Canon*, 389; and Johnson, *Delegates*, 55.

[28] Lohfink, "Paulinische Theologie in der Rezeption," 97–98.

[29] Ibid., 98–99.

extent, it is insufficient simply to say that his gospel is sanctioned by divine authority but his teaching only by personal authority. As apostle and pro-claimer of the gospel, Paul also operates with the authority of God. The distinction between divine authority and Pauline authority is not so clear-cut.[30] Hence, it is difficult to exclude entirely Paul's teaching from the "good deposit," which also includes the gospel. In light of the definition of theology given in chapter 1, the discussion in chapter 2 suggests that in the Pastorals gospel and instruction, as well as theology and ethics, are more intricately interwoven than a sharp distinction between Paul's gospel and his teaching might imply. Therefore, it is probable that παραθήκην in the Pastorals identifies, at the very least, a concept of authorized teaching that begins to take shape in rudimentary form.

On the historical level, Donelson is probably right that there never was a discrete, largely fixed, deposit of doctrinal and moral teachings (as suggested by this imagery) handed down, but that may also be beside the point when it comes to the theological world of the texts.[31] The concept and perception of an authoritative body of teachings and moral standards is already being shaped within the epistles and within the larger theological world of the Pauline tradition. Even if this is a fiction, it is a fiction with important and real consequences for the remembrance of Paul in the church. We will need to examine this more closely below,[32] but it is worth noting that in Child's view the content of the gospel of Paul has not changed in the Pastoral Epistles but the manner in which the content is guarded. The proclamation and teaching of Paul have become the medium through which truth and error are now to be confronted.[33]

First Timothy also makes reference to guarding the παραθήκην in 6:20, but beyond that there are some clear differences when 1 and 2 Timothy are compared. In 1 Timothy, the tradition is conveyed primarily to Timothy through the plea to instruct the people in the sound teaching (e.g., 1:3, 18; 3:14; 4:6, 11, 13, 16; 5:21). Read on its own terms, this suggests that the tradition to be guarded in 1 Timothy is more clearly the correct doctrine to be taught than may be the case in 2 Timothy with its emphasis on preserving and handing on the tradition.[34] This is indicated in 2 Timothy primarily by the personal tone of the letter and the imagery of remembrance. As we have seen,[35] however, this does not mean that 2 Timothy has no concept of sound teaching. The view exhibited by 1 Timothy is also reflected in Titus 2:1: "But as for you, teach what is consistent with the sound teaching." In Titus 1:3 the entrusting of the kerygma to Paul is expressly said to be by the

---

[30] Ibid., 99.
[31] Donelson, *Pseudepigraphy and Ethical Argument*, 164.
[32] See below, pp. 97–100.
[33] Childs, *New Testament Canon*, 389–90.
[34] Cf. Johnson, *Delegates*, 55.
[35] See above pp. 45–46, 73–78.

command of God the savior, which highlights the divine origin of the proclamation as well as its authority as passed from Paul to Titus and on to the other members of the church.

What seems to separate 1 Timothy and Titus from 2 Timothy even more conspicuously is the concept of offices, qualifications for holding office, and the implicit handing on of the sound teaching of the church through people who hold pastoral positions (see 1 Tim 3:1–8; 4:14; 5:17, 22; Titus 1:5–9; cf. 1 Tim 1:12; 2:7), something only hinted in 2 Tim 1:6. Hence, in 1 Timothy and Titus the idea of an authoritative Pauline concept of sound teaching, perhaps even a canonical tradition, develops alongside an emergent ecclesial structure that also has authority. In 1 Timothy and Titus, an incipient canonical process and a community structure are both in view and appear to work in tandem in the transmission and preservation of the Pauline tradition.[36] In that way, sound teaching can be preserved, error identified and hopefully corrected.

Even within these theological frames of reference, it would be inaccurate to portray the Pastorals, 2 Timothy in particular, as benignly passing on a fixed, received Pauline deposit of authoritative preaching and teaching. The issue of Christology in the Pastorals is a good illustration of this dynamic. As we saw earlier,[37] the expression ἐν Χριστῷ (in Christ) in 1 and 2 Timothy is clearly reminiscent of Pauline language and Christology, and appears to root the Christology of the Pastorals in the wider Pauline tradition. However, the Christology of the Pastorals is also dramatically different from the undisputed Paulines and much of the rest of the New Testament. This is the case in primarily two ways: the designation "savior" for both God and Christ, a designation for Christ found only in Phil 3:20 in the undisputed Pauline Epistles, and the language of "epiphany" to describe the coming of Christ, once again terminology not found in the undisputed Paulines. To be sure, Christology anchors the Pastorals in the Pauline kerygma of the early church, but the way it is expressed and developed in the three Pastoral Epistles is peculiar.

Considering first the "savior" terminology, to rehearse what was said above,[38] it is noteworthy that in 1 Timothy, God alone is referred to as "savior," whereas in Titus the designation alternates between God and Christ. The single appearance of the term in 2 Tim 1:10 is also used in connection with Christ. In 1 Timothy 1:1 and 2:3 God is simply referred to as "our savior" and in 4:10 God is identified as a living God who is "savior of all people." The verbal form of the word in 1 Tim 2:4 has God as the subject, whereas in 1:15 Christ is clearly the subject of the infinitive verb: "Christ Jesus came into the world to save sinners." In Titus 1:3, 2:10, and 3:4, similar to 1 Tim 1:1 and 2:3, God is designated "our savior," whereas in 1:4,

---

[36] Donelson, *Pseudepigraphy and Ethical Argument*, 163, 166.
[37] See above, p. 94, note 20.
[38] See above, pp. 58–59.

2:13, and 3:6, Christ carries this designation. In Titus 3:5 the subject of the verb "to save" also has God as the subject. In 2 Tim 1:9 and 4:18 the verb "to save" is used; and in the first case God is the subject, whereas in the second the designation "Lord" functions in that capacity. With regard to the identification of the savior, the Pastoral Epistles consistently apply that designation to God or Christ, unlike the remainder of the New Testament Pauline tradition where the noun form of the term appears infrequently.[39] The important point is that Paul's theological and christological language is thoroughly transformed into savior terminology, especially in 1 Timothy and Titus, but to a lesser extent in 2 Timothy as well. A received christological tradition is not merely being handed on. Whatever the "good deposit" is, it is clearly connected to the christological traditions represented by Paul, but it is by no means a static replication of them either.

While most of the New Testament writings, Paul's included, use παρ-ουσία (coming) to refer to the return of Christ, the Pastorals use ἐπιφάνεια (appearing, appearance) to designate the appearances of Christ, both past and future.[40] This feature of the Pastorals has long been recognized,[41] and as Jouette Bassler indicates these epiphanies do not designate a process that moves from lowliness to exaltation but rather a revelation of something previously hidden. She writes:

> The two epiphanies do not define a process—for example, from lowliness to exaltation. Instead, each reveals a previously hidden divine reality. . . . At least when applied to Jesus' first coming, the epiphany language does not refer primarily to a revelation or manifestation of Christ but to the revelation, through the Christ event, of a reality about God. This does not mean that we should not speak of an epiphany Christology, but that when used of the Pastorals, we must understand it to refer primarily to Christ as the vehicle, and not the content, of the epiphany.[42]

If this epiphany framework not only expresses the Christology of the Pastorals but in some way restructures whatever received Pauline traditions the author(s)—assuming the letters are not from Paul—may have had,[43] this illustrates once again the dynamic and creative quality of the deposit that is to be guarded. From an authorial perspective, we perhaps might conclude that the imitation of Paul in the Pastorals is simply not very good. On the other

---

[39] The only other New Testament document outside the Pastorals where "savior" occurs with some regularity is 2 Peter (five times), and in that epistle the term is used consistently of Christ. In that series of occurrences the only ambiguous reference is 3:2, but even there it is most assuredly a reference to Christ as well.

[40] 1 Tim 6:14; 2 Tim 1:10; 4:1, 8; Titus 2:13; cf. Titus 2:11; 3:4. This term also occurs in 2 Thess 2:8.

[41] See Jouette M. Bassler, "A Plethora of Epiphanies," 310–25; Collins, *1 & 2 Timothy and Titus*, 202–3; and Oberlinner, "Die 'Epiphaneia' des Heilswillens," 192–213.

[42] Bassler, "A Plethora of Epiphanies," 313.

[43] Oberlinner, "Die 'Epiphaneia' des Heilswillens," 192–313.

hand, we might also conclude that the writers are much more creative and transformative of the prior tradition than appears at first reading. This also indicates that the issue must be considered on two different levels: the imagery of the deposit to be guarded in the theology of the Pastoral texts, which might suggest a rather static image, and the reality of what happens to the Pauline tradition in the Pastorals as the larger theological world of Pauline Scripture begins to come into view, which is considerably more innovative.

Lest we incline to the view that the Pastorals are simply works of creative fiction with no reflection of Paul's theology or his controversies, we need to note some other Pauline images that surface in the theological frameworks of these three epistles—that is in addition to those connections between 2 Timothy and Philippians already identified. As we have seen in Titus 1:10–16, the Jewish character of the opposition in this epistle is identified in general terms. These problem people come primarily from the "circumcision." They teach that which is improper to teach for shameful gain. The text goes on in 1:14 to say that those grounded in the true testimony should pay no attention to the Jewish myths and commandments of the people who reject the truth. In this regard, the literary structures of Galatians and Titus have one thing in common. There is a problem with the Jewish law in both. Yet two chapters are devoted in Galatians to the issue of faith and works of law, but only three verses address the issue of the commandments in Titus. The place of the Gentiles in God's covenant, so critical to the discussion in Galatians, is not found at all in Titus. While "faith in Christ" is not juxtaposed opposite "works of law" in Titus, the author of Titus makes it clear in 3:5 that salvation is the result of divine mercy, not works of righteousness. The Pauline image at this point is unmistakable.[44]

To reiterate,[45] 1 Timothy identifies an opposition that is concerned with "myths," "genealogies," and "speculations" (1:4). Furthermore, the author writes against teachers who apparently teach about things that they do not understand (1:7). Similar to Titus, the law is the point at issue. In reply, the writer says the law is good if it is used correctly and if people understand that the law is set forth for the lawless and not the innocent (1:8–10). Galatians 3:19 appears to suggest a view of the law that is similar: "Why therefore the law? It was given because of transgressions. . . ." In both letters, the purpose of the law is to deal with lawlessness and transgressions. In the theology of 1 Timothy this is related to the issue of forbidding marriage and not eating certain foods. That is a misunderstanding and misuse of the law. To be sure, there is an emphasis on training oneself in godliness in 1 Timothy (4:7), but there is no correlation between the law and a παιδαγωγός (mentor). Although there is a basic connection in the way the law is understood in 1 Timothy and in Galatians (the law is given for transgressions and lawlessness) it should be observed again that the law in Galatians is given "because of" or "on account

---

[44] Cf. Rom 4:1–24; 9:30–10:4; Eph 2:8–11.
[45] See above, pp. 64–66.

of" transgressions (τῶν παραβάσεων χάριν), whereas in 1 Timothy it is laid down for the lawless and disobedient. Once more, we hear the echo of Paul's words resounding through the words of 1 Timothy and Titus, yet at the same time we can hear them reverberate in quite new ways in the Pastorals.

It is not necessary to exhaust these parallel images to establish the point that in 1 and 2 Timothy and Titus concepts of sound teaching and the "good deposit" are coming to define how Paul and his teachings are to be remembered, preserved, and passed on. This is not simply a description of how the Pastorals conserved or transformed the Pauline traditions. Neither is it a commentary on the Pastoral Epistles as some type of creative fiction made possible by pseudepigraphy as a type of literature. It is an observation about how an understanding of Pauline doctrine as a deposit is becoming a factor in the larger theological world of Paul's teaching and its legacy. Of course, if there is ever to be a collection of Pauline scriptures and in due time a Pauline canon, there must be a remembrance of Paul and his teaching that is preserved. The claim that this Pauline legacy also has theological and christological authority only underscores its importance and urgency. But the point is that in the Pastorals we are witnessing the early formation of a larger literary world that we might call the Pauline scriptures or the Pauline canon. To that world, each of the epistles eventually included in the Pauline legacy will contribute, but perhaps even more importantly each of the epistles will be read ultimately in light of that larger theological world. The Paul of the Pastorals and the Paul of the undisputed letters will start to be read in light of each other. When that happens, a Pauline collection of writings will start to function as a canon. It is at that point that the notion of a body of sound teaching or a Pauline deposit also has the potential to affect how the church reads the larger Pauline tradition. The letters may now be read in church communities primarily for their doctrines or moral principles or authoritative instruction—in other words for the deposit of sound teaching—rather than for their contingent applications of the gospel in the context of the apostle's missionary work.

## For Teaching, Reproof, Correction, and Training

The author of 2 Timothy writes in 3:14–16:

> But for you, remain in what you have learned and believed, knowing from whom you learned it, and that from childhood you have known the sacred writings (γράμματα) that are able to make you wise for salvation through faith in Christ Jesus. All scripture (γραφή) is God-breathed and profitable for teaching, for reproof, for correction, for training in righteousness.[46]

---

[46] For a brief discussion of the translation issue relating to "all" Scripture being God-breathed or "each" Scripture that is God-breathed, see Bassler, *1 Timothy 2 Timothy, Titus*, 167.

There is little doubt that what the author meant by "sacred writings" or "God-breathed Scripture" are the Scriptures of Israel. Even though we know that authoritative writings were beginning to emerge quite early in the church, it may well be anachronistic to think that the author had in mind a body of church produced writings that were now being referred to as God-breathed.[47] In any case, the text gives us rather direct clues about the utility of Scripture for the author: to make wise for salvation—for teaching, reproof, correction, and training.[48] It may not be too much of a stretch to suggest that as an authoritative Pauline canonical world began to come into view, it was precisely the types of assertions in 2 Timothy about the usefulness and the divine authority of the texts that started to have an effect on how the Pauline texts and the "good deposit" were thought to function—at least among those inclined to include the Pastorals in the Pauline canon.[49] To develop this last claim would take us beyond the scope of the immediate discussion, but the great—and much later—theological debates over this text from 2 Timothy and the inspiration of Scripture would seem to indicate that they were conflicts over claims about the sacred texts, how these claims were to be understood as pertaining to the whole of the Bible and its theological world (not just Paul), and how Scripture was thought to function. In other words, they were conflicts over how the Bible was thought to operate as canon. One may think that on this level these debates were simply a larger version of what had already happened in a more limited and special way within the Pauline writings collection over what it meant to preserve the "good deposit" of the apostle's sound teaching.

In light of 1 Timothy with its concern for not only passing on and preserving Paul's legacy through instruction but also through the people who occupy church positions, we seem to be witnessing the laying of a structural foundation between Scripture and community (church) that would erupt

---

[47] Ibid., 166–67. Wolfe argues that the language of 2 Tim 3:15–17 points to a broader authoritative tradition than simply the Old Testament, "Scripture in the Pastoral Epistles,"13–15. We cannot know for sure whether or not the Pauline community letters were thought of as Scripture by the time 2 Tim was written (cf. 2 Pet 3:15–16), but it is tantalizing to consider this possibility. In any case, they were considered to have authority, and the writer (s) of the Pastorals intended to frame an understanding of Paul's teaching and legacy. In that sense, we can be sure the writer(s) thought of themselves as framing and extending an authoritative Pauline tradition, but we doubt they thought of themselves as writing Scripture in any strict definition of the term. This may have some similarity to the way certain Jewish and perhaps even NT writers saw themselves as extending Hebrew biblical tradition in light of new circumstances and revelation. In light of the two-source hypothesis, it may also have some similarity to the way Matt and Luke reframed, reinterpreted, and extended the Jesus tradition of Mark.

[48] Cf. 1 Tim 4:13. See also Johnson, *First and Second Letters to Timothy*, 422–25.

[49] For a brief discussion of the attestation to the Pastoral Epistles in the early church and by implication the complexity of the formation of the Pauline canon, see Knight, *The Pastoral Epistles*, 13–14. Cf. also 2 Pet 3:15–16.

full-blown into conflict in the early church and again centuries later in the great Reformation debates over the relative authority of the Scriptures and the tradition of the church. It would be simplistic to think that a Pauline canon could function without an interpretive community, in this case the church or churches. Communities revered these texts and were also guided by these sacred texts and traditions that were thought to be authoritative, profitable for teaching, for reproof, for correction, and for training. In various ways, church communities early on were drawn into the canonical world produced by Paul and the literary texts that bore his name. However, the question soon became for the church, how are Paul's letters to be understood and who has the authority to decide? But before we can pursue this issue, we must juxtapose the images of Paul and his authority in other New Testament texts alongside the images, theologies, and patterns that emerge in the lines of development represented by the Pastoral Epistles.

## PAUL AND IMAGES OF PAUL IN ACTS

Having identified the shape of Pauline authority in the Pastorals and having argued that we can discern already in these three letters the earliest traces of a concept of the Pauline Scriptures, perhaps even a Pauline canon, we now turn our attention to other New Testament images of Paul, his authority, and his theology. Once again, the goal is to bring these other New Testament images into juxtaposition with those from the Pastoral Epistles in order to situate more precisely the various lines of Pauline development. Apart from the indisputably authentic Pauline letters, the Acts of the Apostles presents more information about Paul than any other New Testament book, albeit this information is thoroughly shaped to fit the author's historical and theological agenda. There is no need in this discussion to focus extensively on the personal and theological differences between the historical Paul and the Lukan Paul, because the main point of interest in this discussion is the view of Paul presented by the author of Acts. Moreover, unlike the Pastorals, Acts makes no claim to being written by Paul, even though it does purport to tell the story of Paul and his missionary activity. The peculiar blend of historical information and theological shaping, long debated in scholarship on Acts, need not detain us here, except when it pertains to the way the various images of Paul are developing in the New Testament period and beyond.

### *Images of Paul: An Overview*

According to Acts, an apostle is one who was a disciple of Jesus, a witness to the resurrection, and is now sent forth to spread the name of Christ.[50] In the theological geography of Acts, the message of Christ goes

---

[50] Collins, "Image of Paul," 156.

forth from Jerusalem, to Judea, on to Samaria, and ultimately to the "ends of the earth" (1:1–26). Hence, Luke does not organize his narrative according to historical chronology but according to theological meaning.[51] Of the 28 references to ἀπόστολος (apostle) in Acts, only 14:4 and 14, accounts of Paul's work in Iconium and Lystra, is Paul referred to as an apostle. Paul, of course, was not an original disciple of Jesus, but according to Acts he saw a vision of the risen Christ at his conversion and was sent forth in Jesus' name. Despite 14:4 and 14, references which seem to be exceptions to the Lukan pattern, Paul in Acts is not strictly speaking an apostle,[52] even though from chapter 13 on he is the main figure in the narrative and the one around whom the expansion of Christianity turns.[53] According to Luke, the missionary exploits and successes of Paul are the striking features of this early period in the church.[54] As Blasi says, the travels of Paul are of primary interest to the author of Acts, whereas his letters have no particular intrinsic value to him.[55] Throughout the narrative of Acts, the picture is consistent, Paul is a preacher and not a letter writer.[56] It is even debatable if Luke knew the letters of Paul. If he did, why did he not display evidence of them?[57] Even as a preacher, it is not necessarily the distinctiveness of Paul's preaching that marks his presence in any particular location, but rather the success of his mission.[58] The gospel content of his preaching is virtually the same wherever he goes and is only slightly tailored to fit the circumstances of the Lukan narrative.

With the apparent exception of 20:29–30, where Paul addresses the Ephesian elders in Miletus, the Lukan Paul does not seem to be concerned about backsliding and heresy.[59] Paul calls his hearers to faith in Christ, but does not exhort them to proper conduct, as we see in the case of the Pastorals. Yet it is fair to say that Luke's Paul is a pillar of correct belief, as his concern that his missionary activities have the endorsement of the

---

[51] Daniel R. Schwartz, "The end of the Line: Paul in the Canonical Book of Acts," in *Paul and the Legacies of Paul* (ed. William S. Babcock; Dallas: Southern Methodist University Press, 1990), 4–5.

[52] Beker, *Heirs of Paul*, 51.

[53] See Stanley E. Porter, *Paul in Acts* (Library of Pauline Studies; Peabody, Mass.: Hendrickson Publishers, 2001), 196–97. Though concerned primarily with the connection between Paul in Acts and in the letters, Porter concludes that there is a high degree of similarity between the term "apostle" as used in Acts and the letters. The two usages allow for differences of meaning but not contradictions.

[54] Martinus C. DeBoer, "Images of Paul," 365.

[55] Blasi, *Making Charisma*, 77; and Porter, *Paul in Acts*, 100–101, 194–95.

[56] Beker, *Heirs of Paul*, 50.

[57] C. K. Barrett, "Acts and the Pauline Corpus," *Expository Times* 88 (1976–1977): 2–5. Cf. also Blasi, *Making Charisma*, 77, who claims that the letters themselves were not yet necessary to guarantee faithfulness to the Pauline tradition.

[58] Ibid., 86; cf. Beker, *Heirs of Paul*, 51.

[59] Blasi, *Making Charisma*, 80.

apostles in Jerusalem would suggest.[60] In general terms, Luke also illustrates the transformation of Christianity from a Palestinian, Jewish, Torah-observant movement into a Diaspora, Gentile, non-observant religion that is rapidly becoming a universal community.[61] The Jews themselves in Acts drive Paul to the Gentiles,[62] and in the scope of salvation-history Paul more obviously expects the resurrection of the dead than he does the restoration of Israel.[63] This does not mean that the Paul of Acts rejects the Jewish context of the gospel and the church or that he sees no connection between the Jewish and Gentile expressions of Christianity.[64] As a Jew and missionary who preaches to the Gentiles, Paul functions as the connecting link between them.

John Lentz, in his portrait of the Lukan Paul, argues that the author wants to depict Paul as a Tarsian Roman (cf. 9:1; 21:39) who is at ease with the people of power and status in Greco-Roman society.[65] He himself is a man of some social standing and moral virtue,[66] and after his conversion he displays both courage and sobriety.[67] While Paul has a strict Jewish background and is righteous before the Jewish law, he is also a man of significant secular status and prestige.[68] The point Luke makes, according to Lentz, is that the church is a community open to all and that those of high status in particular who want to join the church need not give up their social standing to do so (see 17:12). To those people, the Lukan Paul serves as an example.[69] Galatians 3:28 indicates that the historical Paul relativizes social barriers, whereas the Lukan Paul demonstrates that Christians can follow the example of Paul, raise their social standing, and be good citizens of the

---

[60] Beker, *Heirs of Paul*, 52. See also Acts 15:1–29; 20:29–32.

[61] Schwartz, "End of the Line," 4. Cf. also Ernst Haenchen, *The Acts of the Apostles: A Commentary* (trans. by Bernard Noble and Gerald Shinn et al; Oxford: Basil Blackwell, 1971), 630–31.

[62] The pattern of Paul's preaching is that he enters a town, goes into the synagogue to preach, meets hostility from some Jewish hearers, and is forced to flee, sometimes under threat for his life.

[63] Schwartz, "End of the Line," 21.

[64] See, e.g., Paul's speeches in Acts 22:1–16; 26:1–23. On the issue of Jewish-Christian relations, Porter argues that there is much greater continuity between the Pauline letters and Acts than Haenchen claims. He writes: "To the contrary, the evidence above suggests that there is a surprisingly large amount of continuity and similarity between the two bodies of material. A fresh analysis of this evidence seems, rather, to indicate that there must have been some close lines of connection between the authors of the book of Acts and of the Pauline letters" (*Paul in Acts*, 197–99, 205–6).

[65] See Acts 13:12; 21:37–40; 22:22–30; 24:1–27; 25:1–26; 27:43.

[66] John Clayton Lentz, Jr. *Luke's Portrait of Paul* (SBLMS 77; Cambridge: Cambridge University Press, 1993), 2–3. Cf. also Beker, *Heirs of Paul*, 52.

[67] Lentz, *Luke's Portrait*, 15. See Acts 13:46; 14:1–18; 16:19–40; 17:16–34; 19:8–10; 22:30–23:10; 24:1–27; 25:13–26:32; 27:13–28:31.

[68] Ibid.,19, 23.

[69] Ibid., 19.

empire all at the same time.[70] In Acts, Paul is a man in control of his situation, and even though he suffers beatings and imprisonment, he is still an example of strength rather than weakness.[71] Overall, Luke tells the story of Paul as much for non-believers as for believers, and in that telling he universalizes his portrait of the church's mission. Under the direction of the Holy Spirit, according to Acts, the expansion of Christianity is unstoppable.[72]

As Steve Walton points out, however, scholarly opinion on Luke's view of the Roman empire is more complicated than Lentz's argument might suggest.[73] Walton summarizes the various positions as follows: (1) a political apology for the church to Rome, (2) an apology for Rome to the church, (3) an effort at legitimation whereby the Christians are assured that their faith is not incompatible with loyalty to Rome, (4) an attempt to equip the faithful to live in the empire and face trials before the authorities, and (5) Acts is not interested in politics at all.[74] Walton concludes that Luke writes in order to help his readers see what forms Christian discipleship in the empire might take, offering them a variety of points of view on how the empire might act and how they should respond, recognizing all the while that Christ reigns supreme, even over Caesar.[75] While Lentz's portrayal of Paul and empire relates most directly to positions one and three, Walton provides for us a word of caution about over simplifying Luke's openness to Rome and the Lukan Paul's embrace of the empire. Paul in Acts turns outward to address the empire, but he also turns inward to the faithful in the church.

In describing the making of Paul's charisma in Acts, Anthony Blasi summarizes succinctly Luke's portrayal of Paul. As a larger than life figure, Paul sees visions, makes converts, takes charge of his circumstances, gives speeches, offers advice, cures the sick, and fulfills prophecies. He observes Jewish religious requirements and conducts Christian worship. He is an exemplar of Judaism and a Christian founder.[76] Paul is also a person of worldly affairs, he addresses political leaders and debates with philosophers, and he practices a trade and advises sea captains.[77] In terms of charisma, Luke portrays Paul as a personage in his own lifetime.[78] He is nothing short of heroic. Yet as heroic as Paul may be in Acts, he is also one who is beaten,

---

[70] Ibid., 67.

[71] Beker, *Heirs of Paul*, 53–54. Beker, however, argues that Luke also develops a theology of suffering in the book of Acts. See 9:16 and 19:21–20:31 for what Beker calls Paul's *via dolorosa*.

[72] Lentz, *Luke's Portrait*, 171–72.

[73] Steve Walton, "The State They Were In: Luke's View of the Roman Empire," in *Rome in the Bible and the Early Church* (ed. Peter Oakes; Grand Rapids: Baker Academic, 2002), 1–41.

[74] Ibid., 2–12.

[75] Ibid., 33–35.

[76] Blasi, *Making Charisma*, 69.

[77] Ibid., 75.

[78] Ibid., 69.

imprisoned, and suffers great distress for the sake of his missionary work. On that level, Luke clearly does not romanticize Paul and his life.

## Paul the Convert

The first and primary account of Paul's so-called conversion in Acts 9:1–19 depicts Paul as Christ's chosen instrument (σκεῦος ἐκλογῆς) to carry his name before Gentiles and kings and the children of Israel. In this three-fold destination, Luke identifies in triangular fashion Paul's three most significant audiences: Gentiles, Jews, and those of status and power. Between Christ and those three audiences stands Paul, the chosen instrument. The mission of Paul is divinely commissioned and authenticated. Luke uses terminology that heightens the sense of divine involvement in bringing about this dramatic change in Saul's life.[79] Luke further illustrates this transformation in the way he portrays Saul as a staunch hater and persecutor of the "Way," and yet Christ calls him to be an evangelist at the very moment he is on a mission of persecution. In Luke's narrative, this is a divine event with profound consequences for Paul and the disciples, for the Jews and the Gentiles, and for the church and the empire.

Played out against the backdrop of a controversy over the mission to the uncircumcised in the early church, the Lukan narrative establishes the idea that Paul and his mission are in accord with divine intention. Paul, filled with the Holy Spirit (9:17), goes forth as Christ's chosen instrument, and by this point in the narrative the reader glimpses the impending mission to the Gentiles, authorized and empowered by God.[80] Paul the convert and missionary personifies the connecting link between apostolic time and Luke's time;[81] and, as such, he is a linchpin in the worldwide mission of Christianity. Luke incorporates Paul, the Pharisaic convert, into his own theological vision and into his own overarching view of salvation-history. Distilled from some tradition or record of the historical Paul, Luke reconfigures his image into that of a man of theological and historical proportions who, struck

---

[79] Luke uses ἐξαίφης (suddenly, unexpectedly) twice in Acts (9:3; 22:6). In Luke's Gospel he uses this word to refer to the appearance of the "multitude of the heavenly host" in the nativity account of Jesus' birth (2:13) and to describe how a spirit seizes an epileptic child (9:39). The implication of this word in Luke's account of Paul's conversion is to convey extreme suddenness. It is more than immediate, it is unexpected and striking in its interruption. Περιαστράπτω (shone around), another word Luke uses in both 9:3 and 22:6, dramatizes the extraordinary effect of God's presence on Paul (Saul) in the Damascus Road experience. Coupled with φῶς (light), the term conveys the sense of surrounding him with divine power. From heaven this power has come. Likewise, ὅραμα (vision) connotes this heavenly experience, and in the 11 times Luke uses it the term, it conveys divine communication.

[80] See Hans Conzelmann, *A Commentary on the Acts of the Apostles* (Hermeneia; trans. by James Limburg, A. Thomas Kraabel, and Donald H. Juel; Philadelphia: Fortress, 1987), 84.

[81] Ibid., 73.

down by a vision of Christ on the Damascus Road, epitomizes the inexorable expansion of the church.

Luke also incorporates the account in 9:1–19 into its larger literary context in a manner meant to bolster the Gentile mission. In 8:4–40, the author describes the missionary activity in Samaria, and instead of proceeding directly to the conversion of Saul recounts the proclamation of the gospel to the Ethiopian eunuch by Philip. Even before Saul's encounter on the Damascus Road, the gospel went to this Gentile. With the skill of a master redactor and author, Luke lays the groundwork for the mission to the uncircumcised prior to Saul's conversion. In chapter 10, Luke also records the account of Cornelius' conversion and baptism. Before Paul goes to the Gentiles, Peter is ordered by God to do so. Commanded by the voice from heaven in a vision not to declare unclean what God made clean, Peter, the disciple of Jesus and the apostle of Christ to the Jews, eats food that is not permitted under Jewish law, goes to Cornelius' household, relates the gospel to them, and when they have received the Holy Spirit commands them to be baptized (10:15–48).[82] In this narrative sequence, Paul appears to be less the innovator than the one who goes to the Gentiles according to the precedent established by Peter, who likewise acted only with the prodding of the Holy Spirit. Peter, the preeminent of Jesus' disciples, instructed by the Holy Spirit opens the gate of the Gentile mission, a gate through which Paul walks with astonishing results.[83]

In this subtle narrative construction, Luke sets Paul up as the model for conversion, especially Gentile conversion.[84] He confesses that Jesus is the son of God and confounds the Jews by showing that he is also the Christ. Christians, whether Jews or Gentiles, are the ones who make this confession and in that way follow Paul's example. Though told he will be shown how much he will suffer for the name of Christ (9:16), Paul is not in the first instance a model for Christian suffering. Christians may suffer but that does not seem to be Paul's primary witness. The Lukan Paul does not call converts to suffer as he has suffered. He calls them to a new confession and a new status, a status that warrants respect and honor in the Roman imperial world, even though it may not always be accorded to them. As in the case of Paul, the convert can be at home and feel at ease in the cosmopolitan world of the Roman empire and at the same time remain faithful in the face of imperial threat.

In 22:14–15, Luke reports in the words of Ananias a somewhat altered form of the purpose for Saul's election: "The God of our fathers chose you

---

[82] Later in Jerusalem, Peter is criticized for his actions, especially eating with Gentiles, and is forced to defend himself (11:1–18).

[83] See Haenchen, *Acts of the Apostles*, 327; and Richard Pervo, *Luke's Story of Paul* (Minneapolis: Fortress, 1990), 39–40.

[84] Alan F. Segal, *Paul the Convert: The Apostolate and Apostasy of Saul the Pharisee* (New Haven: Yale University Press, 1990), 14. Cf. 1 Tim 1:12–17.

to know his will and to see the righteous one and to hear his voice for you will be a witness of him to all people of what you saw and heard." In a speech tailored to establish his Jewish credentials, the Lukan Paul, speaking in Hebrew, recounts his record as a good Jew, educated in the law, zealous for God, and a persecutor of the "Way" (22:3–5). This introduces Luke's second account of Saul's encounter on the Damascus Road (22:6–11), which is followed by Ananias' words to the blind Saul (22:12–15). There is no distinction here between Israel and the nations and kings. Paul will be a witness to all people. The moderating of the threefold distinction may simply be the result of the audience and the circumstance under which he is speaking to them. In this situation Paul must present himself as a good Jew and account for his association with Gentiles.[85] In both 19:1–19 and 22:3–16, however, the healing of Saul's blindness sets up his commissioning to go to the Jews, Gentiles, and kings, or simply to all people.[86]

In the speech before King Agrippa in 26:16–18, the purpose of Paul's election is stated directly by Christ on the Damascus Road: "For this reason I have appeared to you to appoint you a servant and witness of the things I have shown to you and of the things in which I will appear to you. I will rescue you from the people and the Gentiles to whom I am sending you." With no reference to Saul being struck blind, Luke makes this account strictly a commissioning story where the Gentiles reappear as the object of Paul's impending testimony.[87] In Paul's reply to Agrippa in 26:19–23, Luke makes the mission of Paul a matter of obedience to God that began first with the Jews but was also destined to go forth to the Gentiles.[88] Like Paul, who under divine command stepped out into world history and imperial culture,[89] the church is destined to make its home in the empire as well. And like Paul, who had help from God (26:22), so too God helps the church. Paul is the obedient servant of God and witness to Christ, and as such is a model for the church in Luke's own day.

According to Conzelmann, Luke does not perceive his task to be a matter of getting Christians ready for martyrdom but of preparing them for life in the empire.[90] From the portrait of Paul in his own letters to the portrait of Paul in Acts, the image of the church in the world and Paul's role in it has shifted. No longer preoccupied with pastoral and theological matters internal to the respective churches, the Lukan Paul now also operates on a larger stage of secular history and imperial affairs. As God's chosen instrument and missionary carrying the name of Christ to the ends of the earth, he

---

[85] Conzelmann, *Acts of Apostles*, 186.

[86] See the comparison of the three conversion accounts by Charles W. Hedrick, "Paul's Conversion/Call: A Comparative Analysis of the Three Reports in Acts," *JBL* 100 (1981): 417–19.

[87] Ibid., 417.

[88] Conzelmann, *Acts of the Apostles*, 211.

[89] Ibid., 692.

[90] Ibid., 693.

points the way to what the church is to become and becomes himself a lens through which Christians are to view and situate themselves in society and history. Not only is the Lukan Paul the model convert, but he is the key to understanding the church in salvation-history and secular history as well as in relation to both Jews and Gentiles. Just as with Paul, the Holy Spirit guides the church as it comes to operate on the stage of human affairs.

### Paul the Preacher

In 13:16–41 the Lukan Paul launches into the first of his great sermons. Having arrived in Psidian Antioch (13:13–15), Paul and his companions enter the synagogue where the local leaders invite the brothers to bring a word of exhortation. The opening of this address is marked by a recitation of the history of salvation from the election of Israel and the Egyptian sojourn to king David (13:17–22). From the posterity of David, God delivered to Israel the savior Jesus, before whose coming John had already proclaimed a baptism of repentance to all the people of Israel. The Davidic connection is taken up once again in 13:34 with a reference to the promises made to David according to Isa 55:3 and again in 13:36–37 in connection with the corruption of David's body (unlike the incorruption of the resurrected Christ's body). In a very un-Pauline fashion,[91] Luke's Paul announces that it is through Jesus that forgiveness of sins is proclaimed to the people. The salvation that Jesus brings to the people is forgiveness and the opportunity to be freed from the sins that the law of Moses could not provide. Turning specifically to the fate of Christ in Jerusalem, Paul announces that since the people of Jerusalem and their leaders did not understand their own prophets, read every Sabbath, they fulfilled their prophecies by condemning him to death (13:27). For no reason, they asked Pilate to kill him and thus fulfilled the prophet's words. What God promised, God has now fulfilled in Jesus' death and resurrection, announces Paul to the assembled audience.

Unlike Paul's method of argumentation in the epistles, Luke's Paul surveys a number of the acts of God in Israel's history and relates these and the witness of the prophets to Christ's appearance, death, and resurrection. While the historical Paul may operate with an implicit promise/fulfillment theological understanding, the Lukan Paul makes this explicit.[92] Moreover, Jesus as savior brings God's forgiveness of sins to all the people, an image of redemption virtually absent from the historical Paul's theological vocabulary.[93] And unlike the historical Paul who by his own admission is not a

---

[91] Ibid., 106. Cf. Rom 4:7–8, a quote from Ps 31, which is the only place in the undisputed Paulines where forgivness of sins is the image for atonement leading to righteousness and salvation.

[92] See my book, *Written Also for Our Sake: Paul and the Art of Biblical Interpretation* (Louisville: Westminster John Knox, 1993), 73–87.

[93] See Krister Stendahl, "Paul Among Jews and Gentiles" in *Paul among Jews and Gentiles, and Other Essays* (Philadelphia: Fortress, 1976), 23–24.

person of great oratorical skill (1 Cor 2:1–5), the Lukan Paul commands his situation in Antioch and appears to be an orator of some consequence, so much so that he and Barnabas are invited back the following Sabbath. When they return, the predictable ruckus ensues (13:44–52); and speaking with boldness Paul and Barnabas announce to the crowd that God's word needed to go first to the Jews, but since they have rejected it, they will now turn to the Gentiles. Predictably in Acts, the Gentiles rejoice at this news and the Jews arouse opposition to Paul, Barnabas, and their message.

In 17:16–34, Paul is in Athens debating with the Jews in the synagogue and with the pious people and philosophers (Epicureans and Stoics) who come to the agora. Assuming he is a proclaimer of alien powers, the listeners bring Paul to the Areopagus where they inquire as to the meaning of his strange new teaching. Unlike the Greeks who worship unknown gods, Paul claims to proclaim the God who made the world and everything in it, is the Lord of heaven and earth, does not live in shrines made with human hands, has no need to be served by humans, and gives life to all living things. But now this God demands repentance, because the day of judgment brought about through Christ has been set in motion. Through the resurrection of this one man, God gives all people assurance in the face of this impending judgment. Conforming his words to the situation in Athens, the heart of the Greek intellectual and religious world, Luke's Paul faces down his interlocutors. One man, with his witness to the God of all creation, courageously engages the representatives of the Greek world, and at least some people are open to hearing more about this new message. In this episode, Luke implicitly portrays the encounter of the church with the Hellenistic world of his own day and models through the example of Paul the way for the church to engage that world. In Psidian Antioch, Paul confronted Jewish opposition incensed by his condemnation of their failure to heed the words of the prophets, whereas in Athens he encounters Greeks who are incredulous when they hear the account of Jesus' resurrection. Clearly Paul, according to Luke, is a man on the cusp of Christianity's encounter with both the Jewish and the Greek worlds.

## Paul's Farewell Discourse

On his final trip to Jerusalem, Paul summons the elders from the church in Ephesus to meet with him in Miletus (20:17).[94] Reciting to them his autobiography as a missionary for Christ and his expectation that imprisonment awaits him in Jerusalem, Paul longs only to follow the course of his ministry to its natural end. It is apparent that this is Paul's farewell discourse to the elders of the church, and in it we find clues to Luke's perception of

---

[94] This is the only speech directed to church leaders in Acts. Cf. 1 Tim 3:1–13; Titus 1:7–9.

Paul's legacy.[95] Paul exhorts the elders in 20:20–28 to watch not only over themselves but also the flock over which the Holy Spirit has made them overseers (ἐπισκόπος) and shepherds. There is no distinction here between a πρεσβύτερος and ἐπίσκοπος, for the elders identified in 20:17 are the overseers addressed in 20:28. For Luke, the referent of the two terms is apparently not yet distinguishable. Furthermore, consistent with Luke's pneumatology, it is the spirit that charged these elders with their responsibility for the church. Yet it is also clear in this account that Paul is passing the mantel of ecclesiastical authority to the post-Pauline generation in the church and exhorting them to be alert in his absence, for the flock will be threatened by "wolves" from without and distorters of the truth from within. Paul, the arbiter of normative teaching, passes this authority to the post-Pauline leaders of the church, and in this account Luke links this teaching authority with the concept of an office.[96] He elaborates neither the nature of this normative teaching—apart from remembering the words of Jesus (20:35)—nor the character of the office that these leaders occupy. The author is content to leave them both undefined. What Luke does reinforce is the idea that Paul has shown all things to them and now leaves that example as his bequest (κληρονομίαν, 20:32, 35) to them. There is no hint that Paul's example involves anything written, such as a body of letters or instructions, or anything else for that matter. His example is his own life, he coveted nothing and worked with his own hands.

## *Paul in the Pastorals and Acts: A Comparative Summary*

The obvious difference between the three Pastoral Epistles and Acts is the literary difference. The Pastorals are letters apparently written to churches in Ephesus and Crete in the name of Paul, and Acts is a story, much of which is about Paul and his missionary work. However, this difference in literary genre need not prevent us from comparing the Pastoral Pauline theological patterns identified in chapters 2 and 3 of the present volume with Luke's story of Paul. By doing so, we can compensate for the genre differential among the various texts and situate the materials in their respective places in the developing Pauline tradition.

If 1 Timothy, and also to a lesser extent Titus, direct attention largely to life within the household of God,[97] Luke expands the horizon to address the church and its place in the Greco-Roman imperial world. The Pastoral Paul exhorts his readers to live appropriately in the household of God—to a life of godliness, whereas Luke uses Paul to exemplify how the church is to engage the world and to find a home in it. If the Paul of 1 Timothy and Titus looks primarily inward, the Lukan Paul clearly looks outward. This does not

---

[95] Haenchen, *Acts of the Apostles*, 596.
[96] Conzelmann, *Acts of the Apostles*, 175.
[97] See above, pp. 23–25.

mean that there is no concern for the outside world in these two Pastoral letters, [98] or that there is no concern for domestic matters in Acts, as Paul's speech to the Ephesian elders in Miletus indicates. However, the theological horizon and orientation is clearly different. From this structural difference flows another contrast. Paul in 1 Timothy and Titus, and to large extent 2 Timothy as well, is one who exhorts his readers to correct belief and proper conduct. He is concerned about heresy, and he is concerned about internal behavior that threatens the household of God. With the exception of 20:29–30, Luke's Paul is not preoccupied with heresy or backsliding from the faith.[99] He does not portray correct doctrine as a παραθήκην, and he does not strictly charge his hearers to "guard the good deposit." Rather, he confronts people, religious forces, ideas, powers and principalities on the larger plane of history and culture. Hence, he debates with religious opponents and philosophers, encounters rulers and secular authorities, and moves extensively through the empire as an instrument of God carrying the name of Christ first to the Jews and then to the Gentiles. The Lukan Paul is a public speaker, not a letter writer; he is a man of missionary achievements, not one who exhorts others to follow his example of suffering (as in 2 Timothy); he is a figure of significant proportions, not narrowly speaking an apostle.

In Acts, Paul's opposition is transparent. It varies, with the Jews being the most consistent opponents of Paul and his preaching, but also includes secular authorities, mobs, and other followers of Christ. The Lukan Paul suffers beatings and imprisonment, but unlike the Paul of 2 Timothy he does not appeal to his followers to join him on the path of suffering. In all cases, however, Paul's religious opposition in Acts turns on general issues—dislike or jealously of what Paul preaches, his interpretation of prophetic fulfillment, teaching against the law, the reality of the resurrection, fear of him because of his former life as a persecutor of the church, disagreement over the Gentile mission, and the threat his message poses to the Ephesian idolmakers. In the Pastorals, the opposition involves teachers of the law who do not understand what they teach, Jewish opposition in the churches, a problem with those who claim the resurrection has already come, and what appears to be an ascetic problem with some people over the issue of eating certain foods and abstinence from marriage.

In Acts, there is no discussion of the appropriate qualities for those who hold positions of leadership in the church, as there is in 1 Timothy and Titus. The closest we get to any recognition of offices in the church, apart from possibly that of an apostle, is the reference to the elders and overseers in Paul's valedictory address in Miletus and the choice, at the behest of the

---

[99] E.g., ἀλήθεια (truth) appears only in Acts 4:27; 10:34; 26:25, and ἀληθής (true) only in 12:9. In none of these references are the terms used to refer to correct doctrine.

apostles, of the seven servers in 6:1–7. In the Miletus speech, however, there is no apparent distinction between elders and overseers. The same people are described using both terms. And the duties of the servers in Acts 6 are not much different from the duties one might expect of the elders and overseers as described in Acts 20. While the apostolate is prominent in Acts, especially in the opening chapters of the narrative, Paul is not strictly speaking included in that number, as important and heroic as he is in Luke's account. In the world of the Pastorals, Paul is *the* apostle. He, himself, fully embodies the apostolate and its authority.

Known as a speaker and not a letter writer, the Lukan Paul gives no evidence of leaving anything for future generations, except his personal example, his words of encouragement, and the communities he began. There is no hint of anything that could be identified as Pauline Scripture. For the Lukan Paul, however, there is an important concern for Scripture. For example, in Acts 17:1–3 Paul, in Thessalonica for three Sabbaths, argued with the Jews and explained to them from Scripture that it was necessary for the Christ to suffer and rise from the dead. Likewise, in 26:23 Paul announces to King Agrippa that he witnessed to the testimony of the prophets and Moses that the Christ must suffer. For Luke's Paul, the Scriptures are the Jewish Scriptures, they testify to Christ's death and resurrection, and he uses them to demonstrate this Christian claim. Although the historical Paul undoubtedly thought the Jewish Scriptures foretold Jesus' life and death, he does not use scriptural quotations to demonstrate this in his epistles.[100] Thus, for the Lukan Paul, the Scriptures are important as a testimony to Christ, and the words of the prophets set up his claim that by rejecting Christ the Jews have fulfilled the words of Scripture, words they hear read to them repeatedly. For the Lukan Paul, the Scriptures are important in making the case for Christianity to unbelievers. On the face of it, they do not appear to serve for reproof, correction, or training. Perhaps because of the Lukan Paul's looking outward to the world and his encounter with potential converts in that larger world, there is little substantive indication of any tension between the relative authority of Scripture on the one hand and the authority of the church's kerygmatic tradition on the other. Through the eyes of the Lukan Paul, the two are in substantial agreement, and the one corroborates the other. And clearly the Holy Spirit in Acts plays a critical role in guaranteeing the faithfulness and expansion of the church.

Acts represents a different expression of the Pauline legacy from that found in the Pastoral Epistles. It is driven by different concerns, different images, and a different orientation to the church and the world. Moreover, its mode of literary expression is fundamentally different. In the Pastorals, we encounter the domestic Paul, concerned about correct doctrine, the well-being and unity of the household of God, and the character of those chosen

---

[100] Aageson, *Written Also for Our Sake*, 38–39.

to lead the church. In Acts, we engage a more cosmopolitan Paul, the man on the sharp edge of the church's encounter with the Greco-Roman world, and the one who holds a strategic place in the history of the church's expansion into the Roman empire. The Lukan Paul is a man of affairs with whom both Jews and Gentiles must reckon.

A line of scholarship, represented perhaps most poignantly by Stephen Wilson, has sought to claim a direct connection between Luke and the Pastoral Epistles.[101] Wilson argues that Luke wrote the Pastorals after he finished Acts, and though he did not know of Paul's letters when he wrote Acts he likely had read some of his epistles and learned something about his travels before he produced the Pastorals. Moreover, when Luke wrote Acts he sought to defend Paul and his churches against attacks from Jews and Jewish Christ believers, whereas by the time he wrote the Pastorals the threat to the church was largely from the gnostics.[102] Beyond seemingly over drawing the similarities and downplaying the differences between the Pastoral letters and Acts, Wilson has had to claim, in order to make his argument, that similarities in language, style, and theology are sufficient to establish common authorship. While a common scholarly procedure when his book was written, this approach seems increasingly problematic without some corroborating evidence. Likewise, the claim that the author of the Pastorals is contending with gnostics represents an earlier view of the opponents in these three letters, a view not unequivocally supported by the textual evidence or much recent scholarship.[103] For these reasons, the claim of Lukan authorship of the Pastorals is unlikely and cannot be corroborated.

## PAUL AND HIS THEOLOGY IN THE DEUTERO-PAULINE EPISTLES

We now turn to the other New Testament representations of Paul, those found in the so-called Deutero-Pauline letters of Ephesians, Colossians, and 2 Thessalonians to see how they fit into this emerging legacy. As before, the goal here is to focus on the images of Paul and his theology found in the literary patterns of the respective epistles. Although debates about the relationship between the authentic Pauline letters and the Deutero-Paulines are interesting, they are not the focus of this discussion. Similarly, Ephesians may be dependent on Colossians,[104] but once again that is not the primary focus of this analysis. The operating assumption is that Colossians,

---

[101] Stephen G. Wilson, *Luke and the Pastoral Epistles* (London: SPCK, 1979), 1–4.

[102] Ibid., 3–4.

[103] See above, pp. 64–66.

[104] Joachim Gnilka, "Das Paulusbild im Kolosser-und Epheserbrief," in *Kontinuität und Einheit: Für Franz Mussner* (ed. Paul-Gerhard Müller and Werner Stenger; Freiburg: Herder, 1981), 180–81 and Andrew T. Lincoln, *Ephesians* (Word Bible Commentary; 42; Dallas: Word Books, 1990), lxvii–lxxiii.

Ephesians, and 2 Thessalonians were written, in all likelihood, by someone other than Paul. However, this discussion is not dependent finally on the question of authorship, because the point is to examine the images of Paul and the theology attributed to him in order to determine how the Pauline tradition was developing. No matter whether Paul wrote these letters or someone wrote in his name, the images and the theologies represented by them have their own reality as part of the emerging Pauline matrix of ideas. To be sure, if Paul actually wrote these letters we might presume that the images and theologies represented by them are closer to the undisputed letters than to the Pastorals and the other post-Pauline texts that bear his name (e.g., *Acts of Paul*). That, however, does not change the fact that these three letters, whoever may have written them, exhibit a number of ideas and images that are not strictly speaking identical to the ideas and images in the undisputed Pauline letters.

## Paul, Servant and Apostle in Colossians and Ephesians

Colossians and Ephesians open with a greeting typical of other Pauline greetings, such as that found in 2 Corinthians: Παῦλος ἀπόστολος Χριστοῦ Ἰησοῦ διὰ θελήματος θεοῦ (Paul, apostle of Christ Jesus by the will of God). In Colossians, this greeting is supplemented with the words καὶ Τιμόθεος ὁ ἀδελφὸς (and Timothy [our] brother), which suggests a joint greeting from Paul and Timothy, even though at the end of the letter Paul is said to write the epistle with his own hand. Ephesians, in contrast, portrays the greeting as coming from Paul alone.[105] Consistent with the rest of the New Testament Pauline tradition, Colossians and Ephesians reaffirm the apostleship of Paul according to divine intention. In Eph 3:2, the stewardship (οἰκονομίαν) of God's grace, referring to the revelation of the divine mystery to Paul for the sake of the Ephesians (see 1:9), reaffirms the place of Paul in the scope of divine intention and his place in the Ephesian community. As if to confirm his role on behalf of the Gentile Ephesians, Paul is a prisoner for the sake of Christ Jesus and for the community in Ephesus. Revelation, divine grace, imprisonment, and a special role on behalf of the Ephesians all come together to establish an image of Paul as the recipient of divine favor and wisdom, as an imprisoned apostle, and as the conduit of divine grace for the community at Ephesus. The text of Ephesians adds yet another image, ". . . a servant (διάκονος) according to the gift of God which was given to me by the workings of his power (3:7)." Servanthood, too, is a result of God's grace given to Paul, servanthood both for the church more broadly and for the Ephesian community specifically.

Servanthood and the stewardship of God (οἰκονομίαν τοῦ θεοῦ) are also linked in Col 1:25 (see also 1:23). Moreover, in this text the gift given is

---

[105] Ibid.,181. See 2 Cor 1:1; 1 Tim 1:1; and 2 Tim 1:1.

connected with the word of God, which is identified as the mystery.[106] And as in Ephesians, this is for the sake of the community to which the author is writing. The imagery is strikingly similar in the two texts, which would appear to support the argument for common authorship or some type of dependence. Yet the point is that Paul's ministry depends on the activity of God in revealing to him the mystery of the gospel and in setting him apart for work among the Gentiles. In both Ephesians and Colossians, Paul is apostle of the mystery of God for Gentiles.[107] He is the recipient of revelation, a revelation now made known also to the saints (Col 1:26) and to the holy apostles and prophets in the spirit (Eph 2:20; 3:5). We might distinguish Colossians from Ephesians by noting that Paul appears to be the sole apostolic link between God's revelation and the saints in Colossae, whereas Ephesians sets Paul alongside a group of apostles and prophets as the foundation of the church.[108] Perhaps this distinction turns on the fact that Colossians presents an image of the church more closely related to the local community, whereas Ephesians projects an image of the universal church.[109] In the broader sense of the church, Paul's uniqueness as an apostle is placed in a wider context, unlike the narrower implication of Paul's more direct apostolic link with the Colossians. Though Eph 3:8 may echo 1 Cor 15:9 in claiming that Paul is the least of all the saints, this does not diminish ultimately the significance of his status as an apostle for the wider church.

## *The Cosmic Christ and the Church in Colossians and Ephesians*

Adding further precision Beker writes: "Whereas the author of Colossians defines the content of the mystery as Christ (1:26–27; 2:2; see 4:3: 'the mystery of Christ'), the author of Ephesians emphasizes its ecclesiological aspect, since here the focus of the mystery (3:3–4; 6:15) is on the power of the gospel to unite Jew and Gentile in the one body of Christ (2:14–22; 3:6; 4:15–16)."[110] Without a doubt, the christological and wisdom focus in Colossians has come to have an ecclesiological emphasis in Ephesians, and this is perhaps most dramatically illustrated by juxtaposing the hymn in Col 1:15–20 with the discussions of the church in Eph 1:22–23; 2:11–22; and 4:1–16.

In Col 1:15–20, the writer elaborates christological imagery that touches on creation, cosmology, reconciliation, soteriology, and ecclesiology.[111] But in each case Christ is central to the imagery. Christ is the image of the in-

---

[106] See Col 1:26–27; 2:2–3; 4:3; Eph 1:9; 3:2–6, 9.

[107] See the discussion of Colossians in this regard by Beker, *Heirs of Paul*, 67–68.

[108] Gnilka, *Paulusbild*, 184.

[109] Ibid., 184.

[110] Beker, *Paul's Legacy*, 70.

[111] Eduard Lohse, *A Commentary on the Epistles to the Colossians and to Philemon* (trans. by William R. Poehlmann and Robert J. Karris; Hermeneia; Philadelphia: Fortress, 1971), 42.

visible God, the firstborn of all creation. In Christ, all things were created in the heavens and upon the earth. Through Christ, God reconciles all things, and makes peace through the blood of the cross. And finally, Christ is asserted to be the head of the body, the church. By appropriating wisdom imagery in the service of Christology, the author has universalized Christ and what he represents for the world, the church, and redemption.[112] As the one who stands as firstborn of all creation and as head of the church, Christ unites creation and church under his rule. Christ the preexistent one is also the uniquely supreme one (1:18). Standing at the beginning of the epistle to the Colossians, this so-called Christ hymn establishes the christological tenor of the text that follows. As apostle of Christ to the church in Colossae and recipient of the divine mystery, Paul's status is inexorably bound up with the creation and the church in a fundamentally important, if not unique, way. To use Beker's terminology, Paul in Colossians is the theologian of cosmic wisdom, the universal ecumenical theologian of wisdom.[113] But Paul in Colossians is not simply a theologian who speaks about wisdom. He is part of the christological drama playing itself out in the creation and in the church. In this, the text of Colossians appears to move beyond the portrayal of Paul in the undisputed letters.

Christ is said in Ephesians to be head over all things "to" or "for" the church, which is his body (1:22–23).[114] On the face of it, this seems to move ever so slightly beyond the implication of Col 1:18, where Christ is identified as the head of the body, the church, and of creation. In Ephesians, the clear implication is that Christ is made head over all things "to" or "for" the church. All things are put under his feet, and since he is head of the church, we might say all things are put under the church. Not only is this a universalization of Christology, but also a subordination of all things, probably read as all creation, to the church. On a conceptual level, Ephesians has greatly expanded the notion of the church supreme, as compared to the undisputed Pauline letters, and moved it incrementally beyond even that of Colossians.

The shift toward ecclesiology takes yet another step in Eph 2:11–22. While it is much debated whether or not Paul in the authentic letters actually sees the church as a "third entity," no longer Jew or Greek, but one in Christ, there is little doubt that Ephesians makes this conceptual move (cf. Col 3:10–11). The law has been abolished and the two peoples have now been made into one new humanity (2:15), in order that both groups might be reconciled to God. Speaking to the Gentiles, the writer indicates that they are no longer outsiders or strangers but citizens with the saints and the household of God (οἰκεῖοι τοῦ θεοῦ). Though we cannot be certain that Paul was speaking to a mixed Jew and Gentile audience in the epistles to the

---

[112] Ibid., 50.

[113] Beker, *Paul's Legacy*, 65–67.

[114] The preposition "to" or "for" depends on how we translate τῇ ἐκκλησίᾳ (the assembly, church).

Galatians and the Romans, the imagery in Eph 2:11–22 clearly addresses the Gentiles and construes the church in terms of a "third entity," one new humanity built upon the foundation of the apostles and prophets, with Christ as the cornerstone. This effectively eliminates the particularity of both Jews and Greeks. In the spirit, the church grows into a holy temple in the Lord, a dwelling place for God. Jew-Gentile issues, so contested in Galatians and Romans, have receded into the background in Ephesians.

Taken together, these ideas develop Pauline ecclesiology beyond anything found in the undisputed letters or Colossians. Colossians and Ephesians are firmly anchored in Pauline thought but show development beyond the Christology and ecclesiology of the authentic letters. And in terms of ecclesiology, Ephesians—perhaps relying on Colossians—has taken the concept of the church still further, moving it into the realm of a cosmic, universal reality built upon the apostles and prophets, with Christ imagined as both the head and the cornerstone. The idea of the church in Ephesians now approaches the image of "one holy catholic and apostolic church,"[115] which by implication also universalizes the role of Paul. He is clearly situated in Ephesians to become a catholic apostle in terms of significance and authority. He himself plays a role in the cosmic drama, a drama manifested in the church.

In Eph 4:1–16, two aspects of the church are emphasized that make more explicit certain features of Paul's view of the church already addressed in the undisputed Pauline letters. The repetition of the church's oneness and the theological character of that oneness recall the historical Paul's own effort to maintain the unity of the church in Christ (4:4–6). Likewise, in 4:11–12 the enumeration of activities echoes the image of the body with its many members in 1 Cor 12.[116] In comparison to 1 Cor 12:4–26, the emphasis in Ephesians seems to shift from the different members belonging to the one body to the different roles in the church given for the building up of the body of Christ. However, in 1 Cor 12:27–31 Paul makes direct reference to apostles, prophets, and teachers, and these roles clearly overlap those identified in Eph 4:11–12. The highly metaphorical language of 1 Cor 12:4–26 gives way in both 1 Cor 12:27–28 and Eph 4:11–12 to something approaching a literal description of various roles being played out in the life of the church. The characteristics of these God given roles are not enumerated but the terms themselves imply their own function: apostles, prophets, evangelists, pastors, and teachers.[117] The qualities appropriate for these various roles are not given, as is the case for the positions described in 1 Timothy and Titus.

There is no hint that these roles are yet institutionalized as offices into which different individuals are appointed. In that regard, the imagery in Ephesians stands closer to the undisputed Pauline letters than to the Pasto-

---

[115] Beker, *The Legacy of Paul,* 72.
[116] Lincoln, *Ephesians,* 248–54.
[117] Ibid., 252.

rals. When we juxtapose the terms from Eph 4:11–12 with those from 1 Timothy and Titus ("overseer," "elder," and "deacon"), we clearly see differences that suggest development in the institutional organization of the church, but this does not necessarily suggest direct movement from less to more institutional sophistication. As much as historical and institutional development, it suggests diversity in the early church. In other words, to speak about "overseers," "elders," and "deacons" does not rule out other roles and features of ecclesiology, even in the same city and in a relatively similar time frame. And in the case of Ephesians and 1 Timothy, this is especially important because ostensibly both epistles are written to Ephesus, one to the church and the other to an individual. A simple linear notion of development would suggest that Ephesians represents an earlier and the Pastorals a later, perhaps significantly later, stage in the ecclesiological development of the Ephesian church. This in fact may be the case, but by itself does not take into account sufficiently the fluidity, diversity, and complex transformational patterns at work in the early church. Clearly there is institutional development in the church, but just as important to observe is the rich mosaic of images and theologies relating to the early church. They are produced by people representing different regions, different functions, different social positions, different theological commitments, as well as different time periods. They overlap and interact with each other. And in the case of Ephesians, with its possible dependence (assuming two authors) on Colossians and with its connections to 1 Corinthians, we see how one author has apparently reworked the imagery of another author.

## Paul the Sufferer in Colossians and Ephesians

In both Ephesians and Colossians, the author (Paul?) repeatedly identifies himself as a prisoner and sufferer. That becomes one of his identifying marks. Whether he is a prisoner of Christ for the sake of the Gentiles (Eph 3:1), praying that the faithful not lose heart over his sufferings (Eph 3:13), as a prisoner pleading with the people to live a life worthy of their calling (Eph 4:1), an ambassador in chains (Eph 6:20) or through his suffering completing Christ's tribulation for the sake of the church (Col 1:24),[118] Paul frames his suffering in positive theological terms (Cf. also Col 4:18). This image of Paul as one who suffers imprisonment and tribulation is one of the most consistent pictures of the apostle in the early church. It is found in the undisputed letters, Acts, 2 Timothy, as well as Ephesians and Colossians. It also

---

[118] Lohse (*Colossians and Philemon*, 72) thinks this indicates the unique dignity of the office that Paul occupies. The use of the term "office" here seems unnecessary and might better be thought of in terms of Paul's apostolic "calling." Furthermore, we cannot make too much of this being a feature of Paul's unique calling, as it may be understand primarily in terms of his relationship with the Colossian community. See also Gnilka, *Paulusbild*, 192–93.

appears, as we shall see, in Ignatius and the *Acts of Paul.* Deeply rooted in the church's memory of the apostle and in his continuing significance for the life of the church in the first and second centuries, Paul the sufferer embodies an important reality for the community. At the same time, the church uses this to validate his exhortation and to identify him with the work of Christ.[119] Contrary to 2 Timothy, the apostle is not held up in the Deutero-Paulines as one to be imitated in his suffering. Rather, Paul calls on the beloved children to be imitators of God (5:1).

## Paul and 2 Thessalonians

As Beker observes, 2 Thessalonians does not move far beyond 1 Thessalonians thematically, and yet it exhibits a number of post-Pauline features: a different eschatology than 1 Thessalonians where the apostle seeks to defuse misplaced eschatological fervor (2:1–12), a more impersonal and instructive tone, the common use of "Lord" as a christological title, and a concern for forgeries as well as maintaining the tradition taught by Paul (2:1–2, 15; 3:6, 17).[120] To use Beker's language, Paul's voice in 2 Thessalonians is the voice of an authoritarian who calls the Thessalonians to imitate the traditions taught by Paul.[121] In other words, Paul, the revered authority figure, and his teaching are to be obeyed. And on the issue of idleness and freeloading, Paul commands the Thessalonians to imitate the example which he, Silvanus, and Timothy set while they were with the church. In 2 Thessalonians, we find none of the rich theology and imagery that mark Colossians and Ephesians, nor do we discover any of the more interesting ecclesiological themes that mark the Pastorals.

## The Deutero-Paulines and the Pastoral Epistles

In theological and structural terms, Colossians and Ephesians resemble more closely the undisputed Pauline letters than they do the Pastorals. As we find in Romans and Galatians, Colossians and Ephesians tend to be overtly theological/christological and often place theological discussion prior to exhortation (especially in the case of Ephesians).[122] This is much less clearly the case in the Pastorals with their alternating style that moves back and forth between theological claim and exhortation. The fact that the Pastorals are individual rather than community letters may in part account for these features, but this does not appear to be sufficient to explain the differences. These structural differences may also be a tell tale sign that the early church in western Asia Minor was generating quite different Pauline

---

[119] Gnilka, *Paulusbild,* 190–93.
[120] Beker, *Paul's Legacy,* 72–73.
[121] Ibid., 74.
[122] Ibid., 69.

styles, a feature that cannot be reduced to a simple matter of earlier and later stages of development.

In terms of ecclesiology, especially in Ephesians, there is nothing that corresponds precisely to 1 Timothy and Titus. Ephesians clearly echoes and overlaps 1 Corinthians more directly than it does the Pastorals. Moreover, the ecclesiology of Ephesians—the oneness of the church, different roles in the church, one new humanity from Jews and Greeks—more closely resembles the ecclesiology of 1 Cor 12 than it does the concern in 1 Timothy and Titus for the qualities necessary for "overseers," "elders," and "deacons." Hence, in terms of the ecclesiological patterns it is much easier to imagine the historical Paul writing Colossians and Ephesians than it is to imagine him writing 1 Timothy and Titus.[123] To the extent we can see clearly the institutional development of the church, the movement is clearly from 1 Corinthians, to Ephesians, and on to 1 Timothy and Titus. Once again, putting the issue in this way suggests a straight line of development that may not be sustainable historically, but it is helpful in positioning the respective ecclesiological patterns.

In terms of the imprisoned and suffering Paul, an image common in much of the early Pauline tradition, the link between the Deutero-Paulines and 2 Timothy is most clear. Two things, however, distinguish 2 Timothy from Colossians and Ephesians. Second Timothy portrays Paul as being near the end of his life, and he consistently appeals to Timothy to follow his example and suffer as he has suffered. Both in tone and substance, 2 Timothy represents a different image of the suffering apostle and the exhortative value of his suffering than that found in the Deutero-Pauline letters.[124]

The Christology of Colossians is marked by the Christ hymn in 1:15–20, an expansive image clearly not paralleled in the Pastorals. Likewise, the incorporation of Christology into ecclesiology, as found in Ephesians, is not a pattern replicated in 1 Timothy or Titus. With the exception of σωτήρ (savior) in Eph 5:23, none of the peculiar christological features of the Pastorals (savior language for Christ, epiphany terminology to describe Christ's coming, and the portrayal of Christ as a mediator) appear in Colossians or Ephesians. In this respect, these letters once again stand closer to the undisputed Pauline letters than the Pastorals.[125] While Ephesians and Colossians both express a concept of the truth,[126] a notion common also in the Pastorals, they do not seem to present it in the self-contained way found in the Pastoral letters. In terms of Christology and the emerging rule of truth, Colossians and Ephesians appear to represent theological patterns closer to the undisputed Pauline letters than to the Pastoral Epistles.[127]

---

[123] For more detail, see above, pp. 31–35, 52–55.

[124] See above pp. 45, 77.

[125] For a discussion of this Christological terminology, see pp. 98–99.

[126] See Col 1:5, 6; Eph 1:13; 4:21, 24, 25; 5:9; 6:14.

[127] Beker, *Paul's Legacy*, 64.

# ✑ 5 ✑

# PAUL, THE PASTORAL EPISTLES, AND THE POSTAPOSTOLIC CHURCH

## INTRODUCTION

THE PAUL under consideration in this chapter and the next is not the historical Paul of Tarsus, author of the seven undisputed letters, but the Paul who people in early Christianity remembered and publicly portrayed. This Paul is the Paul whose legacy runs through Acts (probably the Pastoral Epistles), the Apostolic Fathers, and on to some of the most important thinkers of the emerging Catholic church: Irenaeus, Tertullian, Clement of Alexandria, Origen, Hippolytus, and Cyprian, to name the most prominent. To use Anthony Blasi's words, this Paul had achieved the status of a personage, a figure representing Christian authority and wisdom, who could be called upon when necessary or useful to address issues and problems facing the church. Ultimately, this Paul was perceived to be the author of all the New Testament epistles that bear his name. These letters and the stories recorded in Acts represented the "real" Paul for much of the postapostolic church, and they contributed to his ongoing and transforming legacy. In the emerging traditions of the church, there was ultimately no thought that the Pastoral Epistles or the so-called Deutero-Pauline Epistles were from anyone other than the "real" Paul, or that the Paul in Acts was somehow different from the Paul of the epistles.[1] These images of Paul had merged in the church's conception and became in their own way the grist for further reflection, interpretation, and application. In short, they gave rise to new images of the apostle. Paul, however, was not only a figure of apostolic authority, he was a writer of letters and a theologian whose ideas significantly shaped the first-century church. Hence, when we speak about Paul's legacy, we need to distinguish, though not completely separate, the legacy of Paul the person from the legacy of his letters, and the legacy of his personal example from the legacy of his theology.[2]

---

[1] See Lindemann, "Writings of the Apostolic Fathers," 25.
[2] See the questions raised by Martinus C. DeBoer, "Which Paul," 45–54.

Among the writings of the Apostolic Fathers, only Ignatius, Polycarp, and the author of *1 Clement* mention Paul, and he appears in these texts more often than any other person from the first-century church. Along with Peter and Mary the mother of Jesus, Paul is one of only three people from the early period of the church identified in the Apostolic Fathers.[3] According to Andreas Lindemann, no other New Testament texts or traditions are used more often by the Apostolic Fathers than the epistles of Paul.[4] *Second Clement* and the *Shepherd of Hermas* display no particular interest in Paul or his theology. The *Epistle of Barnabas* may reflect some Pauline ideas, but the author's primary interest is the allegorical interpretation of the Old Testament.[5] Likewise, the *Didache* may contain some Pauline allusions, but there is no direct substantive connection to the apostle. In the writings of the early church, especially in Irenaeus, Tertullian, and Origen, Paul and his writings play a significant role. Once again, the goal of this chapter and the next is to compare Pauline structural elements from the apostolic and selected ante-Nicene writers to the Pauline patterns found in the Pastoral Epistles in order to highlight the contribution of Paul and these letters to the formation of Christianity. More marginal portrayals of Paul and his letters will be examined but primarily for purposes of contrast and illustration.

## PAUL AND THE APOSTOLIC FATHERS

### Ignatius of Antioch

According to the modern view, Ignatius, while under arrest and en route from Antioch to his anticipated martyrdom in Rome, wrote a series of letters, first from Smyrna to Ephesus, Magnesia, Tralles, and Rome and then from Troas to Philadelphia, Smyrna, and the elder Polycarp sometime during the latter part of the reign of emperor Trajan (98–117 C.E.).[6] Not without its critics, this consensus still prevails into the present, along with the presumed authenticity of the so-called "middle recension" of the letters.[7] It is against this historical background and with this version of the epistles that we investigate the place of Ignatius in the line of Pauline development extending through the Pastoral Epistles.

#### Paul and Ignatius

Various scholars have observed the connection between Paul, Pauline theology, and Ignatius. Helmut Koester claims, for example, that Ignatius

---

[3] Lindemann, "Writings of the Apostolic Fathers," 28.
[4] Ibid., 28.
[5] Ibid., 25–27.
[6] Schoedel, *Ignatius*, 4–5.
[7] Ibid., 5–7; and Christine Trevett, *A Study of Ignatius of Antioch in Syria and Asia* (Studies in the Bible and Early Christianity 29; Lewiston, N.Y.: Mellen, 1992), 14–15.

considers Paul the theologian who most correctly understood the salvation announced in Christ's crucifixion and resurrection.[8] According to Koester, Ignatius was strongly influenced by Paul and represents yet another early Christian attempt at elaborating his ideas.[9] William Schoedel argues that of all the material available to Ignatius, the Pauline writings exercised the most influence on him,[10] and Simon Tugwell sees in Ignatius' episcopate the triumph of a Pauline ecclesiological tendency in the early church.[11] In terms of the authority of the bishop, Schoedel also argues that the churches known to Ignatius have moved beyond the Pastoral Epistles, but only at most a step beyond them.[12] Still others, Robert Grant and Christine Trevett among them, think that Ignatius did in fact know Paul's work and letters.[13] At the very least, there is no reason to think he did not know them.

In both Ign. *Eph.* 12:2 and Ign. *Rom.* 4:3, Ignatius makes explicit reference to Paul. To the Ephesians, Ignatius writes: "You are the passage for those who are being slain for God, fellow initiates of Paul, who was sanctified, approved, worthy of blessing, in whose footsteps may I be found when I reach God, who in every epistle makes mention of you in Christ Jesus." Perhaps referring to the meeting in Miletus in Acts 20:1–38, where the Ephesian elders send Paul off to imprisonment and eventual martyrdom,[14] Ignatius overlays his own imprisonment and impending martyrdom with that of Paul. He praises the Ephesians for being the passage way to martyrdom and sees himself as walking in the footsteps of Paul on the way to his own death. It is as though Ignatius has taken up the very words of 2 Timothy's Paul and followed the apostle's example to suffer as he has suffered.[15] Though it may be implied that Christ is also Ignatius' example,[16] the footsteps are not explicitly said to be those of Christ but Paul. He is the one on whom Ignatius models his highly stylized journey to apparent martyrdom in Rome. And it is Paul, the one who was sanctified, approved, and blessed, with whom the Ephesians are "fellow initiates" (συμμύσται) and who in every epistle makes reference to "you" in Christ Jesus. Clearly, Ignatius holds Paul in the highest esteem, sees his own journey to martyrdom for

---

[8] Helmut Koester, *Introduction to the New Testament: History and Literature of Early Christianity* (New York: Walter DeGruyter, 1982), 2:283.

[9] Ibid., 281.

[10] Schoedel, *Ignatius*, 10.

[11] Simon Tugwell, *The Apostolic Fathers* (Outstanding Christian Thinkers; Harrisburg, Pa.: Morehouse, 1989), 105.

[12] Schoedel, *Ignatius*, 22–23.

[13] Robert M. Grant, "Scripture and Tradition in St. Ignatius of Antioch," *CBQ* (1963): 327; and Trevett, *A Study of Ignatius*, 4, 19–20. Cf. also Daniel Hoffman, "The Authority of Scripture and Apostolic Doctrine of Ignatius of Antioch," *JETS* 28 (1985): 74–75.

[14] Schoedel, *Ignatius*, 73.

[15] Cf. Phil 3:7–21.

[16] Cf. Ign. *Phld.* 8:2; Ign. *Trall.* 10:1.

God as following the pattern of Paul's journey, and visualizes the Ephesians as the passage way of those slain for the sake of God.

In Ign. *Rom.* 4:3, the author refers to Paul once again: "I do not command you as Peter and Paul; they were apostles, I am a convict; they were free, but I until now a slave. But if I suffer I shall be a freedman of Jesus Christ and shall be a free man in him. Now I am learning as one bound to desire nothing." Ignatius distinguishes himself from Peter and Paul on the basis of their apostleship. The context of this statement is the plea to the Romans not to hinder his martyrdom. He goes to his death willingly for God's sake and beseeches the Romans not to intercede on his behalf to prevent the glorious fulfillment of this sacrifice. Ignatius is careful not to command the Romans as Peter and Paul did, for they were apostles but he only a lowly convict. As apostles, they are in a different category from Ignatius. It is likely that Ignatius' imagery in Romans reflects the tradition of Peter and Paul's martyrdom in Rome,[17] a martyrdom he expects to share and which he implores the Romans not to impede. Though the apostles can command the Romans apart from their martyrdom, Ignatius will only truly attain the status of a disciple through his sacrificial death (Ign. *Rom.* 4:2).[18] Though Ignatius expects to attain the status of a disciple, he will do so truly only as a martyr. They were apostles in life, something he will never be. Here we can detect a subtle transition to the postapostolic church. Ignatius, the bishop, does not expect to become an apostle through his sacrificial death, but rather a true disciple. The time for the apostles is now past, but through martyrdom, a martyrdom shared with the apostles Peter and Paul, Ignatius can attain a special status, as well as the authority this status confers. As Schoedel remarks: "Martyrdom frees Ignatius because only so can he be a true disciple."[19] Ignatius presumes Paul's apostolic status and authority, a status he himself will only approach as a true disciple through martyrdom.

From Paul to Ignatius, a postapostolic generational shift takes place, and in the line of 2 Timothy, Ignatius sees suffering and martyrdom as something to be embraced according to the pattern of those apostles who have gone before him. Implicitly, Ignatius sees himself as following the example of Peter and Paul who have gone before him to their deaths in Rome. The references to suffering in Paul's letters to the Roman, Corinthian, and Philippian churches are enhanced in the letter to 2 Timothy. The emphasis is not on following Christ's example but almost exclusively on following Paul's example of suffering.[20] Ignatius extends this even further. He overlays his own imminent martyrdom symbolically with that of the apostle in his epistle to the Ephesians, but he also distinguishes his achievement of true discipleship in his letter to the Romans from the apostleship of Peter and

---

[17] Schoedel, *Ingatius,* 176.
[18] Ibid., 176–77.
[19] Ibid., 176.
[20] See above, p. 45.

Paul. The apostolic age is now at an end historically, but as we shall see it persists theologically in the structure and ministry of the church.

Ignatius perhaps knew Paul's first letter to the Corinthians,[21] but beyond that it is difficult to know which if any of the apostle's letters he actually knew.[22] The references to Paul in Ign. *Eph.* 12:2 and *Rom.* 4:3 may also indicate that Ignatius knew Ephesians (cf. 16:8; also 1 Tim 1:3; 2 Tim 1:18; 4:12). Some sixty years ago, Albert Barnett made the claim that Paul knew Romans, 1 Corinthians, and Ephesians;[23] probably knew Galatians, Philippians, and Colossians;[24] and may have known 2 Corinthians, 1 and 2 Thessalonians, and Philemon.[25] However, as Schoedel remarks, many of the examples identified as evidence of Pauline linkage are today more apt to be attributed to the use of traditional Christian material.[26] Andreas Lindemann claims that Ign. *Eph.*18–20 indicates that Ignatius was influenced by Paul, though the categories are presumed rather than made explicit.[27] He also observes structural similarities (regarding Paul's general style of argumentation) between Ign. *Trall.* 9:2 and 1 Thess 4:13–18, and between 1 Cor 15:15, 32 and Ign. *Phld.* 8:2. Similarly, he sees links between Ign. *Magn.* 8–9 and the arguments in Galatians.

Interjecting a word of caution, Robert Grant has observed that the fact that allusions to the Pauline epistles can be identified in the Ignatian letters may owe more to scholarly ingenuity than to evidence that Ignatius read the apostle's work.[28] Though there may be no good reason to doubt Paul's influence on Ignatius or that Ignatius knew Paul's letters, it is often difficult to identify specific texts that establish this, with the possible exception of certain examples from 1 Corinthians. Hence, we need to probe beneath the surface level of the possible Ignatian allusions or parallels to the Pauline letters to see how Ignatius' own theological and ecclesiological patterns may reflect an extension of the Pauline tradition, and only then to see if those patterns are consistent with the line of Pauline development that extends through the Pastoral Epistles. Although it will not be possible to establish beyond a doubt Ignatius' theological dependence on Paul or the Pastorals, it

---

[21] See Ign. *Eph.* 16:1 (cf. 1 Cor 6:9); 18:1 (cf. 1 Cor 1:18–25); Ign. *Rom.* 5:1 (cf. 1 Cor 15:32); 9:2 (cf. 1 Cor 15:8–9); Ign. *Phld.* 3:3 (cf. 1 Cor 1:10; 11:18; 12:25); Ign. *Trall.* 13:3 (cf. 1 Cor 1:9; 9:27; 10:13).

[22] Hoffman, "Authority of Scripture and Apostolic Doctrine," 72; and Schoedel, *Ignatius,* 9.

[23] See Ign. *Eph.* inscrp, 1:1; 12:2; 20:1; Ign. *Magn.* 7:1–2; Ign. *Smyrn.* 1:2; Ign. *Pol.* 1:2; 5:1; 6:2.

[24] See Ign. *Rom.* 2:1; 5:3; Ign. *Phld.* 1:1; 10:1; Ign. *Magn.* 2:1; 10:3; Ign. *Smyrn.* 4:2; 6:1; 11:3; Ign. *Eph.* 2:1; 10:2; Ign. *Trall.* 5:2.

[25] Albert E. Barnett, *Paul Becomes a Literary Influence* (Chicago: Chicago University Press, 1941), 70.

[26] Schoedel, *Ignatius,* 10.

[27] Lindemann, "Writings of the Apostolic Fathers," 37.

[28] Grant, "Scripture and Tradition," 324–25.

will be possible to illustrate the connections between Ignatius and the line of Pauline development exhibited by the Pastoral Epistles.

True and False Teaching, True and False Teachers

Ignatius' letters display a structural distinction between true and false teachers, correct and incorrect belief. This distinction is pervasive and apart from his letter to the Romans is found in all the letters.[29] In Ign. *Eph.* 6:2, Ignatius acknowledges that Onesimus gives praise to the Ephesians for their good order and for the fact that they all live according to the truth (ἀλήθειαν) and that no heresy (αἵρεσις) dwells in them. Moreover, the Ephesians do not even listen to anyone unless he speaks about Jesus Christ in truth (ἀληθείᾳ). A few lines further on (7:1–2), Ignatius warns the Ephesians against the beasts and dogs who threaten them and against which they must be on their guard.[30] He exhorts them not to be deceived (8:1)—indeed as they have not been deceived but live according to God[31]—and in 9:1 he acknowledges that some have stayed among them who represent "evil teaching." In the epistle to the Ephesians, this division is not simply a matter of opposition to Ignatius or to the Ephesians but a structural, religious distinction between true teaching and false teaching, orthodoxy and heresy, as well as an attempt to ensure that the Ephesians not be lured away by those whose teaching deviates from the truth.

In Ign. *Magn.* 8:1 also, Ignatius exhorts the Magnesians not be lead astray by heterodoxies (ἑτεροδοξίαις) or old fables (παλαιοῖς ἀνωφελέσιν). This statement is immediately linked to living according to Judaism, in which case grace has not been received. Similarly in Ign. *Magn.*11:1, he warns them not to be caught by the hooks of empty doctrine (κενοδοξίας), but to be convinced by the birth, death, and resurrection of Jesus, which took place at the time of Pontius Pilate. Once again, Ignatius is concerned conceptually about false teaching and in particular the false teaching associated with living according to Judaism. Jerry Sumney may be correct that there is no evidence of a judaizing opposition in Magnesia,[32] but there can be no doubt that in the epistle to the Magnesians there is a conceptual distinction between true and false teaching, that the threat of false teachers is acknowledged, and that without extensive argumentation, along the lines of the Pastorals, there is concern about Jewish practices among those who claim to be Christians. Ignatius, like the author(s) of the Pastorals, feels compelled to

---

[29] See especially Ign. *Eph.* 6:1, 2; 7:1–2; 8:1; 9:1; 16:1–2; Ign. *Magn.* 8:1; 11:1; Ign. *Trall.* 6:1; 11:1–2; Ign. *Phld.* 2:1–2; Ign. *Smyrn.* 2:1; 4:1; 5:1–3; 6:1–2; 7:2; Ign. *Pol.* 3:1.

[30] See the discussion by Schoedel, *Ignatius*, 59.

[31] In Ign. *Eph.* 8:2 Ignatius makes a distinction between those who are "fleshy" and those who are spiritual. Those of the flesh cannot do spiritual things and those of the spirit cannot do the things of the flesh.

[32] Jerry L. Sumney, "Those who 'Ignorantly Deny Him': The Opponents of Ignatius of Antioch," *JECS* (1993): 363–64.

warn the recipients of the letter to avoid such empty doctrine. Whether there is in fact a judaizing opposition in Magnesisa may, however, be a debatable point. The elaborate arguments about the law, circumcision, faith, and works found in Paul's letters to the Romans and Galatians are not replicated by Ignatius, just as they are not replicated in the Pastorals. What we find in both 1 Timothy and Titus and in the letter to the Magnesians is the concern that certain Jewish practices (identified only as Sabbath observance in Ign. *Magn.* 9:1) are contrary to the correct teaching of the church, and that it is monstrous to speak of Jesus Christ and practice Judaism (9:3). Unlike the theological and scriptural argumentation of Paul in Romans and Galatians, the response to the Christians who engage in such Jewish practices is simply to declare it heretical and to warn them not to become ensnared in empty doctrine. On that structural and stylistic level, Ignatius and the Pastorals seem to have more in common than do Ignatius and Paul. Though acknowledging a structural connection to Galatians in Ign. *Magn.* 8–9, Lindemann seems to acknowledge the same point being made here when he writes: ". . . although it is highly unlikely, in my judgment, that Ignatius was acquainted with Paul's epistle to the Galatians, he uses surprisingly similar arguments. The first of these ("be not seduced by strange doctrines or antiquated fables, which are profitless" [8:1]) actually resembles arguments used by the author of the Pastoral Epistles."[33] In fact, the style as well as the argumentation appear closer to the Pastorals than they do to Galatians.

In Ign. *Trall.* 6:1, Ignatius appeals to the audience with the words: "I exhort you—not I, but the love of Jesus Christ—make use of only Christian food and stay away from any strange plant, which is heresy (αἵρεσις)." As the context following this statement indicates, the emphasis here is on the false teachers who with their poisonous teaching bring division to the community. More than the content of the false teaching, heresy is the factious result of the false teachers and their teachings.[34] They sow discord. The antidote to such poison for the Trallians is not to be puffed up and to be inseparable from God, Jesus Christ, the bishop, and the ordinances of the apostles. The appeal to flee these wicked people is repeated once again in Ign. *Trall.* 11:1, and here they are referred to as "wicked off-shoots," who bear a "deadly fruit." Their work brings disunion with God and enmity with one another.

Communal unity threatened by false teachers is a common Pauline theme especially in 1 and 2 Corinthians and Galatians, just as it is in 1 and 2 Timothy and Titus.[35] There is nothing particularly unusual about this in the Pauline churches. What is striking is that there seems to be a line of development from Paul to the Pastorals and on to Ignatius. Although Paul exhorts his readers to resist those who seek to lead the people astray, defends

---

[33] Lindemann, "Writings of the Apostolic Fathers," 37–38.
[34] Schoedel, *Ignatius,* 147.
[35] See, e.g., 1 Tim 1:18–20; 4:1–5; 6:3–10; 2 Tim 2:14–19; 3:1–9; Titus 3:8–11.

his apostolic authority, and frequently mounts scriptural and theological arguments to refute his opponents, he does not appeal to his audiences to resist by submitting to or remaining inseparable from the bishop or the apostles more generally. As we shall see below,[36] Ignatius views resistance to the false teachers, in part at least, as a matter of submitting to the bishop. He is less inclined to mount theological and scriptural arguments to refute the perceived threat. From Paul to Ignatius, the emphasis shifts from refutation through exhortation and argumentation underwritten by apostolic authority to exhortation and submission to the authorized leader in each of the churches about whom the bishop has received information and to whom writes. In part, this is due to the postapostolic vantage point of Ignatius and the less intimate relationship he has with the churches to whom he is writing. It also indicates that ecclesiologically the churches in Asia Minor, as seen through Ignatius' eyes, have developed since Paul's day. Authority is now derived and expressed in different ways.

First Timothy and Titus are in this regard mid-way between Paul and Ignatius. The author of these letters still represents, probably pseudepigraphically, apostolic authority directly to the recipients of the letters and in that context exhorts them to remain steadfast in the truth. Scriptural and theological elaboration, however, remain limited. Still the author of these two Pastoral letters also reflects an increasingly elaborate system of leadership and the qualities necessary for those who hold certain positions. The emphasis is on the people who aspire to these positions. As of yet, there does not seem to be in 1 Timothy and Titus a sense of authority resident in these offices to which the congregants ought to submit and in so doing resist the false teachers and their teaching. If in the Pauline Epistles, apostolic authority is immediate and a formal system of ecclesiological authority apart from Paul is yet to develop and if in Ignatius apostolic authority extends from the past ordinances of the apostles and is expressed now through the authority of the bishop (see Ign. *Trall.* 8–11), 1 Timothy and Titus exhibit a transition stage between the immediate apostolic authority of Paul and an emerging formal structure of leadership and authority. In these two Pastoral letters, apostolic authority and an emergent ecclesiological structure stand side by side, and both have a temporal immediacy for the addressees not found in either Paul or Ignatius. When we take up the issue of Ignatius' ecclesiology,[37] this point will be developed further.

The plea to flee false teaching (κακοδιδασκαλίας) appears also in the letter of Ignatius to the Philadelphians (2:1), where the members of the church are identified as the "children of the light of truth." Using imagery of the shepherd, the sheep, and the wolves, Ignatius exhorts the Philadelphians to follow the shepherd and to avoid the wolves who lead to captivity with wicked pleasures. Once again, the answer to false teachers and the disunity

---

[36] See below, pp. 130, 135–36.
[37] See below, pp. 135–38.

they cause is the call to be obedient to the shepherd, the bishop.[38] As he writes in Ign. *Phld.* 3:2: "For all who are of God and Jesus Christ, these are with the bishop." Instead of summoning a theological argument to set the Philadelphians on the path to right thinking, he appeals to them to seek protection through obedience to the bishop reminding them that there is one Eucharist, one cup, one altar, one bishop (4:1).[39] In this context, church unity is both liturgical and episcopal, and the real problem with false teachers is that they lead the church to schism. Ignatius responds with a plea to episcopal obedience rather than with the theological subtleties of doctrinal correction. Perhaps the closest he gets in this letter to a hermeneutical defense in the face of the false teachers is the often quoted statement from 8:2: "But I exhort you to do nothing according to partisanship but according to Christ's teaching. For I heard some men saying, 'if I do not find it in the charters I do not believe (it to be) in the gospel,' and when I said it is written, they answered me, 'that is just the question.' But to me the charters are Jesus Christ, the inviolable charters his cross and death and his resurrection and the faith which is through him. . . ." Rather than arguing the case from Scripture, however, he summarily preempts the question with this assertion about the centrality of Christ and his crucifixion, death, and resurrection. In doing so, he does not elaborate his Christology, but merely repeats the basic contours of Christ's saving work.

Ignatius confronts a Docetist opposition in Smyrna (Ign. *Smyrn.* 2–7),[40] and as is his custom he appeals to the authority of the bishop in maintaining the liturgy and the unity of the church (8–9). By emphasizing the reality of Christ's physical suffering and resurrection in the face of those who deny this (2–3), Ignatius warns the Smyrneans against even associating with these false teachers, who are advocates of death rather than the truth (4–5, 7). Moreover, these heretics do not exhibit Christian behavior as they ought (6), with the implication being that their behavior reveals the falseness of their Christology and their liturgical practice. They do not care for the widow, the orphan, the distressed, the afflicted, the prisoner, the hungry or the thirsty (6:2). And they abstain from the Eucharist and prayer because they do not confess that the Eucharist is the flesh of Christ (7:1). In this case, the opposition is clearly docetic and has fractious consequences for the Eucharistic practice of the church in Smyrna. In this case, christological error, liturgical disharmony, and church disunity all converge as Ignatius witnesses to the problems in the church at Smyrna. And once again, obedience to the bishop is his solution to wrong thinking and false teaching.

---

[38] Schoedel, *Ignatius*, 197.

[39] For an argument concerning the connection between church offices and the liturgy in Ignatius, see Allen Brent, "The Ignatian Epistles and the Threefold Ecclesiastical Order," *Journal of Religious History* 17 (1992): 18–32.

[40] Sumney, "Those Who Ignorantly Deny Him," 351–53.

Writing to Polycarp, bishop of Smyrna, Ignatius approaches the issue of episcopal submission from the opposite direction: "Let those who appear to be worthy of confidence but teach other doctrines (teach heterodoxy) not bring you down. Stand firm as an anvil when struck (Ign. *Pol.* 3:1)." He calls upon the bishop to respond with steadfastness as a great athlete suffers punishment and yet endure everything for the sake of God. Here, Ignatius combines an implied antithesis between true and false doctrine and obedience to the bishop in one statement, and this probably reflects the docetic controversy addressed in the letter to the Smyrneans. As is his pattern, Ignatius exhorts and cajoles, but he engages in little theological elaboration. In this regard, he is much more an ecclesiological than a theological figure. Putting the same point another way, William Weinrich observes that Ignatius' theology is largely ecclesial.[41] What is theological in Ignatius, however, is the fundamental distinction between true or false teaching and true or false teachers. He also appears to imply that orthodoxy is relatively fixed and that heterodoxy requires an ecclesiological response (submission to the bishop) more than theological or scriptural elaboration. True teaching and church unity, closely connected for Ignatius, reside in the figure of the bishop.

Christology

In Ign. *Eph.* 18:2, Ign. *Smyrn.* 1:1–2, and Ign. *Trall.* 9:1–2, Ignatius summarizes in credal form his Christology.[42] In Ign. *Eph.* 18:2, he refers to Christ as "our God" who was carried in the womb of Mary according to the plan of God, is of the seed of David, and was born and baptized in order that by his suffering he might purify the water. In Ign. *Smyrn.* 1:1–2, he writes that Jesus is of the family of David according to the flesh, God's son according to the will and power of God, truly born of a virgin, baptized by John, nailed to a (tree) in the flesh, and raised as an ensign for the saints and believers through the resurrection. In the introduction to 1:1, he also identifies Jesus Christ as ". . . the God who has given you wisdom. . . ." In Ign. *Trall.* 9:1–2, Ignatius rehearses once again the significant features of Jesus' background. He was of David's line of descent, was truly born, ate and drank, was truly persecuted under Pilate, was truly crucified and put to death in the sight of all, and was truly raised up as his father shall raise up all who believe. In all three summaries, especially in Smyrneans with its docetic controversy, Ignatius emphasizes the humanity of Jesus. Yet in the first two texts Jesus is also identified as God,[43] an identification that is explicit or

---

[41] William C. Weinrich, "The Concept of the Church in Ignatius of Antioch," in *Good News in History: Essays in Honor of Bo Reicke* (ed. Ed. L. Miller; Atlanta: Scholars Press, 1993), 139.

[42] Schoedel, *Ignatius*, 8. Cf also Ign. *Eph.* 20:2; Ign. *Phld.* 8:2.

[43] For a discussion of pervasiveness of God language in Ignatius see Bishop Demetrios Trakatellis, "God Language in Ignatius of Antioch," in *The Future of the Early Church: Essays in Honor of Helmut Koester* (ed. Birger Pearson et al; Minneapolis: Fortress, 1991), 423–26.

implied in Ign. *Eph.* 1:1; 7:2; 15:3; 19:3; Ign. *Trall.* 7:1; Ign. *Rom.* Inscription; 3:3; 6:3; and Ign. *Pol.* 8:3.[44] The deity of Christ is firmly established in Ignatius, even where there might be some docetic concern about the humanity of Christ. Apart from an apparent identification between God and Christ in 1 Tim 3:15–16 and Titus 2:13,[45] this is not a formulation common in the Pastoral Epistles. However, as argued above,[46] the ease with which both Christ and God are identified as savior in the Pastorals, which implies a rather high Christology on their part, may also presume an implicit identification of Christ with God.[47] In these christological summaries, Ignatius exhibits a high Christology (Jesus is God),[48] while at the same time stressing repeatedly his true humanity and suffering. As God, Christ is preexistent (Ign. *Magn.* 7:1), he came from the father and he will return to the father (Ign. *Magn.* 7:2).[49] He is God incarnate.[50] What this suggests is that Ignatius' elevated Christology is not put at risk even when certain docetic elements threaten to undermine the humanity of Christ and the unity of the church. Indeed, the unity of the church presumes the unity between God and Christ, which is itself actualized in the Eucharistic gathering of the community.[51]

Perhaps more to the point for our purposes, Ignatius also identifies Christ as savior,[52] a common appellation in the Pastorals but appearing only once in the authentic Paulines.[53] In Ign. *Eph.* 1:1 (". . . Christ Jesus our savior . . ."), Ign. *Phld.* 9:2 (". . . the coming of the savior, our Lord Jesus Christ"), and Ign. *Smyrn.* 7:1 (". . . the Eucharist is the flesh of our savior Jesus Christ . . ."), Ignatius carries forth the identification of Christ as savior found in the Pastorals, an identification that may reflect the influence of the imperial cult. For Ignatius, Christ is not only God but savior. Paul's almost total lack of this terminology may simply be a matter of preference, but it may also indicate that this language had not yet fully taken root in the churches of the Greco-Roman world and would not for some years to come, as exhibited by the Pastorals and Ignatius. If so, this is another thread that indicates Ignatius stands in a line of Pauline development that also includes the Pastoral Epistles.

---

[44] Ibid., 425; also Cullen I. K. Story, "The Christology of Ignatius of Antioch," *Evangelical Quarterly* 56 (1984): 174.

[45] See the variant reading.

[46] See above, pp. 58–61.

[47] Story, "Christology of Ignatius," 174.

[48] As Lindemann observes, in calling Jesus God Ignatius goes far beyond Paul's Christology, "Writings of the Apostolic Father," 37. Once again, Ignatius appears closer to the Pastorals than the authentic Pauline letters.

[49] Trakatellis, "God Language in Ignatius of Antioch," 427.

[50] Ibid. 429. Cf. 1 Tim 2:5–6; 3:16; 2 Tim 2:8, texts which may also reflect early christological credal statements.

[51] Ibid., 429.

[52] Story, "Christology of Ignatius," 178.

[53] See above, p. 58.

Concerning the question, "who is Christ?" Cullen Story writes: "The answer of Ignatius is important and far-reaching. I suggest that it can be expressed under two main headings found in the New Testament pastoral letters. To Ignatius, (1) Christ is God made manifest in the flesh (variant reading of 1 Tim 3:16), and (2) Christ is God our savior (Titus 3:4; 2:10).[54] Story's second point corroborates the claim just made about the christological link between the Pastorals and Ignatius, but the first point is also significant. As indicated above,[55] Paul uses παρουσία (coming) language to describe the coming of Christ, whereas the Pastorals use ἐπιφάνεια (appearing, appearance) terminology, once again terminology that may have connections to the language of the imperial cult. In Ign. *Eph.* 19:1, 3 and Ign. *Magn.* 8:2, Ignatius uses "appearance" language to describe God's manifestation in the flesh (Ign. *Eph.* 19:2, ἐφανερώθη; Ign. *Eph.* 19:3, φανερουμένου; Ign. *Magn.* 8:2, φανερώσας). In the Pastorals, this language expresses the coming of Christ, both past and future, and thus implicitly the coming reality of God, whereas Ignatius uses it explicitly in terms of the manifestation of God in the flesh in Jesus Christ. Jesus the savior is the manifestation of God. Though these emphases are not precisely identical, they are very close, and they put both the Pastorals and Ignatius in a common line of early christological development, a line predicated on a notion of divine revelation.[56] As Ign. *Phld.* 9:2 also indicates, however, Ignatius can use parousia language, terminology more common to Paul himself, to describe the coming of Christ the savior.

This suggests that Ignatius is heir to the christological language and concepts of both the historical Paul and the Paul of the Pastoral Epistles, as well as perhaps to the gospel tradition represented by John and Matthew.[57] But rather than simply repeating them, he fuses and extends them into his own situation in the early second century among the churches of Asia Minor. Whether or not Ignatius actually knew the Pastoral letters, he is clearly heir to a christological tradition represented by them, and at certain points that tradition is at variance with the undisputed Pauline letters. That christological tradition represents Christ as God and savior; and, though completely human, he is the epiphany of divine revelation. This does not mean that Paul's own unique Christology does not also leave its imprint on Ignatius. It is as though the imagery of Paul's Christology is double exposed in Ignatius (to use photographic imagery), with the imagery of the Pastoral Epistles overlaying and shaping aspects of Paul's own imagery as the traveling prisoner addresses the various churches and makes his way to Rome. For Ignatius, this is a dynamic process and one that makes no conscious

---

[54] Story, "Christology of Ignatius," 174.

[55] See above, p. 98.

[56] Bassler, "A Plethora of Epiphanies," 313.

[57] For the connections to John and Matthew, see Story, "Christology of Ignatius," 174–76.

distinction between the authentic Paul and the Paul of the Pastorals. To the extent there is any thought given to it at all by Ignatius, the entire tradition is Pauline. We, however, can look back and see that the Pauline christological tradition was being shaped in particular ways and that the tradition of the Pastoral letters was instrumental in that process.

Two Ignatian texts, Ign. *Eph.* 7:2 and Ign *Pol.* 3:2, illustrate the progress of Ignatius' incarnational thinking in antithetical terms. He writes in Ign. *Eph.* 7:2: "There is one physician, both fleshly and spiritual, begotten and unbegotten, in man God, in death true life, both of Mary and of God, first passable then impassable, Jesus Christ our Lord." In terms of a series of antithetical statements about Christ, Ignatius underscores both of the incarnational poles and in doing so affirms the two natures of Christ.[58] Schoedel rightly notes the similarity to 1 Tim 3:16, but because of the fragmentary character of the parallels it is not possible to identify a well-formed liturgical tradition behind these two texts.[59] However, Ignatius does anticipate here the later and more complex christological debates over the two natures of Christ. In Ign. *Pol.* 3:2, the bishop makes another series of antithetical christological statements: "Look for him who is above time, timeless, invisible, who for our sakes became visible, who is intangible, who cannot suffer, who for our sakes suffered, who endured in every way for our sakes." The language and structure are clearly different from that found in Ign. *Eph.* 7:2,[60] but the two texts do not appear to be conceptually inconsistent.

Schoedel observes concerning Ign. *Eph.* 7:2: "Our passage also shows that Ignatius interprets redemption primarily in terms of victory over death. The emphasis is on the incarnation (as the point at which divine power is brought to bear on human existence) and the passion is important largely because it is the necessary prelude to deathlessness. There is little about sin and forgiveness in Ignatius (cf. Ign. *Smyrn.* 7:1)."[61] If Schoedel's perception is correct, the lack of emphasis on redemption in terms of forgiveness of sin in Ignatius is entirely consistent with Paul.[62] Though the emphasis on death and resurrection is surely Pauline, the incarnation as the point when divine power comes to bear on human existence may reflect certain gospel traditions more directly than Paul (cf. Mark 1:1–15; Matt 1:1–25; Luke 1:1–2:52; contrast Rom 1:4). Similarly, forgiveness terminology does not figure prominently in the redemption language of the Pastorals either. In 1 Timothy 2:5–6, Christ is the mediator (between God and humankind) who gave himself as a ransom (ἀντίλυτρον) for all. In 1 Tim 3:16, Christ was revealed in the flesh, vindicated in the spirit, seen by angels, proclaimed among the

---

[58] Schoedel, *Ignatius,* 60.

[59] Ibid., 61.

[60] Ibid., 267.

[61] Ibid., 62.

[62] Cf. Rom 4:7–8 for the only reference to redemption in terms of forgiveness of sin in Paul's undisputed letters.

Gentiles, believed, and taken up into glory. And in 2 Tim 2:11, the imagery concerns dying and living with Christ. In none of these Pastoral texts is Christ the forgiver of sins. He is the mediator, the ransom for all, the one revealed in the flesh, vindicated in the spirit, seen by angels, proclaimed, believed, and taken up in glory. At this point, Paul, the Pastorals, and Ignatius are consistent, though not identical, in their christological formulations and understanding of the atonement.

### Ignatius and the Ministry of the Church

The references in Ignatius' letters to bishops,[63] presbyters,[64] and deacons are pervasive and fundamental to his concept of the church.[65] In Ign. *Magn.* 6:1, Ignatius writes: ". . . I exhort you: be eager to do all things in harmony with God, with the bishop set over you in the place of God, and the presbyters in the place of the council of apostles, and the deacons, most dear to me, entrusted with the service of Jesus Christ." Similarly he writes in Ign. *Trall.* 3:1: "Likewise, let everyone respect the deacons as Jesus Christ, as also the bishop is a type of the Father, and the presbyters as the council of God and as the group of the apostles. Without these nothing is called 'church.'" This is extended still further in Ign. *Smyrn.* 8:1–2: "You must all follow the bishop, as Jesus Christ followed the Father, and the presbytery as if it were the apostles; respect the deacons as the command of God. Apart from the bishop, let no one do anything that pertains to the church. Let that be considered a valid Eucharist, which is done under the bishop or to whomever he entrusts it. Wherever the bishop appears, there let the congregation be present; just as wherever Jesus Christ is, there is the whole church (καθολικὴ ἐκκλησία)."[66]

The plain reading of these texts suggests that Ignatius makes the transition to the postapostolic age by seeing the bishop in place of or as the type of God and the presbyters in the place of or as the type of the apostles, and the deacons as entrusted with the service of Jesus Christ. Moreover, without these there is nothing that can be called "church." In the struggle for discipline and unity in the church, Ignatius charges the Smyrneans to follow the bishop as Jesus followed God, the presbyters as if they were the apostles, and to respect the deacons by the command of God. The church's ministry

---

[63] See Ign. *Eph.* 1:3; 2:1, 2; 3:2; 4:1; 5:1–3; 6:1; 20:2; Ign. *Magn.* 2:1–2; 3:1–2; 4:1; 6:1, 3; 7:1; 13:12; Ign. *Trall.* 1:1–2; 2:1–3; 3:1; 7:1; 12:2; 13:2; Ign. *Rom.* 13:2; Ign. *Phld* inscrip; 1:1; 4:1; 7:1–2; Ign. *Smyrn.* 8:1–2; 9:1; Ign. *Pol.* inscrip; 2:1; 4:1; 6:1.

[64] See Ign. *Eph.* 2:2; Ign. *Magn.* 6:1; 7:1; 13:12; Ign. *Trall.* 2:23; 3:1; 7:1; 13:2; Ign. *Rom.* 13:2; Ign. *Phld.* inscrip.; 4:1; 7:1; Ign. *Smyrn.* 8:1–2.

[65] See Ign. *Eph.* 2:1; Ign. *Magn.* 6:1; 13:12; Ign. *Trall.* 2:23; 7:1, Ign. *Phld.* Inscrip; 4:1; 7:1; Ign. *Smyrn.* 8:1–2.

[66] Trevett notes that Ignatius is the first known writer to use the term Catholic, *A Study of Ignatius,* 152. Schoedel, modifying the distinction between "Catholic" as geographical or "Catholic" as pertaining to orthodoxy, argues that it implies "the whole church resistant by its very nature to division" (*Ignatius,* 243–44). Cf. Ign. *Eph.* 5:1. We would simply note, however, that correct teaching and correct teachers are closely connected with Igantius' desire that the church not be wracked by division.

as a spiritual and theological reality takes on the form of a three-fold system of offices.[67] Here, theology and ecclesiology are intimately intertwined, and this is Ignatius' way of connecting the postapostolic church with the apostolic church and of fending off false teachers and false teachings. Whether we can actually see in Ignatius the idea that a heavenly image reflects in the earthly hierarchy of the church (as Simon Tugwell claims; see also Ign. *Eph.* 6:1, Ign. *Phld.* 1:1),[68] or the idea that the bishop does not in fact occupy the place of God or Christ, or that Ignatius is still relatively close to New Testament models of ministry (as William Schoedel argues), are still disputed issues.[69] However, certain things seem clear in this discussion. Even if Ignatius does not adopt a full-blown heavenly/earthly scheme for understanding the character and ministry of the church, he does see a theological continuation from God, Christ, and the apostles to the bishops, presbyters, and deacons in the postapostolic period of the church. Hence, the authority of the bishop, presbyters, and deacons is enhanced, and the bishop becomes a figure in whom the church exhibits its presence and preserves it unity. The bishop not only functions as a figure of discipline in the church, but also a focal point for the liturgy and the celebration of the Eucharist.[70] This suggests that Ignatius invests the bishop with considerable institutional power. In other words, significant power appears to reside in the office of the bishop.[71] What is less obvious is whether Ignatius conceives of the bishop more in terms of charismatic or institutional functions.[72] On the face of it, institutional—that is liturgical, unifying, and disciplining—responsibilities appear to play an important role in Ignatius' view of the bishop and his functions. However, where the line between the bishop's charismatic and institutional function should be drawn in Ignatius' view is difficult to determine. The fact that Ignatius does not seem to be concerned about episcopal succession may indicate that the seat of power has not yet moved extensively from the person of the bishop to the office of the bishop.[73] Thus, we would argue there is still room in Ignatius's view of the bishop for a notion of charismatic authority that is derived theologically.

In the frequency of the terminology,[74] the concept of the church's ministry, the idea of episcopal authority, and the reduced immediacy of the

---

[67] See Hans von Campenhausen, *Ecclesiastical Authority and Spiritual Power in the Church of the First Three Centuries* (trans. J. A. Baker; London: Adam and Charles Black, 1969), 98–99.

[68] Tugwell, *Apostolic Fathers*, 118.

[69] Schoedel, *Ignatius*, 22. He admits that the authority of the ministry is certainly strengthened but that its legitimation is not essentially new. See also Weinrich, "The Concept of the Church," 149.

[70] See Brent, "The Ignatian Epistles," 22, 25.

[71] Koester, *Introduction to the New Testament*, 2:285.

[72] Ibid., 285.

[73] Schoedel, *Ignatius*, 22.

[74] See Phil 1:1; Rom 16:1; 2 Cor 6:4, 11:15, 23; 1 Thess 3:2.

apostolic presence, Ignatius moves well beyond the views of Paul as expressed in the seven undisputed letters.[75] This, of course, is less obviously the case in terms of the Pastoral Epistles. Schoedel writes: "The situation in the Pastoral Epistles is not entirely clear, but it appears that the churches known to Ignatius have moved at most but one step beyond them."[76] This conclusion is most apt if one does not construe in Ignatius' letters, as Schoedel does not, the bishop as occupying the place of God or Christ. This conclusion, however, appears more tenable in the case of Ign. *Magn.* 6:1, but less so in Ign. *Trall.* 3:1. Even so, there are some substantial differences between the representations of the three-fold ministry in Ignatius and the Pastorals.[77] In 1 Timothy and Titus, unlike Ignatius, instructions are given in terms of the qualities appropriate for those who aspire to such positions in the household of God.[78] Clearly the emphasis is on the personal qualities of the individuals who occupy the positions. Hence, the balance of authority for these individuals still appears to rest decidedly on the side of the individual rather than the office. In the Pastorals there are no calls for obedience to the bishop, who himself represents the unity of the church, as we find repeatedly in Ignatius. Neither are the connections between God, Christ, the apostles, and the various offices made explicit in 1 Timothy or Titus. In that same vein, instructions are also given in 1 Timothy and Titus to women— younger and older—(1 Tim 2:9–15, 3:11; Titus 2:3–5), to younger men (Titus 2:6–8), and slaves (Titus 2:9–10). Both Ignatius and 1 Timothy make reference to widows,[79] but in 1 Timothy a distinction is made between older and younger widows and the qualities appropriate for their being put on the list of widows. They are not simply identified as persons not to be neglected by the members of the church (Ign. *Pol.* 4:1).

That being said, however, there is also a fundamental similarity between Ignatius, 1 Timothy, and Titus. In all three, there is a basic concern for the unity of the community, and the important role the respective offices play in maintaining that unity. In 1 Timothy and Titus, the assumption is that if the church is to function as the household of God it must maintain the proper network of relationships within the community.[80] For that to happen, the persons who hold positions of authority must have the right personal qualities. On the other hand, Ignatius' remarks presume that bishops are in place, and he sees the problem of division as a matter of obedience. On that level, the differences are really a matter of the

---

[75] Also Koester, *Introduction to the New Testament*, 2:284.

[76] Schoedel, *Ignatius*, 23.

[77] See 1 Tim 3:1–13; 5:17–20; Titus 1:5–9.

[78] See above, pp. 66–69.

[79] See Ign. *Smyrn.* 13:1; Ign. *Pol.* 4:1; 1 Tim 5:9–16.

[80] Harry O. Maier argues for the house church setting of Ignatius' churches as well, *The Social Setting of the Ministry as Reflected in the Writings of Hermas, Clement, and Ignatius* (Dissertation S R, 1 Waterloo, Ont.: Wilfrid Laurier University Press, 1991), 148–52.

differences in the circumstances between Ignatius and the author of 1 Timothy and Titus. But both authors are concerned fundamentally about the unity of the respective communities and the role of the designated leaders (three-fold office) in that unity. Though Ignatius clearly appears to place more direct authority in the office itself than does the Pastoral author, this is a matter of relative weight, and it probably also suggests a further historical development in the church's ecclesiology. In any case, Ignatius does not mark a break with the ecclesiology of 1 Timothy and Titus but a continuation and extension of it. In that line of development the Pastorals, based on their theological and structural patterns, are positioned closer to Ignatius than to Paul. At different times and under different circumstances, both authors reflect the emerging ecclesiological situation of the church in Asia Minor and Crete.

Scripture and Tradition

The statement cited above from Ign. *Phld.* 8:2[81] (in which Ignatius echoes a conversation where some men were heard to say that if they do not find something in the "charters" [Old Testament] they do not believe it to be in the gospel) illustrates rather starkly the tension in Ignatius between Christian tradition and Old Testament Scripture. Robert Grant has argued that Ignatius, in his arguments with the false teachers, did not find the quotation of scriptural texts a helpful way to reply. He preferred rather the revelatory events of Christian history to the quotation of Scripture.[82] He further asserts that though there is no reason to think that Ignatius did not know the Pauline letters, as well as the gospels of Matthew and John, he attached little direct authority to Scripture as Scripture and viewed apostolic tradition as of paramount importance. In which case, he also saw the New Testament materials as part of that tradition.[83] In that regard, however, it is difficult to know precisely what the practical difference is between seeing Christian material as authoritative Scripture or seeing it as authoritative tradition. Jerry Sumney sees in the Ign. *Phld.* 8:2 text a debate over how the early Christians identify authority and interpret Scripture. Ignatius' opponents, according to Sumney, see the Old Testament as the primary authority, whereas Ignatius accepts a larger canon with Christ as the final authority.[84] Hence, we see in Ignatius a struggle over how to understand Christian Scripture and tradition and where to apply the relative weight of christological authority.

Casting the discussion more generally in terms of the Apostolic Fathers, Daniel Hoffman asserts that "Scripture" for the Apostolic Fathers was the Old Testament and that references to the New Testament writings

---

[81] See above, p. 130.
[82] Grant, "Scripture and Tradition," 323. See also Ign. *Magn.* 8:1–9:2.
[83] Ibid., 327.
[84] Sumney, "Those Ignorantly Deny Him," 353–55.

were rare, even though the content of these documents was often alluded to favorably.[85] Because Ignatius often only alludes to New Testament material without any introductory formulae, it is difficult to determine Ignatius' view of the New Testament writings. However, Hoffman argues that when the allusions are compared to the high value given to the apostles and other Christian writers by Ignatius, it becomes apparent that the apostolic witness testified to in the Epistles and Gospels is the primary authority and is sometimes even placed above that of the Old Testament scriptures.[86] Hence, he concludes that the Apostolic Fathers saw the tradition of the New Testament books as of equal authority to that of the Old Testament.[87] But he makes another insightful point when he says that "tradition," while often thought of as a body of unwritten doctrine passed down through the church which is often contrasted with scripture, is in fact in the Apostolic Fathers better understood as "authoritative delivery." Whether or not it was handed down orally or in textual form, "tradition" referred to the doctrine committed to the church by Christ and his apostles. Hence, scripture and tradition were not considered to be something different or opposed.[88]

What this means for Ignatius and the Pauline tradition is that the Pauline material has familiarity and apostolic authority for him as tradition, if not yet as fully sacred text or canon. In that regard, Ignatius also hints at something detected earlier in the case of the Pastoral Epistles, the early movement of the Pauline material to the level of sacred tradition (writ) where that material begins to exercise an influence on the way apostolic doctrine will be understood, handed on, and used in the future. In that regard, Ignatius' letters appear, as we have seen, to be heir to a Pauline tradition that already reflects the imprint of the Pastoral letters and their handing on of the tradition of the apostle. The guarding of the "good deposit" of the Pastorals is implicit in Ignatius' concept of orthodoxy, correct teaching, and its defense for the sake of church unity. His Christology also exhibits markers that are consistent with the Christology of the Pastorals and at variance with the christological terminology of the undisputed Pauline letters. Moreover, his concept of ministry is clearly an extension and continuation of that represented by 1 Timothy and Titus. Though the theology, Christology, and ecclesiology of Ignatius represent anything but a fixed, unchanging deposit, they appear to be a "good deposit" in the sense of an authoritative tradition authoritatively delivered and applied under the circumstances of the author's grand procession to Rome and martyrdom. The authority of the "good deposit" resides in the continuation of apostolic tradition in the church properly ordered, not in the fixedness of the tradition.

---

[85] Hoffman, "The Authority of Scripture and Apostolic Doctrine," 72.
[86] Ibid., 73.
[87] Ibid., 73.
[88] Ibid., 73–74.

Ignatius and Martyrdom

A. T. Hanson claims that, as in the Pastorals, Ignatius (1) holds Paul up as an example of martyrdom (Ign. *Eph.* 12:2), (2) has a theology of martyrdom where his own death is the fulfillment of his vocation, (3) connects suffering to the lives of all Christians (Ign. *Magn.* 5:2; 8:2, Ign. *Pol.* 3:1; 6:1), and (4) links Christian suffering with the passion of Christ (Ign. *Eph.*18:1; Ign. *Magn.* 5:2).[89] The absence of any reference to the cross of Christ in the Pastorals, however, contrasts with Ignatius who, according to Hanson, had a doctrine of Christian life as a process of sharing the passion, death, and resurrection of Christ.[90] He concludes that the Pastorals stand conceptually between Paul and Ignatius, but that the theology of suffering in Ignatius is more faithful to Paul than are the Pastoral Epistles.[91] The first observation that must be made is that the notion of suffering is only really emphasized in 2 Timothy and that it may be, as we have argued, that 2 Timothy and 1 Timothy & Titus are not written by the same author. Thus, we cannot assume that there is a theology of suffering in all three Pastoral letters. Second Timothy may only hint at suffering with Christ in 2:11 and the letter clearly focuses on Paul's suffering and the plea for Timothy to suffer according to the example of Paul. Ignatius blends these. Paul is a sufferer in whose footsteps Ignatius follows (Ign. *Eph.*12:2) and the suffering Christian participates in the passion and death of Christ (Ign. *Magn.* 5:2; 18:1). In this, Ignatius seems to be influenced by the traditions of suffering represented in both Paul's own letters and in 2 Timothy. Both lines of tradition feed into Ignatius and can be detected in his theology of suffering.

## *Polycarp, Bishop of Smyrna*

Polycarp's letter to the church at Philippi as we have it today may be a composite text, though that question is still debated.[92] For the purposes of this discussion, we will follow the conclusion of Dehandschutter asserting that the critical problems of the text are best solved if we see the text as a unity.[93] Even if the epistle were in fact a composite text, with the so-called

---

[89] A. T. Hanson, "The Theology of Suffering in the Pastoral Epistles and Ignatius of Antioch," in StPatr (ed. Elizabeth A. Livingstone, 17, 2; Oxford: Pergamon, 1982), 695–96.

[90] Ibid., 695.

[91] Ibid., 695–96.

[92] See Boudewijn Dehandschutter, "Polycarp's Epistle to the Philippians: An Early Example of 'Reception' " in *The New Testament in Early Christianity* (Bibliotheca Ephemeridum Theologicarum Louvaniensium, 86; ed. Jean-Marie Sevrin; Leuven: Leuven University Press-Uitgeverij Peeters, 1989), 278; P. N. Harrison, *Polycarp's Two Epistles to the Philippians* (Cambridge: Cambridge University Press, 1936); and Koester, *Introduction to the New Testament*, 2:306.

[93] Dehandschutter, "Polycarp's Epistle to the Philippians," 278.

second epistle written some years after the first,[94] that would not necessarily alter our argument here. Hence, there is no need for us in this discussion to debate that text critical issue once again. Polycarp in all likelihood was martyred in the year 156 C.E.,[95] but his letter to the Philippians was probably written near the time of Ignatius' martyrdom, somewhere between 110–117 C.E.[96] According to the two epistle hypothesis, the Christian community in Philippi had requested from Polycarp a copy of Ignatius' epistles, which he sent to them along with a letter of his own.[97] This letter included chapter 13 and perhaps also 14, which served as a cover letter to the Ignatian epistles. The second letter, including chapters 1–12, was written several years later.[98] In any case, the epistle as we now have it appears to be a real letter written at the invitation of the Philippians to exhort the community to a life of Christian righteousness (Pol. *Phil.* 3:1).[99] It also deals with the troubling case of Valens, a presbyter, who has apparently strayed from proper Christian conduct in his duties to the community (Pol. *Phil.* 11:1–4).

Polycarp and Paul

In writing to a Christian community that Paul established and with which he had an intimate relationship many years earlier, Polycarp's letter quite naturally has a connection to Paul, or at least to the legacy of Paul as rooted in that church. In this light, Polycarp writes in 3:3: "For neither am I, nor any other like me, able to follow the wisdom of the blessed and glorious Paul, who when he was among you formerly face-to-face taught accurately and steadfastly the word concerning truth (word of truth), who also when he was absent wrote epistles to you, from the study of which you will be able to build yourselves up into the faith which was given to you." Polycarp also refers to Paul in 9:1, where he exhorts the Philippians to obey the word in all righteousness and to endure with the endurance they have seen in Ignatius, Zosimus, and Rufus, but also "in others among yourselves, in Paul himself,[100] and the other apostles." And in 11:2–3, he makes reference to a teaching of Paul, who he mentions labored among the Philippians, that "the saints shall judge the world." Dehandschutter observes that Polycarp knows that Paul is "their apostle" and refers implicitly to Paul's letter to the Philippians (11:3).[101] Polycarp clearly held Paul in the highest esteem, recognized him to be a teacher of truth, and acknowledged him to be a writer of

---

[94] Johannes Quasten, *Patrology* (Utrecht-Antwerp: Spectrum, 1966), 1:79–80.
[95] Ibid., 77.
[96] Ibid., 79–80 and Dehandschutter, "Polycarp's Epistle to the Philippians," 278.
[97] Quasten, *Patrology*, 1:79.
[98] Koester, *Introduction to the New Testament*, 2:306.
[99] Dehandschutter, "Polycarp's Epistle to the Philippians," 279.
[100] Charles Merritt Nielsen emphasizes the intensive pronoun as underscoring the special status of Paul for Polycarp ("Polycarp, Paul, and the Scriptures," *AThR* 47 [1965]: 211).
[101] Ibid., 281.

epistles which are able to edify the faith of his Philippian addressees. It is worth observing that Polycarp identifies Paul as a teacher in 3:2 and 11:2, also an important identification for Paul in the Pastoral Epistles.[102] After Paul, the Pauline tradition tends to emphasize, among other attributes, Paul the teacher. This is exemplified in both the Pastorals and Polycarp, but does not appear to diminish for these writers Paul's authority as an apostle. The further recognition by Polycarp that Paul wrote letters that have a role in building up the Philippians in their faith indicates that his letters,[103] especially the letter he wrote to the Philippians, have authority and as such can be referred to as part of the historical background introducing his exhortation to the church. This is direct evidence of the esteem that had accrued to his letters in Polycarp's view and of their value to this community. Whether they are yet considered sacred Scripture may be an open question, but they certainly have significant authority and illustrate an important stage in the process leading to the formation of a Pauline canon. Moreover, we are told they have particular value in building up the faith of the Philippians (cf. 2 Tim 3:14–16).

Harrison concluded in 1936: "Of Philemon we find no trace. But neither this fact nor the relative weakness of the evidence for Polycarp's use of Colossians and 1 Thessalonians alters the incontestable fact, which emerges from a close study of his Epistle as a whole, that he must have been very familiar with a Corpus Paulinum including at least seven of our canonical ten Paulines."[104] He also pointed to evidence that Polycarp knew the Pastorals, especially 1 Timothy.[105] Taking a slightly different view, Dehandschutter claims that Polycarp knows all of Paul's letters except Colossians, 1 Thessalonians, Philemon, and Titus.[106] Lindemann concludes that Polycarp was probably familiar with 1 and 2 Corinthians, Galatians,[107] Ephesians, and with at least 1 Timothy among the Pastorals. He also knew that Paul had written to the Philippians.[108] Concerning the Pastoral Epistles, Koester argues that the language and style of admonition in Polycarp's letter corresponds

---

[102] See above, pp. 29–30, 41, 45, 91–93.

[103] Lindemann thinks the use of the plural (letters) does not mean that Polycarp knew of several letters written by Paul to the Philippians but that the letters to whomever they were written can strengthen the Christians ("Writings of the Apostolic Fathers," 41).

[104] Harrison, *Polycarp's Two Epistles*, 294.

[105] Ibid., 294–95. See also his references to the Pastorals in Polycarp: the savior language in Polycarp's greeting compared to Titus 1:4; 3:6; the "not by works" terminology in Pol. *Phil.* 1:3 to Titus 3:5–7; the expression in the "present age" in Pol. *Phil.* 5:2 to Titus 2:12; and Pol. *Phil.* 12:3 which is conflated in 1 Tim 4:15 and Titus 3:14.

[106] Dehandschutter, "Polycarp's Epistle to the Philippians," 281. Cf. also Pol. *Phil.* 4–6 to the Pastorals.

[107] Pol. *Phil.* 1:3 seems to echo Paul's theology in Romans and Galatians: ". . . by grace you are saved, not by works, but by the will of God through Jesus Christ."

[108] Lindemann, "Writings of the Apostolic Fathers," 43–44.

closely to the Pastorals, though statements that appear to be quotations from the Pastoral letters are rare.[109] Perhaps the most bold and creative, though clearly hypothetical, attempt to connect Polycarp and the Pastorals is Hans von Campenhausen's argument that Polycarp is the author of the Pastoral Epistles.[110] Although this is finally an unpersuasive thesis, there can be no doubt about the strong links between the letter of Polycarp to the Philippians and the Pastoral Epistles. We, however, are interested in seeing how the Pastoral Epistles and their view of Paul have shaped the Pauline legacy in Polycarp.

### Paraenesis and False Teaching

Although Polycarp does not identify any particular group of false teachers or their arguments, he does display a concern for false teaching.[111] In Pol. *Phil.* 7:1–2, he writes: "For everyone who does not confess that Jesus Christ has come in the flesh is an antichrist; and whoever does not confess the testimony of the cross is from the devil; and whoever perverts the words of the Lord for his own desires and says there is neither resurrection nor judgment, this man is the first born of satan. Wherefore, leaving the foolishness of the crowd, and their false teaching (ψευδοδιδασκαλίας), let us turn back to the word that was delivered to us at the beginning." Four doctrinal elements are important for Polycarp: Jesus' coming in the flesh, the cross, the resurrection (cf. Pol. *Phil.* 2:1–2), and judgment.[112] The failure to confess these or their perversion bring from Polycarp the harshest of accusations: such people are an antichrist, from the devil, or the first-born of Satan.

In the structure of Polycarp's theological worldview, there is as we have seen in the Pastorals and Ignatius a fundamental concern for true and false teaching (cf. Pol. *Phil.* 10:1). Although Polycarp does not seek theologically or on the basis of scriptural interpretation to argue for the truth, as Paul might in the face of his opponents, he presumes certain theological tenets that represent the truth and uses these as markers to distinguish false teaching. Moreover, as we saw in 3:2, Polycarp portrays Paul as a teacher of the word of truth, without defining what the content of that truth is. By doing so, he makes a statement about Paul and his place as an esteemed figure in the

---

[109] Koester, *Introduction to the New Testament*, 2:306–7. He points, however, to the instructions concerning women, deacons, young people, and presbyters in Pol. *Phil.* 4–6, the catalogs of virtues and vices in Pol. *Phil.* 2:2; 4:3; 5:2; 12:2, the admonition to pray for the government, and the warning against avarice in 4:1 as all reflecting instructions in the Pastorals.

[110] Hans von Campenhausen, "Polykarp von Smyrna und die Pastoralbriefe," in *Aus der Frühzeit des Christentums* (Tübingen: J. C. B. Mohr [Paul Siebeck], 1963), 197–252.

[111] Koester, *Introduction to the New Testament*, 307.

[112] In the greeting of the letter, Polycarp refers to ". . . Jesus Christ, our savior." The appellation savior is found in the Pastorals and Ignatius, but it is uncommon is Paul's undisputed letters, being found only in Phil 3:20.

church, and in this statement he implicitly reveals his concern for the truth of the church's teaching in the face of false teaching. As Ignatius and the author(s) of the Pastorals, Polycarp expresses this in his own peculiar fashion in light of his circumstances,[113] but in each of these cases there is a sense that the truth, the sound teaching, has been stabilized, perhaps even reduced to certain fundamental tenets that are asserted as constituting the truth. In Paul's own letters, there is a greater sense that the truth, at least in part, is still being discovered or worked out. In Polycarp's letter that sense has receded, and on that level Polycarp represents the theological world of the Pastoral Epistles and the letters of Ignatius more closely than the world of the historical Paul. Perhaps this is what 1 and 2 Timothy mean by the expression the "good deposit."

Polycarp also exhorts the Philippians in Pol. *Phil.* 7:2 to turn back to the word that was delivered in the beginning. From the temporal perspective of this text, there is a sense that the truth was delivered at the origin of things, and from the context that seems to mean that the beginning is christologically oriented for Polycarp.[114] The theological orientation is to the past as the time of delivery, and there appears to be neither an explicit nor an implicit sense of the progressive revelation of truth. What is theologically important in principle was delivered at the beginning, and the problem is that people have turned away from it. The solution is to turn back, and that is what Polycarp exhorts them to do. This may also represent another aspect of the postapostolic period of the church. The greater the church's sense of its past, the more there is in the past to occupy its theological attention, and the greater the impulse to get back to the foundation of the truth. However, there is much theological and apocalyptic thought in the very early period of the church that also focuses on the beginning (for example, the image of the old creation and the new creation).

The tenor of much of Polycarp's letter to the Philippians is paraenetic and exhortative. For example, in 4:1 he warns them against avarice, in 4:2 he calls upon them to teach their wives to remain steadfast in the faith, and in 4:3 he exhorts them to teach the widows to be discreet in the faith and to refrain from all evil. In chapter 5, Polycarp calls upon all Christians and in particular the deacons and younger men to be righteous, which he spells out in a veritable catalog of virtues. He calls for perseverance in hope and the pledge of righteousness in the face of suffering and martyrdom, according to the example of the martyrs who have gone before (Pol. *Phil.* 8 and 9). And in

---

[113] In all of these authors, that expression is most often in terms of exhortation and paraenesis. The historical Paul certainly presumes to speak the truth and he exhorts people to obedience, but in the case of these later authors the relative proportion seems to have shifted from theology to exhortation.

[114] By "the beginning," he may mean specifically the incarnation (Christ in the flesh), the crucifixion (cross), and the resurrection. This, however, would also include the prophetic announcements of Christ in the Old Testament (Pol. *Phil.* 6:3).

chapter 10, he exhorts them to stand fast and follow the example of the Lord, followed by an elaboration of what that should mean for the Philippians. The extent of Polycarp's paraenetic material and his lists of appropriate behavior illustrate the bishop's preoccupation with communal relations in Philippi and has much in common with the Pastoral letters, even though it is not necessarily possible to derive these instructions from specific texts.[115] If Paul is important for Polycarp's paraenesis, as Dehandschutter asserts,[116] we would argue that it is a portrayal of Paul that to some extent has already been refracted through the lens of the Paul of the Pastoral Epistles. That does not mean that Polycarp was familiar with all or some of the Pastorals, but rather that he reflects a church ethos that is more like that of the Pastorals than much of the undisputed Pauline material: that is, a postapostolic historical perspective, a concern for maintaining the true teaching understood in terms of the "good deposit," the greater emphasis on paraenesis than on theological formulation, a more advanced sense of ecclesiological authority and structure, exhortations to obedience, and instructions concerning the qualities appropriate for church leaders.

## The Qualities Appropriate for Church Leaders

Like Ignatius, Polycarp is identified as a bishop, but like the apostle Paul in the Pastoral Epistles he addresses the qualities and characteristics appropriate for deacons and presbyters. Those aspiring to the office of bishop, however, do not figure in Polycarp's discussion. Much like the descriptions in 1 Timothy and Titus, Polycarp addresses most directly the personal qualities and characteristics necessary for persons in positions of special responsibility, as well as other classes of people such as women, young men, and widows. Though Polycarp can advise subjection to the deacons and presbyters (5:3), along the lines of Ignatius' repeated claims to be obedient to the bishop, for the most part he concerns himself with the worthiness of these individuals. In 5:2 he writes: "Likewise be blameless before his righteousness, as servants of God and Christ and not of man, not slanderers, not double talkers, lovers of money, temperate in all things, compassionate, careful, walking according to the truth of the Lord, who was the servant of all." And of presbyters he writes in 6:1: "And let the presbyters also be compassionate, merciful to all, bringing back those who have gone astray, caring for all the weak, not neglecting the widow or the orphan or the poor, but always providing for that which is good before God and man, refraining from all wrath, respect of persons, unjust judgment, being far from all love of money, not quickly believing evil against anyone, not hasty in judgment, knowing that we all owe the debt of sin." Though the language and tone of these descriptions echo those of 1 Timothy and Titus, the lists of qualities

---

[115] Dehandschutter, "Polycarp's Epistle to the Philippians," 281.
[116] Ibid., 282. Cf. Ign. *Phil.* 12:1–3.

and activities are not identical.[117] What is similar is Polycarp's emphasis on the character of the persons rather than the offices, which puts him closer in this regard to the Pastorals than to Ignatius. Given Polycarp's close connection to Ignatius historically, the differences between their discussions of church leaders probably owes more to their respective purposes in writing and the circumstances surrounding their correspondence than to any underlying difference of theological perspective. Polycarp adopts in his letter a tone of intimate encouragement (cf. 3:1–3), rather than the blunt language of obedience characteristic of Ignatius, with its more distant tone underwritten by the authority of the author's upcoming martyrdom. Koester argues that the letter of Polycarp shows how a bishop could conduct himself and order the affairs of the Christian churches in the spirit of Paul and of the Pastorals.[118] But in his admonitory tone and his style,[119] as well as in his concern for the qualities desirable for deacons, presbyters, and others, Polycarp actually resembles more closely the Paul of the Pastorals than the Paul of the seven undisputed letters.

Polycarp and Scripture

Polycarp undoubtedly held Paul in high esteem and attributed to him special apostolic status, but did he yet know a corpus of Pauline writings that he considered scriptural? This issue turns on how we read Pol. *Phil.* 12:1: "For I am confident that you are well versed in the scriptures (*sacris literis*). . . . Only, as it is said in these scriptures (*scripturis dictum*), 'Be you angry and sin not,' and 'Let not the sun go down on your wrath.'" Following the second reference to the Scriptures, Polycarp quotes Eph 4:26. Since the first part of the quotation also appears in Ps 4:5 LXX, the question becomes, did Polycarp refer to this quotation from the Psalm as Scripture or from Ephesians? Helmut Koester suggests the former, in which case there is no implication that Polycarp affirms Ephesians as Scripture.[120] On the other hand, Charles Nielsen argues that it is much more likely that Polycarp was not aware that the first part of the quotation came from the Psalm at all and thus simply reproduced Eph 4:26 as Scripture.[121] How are we to decide between these two positions?

A number of observations suggest that the latter option is the most probable. First, Polycarp displays no particular interest in quoting the Old Testament nor does he display any particular knowledge of it.[122] We know, however, that Polycarp viewed the prophets of the Old Testament as fore-

---

[117] Cf. the descriptions of the Pastorals above, pp. 66–69.

[118] Koester, *Introduction to the New Testament,* 2:307.

[119] Polycarp's humble tone also strikes the reader. See, e.g., Pol. *Phil.* 3:1–2; 12:1.

[120] Helmut Koester, *Synoptische Überlieferung bei den Apostolischen Vatern* (Berlin: Academie Verlag, 1957), 113.

[121] Nielsen, "Polycarp, Paul, and the Scriptures," 201.

[122] Ibid., 202.

telling the coming of Christ (Pol. *Phil.* 6:3), which may mean the Old Testament prophetic texts had the status of sacred literature for him. That, however, would not speak against identifying Ephesians as scripture in 12:1. Second, there are many allusions to Paul's letters in Polycarp's epistle.[123] Pauline material is clearly in Polycarp's mind as he writes to the Philippians. Third, Polycarp holds the apostle Paul in very high regard and this shows through in a number of instances (Pol. *Phil.* 3:3; 9:1; 11:2–3). Paul and what he represents (e.g., his letters) are of extremely high value for Polycarp. Fourth, as we have already argued, a sense of the Pauline scriptures can be detected already in the Pastoral letters.[124] Since there is little doubt that the Pastorals are earlier than Polycarp's letter to the Philippians and since both Polycarp and 1 and 2 Timothy are ostensibly associated with churches in western Asia Minor, it is suggestive to see that region as a Pauline heartland where not only Paul but his letters are of significant authority and status. If Paul is a figure of utmost importance for most of the Christians in this region and if his letters are his continuing legacy to them, it would make sense to think that his epistles are being held in the same esteem as Paul himself. After all, they are the very words of Paul who accurately taught the truth (Pol. *Phil.* 3:2). And if Paul is the apostle of Jesus Christ, his words are true and have an aura of sanctity. Fifth, Polycarp in 3:2 refers to the letters Paul wrote, but more than that the study of these letters is able to contribute to the building up of the faith of the Philippians. Hence, if these letters are the words of the apostle who taught accurately the word of truth and if they are able to edify the faithful, the epistles possess most of the attributes normally associated with sacred scripture. Furthermore, though stated in more general terms, these attributes would certainly be consistent with 2 Tim 3:14–16. For these reasons, it is probable that Polycarp, and perhaps also the people to whom he is writing, consider a body of Pauline writings to have sacred authority, to be scripture.

This, however, does not settle the issue of the nature and extent of his Pauline corpus. There are many allusions to Paul's letters in Polycarp's letter, but it is difficult to translate these into certainty regarding his Pauline corpus.[125] It seem likely, however, that Polycarp knew some form of 1 and 2 Corinthians, Galatians, Philippians, Ephesians, and 1 Timothy. He may have known in some form Romans, 2 Timothy, and Titus as well. It is not clear that he had any knowledge of Philemon, 1 Thessalonians, and Colossians. This would also suggest that the body of Pauline letters Polycarp in fact knew was still fairly fluid as a body of letters and not yet formed into anything resembling a stable, canonical corpus of epistles. And none of this rules out the possibility that Polycarp knew some Pauline material from the oral tradition, which makes it especially difficult to ascertain with

---

[123] See the examples identified above, p. 142.
[124] See above, pp. 93–100.
[125] See the proposals cited above, pp. 142–43.

certainty Polycarp's familiarity with specific Pauline texts. That Polycarp held certain Pauline writings to be scriptural is highly probable, but that we can know with much confidence the limits of that Pauline corpus is improbable.

## *Clement of Rome:* 1 Clement

According to Eusebius,[126] Clement was the third successor of Peter in Rome, and he sets the 12th year of Domitian's reign as the beginning of his office and the third year of Trajan's reign as the end. This would mark his dates in office from 92 C.E. to 101 C.E.,[127] in other words slightly before either Ignatius or Polycarp. A controversy in the church in Corinth, where some people apparently had rebelled against local ecclesiastical authority, caused Clement to write to the Corinthians. Though only a minority of the Corinthian Christians maintained their loyalty to the ousted presbyters, Clement wrote to them in an attempt to restore order and repair the damage done to the community.[128] According to Quasten, there is no reason to believe that the Corinthians appealed to the bishop of Rome to take action against the wayward elements in Corinth,[129] thereby signaling that the Roman church or the bishop in particular had achieved a preeminent ecclesiastical status in ordering the church and settling disputes. It is more likely that word of the difficulty in Corinth had reached Rome as travelers from Corinth arrived bringing their accounts of the dissension.[130] The letter commonly known as *1 Clement* is Clement's attempt to deal with that discord, the report of which has made its way to Rome.

### Clement, Paul, and Scripture

Clement first makes reference to Paul in *1 Clem.* 5:5–7, immediately after he refers to Peter who underwent many trials and went to the place of glory. He reports that Paul showed the way to the prize of endurance through jealousy and strife. He was imprisoned seven times, exiled, stoned, and was a herald in both the East and the West. Clement portrays Paul in this text as showing the way to the prize of endurance (ὑπομονῆς) in the face of affliction, a herald (κήρυξ), one who taught (διδάξης) righteousness and gave testimony (μαρτυρήσας), and who is himself the greatest example of endurance (μέγιστος ὑπογραμμός). Lindemann argues

---

[126] *Hist eccl.* 3,15, 34. See Irenaeus, *Haer.* 3, 3, 3, who also identifies Clement as the third successor.

[127] Quasten, *Patrology*, 1:42.

[128] Ibid., 43.

[129] Ibid., 43.

[130] Ibid., 43. It is, however, true as Tugwell observes that Clement and the Roman church did assume authority to intervene and may have begun to assume some responsibility for other churches (*Apostolic Fathers*, 90).

that Paul is not overshadowed by Peter but the other way around. Clement portrays Paul as the decisive figure, describing him in more impressive fashion than Peter.[131] Lindemann writes: "Paul is presented to the readers in Corinth as a truly unique pattern of patient endurance. He is the antitype of the Corinthian Christians, who had fallen into *stasis* instead of standing firm in *hypomone*."[132]

Paul appears in *1 Clement* again in 47:1–4, where the author writes: "Take up the epistle of the blessed Paul the apostle. What did he first write to you in the beginning of his preaching the gospel? With truth he charged you spiritually concerning himself and Cephas and Apollos for also then you made yourselves partisans. But that partisanship brought less guilt on you for you were partisans of apostles who were of reputation and of a man approved by them. But now consider who they are who have perverted you. . . ." Emphasizing the partisanship of the Corinthians, Clement distinguishes the apostles from the leaders of the partisan factions now threatening to tear the community apart and advises the Corinthians to read the epistle that Paul first wrote. Clement here combines apostolic authority (apostles and the man, Paul, approved by them) with the advice Paul, the blessed apostle, gave the Corinthians in his letter when he first preached the gospel to them. Two things are important: (1) factions remain persistent in Corinth and (2) Clement considers Paul's earlier response to them to be pertinent to the present Corinthian situation. By referring to that earlier epistle, Clement brings together in his letter the authority of Paul and the memory of Paul's words, and applies them to the persistent Corinthian problem a generation or two later. Whether or not that Pauline epistle can be called scriptural, Clement considers it to have real authority, to reveal the persistent Corinthian tendency towards division, to be applicable to the present situation, and to be the truth. Moreover, Clement apparently presumes the Corinthians still have access to a copy of that earlier letter.[133] Perhaps this should not surprise us, but it is direct evidence that Paul's letter—perhaps letters—were extant in Corinth, and that a church authority figure in Rome considered it to have value beyond its own day. Given the laudatory terms the author uses to describe Paul in this text, that earlier Pauline letter is more than a letter containing good advice of which the Corinthians ought to take note. The words of this epistle are the words of a blessed apostle and are the truth spoken in the Spirit.

The most thorough investigation of Clement's use of Old and New Testament texts is that by Donald Hagner.[134] It is not surprising, as he points out, that 1 Corinthians is the most clearly attested New Testament

---

[131] Lindemann, *Writings of the Apostolic Fathers*, 29.
[132] Ibid., 30.
[133] Lindemann, "Writings of the Apostolic Fathers," 31.
[134] Donald A. Hagner, *The Use of the Old and New Testaments in Clement of Rome* (NovTSup 34; Leiden: E. J. Brill, 1973).

writing in Clement,[135] and it is the only one assigned an author by him.[136] The use of 2 Corinthians material is certainly less clear than 1 Corinthians, but according to Hagner there is a strong possibility that Clement also knew 2 Corinthians.[137] There is also an *a priori* assumption that Clement of Rome knew Paul's letter to the Romans, and in light of the virtual citation of Rom 1:29–32 in *1 Clem.* 35:5–6 there is every reason to think he knew that epistle.[138] He also concludes that it is rather likely that Clement also knew and made use of Galatians,[139] though it is somewhat less probable that he knew or was acquainted with Philippians.[140] With regard to Ephesians and Colossians, Hagner concludes that Clement was probably familiar with Ephesians and that a strong possibility exists that he was also familiar with Colossians.[141]

Although P. N. Harrison and others have made the argument that Clement is not dependent on the Pastorals but the other way around,[142] this is not a scholarly position that has normally carried the day. Given the stance that was taken in chapter 4, that the Pastorals were likely written within 20–25 years of Paul's death, and earlier in this chapter, that the Pastorals are still within an apostolic frame of reference where epistles can be written persuasively in the name of Paul, it is unlikely that they are second century documents. Furthermore, the second century dating of the Pastoral letters often goes hand in hand with the identification of the opposition in the Pastorals as gnostic, but there is no hard evidence to identify any of these opponents as gnostic in any meaningful sense of the term.[143] Likewise, to make the Pastorals contemporaneous with or subsequent to the epistles of Ignatius appears anachronistic based on the greater ecclesiastical development and presumed authority of the bishop in his letters. Hence, it is preferable to conclude that the Pastoral Epistles are earlier than *1 Clement* and

---

[136] Ibid., 195–209. See, e.g., allusions and echoes in *1 Clement* to 1 Corinthians: *1 Clem.* 34:8 to 1 Cor 2:9; *1 Clem.* 40:1 to 1 Cor 2:10; *1 Clem.* 7:1 to 1 Cor 4:14; *1 Clem.* 34:2 to 1 Cor 8:6; *1 Clem.* 37:3, 5; 38:1; 46:7; 48:5 to 1 Cor 12; *1 Clem.* 49:5–50:1 to 1 Cor 13:13; *1 Clem.* 24:5, to 1 Cor 15.

[137] Hagner, *Use of Old and New Testament*, 195.

[138] Ibid., 212. See, e.g., allusions and echoes in *1 Clement* to 2 Corinthians: *1 Clem.* 5:5 to 2 Cor 11:23–29; *1 Clem.* 36:2 to 2 Cor 3:18; *1 Clem.* 2:7 to 2 Cor 9:8 (cf. also 2 Tim 2:21; 3:17; Titus 3:1); *1 Clem.* 2:8 to 2 Cor 3:3.

[139] Hagner, *Use of the Old and New Testament*, 215–16. See, e.g., allusions in *1 Clement* to Romans: *1 Clem.* 32:2 to Rom 9:4–5; *1 Clem.* 33:1 to Rom 6:1. Cf. Lindemann, "Writings of the Apostolic Fathers," 32–34.

[140] Hagner, *Use of the Old and New Testament*, 222. See, e.g., allusions and echoes in *1 Clement* to Galatians: *1 Clem.* 5:2 to Gal 2:9; *1 Clem.* 56:1 to Gal 6:1; *1 Clem* 31:2 to Gal 3.

[141] Hagner, *Use of the Old and New Testament*, 228–29. See, e.g., allusions and echoes in *1 Clement* to Philippians: *1 Clem.* 21:1 to Phil 1:27; *1 Clem.* 16:2 to Phil 2; *1 Clem.* 7:1 to Phil 1:30.

[141] Hagner, *Use of the Old and New Testament*, 226, 230.

[142] Ibid., 230.

[143] See above, pp. 64–66.

also earlier than the letters of Ignatius and Polycarp. If that is correct, any references or allusions to the Pastorals in *1 Clement* may indicate Clement's familiarity with those letters as part of a Pauline corpus, or at least familiarity with the traditions represented by those letters.

In that light, Hagner claims that the numerous allusions to 1 Timothy in *1 Clement* taken collectively suggest that the author was influenced by the first Pastoral Epistle.[144] But there are also numerous allusions to Titus and together these, too, may suggest that Clement was familiar with this letter as well.[145] It is perhaps somewhat less likely that he was acquainted with 2 Timothy.[146] In any case, what we find in *1 Clement* is that allusions and echoes to the Pastoral letters abound, but there is no overt attempt on the part of the author to draw these documents directly into his admonition to the Corinthians. Hence, we can see no particular Pastoral slant on his use of the other Pauline material. And more broadly, apart from 1 Corinthians, there is no explicit evidence that he held these or the other Pauline letters to be authoritative, though that perhaps may be inferred from his allusions to these documents and from his obvious esteem for the apostle.

If Hagner is correct, Clement had knowledge of a Pauline corpus including Romans, 1 Corinthians, Galatians, Ephesians, Philippians, 1 Timothy, Titus, and possibly 2 Corinthians, Colossians, and 2 Timothy.[147] In general terms, the value of Hagner's proposal is that it is suggestive of the importance of Paul and his letters for the churches in Rome and Corinth. It is less certain that we can know the precise limits of Clement's Pauline corpus, and even less clear that we can see any particular interpretive slant on Paul's letters or his theology,[148] apart from his desire to use Paul's words in 1 Corinthians to combat the persistent factionalism of the Corinthian church. It would also suggest, however, that in Rome the contours of some kind of Pauline corpus (canon?) were beginning to take shape and that this preliminary corpus also includes Pastoral material. We cannot yet detect that this Pauline corpus or preliminary canon yet functioned with an organizing interpretive center, apart perhaps from some concern for church

---

[144] Hagner, *Use of Old and New Testament,* 232. See, e.g., allusions and echoes in *1 Clement* to 1 Timothy: *1 Clem.* 42:4 to 1 Tim 3:10; *1 Clem.* 29:1 to 1 Tim 2:8; *1 Clem.* 61:2 to 1 Tim 1:17; *1 Clem.* 21:7 to 1 Tim 5:21; *1 Clem.* 60:4 to 1 Tim 2:7; *1 Clem.* 33:7 to 1 Tim 2:9–10; *1 Clem.* 1:3 to 1 Tim 2:9–15; *1 Clem.* 51:3 to 1 Tim 5:24–25.

[145] Hagner, *Use of the Old and New Testament,* 234–36. See, e.g., allusions and echoes in *1 Clement* to Titus: *1 Clem.* 1:3 to Titus 2:3–5; *1 Clem.* 2:7 to Titus 3:1; *1 Clem.* 42:4 to Titus 1:5; *1 Clem.* 32:3 to Titus 3:5; *1 Clem.* 64:1 to Titus 2:14.

[146] Hagner, *Use of the Old and New Testament,* 233–36, See, e.g., allusions and echoes in *1 Clement* to 2 Timothy: *1 Clem.* 44:2 to 2 Tim 2:2; *1 Clem.* 45:2 to 2 Tim 3:15–16; *1 Clem.* 53:1 to 2 Tim 3:15–16; *1 Clem.* 45:7 to 2 Tim 1:3; *1 Clem.* 30:1 to 2 Tim 2:22; *1 Clem.* 27:3 to 2 Tim 1:6; *1 Clem.* 44:5 to 2 Tim 4:6.

[147] Hagner, *Use of the Old and New Testament,* 237.

[148] See Lindemann's exposition of Pauline themes in *1 Clement* ("Writings of the Apostolic Fathers," 32–36).

unity under a kind of episcopal/presbyterian leadership. Even though Clement was not an exegete of the Pauline texts as such, material from them echo through his words as he admonishes the Corinthians and advises them to read the words Paul first preached to them.

That Clement had a dynamic view of Scripture is clear in 45:1–3 and 53:1, where he makes reference to the "sacred scriptures." In 45:2, he acknowledges that the Corinthians have studied the sacred Scriptures, which are true and are given through the Holy Spirit. Likewise there is, he asserts, nothing unjust or counterfeit in them. And in 53:1, he once again affirms that they understand the sacred Scriptures and that they have studied the oracles of God (τὰ λόγια τοῦ Θεοῦ).[149] Immediately following in each case, Clement makes reference to Old Testament material, which he then applies to the Corinthian situation.[150] Although the terminology is different from that found in 2 Tim 3:15–16, these two references share with 2 Timothy an explicit and lofty view of Scripture's sacredness, as well as its value for the present. Clement has yet to elevate any of Paul's epistles to the level of sacred and divine authority found in 2 Timothy, but some of them, at least 1 Corinthians, appear not to be far away in light of 47:1–4.

Clement and the Church

Unlike the Pastoral Epistles, Ignatius' letters, and to a lesser extent Polycarp's letter to the Philippians, *1 Clement* does not address the issue of false teaching and false teachers.[151] The author's prime concern is the dissension in the Corinthian community, precipitated by the ouster from office of certain presbyters (44:1–6, 47:6, 54:2, 57:1). For Clement, where there is strife, the spirit of Christ cannot exist.[152] In 42:1–5, Clement establishes the chain of gospel reception and the church's ministry and order. The apostles received the gospel from Jesus Christ who was sent from God (Christ is from the God and the apostles from Christ), and receiving their commands and being reassured by Christ's resurrection, they went forth preaching the good news that the kingdom of God is coming and appointed their first converts to be overseers (bishops) and deacons. Authority is clearly passed down, which might imply an issue of succession. Furthermore, this is not a new method, for according to Isa 60:17 this procedure of appointing was long established.

---

[149] Cf. Rom 3:2.

[150] In the first case, it is to Daniel, Ananias, Azarias, and Misael, and in the second to Moses. Herbert T. Mayer claims that Clement quotes the Old Testament 166 times but that it is not clear that he had read the Old Testament through and really understood it. He thinks Clement had before him collections of Old Testament quotations ("Clement of Rome and His Use of Scripture," *Concordia Theological Monthly* 42 [1971]: 537).

[151] Koester, *Introduction to the New Testament*, 2:290.

[152] Mayer, "Clement of Rome and His Use of Scripture," 538–39.

Kenneth Steinhauser claims that the designations "overseer" (ἐπί-σκοπος) and "elder" (πρεσβύτερος) are used interchangeably in *1 Clement*,[153] and *1 Clem.* 44:4–5 may indicate that this is in fact the case. Since these terms are used interchangeably only in *1 Clement*, argues Steinhauser, the reason for this should be found in *1 Clement* itself. For him, the reason why Clement uses these terms synonymously is that since the Roman church is primarily Jewish and the Corinthian church primarily Gentile, the author used the terminology distinctive to each community.[154] If this is correct, *1 Clement* stands apart from the Pastorals, Ignatius, and Polycarp, suggesting that the order, ministry, and terminology of the church in Asia Minor is somewhat different from that in the West, Rome and Corinth in particular.[155] Even though *1 Clement* exhibits allusions to the Pastoral letters, it also may be that ecclesiologically the Pastorals are more at home in the tradition of Asia Minor than of the West. In the case of 1 Timothy, this would certainly make sense, with Ephesus being the apparent destination of the epistle. It might also suggest that the author of 1 Timothy and Titus was not located in Rome when he wrote these epistles. This, however, is an argument at the margins, given the limited evidence available from *1 Clement*.

Whether *1 Clement* exhibits a concern for apostolic succession and the primacy of Rome is a much-debated issue. Helmut Koester thinks there is no interest in the issue of apostolic succession in *1 Clement*, but rather a concern about the stability and continuation of the church.[156] Simon Tugwell argues that it would be anachronistic to see in *1 Clement* any developed idea of Rome's primacy or of a Pope, yet Rome did presume some authority to intervene in Corinthian affairs.[157] Quasten states this even more strongly when he claims that the "Bishop of Rome" thought it a matter of duty to take the Corinthian matter in hand (see *1 Clem.* 59:1–2).[158] This would suggest that Rome and its leadership had some level of importance, but not yet primacy, in church affairs. Steinhauser argues that the implication of 42:1–5 is that, rather than the intervention of the Holy Spirit, succession itself is what is important. Apostolic succession is the foundation of authority and is important because it is according to God's plan.[159] In this regard, once again,

---

[153] Kenneth B. Steinhauser, "Authority in the Primitive Church," *Patristic and Byzantine Review* 3– (1984): 93. See also Tugwell, *Apostolic Fathers*, 91.

[154] Ibid., 94.

[155] See Peter Lampe, *From Paul to Valentinus: Christians at Rome in the First Two Centuries* (trans. by Michael Steinhauser; Minneapolis: Fortress, 2003), 397–408, 410. Lampe argues that the diversity of Christian groups and the diversity of doctrines in Rome is linked to the delay of the rise of the monarchical episcopacy in the capital. The monarchical office of bishop established itself in Rome later than in the East, but when it did establish itself it soon achieved a position of primacy.

[156] Koester, *Introduction to the New Testament*, 2:290.

[157] Tugwell, *Apostolic Fathers*, 90.

[158] Quasten, *Patrology*, 1:46–47.

[159] Steinhauser, "Authority in the Primitive Church," 94.

the author of 1 Timothy and Titus, Ignatius, and Polycarp display no concern for the issue of succession as such. 1 Timothy and Titus (also Polycarp to some extent) are concerned, in contrast, with the qualities and characteristics of the persons who aspire to these offices, which is a significantly different issue.[160]

## Conclusion

Ignatius, Polycarp, and Clement all hold Paul in the highest esteem. For Ignatius, Paul was "sanctified," "approved," "worthy of blessing," an example to be followed on the way to martyrdom. He, along with Peter, is an apostle and thus in a special category never to be attained by Ignatius, even in martyrdom. Polycarp lauds him as "the blessed and glorious Paul" who taught the word of truth and who wrote epistles that can build up the faith of the Philippians. In humble recognition, Polycarp confesses that neither he nor any like him can follow the wisdom of Paul. For Clement, Paul showed the way to the "prize of endurance" and once wrote a letter that is, even now, important to the troubled and divided Corinthians. In each case, the meaning and value of Paul conforms to the needs and circumstances of the author—the journey to martyrdom, the edification of the faithful, and the overcoming of division. Paul, the person, functions as an example, and Paul the letter writer, brings the word of truth that can edify the faithful and curb dissension. Implicit in all three of these descriptions, the temporal perspective is that of the postapostolic period. Unlike the Pastoral Epistles, where Paul is presented as an older contemporary of Timothy and Titus, these writers see the age of the apostles, notably Paul and Peter, as having given way to the postapostolic period of the church. They write in their own names and refer back to Paul. Still, both 1 Timothy and Titus, in their concern for church leaders, reflect and anticipate this development of the church, just as 2 Timothy in the plea to suffer as Paul has suffered anticipates the enduring and martyred Paul, who is revered by those called upon to suffer for their faith. In their representations of Paul's voice, the Pastorals stand closer, both theologically and historically, to the Paul of the undisputed Pauline epistles. But in terms of their concern for the good order and leadership of the household of God and for the church that suffers, they stand closer to the church of the Apostolic Fathers, especially the church of Ignatius and Polycarp.

A structural and conceptual divide runs through Ignatius' letters, and also to a slightly lesser extent through Polycarp's letter to the Philippians, between true and false teaching and between true or false teachers. This is not evident in *1 Clement*. In terms of theological structure, the letters of Ignatius and Polycarp represent a world similar to that found in the Pastoral

---

[160] Cf. the argument about the development of the church by Lampe, *From Paul to Valentinus*, 410.

letters. Though manifested in different ways, all of these letters presume a notion of truth that is not argued but asserted in order to combat false teaching and false teachers. 1 and 2 Timothy represent this as the "good deposit" that is to be guarded. At least conceptually, this seems to be in effect what Ignatius and Polycarp also represent. They appeal to the gospel, true doctrine, and true teachers, but they do not attempt theologically or on the basis of Scripture to defend and elaborate the truth. The authors of all of these letters exhort their addressees to the truth more than they persuade them of it, and these exhortations rest on certain foundations of authority—apostolic (Pastorals), episcopal (Ignatius and Polycarp), prospective martyrdom (Ignatius), tradition (all three). Clement also appeals to Paul's authority in his attempt to overcome the division in the Corinthian church, but in his case this may also represent the authority of the Roman church, which presumes some right to intercede in the affairs of the community in Corinth. In Clement's case, however, this concerns primarily ecclesiastical rather than doctrinal issues. In the Pastorals, as well as in the letters of Ignatius and Polycarp, we see a definite movement toward orthodoxy, which on the level of literary depiction has a defined and circumscribed quality. It is something to be guarded and handed on, not altered or deviated from.

The authors of 2 Timothy and *1 Clement* both make direct reference to the sacred Scriptures (the Old Testament) as authoritative and meaningful in the present. Ignatius, Polycarp, Clement, as well as the author(s) of the Pastorals also allude to and echo New Testament material, but most importantly for our purposes they are all influenced by Paul. As we have argued, the Pastorals, Polycarp, Clement, and to some extent also Ignatius all begin to attribute considerable authority and utility to Paul's letters and probably also reflect a corpus of Pauline material. If these authors did not yet consider Paul's writings technically to be Scripture, they certainly considered them to be part of the authoritative tradition, which, as we have seen,[161] is not necessarily differentiated from or opposed to Scripture. Scripture is part of the authoritative tradition, authoritatively passed on, and Paul's letters are clearly becoming part of that tradition. For all of these writers, that tradition is christologically shaped (see, e.g., Ign. *Phld.* 8:2). In the case of Ignatius' Christology, that tradition reflects elements of the Christology found in the Pastorals, namely the attribution of the title "savior" to Christ and the use of "appearance" language to describe the revelation of Christ. However, these writers are consistent with Pauline theology in that they do not portray the atonement in terms of the forgiveness of sins. This is not by and large a Pauline idea, and neither is it a feature of the theologies of these postapostolic writers. Righteousness by faith and not works, a conspicuous and powerful theme in Romans and Galatians, is reduced in the Pastorals, Ignatius, Polycarp, and Clement to the odd statement here and there. The

---

[161] See above, pp. 138–39.

poignant circumstances that gave rise to those arguments have now receded, though there is still concern in the Pastorals and Ignatius for those
who continue to observe Jewish law and practice.

In terms of the church and its ministry, 1 Timothy, Titus, Ignatius, and
Polycarp are consistent in their reflection of various church offices. Whereas
Ignatius focuses on obedience to episcopal authority, 1 Timothy, Titus, and
Polycarp emphasize the personal qualities appropriate for the individuals
who occupy these positions. Given the geographical and temporal proximity of Polycarp and Ignatius, these different emphases are not necessarily
inconsistent or indicative of substantive ecclesiastical differences, but probably represent the different perspectives and circumstances of the authors.
In that regard, Ignatius appears to represent a somewhat more mature
ecclesiology than does 1 Timothy or Titus, but they are clearly in the same
line of development. The ecclesiology found in the letters of Ignatius is an
extension of that found in 1 Timothy and Titus. In the case of *1 Clement,*
there is a terminological difference—the terms "bishop"/"overseer" and
"presbyter" are interchangeable—which may suggest a different level of ecclesiastical development along the Rome-Corinth axis than that found in
the eastern empire. If this is the case, the Pastorals are more reflective of the
development in the East.

At all of the critical points identified above, the theological worlds of
the Pastorals reflect, intersect, and in some cases presage the development
of orthodox Christianity as it emerges in the postapostolic period of the
church. Paul, his letters, and his theology are significant contributors to this
tradition, but more to the point for our purpose, the Pastoral Epistles are a
critical link in this continuing and expanding early church tradition. In certain cases (the strong emphasis on paraenesis, the abiding concern for correct belief and orthodox doctrine, the urgent desire for unity in the face of
divisive individuals, the persistent matter of church officers and ministers),
the Pastoral letters both reflect and shape the way important aspects of
Paul's legacy are being formed and passed on to the next generations of the
church. Paul, as we are beginning to see, is not only the hero of Christian
heretics—e.g., Marcion and the gnostics—but of important figures in the
"great church" traditions as well, and in that line of development the Pastoral Epistles figure prominently.

# ∿ 6 ∿

# PAUL, THE PASTORAL EPISTLES, AND THE EARLY CHURCH: IRENAEUS, TERTULLIAN, CLEMENT, ORIGEN, AND OTHER EARLY FIGURES

## INTRODUCTION

IN THIS chapter, we will explore the way the theological and ecclesiastical patterns of thought reflected in the Pastoral Epistles overlap and correspond (or do not overlap and correspond) to patterns found in important figures from the second and third centuries of the early church. Irenaeus, Tertullian, Clement of Alexandria, Origen, and other figures (Justin Martyr, Hippolytus, and Cyprian) represent different geographical locations and intellectual traditions, different ecclesiastical concerns and approaches, different ways of dealing with perceived heresy, and different roles within the church. The Pauline legacy, shaped through the tradition of the Pastorals, overlaps most significantly with the work of Irenaeus and Tertullian and less so with the extant writings of Clement and Origen. In part this is because of their respective positions in the church, their differing theological concerns, and their own particular sense of the church and its authority. In the case of Clement and Origen, their Alexandrian intellectual legacy and their roles as teachers, catechetical guides, and exegetes appear to lead them in different theological directions from those represented by the Pastorals. This is in contrast to Irenaeus who is deeply concerned about incorrect belief, the authority of the church, the rule of truth, the line of apostolic tradition, and correct behavior, concerns more amenable to those of the writer(s) of the Pastoral Epistles. In the case of Irenaeus, there is also his connection with Polycarp and the church in Asia Minor, a link that connects the church in the East with the church in the West.

# EAST MEETS WEST: IRENAEUS

## Introduction

Born in western Asia Minor, probably Smyrna, in the middle of the second century, Irenaeus became bishop of Lyon in southern Gaul shortly after his arrival in that city—in perhaps 177 or 178.[1] Irenaeus testifies as a youth to having seen Polycarp, the bishop of Smyrna and a man who until he was martyred taught the things he learned from the apostles, things which the church has handed down and which alone are true.[2] Not only does Irenaeus assert the line of Christ's truth passed down from the apostles to Polycarp and on to the church, but he also connects himself to that line of truth through the venerable martyr, a man whom he observed as a youth and a man who was steadfast in the service of the truth in the face of Valentinus, Marcion, and the other gnostics. Though a bishop of the church in the West, Irenaeus himself is rooted in the church of western Asia Minor,[3] and his conception of the church and its preservation of the truth is clearly shaped by his perception of the apostles, presumably Paul and John. Hence, theologically, ecclesiastically, and geographically Irenaeus is linked to the legacy of Paul, Polycarp, and more generally to the experience of the church in western Asia Minor (perhaps also to 1 and 2 Timothy and Ignatius).

Irenaeus is the first Christian author to display a comprehensive reception of the Pauline epistles,[4] and according to Rolf Noorman, his use of Paul stands already in a tradition of Pauline usage.[5] Hence, the claim that by the middle of the second century there was a "Pauline silence" or that Paul and his epistles had become the exclusive possession of the so-called heretics must be rejected.[6] For Irenaeus, Paul is not the only person considered an apostle.[7] Neither are Paul and his theology simply imposed on Irenaeus by the gnostics' appeal to the Apostle and his letters.[8] Irenaeus is an experienced Pauline exegete in his own right and a formative influence on the developing legacy of Paul.[9] Given Irenaeus' association with the church in

---

[1] Andrew J. Bandstra, "Paul and an Ancient Interpreter: A Comparison of the Teaching of Redemption in Paul and Irenaeus," *Calvin Theological Journal* 5 (1970): 46; and Quasten, *Patrology*, 1:287.

[2] *Haer.* 3:3:4.

[3] Bandstra, "Paul and an Ancient Interpreter," 46.

[4] Rolf Noormann, *Irenäus als Paulusinterpret*, 517.

[5] Ibid., 520.

[6] Ibid., 520.

[7] See *Haer.* 3:13:1; Noorman, *Irenäus als Paulusinterpret*, 517, 530.

[8] Ibid. 520–21; Richard A. Norris, Jr. "Irenaeus' Use of Paul in His Polemics Against the Gnostics," in *Paul and the Legacies of Paul* (ed. William S. Babcock; Dallas: Southern Methodist University Press, 1990), 79–80.

[9] Noorman, *Irenäus als Paulusinterpret*, 518, 531.

western Asia Minor and with Polycarp, this is not surprising. In the theological memory of Irenaeus, that region of the church and its link with Paul plays a crucial role in his attempt to assert the unity of the church. It also shapes his perception of the truth of the church's teaching in the face of gnostic opposition.[10] As Paul himself dealt with opposition in Asia Minor,[11] and as the writer(s) of 1 and 2 Timothy struggled to maintain what he (they) considered to be the true teaching of the church, so Irenaeus several decades later sought to use Paul and the Pauline letters to fend off gnostic claims. He did so by appealing to the unity of the church and the trustworthiness of the tradition passed on by the apostles and guarded by the church.

Though Irenaeus introduces *Adversus haereses* with a quote from 1 Tim 1:4, the Pastorals play only a small exegetical role in Irenaeus' attempt to interpret Paul. On the surface they appear to serve as little more than a source for the author's polemical statements.[12] Furthermore, according to Noorman, Adolf Harnack's claim that the Pastorals eased the church's reception of Paul's letters finds no basis in the evidence.[13] Although Irenaeus assumes the Pastorals are among the authentic letters of Paul, he does not rely on them for exegetical material, and they clearly play a subsidiary role in his use of the Pauline texts.[14] However, this is not the entire story, and though the argument that the Pastorals made possible the church's reception of Paul's letters is not supported by the evidence, it is the case that the Pastorals foreshadow already in the first century some of the major ecclesiological issues that will confront the church in the latter half of the second century and beyond. Hence, Irenaeus is not so much an exegete of the Pastoral Epistles as he is one who stands in a line of Pauline tradition that extends from Paul through the Pastorals and on into the early Christian community in Asia Minor and Gaul as the church struggles for self-definition, clarity of thought, and unity. The crucial point is that important structural patterns in Irenaeus' thought converge with themes, concepts, images, and patterns (a symbolic matrix of ideas and images) that appear already in rudimentary form in the Pastoral Epistles. In Irenaeus these are now extended and developed in the context of a second century church that, in the case of the bishop of Lyon, tries to defend itself in the face of the threat posed by Valentinus, Marcion, and the other gnostics. Even if Irenaeus does not turn exegetically to any great extent to the Pastorals, he does develop certain Pastoral theological themes and patterns that prove to be crucial to his perception of the

---

[10] Cf. also *Haer.* 3:3:3 for the preservation of the truth through the episcopal line and also the connection with Clement of Rome.

[11] See William R. Farmer, "Galatians and the Second-Century Development of the Regula Fidei," *SecCent* 4 (1984): 143–70. Cf. Gal 2:5, 14.

[12] Noorman, *Irenäus als Paulusinterpret*, 521–22.

[13] Ibid., 521.

[14] For a distribution of Pauline exegetical themes and texts in Irenaeus see the discussions by Noormann (*Irenäus als Paulusinterpret*) and Norris ("Irenaeus' Use of Paul" *AThR* 76 [1994]: 285–95).

church. Hence, Irenaeus represents conceptually and symbolically a Pauline tradition that corresponds in a number of respects to the Pastoral letters and the images of Paul contained in them.

## One God, One Christ, and a Unified History

Irenaeus defends the principle of one God, one Christ, and an ordered, unified notion of history on the basis of Pauline material.[15] Richard Norris writes:

> There are at least two places in *Adversus haereses* where Irenaeus sums up what he takes the essential message of Paul to have been. In both passages the summary follows the outline suggested by 1 Corinthians 8:6 but in each case with significant importations and additions. Paul is said first to have taught that there is *one God* (emphasis mine)—an element that, Irenaeus argues, was necessary in the preaching of one who brought the gospel to Gentiles uninstructed in the first principle of Jewish faith. Second, Paul is said to have taught the doctrine of the *Incarnation of the (preexistent) Son or Word of God* (emphasis mine). This is, no doubt, Irenaeus' interpretation of the phrase "one Lord Jesus Christ"—an interpretation that is indebted, as we have seen, to Galatians 4:4–6 read in conjunction with John 1:1–14 and certain other Pauline passages. But to this Irenaeus adds, in each case, a statement of aim or purpose of the incarnation, which turns out to be not only the conquest of Satan, the *inimicum hominis*, but also the re-formation of the human race (AH 4.24.1) or "the adoption of sons" (AH 3.16.3).[16]

In *Haer.* 3:16:3, Irenaeus cites in serial fashion Rom 1:1–4; 9:5; and Gal 4:4–5 and, along with an allusion to Col 1:14–15, finds in these texts clear evidence of the one God who, through the prophets, promised the one Son, Jesus Christ—the one through whom humanity receives adoption. The Pauline expressions "fullness of time" and "adoption" appear regularly in Irenaeus, which suggests that these images are critical to him.[17] The incarnation of God's Son, for Irenaeus, is the central redemptive event of history, which is itself united and tied together by divine providence. Undoubtedly part of his anti-gnostic polemic, the emphasis on the oneness of God, the centrality of the incarnation, and the unity of history under God's providence, are also part of the inner dynamic of Christian faith and theology for Irenaeus.[18] Oneness and unity, both theologically and historically, express a central feature of Irenaeus' pattern of thought about God and divine providence, and they serve his effort to combat the gnostics who have challenged the oneness of the creator and redeemer God and hence the unity of

---

[15] Roch Kereszty, "The Unity of the Church in the Theology of Irenaeus," *SecCent* 4 (1984): 202; and Norris, "Irenaeus' Use of Paul," 89–91, 97.

[16] Norris, "Irenaeus' Use of Paul," 97–98.

[17] Ibid., 89–90.

[18] Kereszty, "The Unity of the Church," 202.

history under the one God's providential direction. This complex of theological and christological ideas, central to the discussion in *Adversus haereses*,
informs and undergirds his conception of the church's unity in the face of
gnostic opposition.

As Richard Norris describes it, Irenaeus indicates what the Pauline
phrase "in the fullness of time" means for him in *Haer.* 3:16:7, where he asserts that all things were foreknown by God and that the Son works each out
at the proper time and in the proper order.[19] Quoting here a series of
Johannine texts, Irenaeus makes clear that God foreknew all things and he
accomplished them in their strict order and proper time. For Irenaeus, "in
the fullness of time" the word of God became incarnate, the time when the
word of God needed to become the son of man. In the divine economy,
everything has its place, and "in the fullness of time" this divine scheme is
punctuated by God's redemption culminating in the incarnation of the divine word.[20] Norris concludes: "It seems to be Paul, moreover, who supplies
Irenaeus with a way of envisaging the unity of this history in all its variety.
The bishop's basic theme, of course, is simply that the one God is the single
source of all things."[21]

## The Unity of the Church and the Canon of Truth

The oneness of God and the unity of history provide the conceptual
structure for Irenaeus' understanding of the church and the canon of truth.
If God is one, Christ is one, and history is structured according to the providence of the one God, it is not surprising that Irenaeus also sees the church
as united, as one. The one God of the Old and New Testaments enables the
person of faith to participate in the harmony of the one church. According
to John Coolidge, where Irenaeus claims that Scripture, both Old and New
Testaments, testifies to the one God, ". . . he describes the reader's perception of this unity in Scripture in the terms which Paul uses to describe partic-
ipation in the unity of the church."[22] Hence, for Irenaeus, theological unity
and ecclesiastical unity interlock, and they manifest themselves in the
church as a harmonious whole that cannot brook doctrinal disunity of the
type now posed by the gnostic opponents.

But if the unity of the church fits together seamlessly with the unity of
God as testified in the Scriptures, how do the theological and doctrinal unity
of the true church relate to the history of the church as a manifestation of
God's providence? For Irenaeus, the true church and the true teaching are

---

[19] Norris, "Irenaeus' Use of Paul," 90.

[20] Ibid., 90–91.

[21] Ibid., 91.

[22] John S. Coolidge, "The Pauline Basis of the Concept of Scriptural Form in
Irenaeus," in *The Center for Hermeneutical Studies in Hellenistic and Modern Culture*, 8th
Colloquy (ed. W. Wuellner; Berkeley: The Center, 1973), 2. See *Haer.* 4:32:1.

inseparable. Both derive from Christ and the apostles who have transmitted this truth to the church, which is now passed on historically through the line of episcopal succession.[23] Quasten claims that for Irenaeus the teaching of the apostles continues on without alteration and as such is the source and norm for the church.[24] Through the line of succession, the church preserves the truth of apostolic teaching, and only those churches founded by the apostles can reliably testify to the correct teaching of the faith and the true doctrine of Christ.[25] The so-called gnostic heretics are not recipients of this succession and hence are not recipients of the truth.[26] Where succession from the apostles becomes the criterion for orthodoxy, as appears to be the case in *Adversus haereses*, the ability of a church to trace its line of succession back to an apostle is critical for its claim to being a repository of true faith and teaching.[27] The stature of Peter and Paul among the apostles and in the church's memory, for example, clearly enhanced the apostolic stature and foundation of the Roman churches.[28] Likewise, for Irenaeus the link between Paul, Polycarp, and the churches in western Asia Minor,[29] perhaps especially the church in Smyrna,[30] presumably enhanced in the eyes of some people the image of those churches as repositories of true teaching as well—even though they may not now rival the authority of Rome.

In *Haer.* 3:2:2, Irenaeus, responding to the gnostics, writes: "But, again, when we refer them to that tradition which originates, and which is preserved by means of the successions of presbyters in the churches, they object to tradition, saying that they themselves are wiser not merely than the presbyters, but even than the apostles, because they have discovered the unadulterated truth."[31] And in 3:3:1 he continues: "It is within the power of all, therefore, in every church, who may wish to see the truth to contemplate clearly the tradition of the apostles, manifested throughout the whole world; and we are in a position to reckon up those who were by the apostles instituted bishops in the churches, and to demonstrate the succession of these men to our own times; those who neither taught nor knew anything like what the [heretics] rave about." Irenaeus in turn focuses on the church in

---

[23] Kereszty, "the Unity of the Church," 207–8; James F. McCue, "Roman Primacy in the Second Century and the Problem of the Development of Dogma," *Theological Studies* 25 (1964): 175–76; Jeffrey G. Sobosan, "The Role of the Presbyter: An Introduction into the Adversus Haereses of Saint Irenaeus," *SJT* 27 (1974), 139–40; Quasten, *Patrology*, 1:299–302.

[24] Quasten, *Patrology*, 1:299–300.

[25] Ibid., 299; and Sobosan, "The Role of the Presbyter," 139.

[26] Sobosan, "The Roles of the Presbyter," 139.

[27] McCue, "Roman Primacy in the Second Century," 175–76.

[28] Ibid., 178.

[29] Cf. *Haer.* 3:14:1–2.

[30] See above, pp. 123, 140–43.

[31] Cf. also 3:1:1.

Rome as the principle of episcopal succession as the conservator of truth,[32] built upon the foundation of the apostles Peter and Paul, and passed down by the succession of bishops, a point he underscores as he lists the apostolic successors by whom the tradition and truth have come down to the present.[33] This receives additional poignancy in 3:4:1, where Irenaeus likens the apostles to a rich man who deposits his money in a bank account, an account from which everyone who desires can withdraw the "water of life." According to Irenaeus, all things pertaining to God's truth were placed in the safekeeping of the church, and they are guarded and preserved from error by episcopal succession from the apostles to the present day. The church's truth serves as a bulwark against the claims of the gnostics.[34] Moreover, in 4:26:2 he argues that it is important to obey the presbyters who possess succession from the apostles and hence have received the gift of truth from the Father.[35] In the thought pattern of *Adversus haereses*, the church, defined in episcopal terms, and the truth of God are inseparable—guarded from false teaching and preserved from error the truth resides in the church. The faithful are expected to obey those leaders of the church who legitimately stand in the line of apostolic succession.

Seeking to refute the apparent claim of the Marcionites that only Paul was privy to this truth, Irenaeus, referring to Gal 2:8; Rom 10:15; and 1 Cor 15:11, uses Paul's letters to establish Peter's apostolic credentials and to show that the revelation of God's truth was preached not by one but many apostles. Where necessary in his debate with the gnostics, Irenaeus limits the domain of divine truth to the apostles and the line of succession in the church, but he also rejects the notion that apostolic truth resides alone in Paul, the hero of the Marcionites. He refuses to reduce the apostolate to Paul. Neither did the apostles withhold anything from the church: "Thus did the apostles simply, and without respect of persons, deliver to all what they had themselves learned from the Lord."[36] Moreover, Irenaeus argues in another context that anybody who rejects Luke, as a man who knows the truth, also rejects the Gospel for through him important parts of the gospel are known. Luke, too, is part of the apostolic testimony and the chain of gospel tradition.

---

[32] See Lampe, *From Paul to Valentinus*, 397–408. Lampe argues that the monarchical episcopacy did not emerge in Rome until the second half of the second century and that in the first half of the second century presbyterial governance still prevailed. From the middle of the second century, the Roman presbyter who dealt with external affairs gained more and more prominence, until with Victor in 189–99 this position has developed into a strong *monarchos*. This puts Irenaus' Lyon episcopate and his developing ecclesiology as described here in roughly the same time frame as the developments in Rome that Lampe describes.

[33] *Haer.* 3:3:3. See also T. F. Torrance, "The Deposit of Faith," *SJT* 36 (1983): 5.

[34] See above, p. 37, 95–97.

[35] Sobosan claims that Irenaeus uses the terms "presbyter" and "episcopos" interchangeably, "The Role of the Presbyter," 141.

[36] *Haer.* 3:14:2–3.

The universal church, possessing the sure and certain tradition of the apostles, according to Irenaeus, unites all in the one faith, for all receive the same God, the same incarnate Son of God, the same gift of the Spirit, the same commandments, the same church constitution, and they look forward to the same coming of the Lord and the same salvation.[37] Here the church, the faith, and all that follows from them and the gospel are tied together into a unified edifice that stands squarely against the gnostics and their recent theological innovations. They are blind and wander doctrinally here and there without agreement or unity,[38] and they lead away from the truth and the one true God adapting Scripture to suit their own purposes, according to Irenaeus.[39] In contrast to these opponents and their inconsistent claims, Irenaeus writes: "But the church throughout all the world, having its origin firm from the apostles, perseveres in one and the same opinion with regard to God and his son."[40] For Irenaeus, the church is one both in time and space.[41]

Irenaeus, however, specifies the one truth of the one church with the well-known expressions "canon of truth" and "body of truth." In *Haer.* 1:22:1 he writes: "The *rule of truth* (regulam veritatis) which we hold, is, that there is one God almighty, who made all things by his word, and fashioned and formed, out of that which had no existence, all things which exist." And in *Haer.* 1:9:4, continuing his polemic against the gnostics, he displays confidence that those who adhere to the truth will see through their perversions when he writes:

> In like manner he also who retains unchangeable in his heart the *rule of truth* (regulam veritatis) which he received by means of baptism, will doubtless recognize the names, the expressions, and the parables taken from the scriptures, but will by no means acknowledge the blasphemous use which these men make of them. . . . But when he has restored every one of the expressions quoted to its proper position, and has fitted it to the *body of truth* (veritatis corpusculo), he will lay bare, and prove to be without any foundation, the figment of these heretics.[42]

Concerning the interpretation of Scripture, Irenaeus also writes in *Haer.* 2:27:1 about the harmony of the body of truth: "And therefore the parables ought not to be adapted to ambiguous expressions. For, if this be not done, both he who explains them will do so without danger, and the parables will receive a like interpretation from all, and the *body of truth* remains entire, with a harmonious adaptation of its members, and without any collision." The unmistakable implication of these references is that the truth for Irenaeus is more than a concept of general reference, but clearly designates and refers

---

[37] *Haer.* 5:20:1.
[38] *Haer.* 5:20:1.
[39] *Haer.* 1:3:6.
[40] *Haer.* 3:12:7; see also *Haer.* 1:10:2.
[41] Kereszty, "The Unity of the Church," 207.
[42] See Richard A. Norris, "Theology and Language in Irenaeus of Lyon," 290.

to the church's teaching and presumably also its liturgical practice—both of which have doctrinal substance and form. Anchoring the canon of truth is the one creator God, who by his word made all things and through whom all things exist. Moreover, this body of truth is consistent with the correct use and interpretation of scripture and stands as a hedge against his gnostic opponents who, according to the bishop, try to turn scripture to their blasphemous ends.

The church, as it is reflected in the thought of Irenaeus, regarded itself as the repository of the truth and the preaching of the gospel that in turn were its only source and norm.[43] "The faith that was once for all entrusted to the saints" (Jude 3),[44] for Irenaeus and other mainstream church writers, came to be enshrined in the apostolic foundations of the church, which preserved unaltered the truth of the gospel.[45] Torrance argues that for Irenaeus the content of this deposit was marked by an order and structure that reflected the design of God's redeeming activity in Christ. Furthermore he writes: "It is by uncovering this internal structure of the Faith and bringing into clear relief the essential arrangement of the 'body of truth and the harmonious adaptation of its members', that the Deposit of Faith can be used both as an instrument of inquiry in the interpretation of the Holy Scriptures and as a canon of truth enabling the Church to offer clear demonstration of the Apostolic *kerygma* whereby it can be distinguished from all heretical deviations and distortions and shine forth in its own self-evidence."[46] Hence, the canon or body of truth is inseparable from the substance of the gospel and becomes the plumbline according to which orthodoxy is preserved and heterodoxy exposed.[47] For Irenaeus, as Norris says, the real plot of Scripture is found in the rule of truth,[48] and, as Coolidge puts it, the rule of truth is in essence the form of the truth that appears in Scripture.[49] Coolidge writes: "The rule of the truth might be called the idea of scripture. It is drawn from the scriptures themselves, not imposed upon them; it is a conception of the whole, governing the interpretation of the parts. What is imposed, however, is the assumption that every part of scripture will exhibit this essential form of the whole in some way."[50] From the first, argues Torrance, the deposit of

---

[43] Quasten, *Patrology*, 1:299.

[44] Cf. 1 Tim 4:6; 6:20; 2 Tim 1:12–14; 2:2; 4:3; Titus 1:9, 13.

[45] Torrance, "The Deposit of Faith," 1.

[46] Ibid., 6. Noorman states that fundamental feature of Irenaeus' theology, grounded as the canon of truth, is faith in one God, who is creator, God of Israel, and the father of Jesus Christ who became flesh, (*Irenäus als Paulusinterpret,* 529–30).

[47] See Farmer, "Galatians and the Second Century Development of the Regula Fidei," 159. Farmer argues that Irenaeus used the "rule of truth" to expose the false teachers just as Paul did to expose his opponents (cf. Gal 2:5, 14; 6:16).

[48] Norris, "Theology and Language," 290

[49] Coolidge, "The Pauline Basis of the Concept of Scriptural Form in Irenaeus," 6.

[50] Ibid., 7.

faith operated on two levels, the deepest level being identified with the re-demptive activity of God in Christ and the other with its faithful reception as it took form in the apostolic foundation of the church.[51] To this we need to add that for Irenaeus it was critical that God the creator and God the re-deemer were the one and same God, and to separate them as the gnostics had done was to deviate from the canon of truth.[52]

William Farmer seeks to find a line of development connecting the post-Pauline church to Paul when he asks about the historical relationship between Paul's doctrinal norm, "the truth of the gospel," (Gal 2:5, 14) and the rules of faith that emerged in the second century.[53] He observes that these rules developed from an apostolic desire to remain faithful to the truth of the gospel and that the epistle to the Galatians was also decisive in the de-velopment of Marcion's own heterodox regula. In response, Irenaeus and Tertullian rejected Marcion's rule first by appeal to Galatians and in turn to the other letters of Paul as well as to the other writings of the New Testament. These rules of truth and faith as found in Irenaeus, Tertullian, and Origen—the most likely foundation of which derives from Gal 2:14 and 6:16—reflect the response of the church to Marcion's regula.[54] Struck by the absence of this type of normative concept in the Christian literature between Paul and Irenaeus, and by its sudden appearance after Marcion, Farmer finds the key to the emergence of these rules in Marcion's challenge to the church and its developing sense of orthodoxy.[55] However, if 1 and 2 Timothy are not from the hand of Paul, as we have argued seems likely,[56] then the concept of the "good deposit" and the emphasis on the true faith or correct belief found in the Pastoral letters appear to be another link in the historical development of this concept. Furthermore, the opposition appears in the Pastorals to be related to Jewish and ascetic concerns, it is not identifiably gnostic.[57] Hence, the common denominator (common function) that gives rise to this notion may be the refutation of theological opposition—whatever the pre-cise nature of that opposition may be. In the second century Marcion is simply a prime example of the opposition and one of the powerful voices who requires the defenders of orthodoxy to develop their thinking beyond what had gone before them. Irenaeus, of course, sees all of the material at-

---

[51] Torrance, "The Deposit of Faith," 14–15.

[52] Richard Norris asserts that the oneness of God is central to Irenaeus' *Adversus haereses* ("The Transcendence and Freedom of God: Irenaeus, the Greek Tradition and Gnosticism," in *Early Christian Literature and the Classical Intellectual Tradition* [ed. William R. Schoedel and Robert L. Wilken; Paris: Éditions Beau-chesne, 1979], 88).

[53] Farmer, "Galatians and the Second Century Development of the Regula Fidei," 144.

[54] Ibid., 156, 170.

[55] Ibid., 159.

[56] See above, pp. 86–89.

[57] See above, pp. 64–66.

tributed to Paul as authentically Pauline, which tends to obscure any sense of historical development in the Pauline corpus, when in fact according to this scenario the Pastorals are themselves later extensions and further developments of the historical Paul's thinking.

## *Irenaeus and the Pastorals*

Though Irenaeus' exegesis of the Pastoral Epistles is limited and his reference to specific Pastoral texts is incidental to his use of the larger Pauline corpus, there are nevertheless links between the two that suggest a line of experience and symbolic continuity that extends from Paul to the Irenaean form of Christianity taking shape in the late second century. The common functional thread between them is opposition to some other form of theology, whether that be some form of Jewish ascetic opposition, as appears in the Pastoral letters, or Marcion and the gnostics, as in the case of Irenaeus. Much of Paul's theology was forged in controversy with his opponents. This is especially evident in Galatians. The writer(s) of the Pastoral letters—assuming they were not written by Paul—and Irenaeus each adapt their apologetic use of Paul to the peculiar circumstances of their own controversies. In the Pastorals, Paul and his letters have already come to have apostolic authority, if not also a rudimentary form of canonical authority. For Irenaeus this authority also includes the Pastorals as part of the Pauline corpus and clearly enhances Paul's legacy as a figure of apostolic authority who, along with the other apostles, transmitted the truth of the gospel to the church, a truth which is now passed down through the line of succession.

From the Pastorals to Irenaeus, the Pauline legacy continued to develop and serve different branches of the early church. The developing mainstream traditions of Christianity never entirely abandoned Paul or his letters; nor did they, as demonstrated by the example of Irenaeus, merely turn to Paul because the opponents had used him, thus requiring some form of counter-Pauline interpretation.[58] Paul remained an authority figure for much, if not all, of Christianity, but the questions were: What role would Paul play for the church and how would his letters and theology be understood? As in the case of Ignatius, Polycarp and the writer of *1 Clement* (but unlike the Pastorals and perhaps also the narrative of Acts), the historical Paul for Irenaeus had receded into history. Though Paul's legacy continued to shine brightly he and his preaching were firmly anchored in the apostolic past, now connected most directly to the present-day church by the line of succession.[59] Paul, now reimaged as the protector of the faith, testified to the truth of the gospel and served as an apostolic pillar for the one true church.

---

[58] This is a point made persuasively by Rolf Noorman (*Irenäus als Paulus-interpret,* 517–31), Richard Norris ("Irenaeus' Use of Paul," 79–98, and Andreas Lindemann ("Writings of the Apostolic Fathers," 27–30, .

[59] See above, pp. 161–64.

As we have seen above, one of the consistent elements in the theological contour of the three Pastoral Epistles is the concept of sound teaching,
correct faith, and the truth. Though the content of this truth often remains
submerged beneath the surface of the texts, several features of the sound
teaching were identified already in chapter 2 and need not be repeated
here.[60] However, the emphasis in Irenaeus on the canon or body of truth,
critical elements in the pattern of his argument in *Adversus haereses*, follows
the general structural pattern found also in the Pastorals, though the concept
is now more defined. Its content is more explicit and begins in Irenaeus to
function as a hermeneutical principle for understanding Scripture. But more
to the point, the reference in *Haer.* 3:4:1 to the apostles being like a rich man
who deposits the truth in a bank account (the church) is more than
coincidently related to 1 Tim 6:20–21 ("O Timothy, guard the deposit that
has been entrusted to you . . .") and 2 Tim 1:14 ("Guard the good deposit
through the holy spirit which dwells in us").[61] The similarity between the
Pastoral texts and *Adversus haereses* is remarkable in two respects: the authors
liken the true teaching to a deposit or a treasure that must be protected, and
the apostle or apostles hand over this good deposit to others—Timothy in
the two Pastoral letters and the church in Irenaeus. In both cases, the authors imagine the true doctrine of the church in terms of a relatively fixed
body of teaching or truth that requires safeguarding, a body of teaching
passed down and kept safe from the time of the apostle(s) to those in the
church who come after. There is clearly a convergence of images in these
Pastoral texts and *Adversus haereses*.[62]

Furthermore, the author in 2 Tim 2:2 states: ". . . and what you have
heard from me through many witnesses entrust to faithful people who will
be able to teach others as well."[63] Though not a full-blown concept of apostolic succession, as we find in Irenaeus, the Pastoral imagery establishes the
necessity of transmitting the true teaching and, in light of 1:12–14, implies
the faithful preservation of that teaching. In the Pastoral Epistles the church
is conceived in terms of the household of God,[64] but with the emphasis on
the qualities for church leadership in 1 Timothy and Titus, there is an implicit sense that these leaders are important links in the faithful preservation
and transmission of the true teaching.[65] Far from the more developed concept of succession prominent in Irenaeus, the writer of 1 Timothy and Titus
suggests only obliquely that these leaders are critical links in the preservation of apostolic truth, but they are links nonetheless. This set of Pastoral im-

---

[60] See above, pp. 28–31, 39–40, 50–52.

[61] See above, pp. 37, 95–97.

[62] In their own way, Ignatius and Polycarp suggest a similar view of the
church's truth. It is something to be preserved, guarded, and transmitted without
alteration.

[63] See also 2 Tim 1:6, 13; 3:10, 14.

[64] See above, pp. 19–25.

[65] See 1 Tim 3:9; 4:14; 5:17, 22; Titus 1:5–9.

ages clearly foreshadows the more developed ecclesiastical ideas found in Irenaeus almost a century later.[66] While the focus in 1 Timothy and Titus is on the qualities of the individuals who hold positions of leadership, Irenaeus appears to have shifted the emphasis to the episcopal offices and the ecclesiatical structure as the guardians of apostolic truth. This is a significant development in the formation of Christianity, but one that also clearly indicates the gradual development of an early Christian ecclesiology. As the episcopal structure of the church developed and came to represent, in the eyes of increasing numbers of Christians, the one church in which the true faith resides, it is not surprising to see the subtle shift in images from the qualifications for church leaders to the offices (and office holders) of the church. In *Adversus Haereses*, apostolic truth does not appear to be preserved merely by individual leaders, no matter what their personal qualifications, but by people who as office holders fit into the official structure of the one church and as such represent that church.[67] It seems clear that 1 Timothy/Titus and Irenaeus are in a similar ecclesiological matrix. What distinguishes Irenaeus most immediately from the Pastorals, Ignatius, Polycarp, and *1 Clement,* however, is the depth and thoroughness of his argumentation in defense of the canon of truth. He does not simply assert a notion of truth or exhort the church to obey this truth but argues for a way of understanding the truth now lodged in the one church.

There are, however, still other suggestive verbal and theological links between Irenaeus and the Pastoral Epistles. In *Haer.* 3:18:7, Irenaeus portrays the Lord as the mediator ($\mu\epsilon\sigma(\tau\eta\nu$ fr.gr.26:8–11) between God and human beings,[68] and in 5:17:1 he describes Christ as the mediator who brought friendship and harmony between God and humanity (*mediatorem Dei et hominum*). This is virtually the same expression used by the writer of 1 Timothy in 2:5 (". . . one mediator between God and humanity"), but it is not a term used of Christ elsewhere in the Pauline writings.[69] Whether Irenaeus adopted this christological image from 2 Timothy or from someone else we cannot know, but it is striking that the writer of 1 Timothy and Irenaeus both use this image and language for Christ. Irenaeus also hints at an epiphany Christology—expressive of the Christology of the Pastorals but not the undisputed Paulines—[70]when he writes in 2:20:3 that the Lord destroyed death, ended corruption, and destroyed ignorance while he manifested (*manifestavit*) life and revealed truth.[71] This is hardly evidence of a

---

[66] See above, pp. 66–69.

[67] This point holds no matter how Irenaeus understood the relationship between presbyters and bishops. See Jeffrey Sobosan's argument about the relationship between presbyters and bishops in Irenaeus ("The Role of the Presbyter," 129–46).

[68] Noorman, *Irenäus als Paulusinterpret,* 140–41.

[69] Torrance, "The Deposit of Faith," 8, 10.

[70] See above, pp. 98–99.

[71] Noorman, *Irenäus als Paulusinterpret,* 96. Cf. also *Haer.* 1:10:1.

deep and abiding connection between the Christology of the Pastorals and Irenaeus, but it suggests perhaps some conceptual christological link between them, a link not found between Irenaeus and the Paul of the undisputed letters. Furthermore, Irenaeus frequently refers to Christ as savior,[72] once again, a common Pastoral designation but not one that is commonly found in the authentic letters of Paul. These verbal and theological connections do not indicate necessarily a direct connection between the Christology of Irenaeus and the Pastorals, but taken together they suggest that Irenaeus reflects a stock of christological words and images also reflected in the Pastorals and to which these three epistles, almost a century before the bishop, contributed.

## IMPORTANT FIGURES IN ROME: JUSTIN MARTYR AND HIPPOLYTUS

### *Justin Martyr*

Justin may have known Paul's epistles, but he does not quote from them or the Pastoral letters.[73] Born in Palestine near Flavia Neopolis, some think he went to Ephesus where his *Dialog with Trypho* is set, later appearing in Rome in the middle part of the second century. He was martyred some ten years later.[74] Since he perhaps spent time in Ephesus as well as Rome, it is hard to imagine that he did not know Paul's letters. But in the *Dialog with Trypho*, because of the nature of the debate with Judaism, it is evident why the focus is on the Old Testament and not Paul. Justin may also have avoided citing Paul because of what Marcion had done with him and his theology.[75] For Justin, the true philosophy is encountered in the words of Scripture. The prophets had seen and heard the truth, and in the Scriptures, one encounters the word of God.[76] They announce what has been fulfilled in Christ and what is still to be fulfilled.[77] In that sense, the Scriptures are unlike all other forms of literature.

---

[72] See, e.g., *Haer.* 1:3:1; 1:10:1; 3:2:2; 3:4:2.

[73] For allusions and similarities to the Pauline letters, see Eric F. Osborn, *Justin Martyr* (BHT 47; Tübingen: J. C. B. Mohr [Paul Siebeck], 1973), 155–56. See also the discussion of Justin's use of Abraham by Jeffrey S. Siker, *Disinheriting the Jews: Abraham in Early Christian Controversy* (Louisville: Westminster John Knox, 1991), 163–83. On Justin's concept of a canon, see Charles H. Cosgrove, "Justin Martyr and the Emerging Christian Canon," *VC* 36 (1982): 209–11.

[74] Hans von Campenhausen, *The Fathers of the Greek Church* (trans. and revised by L. A. Garrard; London: Adam and Charles Black, 1963), 6–7.

[75] Cosgrove, "Justin Martyr," 219–20.

[76] Osborn, *Justin Martyr*, 70–71, 89.

[77] Ibid., 93.

Justin's early desire to be a philosopher found expression in Christianity, which became for him the true philosophy. For the new faith, he became perhaps the greatest early apologist, and as an apologist he raised many of the questions that Irenaeus, Tertullian, Origen, and Clement later expounded.[78] As Eric Osborn describes it, whereas Irenaeus sees the continuity of God's saving work and the summation of all things in Christ, and Tertullian considers the wonders of God's creation, and Origen probes the meaning of Scripture and the word made flesh, and Clement contemplates God and the divine image in human beings, it is Justin Martyr who opened the theological door for these great figures of the early church.[79] Even though Justin's work may not tell us much in detail about how the Pauline tradition was developing, he must be recognized for his contribution to the early church's theology and perhaps indirectly to the developing image of Paul and his theology.

## *Hippolytus*

Hippolytus' background and location are elusive, hampered by a lack of references to him in the writings of his contemporaries and by the diversity of opinions about the location of his bishopric. The place and date of his martyrdom is also uncertain: Rome, Porto, Alexandria, Antioch, or Spain, with his death coming as early as the rule of Alexander Severus (222–235) or as late as Claudius II (268–270).[80] In 1551, a statue of a seated person was found near the Tiburtine Way, and the majority scholarly opinion is that this statue represents Hippolytus and indicates the area of his activity.[81] With the discovery in the nineteenth century of *The Elenchos*, sometimes referred to as the *Refutation of All Heresies*, debate ensued regarding the authorship of the document with Hippolytus being the most likely candidate.[82] Given the autobiographical details of the text, this is an important document for information about Hippolytus, should he in fact be the author. As Dunbar writes:

> In Book IX he presents himself as the champion of Trinitarian orthodoxy and the moral integrity of the Church and the active opposition of popes Zephyrinus (198–217) and Callistus (217–222), whom he regards as Monarchian in theology and lax in discipline. If we may accept, at least tentatively, Hippolytean authorship of the *Refutation*, then we have solid grounds for placing our author in Rome at the beginning of the third century. Further, he lays claim to being a member of the ecclesiastical hierarchy, a doctor and very probably, a bishop of the church.

---

[78] Ibid., 16.
[79] Ibid., 16.
[80] David Dunbar, "The Problem of Hippolytus of Rome," *JETS* 25 (1982): 63–65.
[81] Ibid., 65.
[82] Ibid., 66.

It is this determined opposition to the lawful bishops of Rome that has become the key to the modern reconstructions of the life of Hippolytus. Although virtually nothing is known of his origins (except that he was probably a student of Irenaeus), it is clear that in the beginning of the third century he was a great luminary in the Roman Church. . . . The running battle with Zephyrinus and Callistus is thought to have led him eventually into open schism in which Hippolytus established himself at the head of his own group of disciples. The schism apparently continued during the pontificates of Urbanus and Pontianus.[83]

In the *Refutation of All Heresies,* the church is both hierarchical and spiritual, and in terms of the former the similarity with Irenaeus is clear. In this argument, the author claims that the church is the vehicle of truth and that the succession of bishops is the guardian of the church's teaching.[84] Hippolytus, as Irenaeus before him, has a concept of the rule of truth, though it does not appear to play as dynamic or important a role in his refutation of heresy as it does for his predecessor.[85] By the time of Hippolytus, the gnostics were probably less of a threat to the emerging orthodoxy in Rome, and he could recognize the rule of truth but felt no compulsion to use it as a weapon against the so-called heretics.[86] The perspective of Irenaeus lived on in Hippolytus, but the circumstances in which it was applied were changing in third century Rome. Continuity with a line of ecclesiology extending from the Pastorals and Irenaeus appears in the *Refutation of all Heresies* but now operates in a new and changing Roman church environment. For example, schism at this point was not merely a matter of one group breaking away from another but of a break away group obtaining the consecration of a bishop to lead them. Competing groups would follow different bishops, as there was by the end of the second and the beginning of the third centuries no centralized means to adjudicate conflicting theological and ecclesiastical claims.[87] Only later, in light of Cyprianic language would schism and its remedy become formalized in the church.[88] If different groups in the church each having their own bishop could not guarantee the truth, the

---

[83] Ibid., 66.

[84] Quasten, *Patrology,* 2:202.

[85] Gérard Vallée, *A Study in Anti-Gnostic Polemics: Irenaeus, Hippolytus, and Epiphaniu* (Studies in Christianity and Judaism; Waterloo, Ont.: Wilfrid Laurier University Press, 1981), 57–62. In *Refutatio omnium haeresium* and *De antichristo* he cites 1 Tim 6:20 (guard what has been entrusted to you) and in the latter he also quotes 2 Tim 4:8 (you hold the crown of life and immortality which is laid up for you). He also refers to 1 Tim 3:5 (Christ the mediator) in fragments from the *Commentaries* (Numbers).

[86] See the arguments he uses against heretics (ibid., 48–55).

[87] Allen Brent, "Was Hippolytus a Schismatic," *VC* 49 (1995): 216, 222.

[88] Ibid., 238; see also Allen Brent, *Hippolytus and the Roman Church in the Third Century: Communities in Tension Before the Emergence of a Monarch-Bishop* (Supplements to Vigiliae Christianae 31; Leiden: E. J. Brill, 1995), 455–56.

church needed means to decide conflicting episcopal claims. By the third century, the concept of authority in the western church was clearly in a state of transition yet again.

## THE NORTH AFRICAN CONNECTION: TERTULLIAN

### *Introduction*

As one of the most important church thinkers of the Latin West, Tertullian was born in Carthage in 155, and in 207 publicly became part of the Montanist movement. He produced most of his writings between 195 and 220, which means they can be categorized according to his pre-Montanist and Montanist phases, though there is much debate over what this change actually meant for him and his theology.[89] According to Quasten, apart from Augustine, Tertullian is the most important church thinker in Latin, and especially during his earlier period strongly resembles Irenaeus.[90] Concerning the apostle Paul, Robert Sider rejects the idea that we can limit Paul's legacy in Tertullian to his use of the apostle's thought, for Tertullian also includes a vivid image of the person of Paul drawn from both Paul's letters and Acts.[91] Tertullian's method, according to Sider, is not that of the systematic theologian but the "literary artist and master of rhetoric" in which the life and person of Paul is as important as his thought.[92] Hence, to understand Paul's legacy in Tertullian, we need to attend to the images of Paul as he appears in both the events of his life and his thought.[93]

Among events from Paul's life, Tertullian focuses especially on the apostle's Damascus Road experience (conversion and loss of sight), his confrontation with Peter in Antioch, his missionary journeys, and his sufferings through which Paul shows himself to be a model of courage.[94] For anti-gnostic purposes, Tertullian can portray Paul as dependent on the other apostles, but he can also distinguish him from them on other occasions as an apostle of peace and teacher of the nations.[95] The holy apostle possesses the Holy Spirit, and as one who desires to depart this life to be with Christ, he serves as a model.[96] The later Tertullian, not surprisingly,

---

[89] Quasten, *Patrology,* 2:246–47.

[90] Ibid., 247, 331.

[91] Robert D. Sider, "Literary Artiface and the Figure of Paul in the Writings of Tertullian," in *Paul and the Legacies of Paul* (ed. William S. Babcock; Dallas: Southern Methodist University Press, 1990), 100.

[92] Ibid., 100.

[93] Ibid., 100.

[94] Ibid., 102–6.

[95] Ibid., 107–8.

[96] Ibid., 110.

depicts Paul as a proclaimer of the Spirit and the gifts of the Spirit, and he sees Paul claiming that knowledge of God comes through both natural and divine revelation.[97] Eschatology is another Pauline theme important in Tertullian's portrayal of the apostle, for Paul also understood himself to be living in the end-time.[98] In Tertullian's depiction of Paul, we find a fusion of the historical Paul remembered and the apostle revered as a saint of the church.

## *The Paradox of the Pastorals, the* Regula Fidei, *and the Church*

Paradoxically, when Tertullian cites material from the Pastoral Epistles that deals with matters of the ministry, church order, authority, and polity, he relates that material to different kinds of concerns.[99] Although the early Tertullian follows closely Irenaeus' view of sound doctrine and its transmission in the church, he does not turn in fact to the most conspicuous and appropriate Pastoral texts to defend his view of the church.[100] David Rankin suggests that the reason for this reluctance may be that Tertullian, especially in his later phase, found the Pastoral Epistles to be too supportive, at least in appearance, of those who wanted an even more authoritarian form of episcopal government. Not wanting to support those people and that argument, he avoided using the Pastoral texts relating to these kinds of ecclesiastical concerns.[101] Whether this explanation is persuasive or not, it highlights an important feature of Tertullian's use of the Pastoral letters and his own sensibilities concerning the nature and power of the church.

L. William Countryman identifies three prime *regula fidei* (rule of faith) texts,[102] and he argues that, as for Irenaeus, Tertullian saw Christian truth in *De praescriptione hereticorum* as a deposit left behind for us by Christ and passed on through the line of succession in the church. Hence, this truth is not something to be discovered anew.[103] Countryman writes: "Tertullian expected catholic Christians to accept the idea that there are certain

---

[97] Ibid., 114–16.

[98] Ibid., 117–18.

[99] David Rankin, "Tertullian's Use of the Pastoral Epistles in His Doctrine of Ministry" *ABR* 32 (1984): 19.

[100] Ibid., 22, 25–27, 35. Concerning the proper transmission of the truth, Tertullian in *Praescr.* 25 cites 1 Tim, 6:20, 14; and 2 Tim 1:18 in order to make the case that the apostles did not withhold part of the truth, which only later they revealed secretively to a select group of people now identified with the heretics. Instead, Tertullian sees Paul in these Pastoral texts charging Timothy not to accept any other teaching than that preached by Paul himself. They are not texts about special knowledge secretly revealed.

[101] Rankin, "Tertullian's Use of the Pastoral Epistles," 33.

[102] For his discussion of these three texts see L. William. Countryman, "Tertullian and the Regula Fidei," *SecCent* 2 (1982): 208–14. The three texts are *Praescr.* 13, *Virg.* 1, and *Prax.* 2

[103] Ibid., 211.

irreformable truths of the faith and that these are summarized in a brief, recognizable composition."[104] Furthermore, he argues that the formulation of this truth has a bipartite structure—belief in the creator and in Jesus as the son of the creator—and when mention of the Spirit occurs it is as a subheading of Jesus.[105] From a different perspective, Anthony Guerra claims that the most common religious sense of *fides* in Tertullian, as in the term *regula fidei*, is of a body of religious truths.[106] Stated even more forcefully, Eric Osborn writes that the *Regula Fidei* for Tertullian is a fixed form, identical with the full revelation from God, prior to heresy, and in a direct line running back to the apostles.[107] Thus, the truth of the *Regula Fidei* precedes the falsehood now being taught by the opponents.[108] Moreover, the true teaching that Jesus left for the church is plain to see and understand, it is not an esoteric teaching to which only a few initiates are privy as the gnostics claimed.[109]

For Tertullian in *De praescriptione hereticorum*, the church is the repository of this truth and the guardian of revelation.[110] He writes in 20–21:

> [A]nd after first bearing witness to the faith in Jesus Christ throughout Judea, and founding churches there, they next went forth into the world and preached the same doctrine of the same faith to the nations. They then in like manner founded churches in every city, from which all the other churches, one after another, derived the tradition of the faith, and the seeds of doctrine, and are every day deriving them, that they may become churches. . . . Therefore the churches, although they are so many and so great, comprise but the one primitive church, founded by the apostles from which they all spring. In this way all are primitive, and all are apostolic, whilst they are all proved to be one, in unbroken unity. . . . Since the Lord Jesus Christ sent the apostles to preach, our rule is that no others ought to be received as preachers than those whom Christ appointed. . . . If, then, these things are so, it is in the same degree manifest that all doctrine which agrees with the apostolic churches—those moulds and the original sources of the faith must be reckoned for truth.[111]

---

[104] Ibid., 213.

[105] Ibid., 209–10.

[106] Anthony J. Guerra, "Polemical Christianity: Tertullian's Search for Certitude," *SecCent* 8 (1991): 109. See also Gal 1:6; 6:16.

[107] Eric F. Osborn, "Reason and the Rule of Faith" in *The Making of Orthodoxy: Essays in Honour of Henry Chadwick* (ed. Rowan Williams; Cambridge: Cambridge University Press, 1989), 45. See also Robert B. Eno, "Scripture and Tradition in Tertullian," in *The Quadrilogy: Tradition and the Future of Ecumenism* (ed. Kenneth Hagen; Collegeville, Minn.: Liturgical, 1994), 17–18.

[108] See Eno, "Scripture and Tradition," 14; and Countryman, "Tertullian and the Regula Fidei," 213.

[109] Eno, "Scripture and Tradition,"16. See Countryman's argument for the context of the *Regula Fidei* ("Tertullian and the Regula Fidei," 217–23).

[110] Quasten, *Patrology*, 2:331.

[111] See also *Praescr.* 22, 25, 37.

For Tertullian, God sent his son, Christ sent the apostles, the apostles formed the church, and this one church stands in a direct line with the apostles.[112] David Rankin observes that Tertullian does not explicitly affirm, any more than any other orthodox church writer before him, the "one holy, catholic, and apostolic church," but he does come closer by implication.[113] Furthermore, in *Cor.* 13 and *Mart.* 3 Tertullian, echoing Paul's comment in Phil 3:20, asserts that the citizenship of the Christian (martyr) is in heaven,[114] and in that sense he claims that those in the one true church belong ultimately to a different realm.

### Tertullian and the Pastorals

As in the case of Ireneaus, Tertullian clearly reflects the now familiar pattern of sound doctrine (*Regula Fidei*) and deposit of the truth, a theological pattern found also in principle in the Pastoral Epistles. The picture of Tertullian, however, is complicated by his later Montanist leanings and by the impression that the *Regula Fidei* is for him a fixed formula of truth handed down unchanged from the apostles as a virtual compendium of doctrines to be believed in order to obtain salvation.[115] Whether or not Tertullian consistently held fast to such static notions of orthodox Christian doctrine does not diminish his commitment to the one creator God and to Jesus his son. The church is the repository of this truth and guards it from all deviation. In his later phase, he may have broken with the church and the role of the Spirit obviously became more important in his thinking. Yet it is by no means clear that he abandoned these notions of orthodox truth to which he had committed himself earlier in life. The earlier Tertullian stands closer to Irenaeus than to the Pastoral Epistles on the question of sound truth, but like the bishop of Lyon he is part of the same frame of reference that the Pastorals foreshadow already in the Pauline corpus.

Paul's life and thought are important for Tertullian, but as we observed he does not use the Pastorals, as one might expect, to defend the ministry, the order and the authority of the church. Though he cites Pastoral material that in fact might support his claims about the church, he does not use this material for these purposes. If Rankin is correct, Tertullian may in fact refrain from using these Pastoral texts in addressing these ecclesiastical issues in order not to play into the hands of still more authoritarian forces in the church.[116] As with Irenaeus, Tertullian also reflects the image of Christ as the mediator between God and human beings found in the Pastoral

---

[112] David Rankin, *Tertullian and the Church* (Cambridge: Cambridge University Press, 1995), 101; and Eno, "Scripture and Tradition," 21.

[113] Rankin, *Tertullian and the Church*, 92.

[114] Ibid., 98.

[115] Torrance, "The Deposit of Faith," 15.

[116] Rankin, "Tertullian's Use of the Pastoral Epistles," 25.

Epistles.[117] Whether through direct quotation or allusion, Tertullian expresses a christological image and pattern of thought emanating from the Pastorals—though not found in the undisputed letters of Paul. The Pastorals are part of the Pauline corpus for Tertullian, and he reflects the image of Christ the mediator as a Pauline image, though it is an image that already in the Pastoral letters bears the stamp of being incorporated into the historical Paul's Christology. And as Irenaeus, Tertullian can also employ "savior" language for Christ,[118] terminology that as we have seen figures prominently in the Pastoral letters.[119] Not only in the broader contours of emerging Christian theological formation but also in these terminological clues we find evidence that Irenaeus, Tertullian, and the Pastorals all represent features of a symbolic frame of reference that includes the Apostolic Fathers and certain developing mainstream Christian traditions in Gaul and North Africa of the second and third centuries.

## THE NEXT GENERATION IN NORTH AFRICA: CYPRIAN

A generation following Tertullian, the church in North Africa came to struggle with a host of new issues, and Cyprian became the point person for many of these struggles and the ecclesiastical issues prompted by them. A man of some social prominence and wealth, Cyprian converted to Christianity and almost immediately assumed a leadership role in the North African church, becoming bishop of Carthage in about 249.[120] Following the order by emperor Decius in 249 or 250 that all people in the empire should make sacrifices to the gods, Cyprian went into hiding only to be criticized for fleeing. Once the persecution subsided, the church faced the problem of what to do with those who had lapsed under threat of harm and now desired to return to the church. Different attitudes to that issue tore at the fabric of the church, threatening to divide it. Cyprian wrote two treatises in response, *De lapsis* and *De Catholicae ecclesiae unitate*, and has often been viewed as taking a compromise position between the rigor of Novatian and the laxity of Fortunatus, between protecting the holiness of the church and the hope of salvation for the fallen.[121]

---

[117] See *Carn. Chr.* 15 (citing the 'apostle Paul' and 1 Tim 2:5); *Res.* 51, 63; and *Prax.* 27 (citing the 'apostle').

[118] See, e.g., *Pud.* 2.

[119] See above, pp. 58–61.

[120] G. W. Clarke, "Cyprian," 1:1226–28; Theodore Damian, "The Unity of the Church in the Theology of St. Cyprian of Carthage and that of Karl Barth," *Patristic and Byzantine Review* 13 (1994): 88–89; and Roy Griggs, "Christ's Seamless Robe: A Study of Cyprian's Concept of the Unity of the Church," *Mid-Stream* 16 (1977): 399–400.

[121] J. Patout Burns, "The Holiness of the Churches," in *The Unbounded Community: Papers in Christian Ecumenism in Honor of Jaroslav Pelikan* (ed. William Caferro

This problem raised the larger concern of the church's unity and forced the issue of how to understand the church, the place of bishops, and the role of presbyters and deacons.[122] As Charles Bobertz notes, Cyprian's writings represent the culmination in the West of episcopal and priestly leadership, in large part provoked by persecution and the responses to it.[123] Whether Cyprian held a notion of Petrine supremacy or not,[124] the operative concept in his ecclesiology is the notion of equal sharing of power by those who stand in the line of succession. In that sense, the church is one and undivided, it is extended and held together by the individual bishops.[125] For Cyprian, apart from the church there is no salvation, and that meant in effect apart from unity with the bishop there is no hope of salvation.[126] For our purposes, M. F. Wiles may have summed up the church's developing ecclesiology best when he claimed many years ago that Ignatius stressed obedience to the bishop with little theoretical development and Irenaeus emphasized the succession of the living tradition guarded by "episcopoi" and *presbyteroi,* whereas Cyprian combined both.[127] Unlike Irenaeus, however, who grounded the succession of bishops in the succession of the church, Cyprian saw it the other way around.[128]

From the Pastorals to Ignatius, Irenaeus, and on to Cyprian in the middle of the third century, we can see the shape of the church's episcopal development in the first two centuries. Cyprian has moved well beyond his predecessors, but we might also say that his ecclesiology is a logical extension of the ideas and claims made by them. Hence, there may well be a trajectory of institutional development that comes into view and extends all the way back to the earliest efforts of the church to work out an institutional arrangement for the maintenance of a universal church, even back to the time of 1 Timothy and Titus.

In his writing, Cyprian eliminated all references to the classical authors, references that would have been expected to lace the work of any

---

and Duncan G. Fisher; New York: Garland, 1996), 4–6. Novatian was a Roman priest, perhaps from Phrygia, who by 250 had become a leading figure among the clergy in the city. A contemporary of Cyprian, he was noted for his strict stance regarding return of the lapsed to good standing in the church. We have a few surviving works from Novatian in which he quotes from the Pastorals (e.g., *De cibus Judaicus* 5; cf. Titus 1:15; 1 Tim 4:4–5, 1–3; 6:8), but they are limited and do not give us much insight into the developing Pauline tradition.

[122] Charles A. Bobertz, "The Development of Episcopal Order," in *Eusebius, Christianity, and Judasim* (ed. Harold W. Attridge and Gahei Hata; Detroit: Wayne State University Press, 1992), 194.

[123] Ibid., 194.

[124] Cf. ibid., 199; and Griggs, "Christ's Seamless Robe," 402–3.

[125] Griggs, "Christ's Seamless Robe," 402–5. Cf. also R. J. Halliburton. "Some Reflections on St. Cyprian's Doctrine of the Church," StPatr 11 (1972): 195–97.

[126] Ibid., 405, 407.

[127] M. F. Wiles, "The Theological Legacy of St. Cyprian," *Journal of Ecclesiastical History* 14 (1963): 143.

[128] Ibid., 144. See also Damian, "The Unity of the Church," 95.

trained rhetorician, only to be replaced by scriptural references.[129] Strongly influenced by Tertullian, Cyprian treated the biblical text with great respect, preferring direct biblical quotations to vague allusions. His Christianity was very much a religion of the book,[130] and unlike Clement of Alexandria, Cyprian seems to have cared little about philosophy. As seen in his *Ad Quirinum testimonia adversus Judaeos* and other writings, he preferred to assemble a series of texts from which to glean answers to practical theological and ecclesiastical questions.[131] In *Test.* book 3, a manual of Christian duties, this is clearly the way he uses the Pastoral Epistles.[132] Similarly, in *Ad Fortunatum*, Cyprian uses 2 Timothy to address those who face death.[133] This pattern of scriptural usage continues in other treatises and epistles as well.[134] He did not use Scripture to develop grand theological schemes or chart new systems of thought. Such was not his contribution to the church. Yet along with the other Pauline texts, the Pastorals were for Cyprian sacred Scripture, good for instruction and training in righteousness much as the author of 2 Timothy had written many decades earlier.

## FROM ALEXANDRIA TO CAESAREA: CLEMENT AND ORIGEN

### Clement of Alexandria

Introduction

Teaching and writing in Alexandria during the last two decades of the second century and the beginning of the third century, Clement sought to reconcile faith and philosophy and to show that the gospel and classical

---

[129] G. W. Clarke, "Cyprian," 1:1227; and Wiles, "Legacy of St. Cyprian, 141.

[130] G. W. Clarke, "Cyprian," 1:1227.

[131] Wiles, "Legacy of Cyprian," 141.

[132] See *Test.*, book 3, #36 / 1 Tim 2:9–10 (adornment of women); #46 / 1 Tim 2:11–14 (silence of women); #74 / 1 Tim 5:3, 6 (honor of widows); # 76 / 1 Tim 5:19 (not to receive an accusation against an elder); #77 / 1 Tim 5:20 (rebuke of sinners); #78 / 2 Tim 2:17 (not to speak with heretics); #61 / 1 Tim 6:7–10 (not seek money and lust for possessions); #11 / 2 Tim 2:4–5 (give heed to spiritual things); #53 / 2 Tim 2:23–24 (faith ought to be simple and avoid foolish questions); #67 / 2 Tim 4:3–4 (time when people will not endure sound doctrine); # 16 / 2 Tim 4:-6–8 (benefits of martyrdom).

[133] *Fort.* # 8 / 2 Tim 2:4–5 and # 5 / 2 Tim 2:11–12; and *Martyrs and Confessors* / 2 Tim 4:6–8.

[134] Treatises: *Pat.* / 1 Tim 1:3; *Hab. virg.* / 1 Tim 2:9–10; *Mort.* / 1 Tim 6:6 and 2 Tim 3:12; *Dom. or.* / *1 Tim* 6:7; *Eleem.* / 1 Tim 6:7–10; *Exhortation to Repentance* / 2 Tim 2:16; *Laps.* / 2 Tim 2:17; *Unit. eccl.* / 2 Tim 3:9; *Mort.* / 2 Tim 3:12; *[Idol.]* / 2 Tim 3:13. Epistles: *Julianos* / 1 Tim 1:13; *Rogatianus* / 1 Tim 4:12 (cf. 1 Tim 5:22); *Moyes and Maximus* / 1 Tim 4:17; *People* / 1 Tim 6:3–5; *Pompey* / 1 Tim 6:3–5; 2 Tim 2:24; Titus 3:5, 11; *Clergy* / 2 Tim 2:4; Titus 1:7; *Stephen* / 2 Tim 2:17; *Confessors* / 2 Tim 2:20; *Cornelius* / Titus 3: 10–11.

learning are not opposed to each other.[135] Whereas Irenaeus was deeply rooted in the apostolic tradition of the church and sought to use doctrine derived from this tradition to combat ideas he deemed heretical, Clement attempted to bring faith and knowledge together.[136] Though not officially a public teacher of the church, he was a man of the Spirit who taught, guided, and exhorted the souls of those who came as catechumens to his school.[137] Clement's virtual lack of concern for ecclesiastical organization suggests that whether or not he and his teaching had institutional church support, he did not simply teach doctrines already approved by the church in Alexandria. Rather, he constructed his own vision of the Christian faith, a vision in which faith serves as the foundation of philosophy.[138] Of the ten works attributed to Clement by Eusebius, five are extant, and these constitute the main surviving body of his written work.[139]

Estimates of Clement's scriptural references and allusions range has high as 3,200 to the Old Testament and 5,000 to the New, and these are matched by numerous references to classical texts.[140] Pauline quotations figure prominently among Clement's New Testament citations, and these are frequently connected with the name Παῦλος (Paul) or the title ἀποστολός (apostle).[141] Of the epistles in the New Testament Pauline corpus, Romans, 1 and 2 Corinthians, Galatians, Ephesians, Philippians, Colossians, 1 and 2 Timothy, and Titus are all cited by name and attributed to Paul or "the apostle." First and Second Thessalonians are not identified by name but are quoted directly and attributed to "the apostle," unlike Philemon, which does not appear anywhere in Clement's writings.[142] Not only are the Pastoral Epistles seamlessly integrated into the Pauline corpus in Clement, but Paul and his epistles exhibit an authority virtually equal to that of the four Evan-

---

[135] Quasten, *Patrology*, 2:7.

[136] Ibid., 20.

[137] Campenhausen, *The Fathers of the Greek Church*, 25.

[138] Denise Kimber Buell, *Making Christians: Clement of Alexandria and the Rhetoric of Legitimacy* (Princeton: Princeton University Press, 1991), 12.

[139] Ibid., 10.

[140] Eric Osborn, "Clement and the Bible," in *Origeniana Sexta: Origene et la Bible* (BETL 118; Leuven: Leuven University Press, 1995), 121. Quasten identifies 1,500 passages in which Clement alludes to the Old Testament and 2,000 passages in which he refers to the New Testament (*Patrology*, 2: 6). He also identifies 360 quotations from classical texts. James A. Brooks identifies a third of Clement's references as coming from pagan sources and notes that he cites the New Testament approximately twice as often as the Old Testament ("Clement of Alexandria as a Witness to the Development of the New Testament Canon," *SecCent* 9 [1992]: 47).

[141] Annewies van den Hoek, "Techniques of Quotation in Clement of Alexandria: A View of Ancient Literary Working Methods," *VC* 3 (1996): 230. She notes that according to Stahlin there are 1,273 borrowings from Paul and 24 percent of the references to Paul mention the name. Brooks argues that 40 percent of the New Testament references in Clement are from Paul as opposed to 45 percent from the gospels (ibid., 47).

[142] Brooks, "Clement of Alexandria," 42–43.

gelists and the Gospels. But more importantly, if critical theology began, as some claim, with Paul's distinction between letter and spirit in Romans and 2 Corinthians, a distinction that rooted exegesis in Christology and made interpretation a critical exercise, Clement advanced this procedure by incorporating Greek philosophy and logic into the process and by linking God with rational argument.[143] If so, Clement was in fact heir to a process set in motion by Paul a century and half earlier.

Scripture and Truth

For Clement, Scripture functions as divine oracle and true philosophy, and as such it is the very mind and will of God.[144] He writes in *Strom.* 2:2:9: "He who believes the divine scriptures with sure judgment, receives the voice of God, who bestowed the scriptures, a demonstration that cannot be impugned." And in *Strom.* 2:11:49 he writes: "For the highest demonstration, to which we have alluded, produces intelligent faith by the adducing and opening up of the scriptures to the souls of those who desire to learn; the result of which is knowledge." As Eric Osborn observes, the Scriptures provide proof producing ἐπιστήμη (understanding), which leads ultimately to γνῶσις (knowledge). Moreover, faith cannot be refuted because it is God who comes to us in Scripture.[145] For Clement, the authority of Scripture to settle controversy is primary and final, whereas the wisdom and authority of philosophy is derivative.[146] He writes in *Strom.* 6:5:125: "'But all things are right,' says scripture, 'before those who understand,' that is those who receive and observe, according to the ecclesiastical rule (ἐκκλησιστικὸν κανόνα), the exposition of the scriptures explained by him; and the ecclesiastical rule is the concord and harmony of the law and the prophets in the covenant delivered at the coming of the Lord." A central feature of Clement's hermeneutic in this text is the unity of the law and prophets with the covenant delivered at the coming of Christ.

But perhaps equally important is the claim that right understanding and exposition of Scripture are in accord with the ecclesiastical rule, which is best understood as the tradition that began with the apostles and comes down to the church authoritatively through the process of transmission.[147] Although "ecclesiastical rule" or "ecclesiastical canon" may not be identical with them, it appears to echo the sense of the terms "canon of truth," "body

---

[143] Osborn, "Clement and the Bible," 123–24.

[144] Ibid., 125. See also Quasten, *Patrology*, 2:25–26; and Brooks, "Clement of Alexandria," 48.

[145] Osborn, "Clement and the Bible," 125.

[146] Brooks, "Clement of Alexandria," 49.

[147] Eric Osborn, "The Bible and Christian Morality in Clement of Alexandria," in *The Bible in Greek Christian Antiquity* (ed. and trans. by Paul M. Blowers, The Bible Through Ages 1; Notre Dame, Ind.: University of Notre Dame Press, 1997): 113.

of truth," and *"regula fidei"* in Irenaeus and Tertullian.[148] Clement's terminology elsewhere ("knowledge of truth," "canon of truth," "canon of
faith"),[149] however, overlaps theirs, and for him this terminology expresses
the church's inner principle of theological truth and the authority that derives from it. Presumably both of these are in accord with the tradition
passed down from Christ and the apostles.[150] In this way, the interpretation
of Scripture and the authority of tradition work together to express the truth.
Clement positions himself as a rightful heir of this tradition of knowledge
and true interpretation, which emerged when the divine logos (wisdom) entered into the earthly realm and came down to the present in the transmitted
tradition of the church.[151]

As Osborn indicates, Clement did not operate with anything like a
modern sense of biblical context or textual integrity. For him, the unity of
biblical truth understood christologically must be uncovered wherever the
various parts of this truth are found in Scripture. They are to be taken from
their immediate contexts and placed in the new context of Christ. By recol-
lecting these various elements of scriptural truth, the whole body and unity
of the truth can be restored.[152] Hence, the truth of Scripture is anchored in
God's revelation in Christ, and the harmony between the law, the prophets,
and the covenant delivered through God's incarnation in Christ expresses
this one truth of Scripture and the church. As Irenaeus before him, Clement
too was involved in combatting what he considered to be heresy, and the
formation of the biblical canon progressed in tandem with the church's attempt to clarify the truth of Scripture and the authority of tradition.[153] In
terms of the Pauline canon, the Pastoral Epistles are fully integrated into the
corpus of thirteen epistles, and the limited role they play in Clement's use of
Pauline material appears related to his sense of their relative significance.
Given Clement's commitment to critical argumentation, speculative theology, and the interface between faith and philosophy, this makes sense, as it
can hardly be suggested that the Pastorals rival Romans, 1 and 2 Corinthians, or Galatians in theological depth. Having said this, however, Clement's

---

[148] See L. G. Patterson, "The Divine Became Human: Irenean Themes in
Clement of Alexandria," StPatr 31 (1997): 509. He argues that throughout his writings but primarily in *Strom.* 6 and 7, Clement uses the familiar Irenaean expressions
"rule of truth" and "rule of faith" to describe the accessing of the basic theology of
Scripture.

[149] See also the expressions "canon of the church" in *Strom.* 7:16:105; "knowledge of truth" in *Protrept.* 9:85:71; "canon of truth" in *Strom.* 7:16:94; and "canon of
faith" in *Strom.* 4:15:98.

[150] Brooks, "Clement of Alexandria," 53.

[151] Buell, *Making Christians,* 12–14. She also argues that Clement uses procre-
ative and kinship imagery when issues of issues of authority and identity are at issue.

[152] Osborn, "The Bible and Christian Morality," 113–14.

[153] Brooks sees only minor variations between Clement, Irenaeus, Tertullian,
and the Muratorian canon, and concludes that on the development of the canon they
are closely related ("Clement of Alexandria," 54–55).

pattern of thought still overlays a number of the theological and ecclesiastical patterns reflected in the Pastoral Epistles, the Apostolic Fathers, Irenaeus, and Tertullian. Since Clement was a critical and constructive thinker, a man concerned about heresy (though perhaps not to the degree that Irenaeus had been), and a teacher removed from the duties of day-to-day church administration, it is not surprising that some of the patterns and images in his writing that intersect with Irenaeus's work appear to be more distant and subdued. Moreover, Clement's orthodoxy was itself questioned, and according to strict distinctions between orthodoxy and heresy, his own legacy was dubious.[154]

### Unity and the Character of the Church

Hans von Campenhausen makes the rather bold claim that Clement was the most unecclessiastical of the early church authors and the most uninterested in the church as an institution. Clement rarely refers to the wider church community, and church officials do not interest him very much.[155] He only mentions ἐπίσκοποι (bishops) eight times, though there were certainly such figures in Alexandria by his time.[156] Yet Clement does attend to the theological character of the church and its authority, and though many heretics rejected the church's authority and the tradition preserved and passed on by it, it is precisely this tradition that Clement sees as the foundation of ecclesiastical authority. As Irenaeus before him, Clement claims that the creator and savior are one and the same and that this pattern can be seen in Scripture itself.[157] This one creating and saving God corresponds to the one church.[158] He uses kinship and procreation imagery to deal with the problem of unity and diversity in the church, and it is this imagery that gives Clement the framework to argue for the church's unity stemming from its originating source, Christ.[159] Further, he pictures the church as a nursing mother who feeds her children with the milk of divine wisdom and likens it elsewhere to a mother who draws her children to herself.[160] In *Strom.* 1:1:11 he uses the image of apostolic seeds and the preservation of truth: "Well, they preserving the tradition of the blessed doctrine derived directly from the holy apostles, Peter, James, John, and Paul, the sons receiving it from the father (but few were like the fathers), came by God's will to us also to deposit those ancestral and apostolic seeds. And well I know that they will exult; I do not mean delighted with the tribute, but solely on account of the preservation of the truth, according as they delivered it." While Clement may not

---

[154] Buell, *Making Christians*, 12.

[155] Campenhausen, *The Fathers of the Greek Church*, 35–36.

[156] U. Neymeyr, "Episkopoi bei Clemens von Alexandrien," StPatr 26 (1993): 292–95.

[157] Patterson, "The Divine Became Human," StPatr 31 (1997): 498.

[158] Quasten, *Patrology*, 2:24.

[159] Buell, *Making Christians*, 13, 18.

[160] See *Paed.* 1:6:42; and 1:5:21.

express much interest in the institutional character and management of the church, he does maintain a theology of the church's unity with which to combat the movements he sees threatening that unity.

Clement, Paul, and the Pastorals

Citing 1 Tim 1:5, 7, 8 (along with Romans 1:22; 3:16–18), Clement in *Strom.* 1:27 asserts the goodness of the law for training in piety, restraining sin, leading to virtue and well-doing, and making some people righteous. To know the law is descriptive of a good disposition and those who seek the law, says Clement, shall understand what is good. In *Strom.* 4:3, he juxtaposes 1 Tim 1:9, which states that the law is not made for the just person, and a statement of Socrates to the effect that the law was not made for the good person. Clement's apologetic for the law here draws together Scripture and Greek insight in order to assert the value of the law, and in that discussion 1 Timothy's statements about the law clearly serve his purpose. The issue of law is important in Romans and Galatians, and in the later Pauline context of 1 Timothy the goodness of the law and its purposes are claimed. Clement collapses these texts into his vision of the divine word and then uses them to underwrite his point that both the law and the gospel are important. In *Strom.* 4:3, he illustrates concretely his attempted fusion of Christian and pagan thought by citing together 1 Timothy and Socrates.

In *Paed.* 3:12, a section filled with scriptural quotations and allusions, many of them from Pauline texts, Clement in his counsel for the appropriate manner of life paraphrases 1 Tim 4:6–8 and the call to exercise to godliness (εὐσέβεια). Likewise, in *Protr.* 9:85:71, in a context where he refers to knowledge of the truth Clement identifies the meaning of knowledge as godliness (θεοσέβεια). Further in that same discussion, he says that the godliness that makes one like God (as far as possible) designates God as our teacher who alone can bring human beings to himself. This is followed immediately by a reference to 2 Tim 3:15–17 and the character and function of Scripture. In *Strom.* 1:1 and 2:11, Clement cites 2 Tim 2:1–2 and 1 Tim 6:20–21 in a plea to be strong and keep pure that which has been committed to the faithful. Savior language for Christ is also relatively common in Clement's work,[161] and the Pastoral image of Christ the mediator (μεσίτης) appears in *Paed.* 3:1:251.

These are but a few examples of Clement's copious references to scriptural texts and images, and they do not indicate any influence peculiar to the Pastorals, except as those texts have been incorporated into the Pauline corpus of writings and judged to be the inspired word of God. In that sense, the Pastoral texts and images are simply incorporated into the wider world of Scripture and cited when germane to the author's purposes. Once again, there is no apparent sense of literary or historical context in these refer-

---

[161] See for example *Strom.* 1:1:7; 5:12:79; 6:15, and compare the citations of 1 Tim 4:10; Titus 2:11–13, 3:3–5 in *Protr.* 9:1.

ences, for the biblical texts have been swept up by Clement into a new context as the word of God and are summoned to give knowledge of divine truth and exhortation to the Christian life. Clement is a speculative theologian, not an exegete on the order of Origen. With the long tradition of Greek philosophy in Alexandria, it is not surprising that Egyptian Christianity produced an abstract thinker in the mold of Clement. Yet it is precisely the imaginative and abstract character of his work, as well as his relative disinterest in the earthly affairs and polity of the institutional church, that make it difficult to assess the role of any particular set of Pastoral texts. References to the canon of truth, knowledge, inspired scripture, godliness, transmitting and preserving the tradition, the goodness of the law, Christ the mediator, and the apostolic authority of Paul are all shadowed in Clement's writing, but their immediacy and clarity are removed at least a step or two from our view. Biblical and textual particularity are merged now into his sense of scripture as the word of God and into his teaching, exhortation, and theological reflection. His project of bringing Greek philosophy to bear on the faith of the church and its theology is far removed from the concerns that motivated the Pastoral Epistles. Hence, it is not surprising that the patterns of thought represented in 1 & 2 Timothy and Titus, with their ecclesiastical concerns and hortatory appeals to those within the community, are only dimly reflected in the extant writings of Clement of Alexandria.

## Origen

### Introduction

In Origen, Clement's successor, Alexandrian Christianity produced its most important scriptural interpreter and original thinker. Born about 185, perhaps in Alexandria to a Christian family, he died in Caesarea in 253.[162] Excommunicated following his conflict with the Alexandrian bishop Demetrius, Origen spent the second part of his life in Caesarea where the bishop, ignoring the actions in Alexandria, invited him to establish a school that he oversaw for almost two decades. Hans von Campenhausen claims that Origen was the only one to present all of Christianity in the form of a workable philosophical system and he achieved a level of integration which none of the later Greek fathers matched.[163] Origen's most important apologetic treatise, *Contra Celsum*, illustrates in mirror image the struggle between Christianity and paganism, whereas *De principiis* is most aptly called a Christian systematic theology or manual of doctrine.[164] As did many before him in the early church, Origen sought to combat and refute his opponents and

---

[162] Quasten, *Patrology,* 2:40; see also Campenhausen, *The Fathers of the Greek Church,* 38.

[163] Campenhausen, *The Fathers of the Greek Church,* 42.

[164] Quasten, *Patrology,* 2:52, 57.

those who had used Scripture to support their own views, among them the gnostics, predestinarians, literalists, Marcionites, Jewish scholars, and pagan intellectuals.[165] Hence, when Origen writes his commentaries on Scripture and his other works, he is not writing into a vacuum. Origen, however, was not satisfied merely to refute his interlocutors, he sought to provide reasoned responses to the serious intellectual challenges they presented, which often forced him to go beyond the church's more narrowly defined doctrines of the faith.[166]

Of the Pauline Epistles, Origen wrote commentaries or homilies (or both) on all of them except 1 and 2 Timothy.[167] Though he was the first Christian exegete to comment systematically on the Pauline Epistles, only a small portion of this material has survived, and in some cases the evidence must be gleaned from the work of others, for example, Jerome.[168] As identified by Hammond-Bammel, Origen's Pauline Prefaces commonly exhibit a sense of the inspiration and difficulty, along with the profundity and usefulness, of the letter to be commented upon, as well as an acknowledgment of the need for divine aid in understanding it.[169] As with Clement, so with our discussion of Origen, we need only identify here the broad contours of his writing and thought in order to see the shadow lines of his sense of Christ, the truth, Scripture, and the church, and to see in what way these intersect with the patterns so conspicuous in the Pastorals—patterns that also ripple out into the post New Testament church.

Christ, Truth, Scripture, and the Church

Christophe Potworowski writes, ". . . truth for Origen refers primarily to a christological title, that is, an ἐπίνοια of Christ. It points to the mystery of Christ. Christ is 'truth itself' (αὐτοαλήθεια)."[170] In the coming of Christ, the true character of the Mosaic law and the Bible is disclosed.[171] For Origen, the function of biblical exegesis is none other than the mediation of

---

[165] R. P. C. Hanson, *Allegory and Event: A Study of the Sources and Significance of Origen's Interpretation of Scripture* (Richmond, Va.: John Knox, 1959), 160–61.

[166] Joseph Trigg, "Origen," *ABD* 5:45.

[167] Caroline P. Hammond-Bammel, "Origen's Pauline Prefaces and the Chronology of His 'Pauline Commentaries,'" *Origeniana Sexta: Origène et la Bible* (1995): 495. Origen wrote commentaries on Romans, Galatians, Ephesians, Philippians, Colossians, and 1 and 2 Thessalonians, Titus, Philemon; and homilies on Hebrews, Galatians, Titus, and probably also 1 and 2 Corinthians, 1 and 2 Thessalonians. See also Richard A. Layton, "Recovering Origen's Pauline Exegesis: Exegesis and Eschatology in the Commentary on Ephesians,"*JECS* 8 (2000): 373.

[168] Because so much of Origen's exposition of biblical books has not survived, Hammond-Bammel sounds an important warning about over generalizing concerning his Pauline exegesis ("Origen's Pauline Prefaces," 495).

[169] Ibid., 501.

[170] Christophe F. Potworowski, "The question of Truth (ἀλήθεια) in the Hermeneutics of Origen and Paul Ricoeur" StPatr 26 (1993): 311.

[171] Ibid., 311.

Christ's teaching and redemption to the hearer,[172] and the questions of the Christian faith not answered by the tradition of the apostles are addressed in Scripture. Since Christ is truth and since his words are found nowhere else than in Scripture, it follows that those who receive the truth receive it from Scripture.[173] In the preface to *De principiis* he writes:

> All who believe and are assured that grace and truth were obtained through Jesus Christ, and who know Christ to be the truth, agreeably to his own declaration, 'I am the truth,' derive the knowledge which incites men to a good and happy life from no other source than from the very words and teaching of Christ. And by the words of Christ we do not mean only those which he spoke when he became man and tabernacled in the flesh; for before that time, Christ, the Word of God, was in Moses and the prophets.

For Origen, Scripture and tradition are both sources for Christian doctrine,[174] and in the face of evident doctrinal differences, he appeals unabashedly to the rule of faith, as he indicates further in the same preface:

> Since many, however, of those who profess to believe in Christ differ from each other, not only in small and trifling matters, but also on subjects of the highest importance, . . . the teaching of the church, transmitted in orderly succession from the apostles, and remaining in the churches to the present day, is still preserved, that alone is to be accepted as truth which differs in no respect from the ecclesiastical and apostolic tradition.

The transmission of the truth and apostolic succession work together to establish in the present the church's canon of faith and to circumscribe legitimate differences of Christian belief. Hence, exegesis of Scripture for Origen is not to be set against the church's rule of faith but is rightly understood as corroborative of it. Exegesis is the process of mediating truth to the souls of Christian hearers as they progress in the purity of heart. Yet it is in Scripture that the hearers encounter most directly the words and teachings of Christ, who is the truth of God itself.

The issue of scriptural interpretation is central to Origen's writing, and in *Princ.* 4 he sets forth most directly his view of Scripture and the means for its interpretation. For him, Scripture is not only inspired, but it is verbally inspired. God is its author,[175] and it is this sense of divine authorship that establishes the unity of Scripture.[176] The Old Testament, whose full meaning is now disclosed in Christ,[177] united with the writings of the New Testament, is intended for the nourishment of the contemporary church and all those in

---

[172] Karen Jo Torjesen, *Hermeneutical Procedure and Theological Method in Origen's Exegesis* (PTS 28; Berlin: Walter De Gruyter, 1986), 12–14.

[173] Ibid., 36.

[174] Quasten, *Patrology*, 2:59.

[175] Hanson, *Allegory and Event*, 187; and Quasten, *Patrology*, 2:93.

[176] Hanson, *Allegory and Event*, 198.

[177] See *Princ.* 4, 6.

it.[178] And if one should doubt the divinity of Scripture, the sheer effectiveness of its power to transform hearers into followers of the truth should dispel those doubts.[179] Not only has Christ uncovered the meaning of the Old Testament for Origen, but the divine character of Jesus' teachings recorded in Scripture further prove for him their inspiration.

Torjesen illustrates the critical importance of Origen's *Logos* Christology for his understanding of Scripture and spiritual exegesis when she writes:

> Origen's Logos doctrine determines his approach to exegesis in several different ways. First of all, it is the presence of the Logos in Scripture which defines the spiritual sense. Everywhere Origen turns in Scripture he always finds this one thing—a teaching activity of the Logos. . . . The doctrine of the Logos as guiding principle of Origen's spiritual exegesis includes the origin of scripture from the Logos, the manifold forms of the Logos activity in Scripture and the pedagogical use of Scripture by the Logos in its present interpretation.[180]

Operating from Prov 22:20, Origen develops this notion of spiritual exegesis in terms of the various categories of hearers when he addresses a Christian teacher:

> The individual ought, then, to portray the ideas of holy scripture in a threefold manner upon his own soul; in order that the simple man may be edified by the "flesh," as it were, of the Scripture, for so we name the obvious sense; while he who has ascended a certain way may be edified by the "soul" as it were. The perfect, again, and he who resembles those spoken of by the apostle, when he says, "We speak wisdom among them that are perfect, but not the wisdom of the world, nor of the rulers of this world, who come to naught; but we speak the wisdom of God in a mystery, the hidden wisdom, which God has ordained before the ages, to our glory," may receive edification from the spiritual law, which has a shadow of good things to come.[181]

For Origen, Scripture contains progressive levels of teaching and nourishment for those at different stages of spiritual growth. The teachings of Christ guide the hearer through the process of purification, leading ultimately to perfection, and it is to this process that Origen's concept of the levels of scriptural meaning is tied. Exegesis is the process of mediating the truth of Scripture to the hearers, thus nourishing them on their spiritual journey. Whether we distinguish in Origen's thought between the physical, psychic, and spiritual meanings of Scripture as Campenhausen does,[182] or between the literal and the nonliteral (in turn subdivided into the moral and the spiritual) as

---

[178] Hanson, *Allegory and Event*, 203.
[179] See *Princ.* 4, 1–2. See also Torjesen, *Hermeneutical Procedure*, 36–37.
[180] Torjesen, *Hermeneutical Procedure*, 108.
[181] *Princ.* 4, 1, 11.
[182] Campenhausen, *The Fathers of the Greek Church*, 48.

Scalise does,[183] allegory plays a key role in bringing the truth of scripture to the hearts and minds of the hearers, guiding them on the journey to perfection. Ultimately it is not the history of scripture but the spiritual meaning disclosed by the procedures of allegory that concerns Origen.[184] For him truth is not called into question by the multiplicity of scriptural meanings. What is threatened is the idea that once attaining the truth, interpretation is no longer necessary.[185]

Paul, the Pastorals, and the Alexandrian Context

In *Contra Celsum*, Origen quotes or echoes a small number of Pastoral texts related to Christology: 1:63 to 1 Tim 1:15; 3:31 to 1 Tim 3:16; 4:38 to 1 Tim 4:10; 3:61 to 2 Tim 1:10; 2:59 to 2 Tim 2:11; 1:64 to Titus 3:3–6. There appear to be no substantive or extensive christological quotations from the Pastoral Epistles in *De principiis*, or on any other topic for that matter. There are a few quotations or allusions in *Contra Celsum* to ethical or practical pastoral issues from the Pastorals, but once again the issues seem to be random and do not exhibit a clear pattern: 8:73 to 1 Tim 2:1–2; 5:63 to Titus 3:10–11; 5:64 to 2 Tim 4:1–3; 8:32 to 1 Tim 4:4–5; 7:21 to 1 Tim 6:17–18; 3:11 to 1 Tim 6:20; 6:24 to 2 Tim 3:6–7; 4:70 to 2 Tim 2:20–21; 3:48 to Titus 1:9–10. These quotations and allusions relate to the character and purpose of the treatise but do not enable us to identify any significant patterns as they might relate to the Pastoral Epistles.

Our quest for Origen's use and view of Paul, his epistles, and more narrowly the Pastoral corpus is, of course, hampered by the loss of most of his biblical commentaries and homilies. But here, too, it is worth noting that Origen apparently did not write commentaries on 1 and 2 Timothy. What that omission means is, however, mere conjecture. The most that we can say is that not being an ecclesiastical figure in the institutional sense of that term, Origen did not think primarily of orthodoxy in institutional terms, but as a teacher he thought in terms of exegesis and argumentation. He was concerned with spiritual development, and his understanding of Scripture and exegesis was informed by and put in the service of that goal. His attempt to refute his opponents was not by simple appeal to the institutional authority of the church and its tradition, but to the interpretation of Scripture, manifested on one level by allegory. Origen also reflects the church's continuing development of Scripture as the inspired word of divine truth. The claim made in 2 Tim 3:14–16 has developed in Origen, and thus the specific historical circumstances of the scriptural texts are removed from his immediate

---

[183] Charles J. Scalise, "Origen and the 'sensus literalis,'" in *Origen of Alexandria: His World and His Legacy* (Christianity and Judaism in Antiquity 1; ed. Charles Kannengiesser and William L. Petersen; Notre Dame, Ind.: University of Notre Dame Press, 1988 ), 122–23.

[184] Ibid., 122.

[185] Potworowski, "Question of Truth," 310.

concern. For him, Scripture represents divine truth, and the purpose of exegesis is to mediate this truth to the hearers on their spiritual journey.

Origen's emphasis on interpretation and argumentation, as well as his concern for spiritual development, is consistent with the Hellenistic legacy in Alexandria. Platonic thought filtered through Philo had already put down the foundations for Clement's interest in bringing faith and philosophy, religion and knowledge, together. But it had also provided a precedent for Origen's spiritual exegesis, marked most conspicuously by his use of allegorical interpretation. Philo, too, had distinguished between literal and allegorical interpretations of Scripture, and he had distinguished as well between different levels of spiritual discernment on the part of individuals. Hence, the intellectual legacy of Alexandria appears to put both Clement and Origen, the two most important early church figures to emerge out of Alexandria, in a line of Hellenistic tradition that precedes the appearance of the church in Egypt. Although both men are within the Christian church, their approach to theology, their use of Scripture, and their view of the church, though different from each other in significant ways, are markedly influenced by that Alexandrian legacy.

## CONCLUSION

Determining the character of Pauline, in particular Pastoral, usage in Irenaeus, Tertullian, Clement, and Origen requires that we consider the interplay of three factors. We can refer to these as location and legacy, ecclesiology and opposition, and function and formation. Our investigation of the Pauline and Pastoral patterns reflected in these early church figures indicates that each of these factors played a role in the way Pauline material was used, interpreted, and reconfigured. But even more importantly for our purposes these categories help us position more clearly the Pastoral Epistles and the theological patterns reflected in them in their proper conceptual and symbolic matrix in the developing Pauline legacy.

### *Location and Legacy*

Coming from Asia Minor to Lyon, Irenaeus bridged the church in the East and the emerging church in the West. His association with Polycarp, his connection with the territory of Paul's early missionary work, and his proximity to the apparent destination of 1 and 2 Timothy, undoubtedly brought him into close contact with the Pauline tradition and the emerging Pauline legacy. It is implausible to think he could have left that tradition and legacy behind when he went to Gaul. The evidence of Irenaeus' Pauline usage confirms that he was part of a tradition of Pauline interpretation and was not merely turning to Pauline texts because his opponents had used them earlier to support their gnostic views. Paul and the Pauline scriptural texts were clearly important for the bishop, and perhaps more importantly for our purposes, he reflects a number of the impulses previously expressed in the Pastoral Epistles: sound teaching, correct faith, truth, guarding the "good deposit," faithful transmission of the tradition, ecclesiology and leadership in the church, and christological images. To be sure, Irenaeus extends, and in some cases, transforms these ideas, but as a bishop defending the church from the gnostics, he reflects a theological framework related to that found in the Pastorals.

The North African Tertullian, too, defends the church's orthodoxy, displays a concern for the rule of faith guarded and preserved by the church, and reflects certain christological formulations found in the Pastorals. At least in his pre-Montanist phase, Tertullian has many things in common with Irenaeus, as we have seen. Determining whether these connections to the Pastorals and Irenaeus are attributable to Tertullian alone or are also reflective of the church in North Africa more broadly is beyond the scope of this discussion, but it is noteworthy that the Latin church in Gaul and North Africa, represented by Irenaeus and Tertullian, display a number of common concerns and formulations.

On the other hand, Clement and Origen, both strongly influenced by their work in Alexandria, represent different interests and concerns. Though troubled by various kinds of opponents, Clement sought to bring Christian faith and Greek philosophy together and to instruct and nurture the souls of his catechetical students, whereas Origen, the scriptural exegete and preacher, tried to bring the word of God to life for those on the spiritual journey to perfection. For both of these writers, Paul is very important, but the concerns that drive the Pastoral Epistles seem to be at least a step or two removed from the concerns of Clement and Origen. They are teachers, not institutional figures like Irenaeus is, and the responses to their opponents are marked more by theological argument and scriptural interpretation than institutional defense, even though on some issues of polity they may have been in sympathy with the claims of Irenaeus and Tertullian. In any case, Alexandria and its Hellenistic legacy undoubtedly influenced the thought and work of Clement and Origen.

## Ecclesiology and Opposition

Another factor is the position of the respective authors in the church and their struggle with opponents who deviate from their perception of the church and the truth. In *Adversus haereses*, Irenaeus, the bishop, sets out to refute the claims of the gnostics, and he does so by developing the theology of the church, the authority of the apostles, the transmission of the tradition, and the sense that correct teaching is preserved in the episcopal structure of the church marked by apostolic succession. Although the Pastoral Epistles may be almost a century earlier than *Adversus haereses,* they are united by a common concern to transmit and preserve apostolic tradition in the face of forces the authors consider a threat to the truth. Irenaeus develops his ecclesiology beyond that of the Pastorals by, for example, shifting the emphasis from the personal qualities of office holders to the offices themselves. This represents a marked development in ecclesiological thought, but it suggests an extension of rather than a break from the tradition of the Pastorals. Though not a bishop, Tertullian also displays concern for the orthodoxy of the church and the preservation of that orthodoxy in the face of opponents who threaten it. The true church is the repository of correct teaching.

Clement is a speculative theologian concerned about bringing faith and philosophy together and nurturing the minds and souls of his catechumens. He is not apparently concerned with the institutional politics and apparatus of the church. Clement is a thinker and not directly an apologist for the institution of the church. Origen, too, was a teacher, and he had his own difficulties with the institutional church in Alexandria, being excommunicated by the bishop there. To be sure, Origen sought to refute his opponents, among them gnostics, predestinarians, literalists, Marcionites, Jewish scholars, and pagan thinkers, but he did not do so from a position of ecclesiastical authority as much as by scriptural exegesis, allegorical interpretation, and reasoned response. As a result, Clement and Origen stand at some distance from the perspectives of Irenaeus and Tertullian, as well as the Pastoral Epistles, even though both men consider the Pastorals to be part of the Pauline corpus.

## Function and Formation

Clement and Origen are church teachers and writers; they are not noted as figures in positions of institutional authority. This clearly affects how they function, for ultimately they are concerned with the minds and faith of their students. Christian spiritual life and formation is clearly important to these two men, and that affects how they rethink the faith and the Scriptures. As we see in Clement's concern for Greek philosophy and Origen's use of allegorical interpretation, these two early church thinkers were pushing the boundaries of Christian thought. They were not mere consolidators of the tradition. It would be unfair to characterize Irenaeus and Tertullian as mere conservators of past tradition, especially in light of Tertullian's later interest in Montanism, but their view of the church, sense of orthodoxy, perspective on the church, and location puts them in different categories from Clement and Origen. While each of these authors may exhibit different perspectives in different writings, certain concerns and ideas characterize their respective approaches and their use of Pauline material. In light of this three-fold categorization of contributing circumstances, we are able to see more clearly the place of the Pastoral Epistles in the developing Pauline legacy of the early church.

# ~ 7 ~

# PAUL, THE PASTORAL EPISTLES, AND
# THE *ACTS OF PAUL (AND THECLA)*

## INTRODUCTION

THE BODY of material collectively known as the *Acts of Paul* comprises a series of stories purporting to describe episodes in Paul's life in various places:
Antioch, Iconium, Myra, Sidon, Tyre, Ephesus, Philippi, Corinth, conclud-
ing in Rome with his martyrdom. In that collection of stories, perhaps the
most intriguing is the account of Paul and Thecla in Iconium and Antioch
(Syrian or Psidian?). In this episode we get a glimpse into the struggle to deal
with women's roles, their authority in the church, and the growing second
century Christian interest in celibacy. According to the story of Paul and
Thecla, at the heart of the Pauline gospel is the oneness of God, the resurrection, and sexual continence, if not also chastity and celibacy. There is a general consensus that these apocryphal accounts derive from the latter part of
the second century, somewhere in Asia Minor. However, the complicated
extant textual tradition makes it difficult to know precisely how the various
episodes fit together, who wrote them, and how we should characterize the
genre of these narratives.[1]

The pre-Montanist Tertullian (sometime before 207) apparently refers
to the story of Paul and Thecla when he writes in *Bapt.* 17:5: "But if the writings which wrongly (falsely) go under Paul's name, claim Thecla's example
as a license for women's teaching and baptizing, let them know that, in Asia,
the presbyter who composed that writing, as if he were augmenting Paul's
fame from his own store, after being convicted, and confessing that he had

---

[1] For discussions of the textual traditions of the *Acts of Paul,* see J. K. Elliott, *The
Apocryphal New Testament: A Collection of Apocryphal Christian Literature in an English
Translation* (Oxford: Clarendon, 1993), 352; and E. Hennecke, *New Testament Apoc-
rypha* (ed. by W. Schneemelcher, trans. and ed. by R. McL. Wilson; Southhampton,
Eng.: SCM, 1965), 2:325–27. See also the comments by Willy Rordorf regarding the
text and the connection between the *Acts of Paul* and the Thecla story, and the *termi-
nus ante quem* for the writing of the *Acts of Paul* ("Tradition and Composition in the
*Acts of Thecla*: The State of the Question," *Semeia,* 38 [1986]: 43–44). Also Sheila E.
McGinn, "The Acts of Thecla," in *Searching the Scriptures: A Feminist Commentary* (ed.
Elisabeth Schüssler Fiorenza; New York: Crossroads, 1994), 2:802–3.

done it from love of Paul, was removed from office."[2] At least by the beginning of the third century, the story of Thecla and her encounters with Paul were known in North Africa, where Tertullian objects to Thecla being used as an example authorizing women to teach and baptize. Although we cannot confirm that the author in fact was a presbyter in the church in Asia Minor, or that he was removed from office thereby bringing disrepute on Thecla and other church women, Tertullian's account suggests that the story of Thecla was circulating rather broadly in the church and was being used by some as an example authorizing women to teach and baptize. At the same time, it also suggests that it generated resistance on the part of those who objected to these roles for women in the church and who, as in the case of Tertullian, sought to undermine the legitimacy of the tradition. Women teachers and baptizers were not thought to be consistent with what Paul was known to have written about women in 1 Corinthians and probably also in 1 Timothy.

## CONFLICTING TRADITIONS OR EXTENDING THE TRADITION

The *Acts of Paul*, along with the apocryphal acts of other apostles, have long invited scholarly attention focusing on how these texts were produced, what they say about the history of the early church, and how they relate substantively and literarily to the Acts of the Apostles.[3] For our purposes, two arguments are especially important because of what they say about the *Acts of Paul*, but perhaps even more so because of how they argue for a connection between the apocryphal text and the Pastoral Epistles. The hypotheses put forth by Dennis MacDonald and Richard Bauckham warrant attention on their own merits, but for the purposes of this argument they can also

---

[2] A. Hilhorst, "Tertullian on the Acts of Paul," in *The Apocryphal Acts of Paul and Thecla* (ed. Jan N. Bremmer; GA Kampen: Kok Pharos, 1996), 150–58. Here, Hilhorst discusses the textual and translation issues associated with the text of *De baptismo* (see also Rordorf, "Tradition and Composition," 44). McGinn rightly cautions against over stating the value of Tertullian's comment for dating the *Acts of Paul* for two reasons: (1) the arguments normally assume a close connection between the *Acts of Paul* and the story of Thecla (the Thecla portion of the larger apocryphal Pauline tradition) and (2) the necessary distinction between knowing a written text and knowing the Thecla story (she is here presumably acknowledging a different text of *De baptismo* that reads "Acta Pauli" [*codex Trecensis*] rather than "scripta" [Mesnartius edition], suggesting that what is being referred to may not be a written text but a story). The most we can say with complete certainty is that the Thecla story, if not a text, was known in North Africa by the beginning of the third century ("The Acts of Thecla," 802–3).

[3] For one of the best accounts of scholarship on the literary and folk tradition character of these texts, see Virginia Burrus, *Chastity as Autonomy: Women in the Stories of Apocryphal Acts* (Studies in Women and Religion 23; Lewiston, N.Y.: Mellen, 1987), 7–20. See also McGinn, *The Acts of Thecla*, 803–4.

serve as interpretive typologies to organize our sense of how to position the respective texts in the developing Pauline tradition. In this regard, the arguments by MacDonald and Bauckham set the categories for our thinking about how Paul was being recast as an apostolic figure and how his gospel was being tailored to new circumstances in the church.

Dennis MacDonald argues that the Pastoral Epistles represent the tradition of those who rejected the so-called old wives tales and the images of Paul told in stories by women.[4] The story of Thecla came from these oral folk traditions of women well known in Greek antiquity, and the Asian presbyter borrowed from this tradition to produce the story of Paul and Thecla known in the apocryphal *Acts of Paul.*[5] Rejecting the idea of literary dependence—either of the *Acts of Paul* on the Pastoral Epistles or the Pastorals on a written source behind the apocryphal *Acts of Paul*— MacDonald argues it is most plausible to conclude that both authors knew the same oral traditions, and that the author of the Pastorals objected to the portrayal of Paul in them. The author of the Pastorals wrote to present an alternative view of Paul and his teaching as the apostle approached his death.[6] The image of Paul and his teaching in the Pastorals prevailed over the Paul of the apocryphal *Acts of Paul* and ultimately these three letters were included in the New Testament canon, although the tradition of Thecla and her miraculous escape from martyrdom, her fierce independence, and her chastity lived on in the church. Hence, the legacy of Paul contained in the Pastoral Epistles and the body of Pauline letters in the New Testament represents only one line of the developing Pauline legacy. It is a line characterized by literate men who supported the developing episcopal authority of the church and rejected the folk traditions of women who remembered a more marginal and undomesticated Paul.[7]

According to MacDonald's view, the author of the Pastoral Epistles represents a socially conservative movement in the church that reacts against the more radical Paul of the folk traditions and women. This argument, of course, addresses the Thecla tradition and its connection with the Pastoral letters, but does not account as well for the other traditions in the apocryphal *Acts of Paul.* In any case, we might characterize the relationship between the Pastoral Epistles and the *Acts of Paul* argued by MacDonald as a conflict model, where conservative forces are contending against more popular and radical elements in the church, elements marked by openness to women and their central place in the church, as well as an ascetic and

---

[4] Dennis R. MacDonald, *The Legend and the Apostle: The Battle for Paul in Story and Canon* (Philadelphia: Westminster, 1983), 14.

[5] Ibid., 19, 21.

[6] Ibid., 62–66. Cf. also W. Rordorf, "Nochmals: Paulusakten und Pastoral-briefe," in *Tradition and Interpretation in the New Testament: Essays in Honor of E. Earle Ellis for His 60th Birthday* (ed. Gerald F. Hawthorne and Otto Betz; Grand Rapids: Eerdmans, 1987), 319–25.

[7] MacDonald, *The Legend and the Apostle,* 85, 89.

celibate way of life. Both of these are played out against the backdrop of the church's martyrdom tradition, which was becoming a conspicuous feature of the church's life in the second century.

Although given high marks for ingenuity, MacDonald's argument is not without its critics, scholars who present compelling alternatives to the conflict model, among them most notably Richard Bauckham. After acknowledging the close relationship of the *Acts of Paul* with the Pastoral Epistles, especially with 2 Timothy, Bauckham compares the places and the names reported in the Pauline itinerary in the *Acts of Paul* and the Pastorals and concludes that the evidence is best explained by claiming that the *Acts of Paul* was intended as a sequel to the Acts of the Apostles. The author sought to continue the story of Paul from the point where the Lukan account leaves off to the time of the apostle's eventual martyrdom in Rome. Because of this, the author of the *Acts of Paul* did not draw characters from Acts but did draw from 2 Timothy and 1 and 2 Corinthians. In the case of both 2 Timothy and the two Corinthians letters, the author of the *Acts of Paul* assumed that the events described in those texts came from the time after the events reported in Acts. Hence, the author of the apocryphal account of Paul drew upon 2 Timothy (perhaps also Titus) and 1 and 2 Corinthians. Unlike MacDonald who argues that both the *Acts of Paul* and the Pastoral Epistles were dependent on a common oral tradition, Bauckham claims that the author of the *Acts of Paul* worked with those Pauline letters thought to come from the end of Paul's first imprisonment in Rome to his martyrdom in the imperial capital sometime later.[8]

Bauckham points to two examples he thinks illustrate the greater plausibility of his hypothesis for literary dependence over MacDonald's claim for a common oral tradition. The first is the connection between 2 Tim 4:17 ("So I was rescued from the Lion's mouth") and the story of Paul's encounter with the lion in Ephesus in the apocryphal *Acts of Paul.* Bauckham concludes that, in light of the allusion to 2 Tim 4:17, it is most likely that the story in the *Acts of Paul* stands in an exegetical relationship with the second letter to Timothy. Operating in the way Jewish interpreters often did, the author of the *Acts of Paul* found a reference to an event in Paul's life, though not actually described, and imaginatively created a story to account for this reference. Although the reference in 2 Tim 4:17 (cf. 1 Cor 15:32) may have been intended metaphorically, the author has taken it literally and constructed a story around it.[9] The second example is the reference in 2 Tim 2:18 (". . . the resurrection has already taken place."), which, according to Bauckham, is exegeted and elaborated in the story of Paul and Thecla (*Acts of Paul and*

---

[8] Richard Bauckham, "The *Acts of Paul* as a Sequel to Acts," in *The Book of Acts in Its Ancient Literary Setting* (ed. Bruce W. Winter and Andrew D. Clarke; vol. 1 of *The Book of Acts in Its First Century Setting;* ed. Bruce W. Winter; Grand Rapids: Eerdmans, 1993), 116–20.

[9] Ibid., 125.

*Thecla* 14). Demas and Hermogenes say to Thamyris, "And we shall teach you about the resurrection which he says is to come, that it has already taken place in the children, and that we rise again, after having come to the knowledge of the true God." Once again, for Bauckham this is most aptly explained as a creative extension of 2 Tim 2:18, in this case brought about by a desire to place the notion of the resurrection as a past event into the context of the Paul and Thecla story.[10]

Thus, in Bauckham's view, the *Acts of Paul* was a continuation of the Pauline story whereby the author searched the texts thought to come from the time in Paul's life following the Acts of the Apostles. Finding only a few references to episodes thought to come from Paul's life and ministry during this period but no actual narrative for these references, the author set out to create in narrative form a story of the final part of the apostle's life. For Bauckham, three things influenced the genre of the *Acts of Paul*: (1) the form, structure, and content of the Acts of the Apostles, (2) Jewish interpretive literature referred to as "rewritten Bible," and (3) the novelistic biography where history and freedom for imaginative expression went together quite naturally. He concludes: "The result is a work of novelistic biographical character (not strictly a biography) suited to telling the story of a particular kind of historical figure: the Christian apostle. We may regard this as a new genre alongside the novelistic biography or as a subgenre of the novelistic biography."[11]

In contrast to MacDonald's conflict model, Bauckham presents a model based on literary dependence to describe the relationship between the *Acts of Paul* and the Pastoral letters. Bauckham rightly distinguishes among the three Pastoral letters and their respective links to the apocryphal *Acts of Paul*. As we have noted, 1 and 2 Timothy are in some ways quite different texts, and it comes as no surprise to suggest that the individual Pastoral letters may relate in different ways to the *Acts of Paul*. What still needs to be stressed, however, is that the apocryphal *Acts of Paul* reflects circumstances of a popular form of second-century Christianity in Asia Minor, emphasizing the authority of women in the church, the importance of sexual continence, and the power of the resurrection.[12] These issues come to the

---

[10] Ibid., 127–28. See also Pieter J. Lalleman, "The Resurrection in the Acts of Paul," in *The Apocryphal Acts of Paul and Thecla* (ed. Jan N. Bremmer; GA Kampen: Kok Pharos, 1996), 134–36.

[11] Ibid., 149–50.

[12] For discussions of various aspects of these circumstances, see Burrus, *Chastity and Autonomy*, 59–60; Willi Braun, "Physiotherapy of Femininity in the Acts of Thecla, " in *Text and Artifact in the Religions of Mediterranean Antiquity: Essays in Honour of Peter Richardson* (Studies in Christianity and Judaism 9; ed. Stephen G. Wilson and Michel Desjardins; Waterloo, Ont.: Wilfrid Laurier University Press, 2000), 209–30; Jan N. Bremmer, "Magic, Martyrdom and Women's Liberation in the Acts of Paul and Thecla," in *The Apocryphal Acts of Paul* (ed. Jan N. Bremmer; GA Kampen: Kok Pharos, 1996), 42–44, 51, 57; McGinn, "The Acts of Thecla," 804, 819–20; Beate Wehn, " 'Blessed Are the Bodies of Those Who Are Virgins': Reflections on the Image of Paul in the *Acts of Thecla*," *JSNT* 79 (2000): 151–57.

fore most clearly in the narrative of Paul and Thecla, whereas (save the topic of bodily resurrection) other issues, perhaps reflective of Paul's conflict with the Corinthian church, seem most clearly echoed in the so-called *3 Corinthians*.[13] Furthermore, there is no compelling reason why more than one authorial hand may not be at work in the texts collectively known as the *Acts of Paul*. And the possibility of later redaction clearly adds yet another complicating dimension to the interpretation of these stories.[14]

Using the insights generated by these formative arguments as the frame of reference for our juxtaposition of the Pastoral Epistles and the *Acts of Paul*, we will proceed in the next section to position the two sets of texts in the developing Pauline tradition with an eye toward the image and message of Paul. Here, the issue is not simply literary dependence, but the symbolic relationships and the way these relationships suggest different trajectories or dichotomies in the early church's representation of the apostle. The approach, once again, is to compare theological patterns, more specifically in this case to compare patterns from the *Acts of Paul* to patterns in the Pastoral Epistles as we have already identified them. In this case, we can see how Paul's theology and charisma have been constructed in remarkably different ways, even though there is a good chance that the author(s) of the *Acts of Paul* may have used some Pastoral material in the writing of the apocryphal acts of the apostle.

## The *Acts of Paul* and Pauline Patterns in the Pastoral Epistles

The Pastoral Epistles, as we have seen from a number of different perspectives,[15] represent a desire to preserve the true faith, and consequently they portray the apostle Paul as the defender of this faith. The contours of the true faith are not usually spelled out in any great detail, but the concept of an orthodox faith is clearly established in the tradition of these three epistles.[16] In the account of Paul and Thecla, the establishment of orthodoxy is not a driving concern of the narrative, but the stories nevertheless give us certain clues to the gospel, if not also the theology, represented by the apostle in the apocryphal tradition.

In the opening words of the story the author notes, when referring to the hypocrisy of Demas and Hermogenes, that Paul did them no harm but loved them "so that he made sweet to them all the words of the lord and the

---

[13] Gerard Littikhuizen, "The Apocryphal Correspondence with the Corinthians and the Acts of Paul," in *The Apocryphal Acts of Paul and Thecla* (ed. by Jan N. Bremmer; GA Kampen: Kok Pharos, 1996), 75–91.

[14] McGinn, "The Acts of Thecla," 801, 805.

[15] See above, especially pp. 193–95.

[16] See above, p. 69.

interpretation of the gospel concerning the birth and resurrection of the Beloved; and he gave them an account, word for word, of the great deeds of Christ as they were revealed to him" (*Acts of Paul and Thecla* 1). These statements lead to the scene in the house of Onesiphorus where Paul pronounces a number of beatitudes, and these blessings give us clues to Paul's image and his gospel in the apocryphal narrative:

> [T]here was great joy and bowing of knees and breaking of bread and the word of God about abstinence and the resurrection (ἐγκρατείς καὶ ἀναστάσεως). Paul said, 'Blessed are the pure in heart (καθαροὶ τῇ καρδιᾳ), for they shall see God; blessed are those who have kept the flesh chaste (ἁγνὴν τὴν σάρκα), for they shall become a temple of God; blessed are the continent (ἐγκρατεῖς), for God shall speak with them; blessed are those who have kept aloof from this world (ἀποταξάμενοι τῷ κόσμῳ τούτῳ), for they shall be pleasing to God; blessed are those who have wives as not having them, for they shall experience God.'[17]

Perhaps echoing and elaborating 1 Tim 5:22 where Paul counsels Timothy to "keep yourself pure (ἁγνόν),"[18] the apocryphal author uses a series of words normally translated as "abstinence," "pure," "chaste," and "continent" in a narrative context pertaining to separation from the world and advising husbands to live as though they have no wives. All of these behaviors are blessed and result in some intimate relationship with God ("see God," "become a temple of God," "speak with God," "pleasing to God," "experience God"). These behaviors are linked to the resurrection and perhaps also in some conceptual way to the intimate relationship the blessed have with God.

With respect both to sexual relations and to involvement in the affairs of this world, the author ties the Pauline gospel to an encratic orientation that clearly seems at odds with the spirit of 1 Tim 4:3–4 and the call not to reject anything created by God, referring to marriage and food. The concepts of purity and self-control are found in both the Pastoral Epistles and the account of Paul and Thecla,[19] but the apocryphal narrative has turned them in the direction of sexual restraint, even in marriage, and withdrawal from the world and its expectations. Regardless of whether or not we claim some exegetical dependence of the apocryphal author on the Pastoral texts (so Bauckham) or a common oral tradition (so MacDonald), the conceptual patterns of the two traditions intersect; yet they ultimately move in very different directions: the

---

[17] *Acts of Paul and Thecla* 5. Wehn ("Blessed are the Bodies," 151) claims that these beatitudes are central to the image of Paul in the narrative.

[18] Cf. σώφρονας (moderate, sensible) and ἁγνὰς (chaste) in Titus 2:5 with respect to proper behavior for older women.

[19] See ἐγκρατῆ (self-controlled) in Titus 1:8; καθαρίσῃ (cleanse, purify) in Titus 2:14; καθαρᾷ (clean, pure) in 2 Tim 1:3; καθαρᾶς (clean) in 2 Tim 2:22; καθαρὰ τοῖς καθαποῖς ("to the pure all things are pure") in Titus 1:15; and ἁγνὰς (chaste) in Titus 2:5.

one toward a settled and stable household and the other toward a counter-cultural relationship with the established social order of the Greco-Roman world. In the respective author's hands, Paul becomes the spokesman for both of these gospels as well as the theologies that support them.

These ideas are reinforced again in the *Acts of Paul and Thecla* 9, where the writer makes clear that Paul teaches that a person must fear only one God and live chastely (καὶ μόνον Θεὸν φοβεῖσθαι καὶ ζῆν ἀγνῶς). Thecla, enthralled by Paul's teaching, refuses to marry Thamyris and rebuffs his overtures toward her, opting instead to adhere to Paul's teaching. The gospel of chastity is linked explicitly in v. 12 to the resurrection, where Paul is said to teach that "there is for you no resurrection unless you remain chaste and do not pollute the flesh (ἀνάστασις ὑμῖν οὐκ ἔστιν ἐὰν μὴ ἀγνοὶ μείνητε καὶ τὴν σάρκα μὴ μολύνητε ἀλλὰ τηρήσητε ἀγνήν)."[20] Here the connection between the resurrection and chastity is made explicit. The one (resurrection) is dependent on the other (chastity), which clearly puts the Pauline gospel in the position of making resurrection the goal of the chaste life.[21]

According to the story of Paul and Thecla, the apostle teaches the gospel of chastity, and Thecla fiercely and courageously resists conformity to patriarchal social norms. In doing so, she is not only miraculously rescued from death by divine intervention, but also supported by other women. For example, Tryphaena in the Antioch portion of the story comes to the aide of Thecla. The unmistakable implication is that her actions are confirmed both by God and other women, and her behavior conforms to the gospel that Paul teaches, not to Greco-Roman household expectations. According to this part of the apocryphal *Acts of Paul*, the proper way of relating to the Greco-Roman world is separation and non-conformity in sexual matters to the common social norms. The Pastoral Epistles on the other hand encourage a version of godliness that presumes conformity to a concept of the household of God that is modeled on the Greco-Roman household, even to the point of saying in 1 Tim 2:15 that women "will be saved through childbearing, provided they continue in faith and love and holiness, with modesty." These opposing versions of the Pauline gospel need not mean that one author is writing to refute the other. It is just as likely that whatever literary connections there are between the two texts they represent quite different manifestations of the developing Pauline tradition corresponding to two different brands of emerging Christianity.

---

[20] In making the turn to the gospel of chastity, the author may be playing off of words and images in 1 Cor 7 and even 2 Cor 7:1. If this is the case, this would support the argument made by Richard Bauckahm (see above).

[21] Bremmer, "Magic, Martyrdom and Women's Liberation", 55; E. Margaret Howe, "Interpretations of Paul in the Acts of Paul and Thecla," in *Pauline Studies: Essays Presented to F. F. Bruce on His 70th Birthday* (ed. Donald A. Hagner and Murray J. Harris; Grand Rapids: Eerdmans, 1980), 35–36, 43–46; Pieter J. Lalleman, "The Resurrection in the Acts of Paul," in *The Apocryphal Acts of Paul and Thecla* (ed. Jan N. Bremmer; GA Kampen: Kok Pharos, 1996), 126, 127–32, 134–35.

It is worth noting, however, that the call by Paul in 2 Timothy to suffer as he has suffered, with the clear implication that the apostle is fast approaching the end of his life (4:6–8), conforms more closely than 1 Timothy and Titus to the near martyrdom of Thecla and the subsequent suffering and martyrdom of Paul.[22] Both 2 Timothy and the Thecla story unfold against a backdrop of prospective martyrdom (*Acts of Paul and Thecla* 15–17 and Paul in Ephesus). Steadfastness in the gospel, meaning quite different things in the two traditions, is the desired mode of behavior in the face of death, with resurrection being the ultimate reward for those who remain obedient. What is especially evident in the Pastorals, including 2 Timothy, is the call to guard the "good deposit" of the church's truth. In the case of 1 Timothy and Titus, this suggests an emerging church structure that will become the cradle and guardian of the true teaching. Whereas in the *Acts of Paul and Thecla* the most that can be said is that the popular stories about the apostle entertain and serve the desires of a countercultural community reluctant to conform to the expectations of Greco-Roman patriarchal society. The message is that, although the dominant society responds to this nonconformity with a vengeance, God stands with those who are obedient, indeed rescuing them from fire and wild beasts.

On the relationship between Jews, Gentiles, and the law, we can see a clear line of progression from Paul to the Pastorals and on to the *Acts of Paul.* In Rom 4, 9–11, and Gal 3–4, the problem of Gentile inclusion and the place of the Jewish law is front and center. These are burning issues for Paul. By the time 1 Timothy and Titus appear, this cluster of issues is subdued dramatically, and 2 Timothy gives no attention at all to these issues.[23] Furthermore, by the time of the *Acts of Paul,* these concerns are nowhere to be found.[24] In the *Acts of Paul and Thecla* the primary issues are women, continence, chastity, and resurrection; in *3 Corinthians* the primary issues are linked to some type of gnostic or spiritualist tendency. There can be no doubt that these three sets of texts reflect broadly the development of the church away from matters of Jew-Gentile concern as the Christian church accepted the Gentile mission and became in fact increasing non-Jewish. Paul and his authority were being put in the service of new concerns and problems. This development, however, was anything but a simple linear progression. It was complicated by local concerns, by social class, and by oppositional forces both inside and outside the church.

The theological pattern of each of these traditions results from a reshaping of Paul's charisma. Paul came to underwrite different responses to current issues in the church; and because he was deemed relevant to the new problems facing the church, his authority was enhanced still further. The charisma of Paul operated in a reciprocal relationship with the concerns

---

[22] Cf. the *Martyrdom of Perpetua.*
[23] See 1 Tim 1:8–11; and Titus 1:10–16.
[24] Pheme Perkins, "Paul, Apocalypse of," *ABD* 5:203.

of the day, and in the *Acts of Paul and Thecla* the theological concerns, such as they were, served the interests of those who wished to opt out of the normal gender and social expectations of Roman society.

The one theological issue that persists through all three traditions is a concern for the resurrection. In 1 Corinthians 15, 2 Timothy 2:18, and throughout the *Acts of Paul*, the topic of the resurrection or some question about it comes to the fore as a matter of controversy. From the time of Paul until the late second century, the resurrection generally was a matter of some debate in the Eastern church, perhaps in the West as well. By the third century this issue may have become less a matter of controversy.[25] In the *Acts of Paul*, unlike the issues of women, marriage, and chastity which are limited largely to the *Acts of Paul and Thecla*, concerns about the resurrection are found in the *Martyrdom of Paul*, in the apocryphal Corinthian correspondence, as well as in the *Acts of Paul and Thecla*.[26] In the story of Paul and Thecla, chastity is a precondition for the resurrection.[27] In the apocryphal Corinthian correspondence, however, Paul learns in the letter from the Corinthians that there are those who are teaching that there is no bodily resurrection (I, 12), clearly a heretical idea as far as the text is concerned. In the apocryphal letter to the Corinthians, the apostle replies: "How much more will he raise you up, who have believed in Christ Jesus, as he himself was raised up" (III, 31). In this text, Christ himself does the raising (cf. III, 6, 16–18). The prospect of future resurrection is not simply a matter of faith and divine grace, for as the text says: "And whoever accepts this rule which we have received by the blessed prophets and the holy gospel, shall receive a reward" (III, 36). Something more than faith seems to be required. However, in the *Martyrdom of Paul*, following his beheading, the apostle is raised from the dead, just as he had promised, and Longus and Cestus come to faith because of having seen the miraculous resurrection of Paul. Pieter Lalleman writes: "Contrary to the *AThe*, in the *MP* it is faith that is the prerequisite for the resurrection, not chastity. It appears that in most other parts of the *AP* the believers' good works are a necessary addition to faith in gaining the resurrection. Among these works, chastity is the most important. The resurrection of the believers cannot be separated from that of Christ."[28]

In the epistle to the Corinthians (III, 4), the apocryphal writer echoes the words of 1 Cor 15:3: "For I delivered to you first of all what I received from the apostles before me who were always with Jesus Christ . . . (III, 4)." What follows this assertion is a kerygmatic summary that is strikingly like the summaries of the sermons in Acts, especially Acts 13:16–41.[29] If the apocryphal Corinthian correspondence was part of the original *Acts of Paul*

---

[25] Lalleman, "The Resurrection in the Acts of Paul," 126.
[26] Ibid., 127.
[27] Ibid., 131.
[28] Ibid., 132–33.
[29] Cf. also Acts 3:12–26.

tradition,[30] this similarity would seem to support the claim by Bauckham that the New Testament Corinthian letters were known and used by the author of the *Acts of Paul.* In its present context, this lengthy recitation, purporting to be from Paul to the Corinthians, is intended to refute those seeking to undermine the faith of the Christians in Corinth. In the face of a gnostic or spiritualizing heresy threatening the foundation of the church,[31] Paul appears as the defender of the true faith.[32] With the caveat that this section may not have been a part of the original tradition, the apocryphal letter of Paul to the Corinthians as it stands and the Pastoral letters converge in presenting the apostle as the guardian of true faith in the face of opponents who threaten to lead the church away from the correct path. In addition to the emphasis on bodily resurrection, a number of features of this summary reinforce the idea that this text was intended to refute some type of gnostic opposition: "Christ was born of Mary of the seed of David" (5), "came into this world to save all flesh by his own flesh" (6), "the Father created humans" (7), "almighty God maker of heaven and earth" (9), "almighty God, being just, and not wishing to repudiate his creation" (12), "by his own body Jesus Christ saved all flesh" (17), "in their unbelief claim that heaven and earth and all that is in them are not a work of God" (19), and the repeated emphasis on the flesh.

If it is the case that the opposition reflected in the apocryphal Corinthian correspondence is gnostic, it leaves open the possibility that this text originated as early as the middle part of the second century. The discussion above concerning Irenaeus' opposition to Gnosticism also confirms the possibility of this early dating.[33] Furthermore, it gives us a clue why interpreters have often dated the Pastoral Epistles well into the second century and have seen reflected in them a gnostic opposition. However, this argument can easily become circular. The Pastoral Epistles date from the second century, therefore they must reflect a gnostic opposition, which only reconfirms their later date. If in the case of 1 Timothy and Titus the opposition touches on Jewish torah issues, the Pastoral texts should be situated significantly closer theologically to the historical Paul than to the apocryphal *3 Corinthians.* This would also appear to be confirmed by the connections between the Pastorals and the letters of Ignatius, which may reflect docetic issues, but are characterized more accurately as early catholic rather than gnostic, and date from the early period of the second century.

Apart from the differences in genre between the Pastorals and the apocryphal *Acts of Paul,* perhaps the most dramatic difference in the theological patterns is the concern repeated in 1 Timothy and Titus for leadership in

---

[30] For a discussion of the textual tradition, see Luttikhuizen, "The Apocryphal Correspondence with the Corinthians," 75–78.

[31] See the so-called Letter of the Corinthians to the apostle Paul, I, 4–16.

[32] Luttikhuizen, "The Apocryphal Correspondence with the Corinthians," 91.

[33] See above, pp. 161–67.

the household of God. The subtext for this concern, of course, is the adaptation of cultural forms for the maintenance and building up of the church, the preservation of the truth, and the conforming of behavior to the author's vision of the gospel. In these two letters, less formal types of leadership are giving way to a more institutional pattern. Even though the Pastorals do not yet give evidence that church authority resides, strictly speaking, in the office of overseer, deacon, or elder, the concern for qualities appropriate for leadership indicates that the movement is in that direction. One of the conspicuous features of these texts is exhortation, whereby the readers are challenged to adhere to a way of living and believing appropriate for those in the household of God. The writer puts Paul's apostolic authority in the service of that message.

In the *Acts of Paul and Thecla*, a very different notion of authority and its manifestation comes into play. Perhaps best described as charismatic authority, Paul comes preaching his countercultural message, survives trial and tribulation, and travels from one place to the next doing wondrous things. Believing Paul's message and living the chaste life, Thecla too survives death by the miraculous intervention of God (represented by a rainstorm, a protective lioness, and other death defying adventures). God is clearly protecting Paul and Thecla, and from this divine protection derives a type of charismatic authority. In the case of Thecla, this authority has gender implications as women rally around her in Antioch. This has the effect of authenticating the Pauline gospel of chastity and of supporting those who suffer at the hands of people who react violently against such countercultural behavior.

If women were already in short supply in Greco-Roman society,[34] the demographic threat of women opting out of marriage was of more than casual interest to those who felt compelled to maintain society's well-being. This was serious business and those unwilling to fulfill their social obligations were a real threat to good social order.[35] For rebuffing the advances of Alexander, an influential citizen of Antioch, Thecla is guilty of sacrilege (Ἱερόσυλος), a term clearly indicating the interconnectedness of religion and societal well-being. The heavy hand of society, not surprisingly, could come down with a vengeance. The statement about women being saved through child bearing in 1 Tim 2:15 can be read as a community relating to society in precisely the opposite way. Bearing children and not bearing children provides an interesting contrast between the two traditions on the level of demographics and social stability. Such countercultural behavior as chastity benefited from having divine sanction and reward, even though it put the group advocating such conduct in social jeopardy. Institutional self-

----

[34] Or we might say, where women were in short supply this was a critical issue. See the discussion by Rodney Stark, *The Rise of Christianity* (San Francisco: Harper Collins, 1996), 103–11.

[35] See my article, "'Control' in Pauline Language and Culture: A Study of Rom 6," *NTS* 42 (1996): 86.

interest, as reflected in 1 Timothy and Titus, pushes the communities toward social conformity and approval, but communities inclined to resist society need some other form of authorization for their action. In the case of the *Acts of Paul and Thecla*, this authorization was rooted in Paul's apostolic authority and in the divine intervention to spare Thecla. If Sheila McGinn and Willi Braun are right,[36] the attempt to tame the story of Thecla can be seen already in the text and its redaction history, which only confirms the threat such traditions posed and the reactions they invited.

The *Acts of Paul* does not present the apostle as a founder of churches as such. He is an itinerant missionary and wonder worker. In the *Acts of Paul and Thecla*, he is not explicitly portrayed as the bearer of apostolic memory,[37] and the interpretation of Scripture is not apparent in the apocryphal text. If Bauckham is correct, the attempt to model the story on the pattern of the Acts of the Apostles may imply some link with an authoritative text, but notions of scriptural authority are not emphasized. In *3 Corinthians*, Paul's kerygma displays a traditional character as he rehearses images from the Old Testament, but here too these images are more limited than one might expect. Training oneself in the disciplines of the household of God is not part of the narrative world of the *Acts of Paul*. With the possible exception of *3 Corinthians*, Paul walks on a bigger stage in the apocryphal narratives and the simple domestic matters of church life in the main do not occupy him or the narrative. Across the stage of this entertaining story strides Paul the general, the Hebrew convert, the preacher, the martyr, the amiable human being, the ascetic, and the divine man, as Peter Dunn points out.[38] His heroic feats play out on a rather public stage, and likewise his demise takes place at the center of Roman power.

## CONCLUSION

In the Pauline heartland, very different perceptions of Paul and his teaching were being generated in the first two centuries of the church, and these rippled throughout Mediterranean Christainity to North Africa, Rome, and Gaul. Intersecting in subtle ways, the Pastoral Epistles and the *Acts of Paul* represent two remarkably poignant and divergent outgrowths of the Pauline legacy. The texts may be separated historically by as much as a century, but more importantly they illustrate two significant polarities or axes that shape Paul's legacy in the church. First, both the Pastoral Epistles and the *Acts of Paul* represent extensions of the Pauline tradition. This is seen in the Pastorals' representation of the apostle, as well as in the actual passing on of the tradition.

---

[36] Braun, "Physiotherapy of Femininity in the Acts of Thecla," 209–30; and McGinn, *The Acts of Thecla*, 800–806.

[37] More broadly in the *Acts of Paul*, *3 Corinthians* III, 4, may be a case where Paul is presented as a bearer of apostolic memory.

[38] Peter W. Dunn, "L'image de Paul dans les 'Actes de Paul,'" *Foi et Vie* 94 (Spring, 1995): 75–85.

This is the case both in the way Paul is portrayed and the way the letters substantively relate to the Pauline tradition.[39] The *Acts of Paul*, too, extend the tradition of Paul. Here, it appears Bauckham is right. Not only does the author(s) of the apocryphal acts in fact extend the Pauline tradition; the author intends to extend the tradition and to portray Paul on a continuum with that authoritative legacy. The author's use of the tradition may or may not involve literary dependence, but the attempt to complete the Pauline story surely implies a vantage point within the tradition. Use of Pauline authority requires that the author tap into the past tradition in order to extend it.

Second, the social situation of the author and the community determines in large measure how the tradition would be reshaped. As we have seen,[40] that is the case with 1 Timothy and Titus, notably in the way they use household imagery to represent godliness. On the other hand, the *Acts of Paul and Thecla* point to a countercultural situation most likely shaped by a community of women who sought places and roles in the church outside of traditional lines of authority. They are challenging the "natural" order of things and in turn inviting the wrath of traditional society on themselves and their community. Here, MacDonald's approach to the *Acts of Paul and Thecla* illustrates something important. While it seems highly questionable to argue that the Pastoral Epistles were written as a direct response in order to counter folk traditions that were mischaracterizing Paul, it seems quite likely that the story we know as the *Acts of Paul and Thecla* emerged among people, mostly especially women, who challenged traditional authority structures and bent the Pauline tradition to their cause. These may have been entertaining stories, but their effect was undoubtedly serious. In short, those without authority or status in the church, though some may have had a measure of both in society generally, were challenging the underbelly of the church's emerging patriarchal authority structure and the portrayal of the Pauline gospel. And this also fed into the church's martyrdom tradition, which in its own way had the potential to challenge Roman imperial power.

The Pastoral Epistles and the *Acts of Paul* turn on both of these axes. Their approaches to extending and/or contesting the Pauline tradition are dramatically different, but both engage on this level in a similar exercise. Despite differences in genre between the two sets of texts, these axes help us understand more clearly how to position the respective traditions in Paul's developing legacy in early Christianity. The issues common to both sets of texts are the roles of women, female sexuality, the resurrection, authority in the church, the nature of the faith, and divine power. Standing closer to Paul historically and theologically than the *Acts of Paul*, the Pastorals already foreshadow many of the issues that will reappear in the apocryphal tradition, but when they do reappear they do so in dramatically different forms reflecting very different social circumstances.

---

[39] See above, pp. 196–98.
[40] See above, pp. 61–63.

# ∾ 8 ∾

# SUMMARY AND CONCLUSION

THE THEOLOGICAL patterns generated by this discussion converge in support of the claim that the Pastoral Epistles were written most likely after Paul's death but before Ignatius of Antioch wrote his letters. These theological patterns are represented in the Pastorals by post-Pauline christological language and development (savior, epiphany, and mediator language), different and also more mature ecclesial concerns (the household of God and qualities appropriate for leadership roles), and more fully expressed notions of correct belief and truth (the "good deposit"). The Pastorals also represent a social context close enough in time to the historical Paul that the letters appearing in his name have credibility, even though their omission from some canonical and textual traditions ($\mathfrak{P}^{46}$, Codex Vaticanus) seems from an early date to call their authenticity into question. They also display only modest concern for Jew-Gentile matters with no apparent concern for the issue of Gentile inclusion, an issue that is a major one in in Romans and Galatians. Likewise, there is no compelling evidence for the direct gnostic opposition in these three letters that is seen in the undisputed Pauline letters. They represent an acute concern for issues related to Christian life in the late first-century empire and seemingly a different perspective from the undisputed Pauline epistles on the important place of women in the ministry of the church (cf. Gal 3:28). Ignatius' apparent echo of some Pastoral material (christological language and texts) suggests they were written before the bishop wrote his letters. Moreover, if 2 Timothy was written by a different author from 1 Timothy and Titus, this further supports the non-Pauline authorship of one or more of the three Pastoral Epistles. None of these considerations by themselves is sufficient to support the non-Pauline authorship of the Pastorals, but taken together they provide a preponderance of evidence to support the likelihood that Paul did not write some or all of these letters.

The primary point of this discussion, however, is not to make a claim about the Pauline or non-Pauline authorship of the Pastoral Epistles, but to achieve greater clarity about the place of the Pastorals and their theology in the developing Pauline tradition. Questions of authorship and dating, of course, affect this issue, but the argument here also moves well beyond these matters. Hence, we have argued for a bifocal approach where we position the Pastorals on a continuum that reflects and passes on the earlier Pauline tradition, as well as shapes and directs the subsequent Pauline legacy. The writer(s) of the Pastorals looked to the Pauline past and used a memory of the past to enact a version of the Pauline tradition in the present. In this functional way, the Pastoral writer(s) contributed to the development of the early church, even as he sought to combat various theological opponents.

Closely related in the early church are the ongoing transformation of Paul's theology and the development of his personal legacy, which included both his image and authority. In the Pastoral Epistles both of these features of Paul's legacy are evident. As we have argued, in the Pastoral letters Paul becomes the one who protects and passes on the "truth," establishes churches, identifies qualities for church leadership and implicitly for appropriate leaders in the church (e.g., the laying on of hands), transmits apostolic memory, defends church unity, and exhorts those in the church to proper behavior. Even more poignantly, the Pastorals portray theological concerns that both reflect and foreshadow critical issues that will occupy the church into the second and third centuries: the nature of the true faith, the church and its relationship to Judaism and the Jewish law, Christian asceticism, the problem of maintaining church unity in the face of disunity, the formation and function of Christian Scripture and tradition, the place of women in the community, and the role of church leaders in maintaining the faith and practice of the church. Even where the Pastorals do not elaborate a particular issue or perspective, they give us clues that suggest that certain concerns are afoot more broadly in the life of the community. We may think in particular of the issues surrounding the resurrection, slavery, eating certain foods, marrying, apostasy, false teachers leading the unsuspecting astray, gossip, and training in the way of righteousness.

Following the period of the New Testament, interest in Paul and his theology was clearly not limited to the gnostics. Paul's reputation flourished among many different groups in the early church, and his epistles were cited by influential church figures from the four corners of the Christian world: Asia Minor, Gaul, North Africa, and Egypt. His influence was pervasive, and his authority came to underwrite a variety of different interests, among them: concern for the unity of the church, different perceptions of correct belief and behavior, authoritative transmission of tradition, hierarchical leadership, martyrdom, chastity, and male and female roles in the church. The question was not whether Paul was authoritative, but how his authority would be reconstructed to address the pressing concerns and interests of a growing church. In this process, Paul's theology, the use of his epistles, and his charismatic persona were tightly interwoven in the development of his apostolic legacy, a legacy that during this period took many different forms.

Asia Minor was the Pauline heartland in the early church, and his legacy had special poignancy in this part of the Mediterranean world. First and Second Timothy, the letters of Ignatius and Polycarp, the Acts of the Apostles, and the *Acts of Paul and Thecla* all testify to this. Even more specifically, however, the church in Gaul also had links to Asia Minor through

Irenaeus, as did North Africa through Tertullian (via his interest in Montanism and his familiarity with *Thecla,* both expressions of early Christianity that were centered in Asia Minor). In Egypt, the influence of Philo and the Alexandrian Hellenists left their imprint on the thought of Clement and Origen in ways that distinguish them from their counterparts in Asia Minor and the western church. There are also indications that ecclesial development took different forms in Rome and Corinth than in Asia Minor, where episcopal development seems to have taken root earlier than at the imperial center. In short, the Pauline legacy displays a regional stamp, as different traditions, issues, and movements developed in different parts of the church.

The important post-New Testament writers who left theological legacies in their own right also represent particular places in the emerging institution of the church, and that fact also leaves its imprint on the Pauline perspective represented by them. We simply need to contrast the perspectives of Ignatius of Antioch and the writer of the *Acts of Paul and Thecla.* The contrasting social locations and circumstances of the two authors, both closely connected to the church in Asia Minor, resulted in very different portrayals of Paul, his gospel, and the character of the church. Furthermore, the form and function of their writings are profoundly different, suggesting quite different notions of how Paul was understood and his authority construed. Letters and stories not only represent different literary genres but they also have different functions. Social location and literary function both play a role in the use of Pauline material and the transformation of his legacy.

In his discussion of the rise of normative Christianity, Arland Hultgren summarizes four scholarly approaches to the development of the church: (1) truth preceded error, (2) heresy preceded orthodoxy, (3) fixed and flexible elements, and (4) diverse trajectories from the beginning.[1] The idea that "heretical" ideas may in fact be earlier than more "orthodox" formulations was argued vigorously by Walter Bauer in his influential book *Orthodoxy and Heresy in Earliest Christianity* published in the 1930's,[2] and this challenged the earlier assumption that "heresy" was largely a corruption of earlier "orthodox" theological concepts and practices. The notion of different trajectories was popularized in the early 1970's by James Robinson and Helmut Koester in their book, *Trajectories through Early Christianity.*[3] Perhaps one of the most enduring legacies of the dichotomy between "heresy" and "orthodoxy," no matter which way they relate to each other, is the dialectical approach to understanding Christian origins. Apart from any value judgments

---

[1] Arland J. Hultgren, *The Rise of Normative Christianity* (Minneapolis: Fortress, 1994), 7–18.

[2] Walter Bauer, *Orthodoxy and Heresy in Earliest Christianity* (trans. by Robert A. Kraft and Gerhard Krodel; Philadelphia: Fortress, 1971).

[3] James M. Robinson and Helmut Koester, *Trajectories through Early Christianity* (Philadelphia: Fortress, 1971).

implied in the terminology, this dialectical approach often goes hand in hand with a notion of conflict or struggle in early Christian development. We can see this most clearly in Elaine Pagel's work on the dialectic between Gnosticism and institutional development, and more recently in the work of Laura Nasrallah on the tension between prophecy and authority in the early church.[4] To be sure, there was conflict and struggle in the early church. But can early Christian development be reduced to any single instance of conflict or tension? Probably not, but neither can theological trajectories through early Christianity be so clearly identified that they portray fixed, precisely discernable lines of development.

In this light, a more complex and variegated approach to Christian origins is suggested by our look at Paul and the Pastoral Epistles. There are lines of development that do come into view in the way Paul's legacy developed in and through the Pastoral Epistles, just as there are identifiable tensions between competing elements, each attempting to define and shape the church. And there are those, among them the writer(s) of the Pastoral Epistles, who try to establish their notion of Christian truth. Yet, no single trajectory or polarity or notion of orthodoxy can capture this complexity by itself. Hence, we need to adopt what might be called a multiplex or multilayered approach to the development of early Christianity in general and Paul's legacy in particular. In this way, we will be able to plot in this material certain theological and ecclesial affinities that suggest lines of development, and we will be able to observe certain adversarial polarities that indicate conflict in the church. And without a doubt, the Pastorals represent an idea of theological truth to which the addressees and the audience are exhorted to conform in the service of church unity.

But these lines of development, conflicts, and ideas of Christian truth are not isolated from each other in the early church. They intersect in complex ways, sometimes in conflict with one another, at other times through adaptation or reinterpretation. Not until the consolidations of the fourth century and beyond do we see an effort to establish correct Christian belief and practice on a grand scale, an effort that was only partially successful in its own day and perhaps even less successful when tried in our time. Nevertheless, Paul, his theology, and letters have continued to shape, nourish, and reform the church from the first century to the twenty-first. To this day, his legacy continues to be transformed through Christian preaching and theology and through serious study of early Christian history. Virtually no one in Paul's day could have imagined the scope and pervasiveness of this legacy, let alone the speed and power with which it developed.

---

[4] Laura Nasrallah, *The Ecstasy of Folly: Prophecy and Authority in Early Christianity* (Cambridge, Mass.: Harvard University Press, 2003), 1–28; and Pagels, *Gnostic Paul*, 1–12.

# BIBLIOGRAPHY

Aageson, James W. "A Theoretical Context for Understanding 1 Cor 1:18–2:16." *Teaching at Concordia* 19 (1996–1997): 1–3.

———. *Written Also for Our Sake: Paul and the Art of Biblical Interpretation.* Louisville: Westminster John Knox, 1993.

———. "'Control' in Pauline Language and Culture: A Study of Rom 6." *New Testament Studies* 42 (1996): 75–89.

Achtemeier, Paul J. "An Elusive Unity: Paul, Acts, and the Early Church." *Catholic Biblical Quarterly* 48 (1986): 1–26.

———. *The Quest for Unity in the New Testament Church.* Philadelphia: Fortress, 1987.

Aymer, Margaret P. "Hailstorms and Fireballs: Redaction, World Creation, and Resistance in the Acts of Paul and Thecla." *Semeia* 79 (1997): 45–59.

Balch, David L. "Household Codes." Pages 25–50 in *Greco-Roman Literature and the New Testament: Selected Forms and Genres.* Edited by David E. Aune. Atlanta: Scholars Press, 1988.

———. *Let Wives Be Submissive: The Domestic Code in 1 Peter.* Society of Biblical Literature Monograph Series 26. Chico, Calif.: Scholars Press, 1981.

Bandstra, Andrew J. "Paul and an Ancient Interpreter: A Comparison of the Teaching of Redemption in Paul and Irenaeus." *Calvin Theological Journal* 5 (1970): 43–63.

Barnett, Albert E. *Paul Becomes a Literary Influence.* Chicago: University of Chicago Press, 1941.

Barrett, C. K. "Acts and the Pauline Corpus." *Expository Times* 88 (1976–1977): 2–5.

———. "The Acts of Paul." Pages 86–100 in *New Testament Essays.* London: SPCK, 1972.

Bassler, Jouette M. *1 Timothy, 2 Timothy, Titus.* Abingdon New Testament Commentaries. Nashville: Abingdon, 1996.

———. "A Plethora of Epiphanies: Christology in the Pastoral Letters." *Princeton Seminary Bulletin* 17, no. 3 (1996): 310–25.

Bauckham, Richard. "The Acts of Paul as a Sequel to Acts." Pages 105–52 in *The Book of Acts in Its Ancient Literary Setting.* Edited by Bruce W. Winter and Andrew D. Clarke. Vol. 1 of *The Book of Acts in Its First Century Setting.* Edited by Bruce W. Winter. Grand Rapids: Eerdmans, 1993.

Bauer, Walter. *Orthodoxy and Heresy in Earliest Christianity.* Translated by Robert A. Kraft and Gerhard Krodel. Philadelphia: Fortress, 1971.

Beker, J. Christiaan. *Heirs of Paul: Paul's Legacy in the New Testament and in the Church Today.* Minneapolis: Fortress, 1991.

Bevenot, Maurice. "Clement of Rome in Irenaeus's Succession List." *Journal of Theological Studies* 17 (1966): 98–107.

Blasi, Anthony J. *Making Charisma: The Social Construction of Paul's Public Image.* New Brunswick, N.J.: Transactions, 1991.

Bobertz, Charles A. "The Development of Episcopal Order." Pages 183–211 in *Eusebius, Christianity, and Judaism.* Edited by Harold W. Attridge and Gahei Hata. Detroit: Wayne State University Press, 1992.

Bollók, János. "The Description of Paul in the Acta Pauli." Pages 1–15 in *The Apocryphal Acts of Paul and Thecla.* Edited by Jan N. Bremmer. GA Kampen: Kok Pharos, 1996.

Borgen, Peder. "From Paul to Luke." *Catholic Biblical Quarterly* 31 (1964): 168–82.

Braun, Willi. "Physiotherapy of Feminism in the Acts of Thecla." Pages 209–30 in *Text and Artifact in the Religions of Mediterranean Antiquity: Essays in Honour of Peter Richardson.* Studies in Christianity and Judaism 9. Edited by Stephen G. Wilson and Michel Desjardins. Waterloo, Ont.: Wilfrid Laurier University Press, 2000.

Bremmer, Jan N. "Magic, Martyrdom, and Women's Liberation in the Acts of Paul and Thecla." Pages 36–59 in *The Apocryphal Acts of Paul.* Edited by Jan N. Bremmer. GA Kampen: Kok Pharos, 1996.

Brent, Allen. *Hippolytus and the Roman Church in the Third Century: Communities in Tension Before the Emergence of a Monarch-Bishop.* Supplements to Vigiliae Christianae 31. Leiden: E. J. Brill, 1995.

———. "The Ignatian Epistles and the Threefold Ecclesiastical Order." *Journal of Religious History* 17 (1992): 18–32.

Bromiley, Geoffrey W. "The Church Fathers and Holy Scripture." Pages 194–220 in *Scripture and Truth.* Edited by D. A. Carson and John D. Woodbridge. Grand Rapids: Zondervan, 1983.

Brooks, James A. "Clement of Alexandria as a Witness to the Development of the New Testament Canon." *Second Century* 9 (1992): 41–55.

Brown, Peter. *The Body and Society: Men, Women, and Sexual Renunciation in Early Christianity.* New York: Columbia University Press, 1988.

Buell, Denise Kimber. *Making Christians: Clement of Alexandria and the Rhetoric of Legitimacy.* Princeton: Princeton University Press, 1991.

Burke, Patrick. "Monarchical Episcopate at the End of the First Century." *Journal of Ecumenical Studies* 7 (1970): 499–518.

Burns, J. Patout. "The Holiness of the Churches." Pages 3–15 in *The Unbounded Community: Papers in Christian Ecumenism in Honor of Jaroslav Pelikan.* Edited by William Caferro and Duncan G. Fisher. New York: Garland, 1966.

Burrus, Virginia. *Chastity as Autonomy: Women in the Stories of Apocryphal Acts.* Studies in Women and Religion 23. Lewiston, N.Y.: Mellen, 1987.

Bush, P. G. "A Note on the Structure of 1 Timothy." *New Testament Studies* 36 (1990): 152–56.

Campbell, R. Alastair. "Identifying the Faithful Sayings in the Pastoral Epistles." *Journal for the Study of the New Testament* 54 (1994): 73–86.

Campenhausen, Hans von. *Ecclesiatical Authority and Spiritual Power in the Church of the First Three Centuries.* Translated by J. A. Baker. London: Adam and Charles Black, 1969.

———. *The Fathers of the Greek Church.* Translated and revised by L. A. Garrard. London: Adam and Charles Black, 1963.

———. "Polykarp von Smyrna und die Pastoralbriefe." Pages 197–301 in *Aus der Frühzeit des Christentums: Studien zur Kirchengeschichte des ersten und zweiten Jahrhunderts.* Tübingen: J. C. B. Mohr (Paul Siebeck), 1963.

Childs, Brevard S. *Biblical Theology of the Old and New Testaments: Theological Reflections on the Christian Bible.* Minneapolis: Fortress, 1992.

———. *The New Testament as Canon: An Introduction.* Philadelphia: Fortress, 1984.

Clarke, G. W. "Cyprian." Pages 1226–28 in vol. 1 of *The Anchor Bible Dictionary.* Edited by David Noel Freedman. 6 vols. New York: Doubleday, 1992.

Collins, Raymond F. *1 & 2 Timothy and Titus: A Commentary.* The New Testament Library. Louisville: Westminster John Knox, 2002.

———. "The Image of Paul in the Pastorals." *Laval Theologique et Philosophique* 31 (1975): 147–73.

———. *The Letters That Paul Did Not Write: The Epistle to the Hebrews and Pauline Pseudepigrapha.* Good News Studies 28. Wilmington, Del: Michael Glazier, 1988.

Conzelmann, Hans. *A Commentary on Acts of the Apostles.* Translated by James Limburg, A. Thomas Kraabel, and Donald H. Juel. Hermeneia. Philadelphia: Fortress, 1987.

Cook, David. "2 Timothy 4:6–8 and the Epistle to the Philippians." *Journal of Theological Studies* 33 (1982): 168–71.

Coolidge, John S. "The Pauline Basis of the Concept of Scriptural Form in Irenaeus." Pages 1–16 in *The Center for Hermeneutical Studies in Hellenistic and Modern Culture.* Edited by W. Wuellner. 8th Colloquy. Berkeley: The Center, November, 1973.

Cosgrove, Charles H. "Justin Martyr and the Emerging Christian Canon," *Vigiliae christianae* 36 (1982): 209–32.

Countryman, L. William. "Tertullian and the Regula Fidei." *Second Century* 2 (1982): 208–27.

Damian, Theodore. "The Unity of the Church in the Theology of St. Cyprian of Carthage and that of Karl Barth." *Patristic and Byzantine Review* 13 (1994): 87–107.

Daniel, Marguerat. "The Acts of Paul and the Canonical Acts: A Phenomenon of Reading," *Semeia* 80 (1997): 169–83.

Danielou, Jean. *The Theology of Jewish Christianity.* Chicago: Henry Regner, 1964.

Davies, Margaret. *The Pastoral Epistles.* Sheffield: Sheffield Academic Press, 1996.

DeBoer, Martinus C. "Comment: Which Paul." Pages 45–46 in *Paul and the Legacies of Paul.* Edited by William S. Babcock. Dallas: Southern Methodist University Press, 1990.

———. "Images of Paul in the Post Apostolic Period." *Catholic Biblical Quarterly* 42 (1980): 359–80.

Dehandschutter, Boudewijn. "Polycarp's Epistle to the Philippians: An Early Example of Reception." Pages 275–91 in *The New Testament in Early Christianity.* Edited by Jean-Marie Sevrin. Leuven: Leuven University Press, 1989.

Dibelius, Martin. *Studies in the Acts of the Apostles.* Translated by Mary Ling. London: SCM, 1956.

Dibelius, Martin, and Hans Conzelmann. *The Pastoral Epistles: A Commentary on the Pastoral Epistles.* Translated by Philip Buttolph and Adela Yarbro. Hermeneia. Philadelphia: Fortress, 1972.

Donelson, Lewis R. *Colossians, Ephesians, First and Second Timothy, and Titus.* Westminster Bible Companion. General editors Patrick D. Miller and David L. Bartlett. Louisville: Westminster John Knox, 1996.

———. *Pseudepigraphy and Ethical Argument in the Pastoral Epistles.* Tübingen: J. C. B. Mohr (Paul Siebeck), 1986.

———. "Studying Paul: 2 Timothy as Remembrance." Pages 715–31 in *Society of Biblical Literature Seminar Papers* 36. Atlanta: Scholars Press, 1997.

Donovan, Mary Ann. *One Right Reading: A Guide to Irenaeus.* Collegeville, Minn.: Liturgical, 1997.

Dunbar, David. "The Problem of Hippolytus of Rome: A Study in Historical Reconstruction." *Journal of the Evangelical Theological Society* 25 (1982): 63–74.

Dunn, James D. G. "The Theology of Galatians: The Issue of the Covenantal Nomism." Pages 125–46 in *Pauline Theology* 1. Edited by Jouette M. Bassler. Society of Biblical Literature Symposium Series 4. Minneapolis: Fortress, 1991.

———. *The Theology of Paul the Apostle.* Grand Rapids: Eerdmans, 1998.

Dunn, Peter W. "L'image de Paul dans les 'Actes de Paul.'" *Foi et Vie* 94 (1995): 75–85.

Elliott, J. K. *The Apocryphal New Testament: A Collection of Apocryphal Christian Literature in an English Translation.* Oxford: Clarendon, 1993.

Ellis, E. Earle. "Traditions in the Pastoral Epistles." Pages 237–53 in *Early Jewish and Christian Exegesis: Studies in Memory of William Hugh Brownlee.* Edited by Craig A. Evans and William F. Stinespring. Atlanta: Scholars Press, 1987.

Eno, Robert B. "Scripture and Tradition in Tertullian." Pages 13–31 in *The Quadrilog: Tradition and the Future of Ecumenism.* Edited by Kenneth Hagen. Collegeville, Minn.: Liturgical, 1994.

Farmer, William R. "Galatians and the Second-Century Development of the Regula Fidei." *Second Century* 4 (1984): 143–70.

Fee, Gordon D. *1 and 2 Timothy, Titus.* New International Bible Commentary on the New Testament. Peabody, Mass.: Hendrickson, 1988.

———. "Toward a Theology of 1 Corinthians." Pages 37–58 in *Pauline Theology* 2. Edited by David M. Hay. Society of Biblical Literature Symposium Series 4. Minneapolis: Fortress, 1993.

Fiore, Benjamin. *The Function of Personal Example in the Socratic and Pastoral Epistles.* Analecta biblica 105. Rome: Biblical Institute Press, 1986.

Fitzmyer, Joseph A. "The Structured Ministry of the Church in the Pastoral Epistles." *Catholic Biblical Quarterly* 66 (2004): 582–96.

Furnish, Victor. "Theology in 1 Corinthians." Pages 59–89 in *Pauline Theology* 2. Edited by David M. Hay 2. Society of Biblical Literature Symposium Series 4. Minneapolis: Fortress, 1993.

Gager, J. G. "Jews, Gentiles, and Synagogues in the Book of Acts." *Harvard Theological Review* 79 (1986): 91–99.

Gamble, H. "The Redaction of the Pauline Letters and the Formation of the Pauline Corpus." *Journal of Biblical Literature* 94 (1975): 403–18.

Gamble, Harry Y. "Canon." Pages 852–61 in vol. 1 of *The Anchor Bible Dictionary.* Edited by David Noel Freedman. 6 vols. New York: Doubleday, 2002.

Gaventa, Beverly Roberts. "The Singularity of the Gospel: A Reading of Galatians." Pages 147–59 in *Pauline Theology* 1. Edited by Jouette M. Bassler. Society of Biblical Literature Symposium Series 4. Minneapolis: Fortress, 1991.

Gnilka, Joachim. "Das Paulusbild im Kolosser-und Epheserbrief." Pages 179–93 in *Kontinuität und Einheit: Für Franz Musser.* Edited by Paul-Gerhard Müller and Werner Stenger. Freiburg: Herder, 1981.

Gorday, Peter ed. *Ancient Christian Commentary on Scripture.* Downers Grove, Ill.: InterVarsity, 2000.

Grant, Robert M. "The Description of Paul in Acts and Paul and Thecla." *Vigiliae christianae* 36 (1982): 1–4.

———. "Scripture and Tradition in St Ignatius of Antioch." *Catholic Biblical Quarterly* 25 (1963): 322–35.

Griggs, Roy. "Christ's Seemless Robe: A Study of Cyprian's Concept of the Unity of the Church." *Mid-Stream* 16 (1977): 399–411.

Guerra, Anthony J. "Polemical Christianity: Tertullian's Search for Certitude." *Second Century* 8 (1991): 109–23.

Haenchen, Ernst. *The Acts of the Apostles: A Commentary.* Translated by Bernard Noble and Gerald Shinn. Oxford: Basil Blackwell, 1971.

Hagner, Donald A. *The Use of the Old and New Testaments in Clement of Rome.* Supplements to Novum Testamentum 34. Leiden: E. J. Brill, 1973.

Halliburton, R. J. "Some Reflections on St. Cyprian's Doctrine of the Church." Pages 192–98 in *Studia patristica*. Edited by Elizabeth A. Livingstone 11. Oxford: Pergamon, 1972.

Hammond-Bammel, Caroline P. "Origen's Pauline Prefaces and the Chronology of His 'Pauline Commentaries.'" Pages 495–513 in *Origeniana Sexta: Origène et la Bible*. Leuven: Leuven University Press, 1995.

Hannah, Jack. "Ignatian Long Recension: Relationship to Pastorals in Household Rules." *Proceedings of the Eastern Great Lakes and Midwest Biblical Societies* 4 (1984): 153–65.

Hanson, A. T. *The Pastoral Letters: Commentary on the First and Second Letters to Timothy and the Letter to Titus*. Cambridge: Cambridge University Press, 1966.

———. "The Theology of Suffering in the Pastoral Epistles and Ignatius of Antioch." Pages 694–96 in *Studia patristica*. Edited by Elizabeth A. Livingstone 17. Oxford: Pergamon, 1982.

Hanson, R. P. C. *Allegory and Event: A Study of the Sources and Significance of Origen's Interpretation of Scripture*. Richmond, Va.: John Knox, 1959.

Harrison, P. N. *Polycarp's Two Epistles to the Philippians*. Cambridge: Cambridge University Press, 1936.

Hartman, L. "Some Unorthodox Thoughts on the 'Household-Code Form.'" Pages 219–32 in *The Social World of Formative Christianity and Judaism*. Edited by Jacob Neusner, Ernest S. Frerichs, Peder Borgen, and Richard Horsley. Philadelphia: Fortress, 1988.

Hayne, Leonie. "Thecla and the Church Fathers." *Vigiliae christianae* 48 (1994): 209–18.

Hedrick, Charles W. "Paul's Conversion/Call: A Comparative Analysis of the Three Reports." *Journal of Biblical Literature* 100 (1981): 415–32.

Hennecke, E. *New Testament Apocrypha*. 2 vols. Edited by W. Schneemelcher, trans. and ed. by R. McL. Wilson. Southhampton, Eng.: SCM, 1965.

Hilhorst, A. "Tertullian on the Acts of Paul." Pages 150–63 in *The Apocryphal Acts of Paul and Thecla*. Edited by Jan N. Bremmer. GA Kampen: Kok Pharos Publishing, 1996.

Hoek, Annewies van den. "Techniques of Quotation in Clement of Alexandria: A View of Ancient Literary Working." *Vigiliae christianae* 3 (1996): 223–43.

Hoffman, Daniel. "The Authority of Scripture and Apostolic Doctrine in Ignatius of Antioch." *Journal of the Evangelical Theological Society* 28 (1985): 71–79.

Howe, E. Margaret. "Interpretations of Paul in the Acts of Paul and Thecla." Pages 33–49 in *Pauline Studies: Essays Presented to F. F. Bruce on His 70th Birthday*. Edited by Donald A. Hagner and Murray J. Harris. Grand Rapids: Eerdmans, 1980.

Hultgren, Arland J. *The Rise of Normative Christianity*. Minneapolis: Fortress, 1994.

Hultgren, Arland J., and Roger Aus. *I, II Timothy, Titus and II Thessalonians.* Augsburg Commentary on the New Testament. Minneapolis: Augsburg, 1984. Jay. Eric G. "From Presbyter-Bishop to Bishops and Presbyters." *Second Century* 1 (1981): 125–62.

Jefford, Clayton N. "Household Codes and Conflict in the Early Church." Studia patristica 31 (1997): 121–27.

Jervis, Ann L. "Paul and the Poet in First Timothy." *Catholic Biblical Quarterly* 61 (1999): 695–712.

Johnson, Luke Timothy. *The First and Second Letters to Timothy.* Anchor Bible 35A. General editors William Foxwell Albright and David Noel Freedman. New York: Doubleday, 2001.

———. *Letters to Paul's Delegates: 1 Timothy, 2 Timothy, Titus.* The New Testament in Context. Valley Forge: Trinity, 1996.

———. "Oikonomia Theou: The Theological Voice of 1 Timothy From the Perspective of Pauline Authorship." *Horizons in Bible Theology* 21 (1999): 87–104.

Karris, Robert J. *The Pastoral Epistles.* New Testament Message 17. Wilmington, Delaware: Michael Glazier, 1979.

Kaufman, Peter Iver. "Tertullian on Heresy, History, and the Reappropriation of Revelation." *Church History* 60 (1991): 167–79.

Kelly, J. N. D. *A Commentary on the Pastoral Epistles: I Timothy, II Timothy, Titus.* Harper's New Testament Commentaries. New York: Harper and Row, 1963.

Kereszty, Roch. "The Unity of the Church in the Theology." *Second Century* 4 (1984): 202–18.

Knight, George W. III. *The Pastoral Epistles: A Commentary on the Greek Text.* The New International Greek Testament Commentary. Grand Rapids: Eerdmans, 1992.

Knoch, Otto. "Petrus und Paulus in Den Scriften der Apostolischen Veeter." Pages 240–60 in *Kontinuitaet in Kontinuität und Einheit: Für Franz Musser.* Edited by Paul-Gerhard Müller and Werner Stenger. Freiburg: Herder, 1981.

Koester, Helmut. *Introduction to the New Testament.* 2 Vols. New York and Berlin: de Gruyter, 1982.

———. *Synoptische Überlieferung bei Den Apostolischen Vatern.* Berlin: Academie Verlag, 1957.

Lalleman, Pieter J. "The Resurrection in the Acts of Paul." Pages 126–41 in *The Apocryphal Acts of Paul and Thecla.* Edited by Jan N. Bremmer. GA Kampen, The Netherlands: Kok Pharos Publishing, 1996.

Lampe, Peter. *From Paul to Valentinus: Christians at Rome in the First Two Centuries.* Translated by Michael Steinhauser. Edited by Marshall D. Johnson. Minneapolis: Fortress, 2003.

Layton, Richard A. "Recovering Origen's Pauline Exegesis: Exegesis and Eschatology in the Commentary on Ephesians." *Journal of Early Christian Studies* 8 (2000): 373–411.

Lentz, John Clayton Jr. *Luke's Portrait of Paul.* Society for New Testament Monograph Series 77. Cambridge: Cambridge University Press, 1993.

Lincoln, A. T. *Ephesians.* Word Bible Commentary 42. Dallas: Word Books, 1990.

———. "The Household Code and Wisdom Mode of Colossians." *Journal for the Study of the New Testament* 74 (1999): 93–112.

Lindemann, Andreas. "Paul in the Writings of the Apostolic Fathers." Pages 25–45 in *Paul and the Legacies of Paul.* Edited by William S. Babock. Dallas: Southern Methodist University Press, 1990.

———. *Paulus im ältesten Christentum: Das Bild des Apostels und die Rezeption der paulinischen Theologie in der frühchristlichen Literatur bis Marcion.* Beiträge zur historischen Theologie 58. Tübingen: J. C. B. Mohr (Paul Siebeck), 1979.

Lohfink, Gerhard. "Paulinische Theologie in der Rezeption der Pastoralbriefe." Pages 70–121 in *Paulus in den Neutestamentlichen Spätschriften: zur Paulusrezeption im Neuen Testament.* Quaestiones disputatae 89. Freiburg: Herder, 1981.

Lohse, Eduard. *A Commentary on the Epistles to the Colossians and to Ephesians.* Translated by William R. Poehlmann and Robert J. Karris. Hermeneia. Philadelphia: Fortress, 1971.

Louw, Johannes P. and Eugene A. Nida, eds. *Greek English Lexicon of the New Testament Based on Semantic Domains,* 2 vols. 2nd ed. New York: United Bible Societies, 1988–1989.

Lull, David J. "'The Law Was Our Pedagogue': A Study of Galatians 3:19–25." *Journal of Biblical Literature* 105 (1986): 481–98.

Luttikhuizen, Gerard. "The Apocryphal Correspondence with the Corinthians and the Acts of Paul." Pages 75–91 in *The Apocryphal Acts of Paul and Thecla.* Edited by Jan N. Bremmer. GA Kampen, The Netherlands: Kok Pharos, 1996.

MacDonald, Dennis R. *The Legend and the Apostle: The Battle for Paul in Story and Canon.* Louisville: Westminster John Knox, 1983.

MacDonald, Margaret Y. *The Pauline Churches: A Socio-Historical Study of Institutionalization in Pauline and Deutero-Pauline Writings.* Society for New Testament Series Monograph Series 60. Cambridge: Cambridge University Press, 1988.

———. "Rereading Paul: Early Interpretation of Paul on Women and Gender." Pages 236–53 in *Women and Christian Origins.* Edited by Ross Shepard Kraemer and Mary Rose D'Angelo. New York: Oxford University Press, 1999.

MacMullen, Ramsay. *Roman Social Relations: 50 B.C. to A.D. 284.* New Haven: Yale University Press, 1974.

Maier, Harry O. *The Social Setting of the Ministry as Reflected in the Writings of Hermas, Clement and Ignatius.* Dissertations SR 1. Waterloo, Ont.: Wilfrid Laurier University Press, 1991.

Malherbe, Abraham J. "Response to Raymond Collins, Donald Hagner, Bonnie Thurston." Paper presented at the annual meeting of the Society of Biblical Literature, Orlando, Fla., November 22, 1998.

Marshall, I. Howard. "Recent Study of the Pastoral Epistles." *Them* 23 (1997): 3–21.

———. "Salvation, Grace, and Works in the Later Writings in the Pauline Corpus." *New Testament Studies* 42 (1996): 339–58.

Martyn, J. Louis. "Events in Galatia: Modified Covenantal Nomism Versus God's Invasion of the Cosmos in the Singular Gospel: A Response to J. D. G. Dunn and B. R. Gaventa." Pages 160–79 in *Pauline Theology* 1. Edited by Jouette M. Bassler. Society of Biblical Literature Symposium Series 4. Minneapolis: Fortress, 1991.

Mayer, Herbert T. "Clement of Rome and His Use of Scripture." *The Concordia Theological Monthly* 42 (1971): 536–40.

McCue, James. "Bishops, Presbyters, and Priests in Ignatius of Antioch." *Theological Studies* 28 (1967): 828–34.

———. "Roman Primacy in the 2nd Century and the Problem of the Development of Dogma." *Theological Studies* 25 (1964): 161–96.

McGinn, Sheila E. "The Acts of Thecla." Pages 800–28 in *Searching the Scriptures: A Feminist Commentary*. 2 vols. Edited by Elisabeth Schüssler Fiorenza. New York: Crossroads, 1994.

Meier, J. P. "The Inspiration of Scripture: But What Counts as Scripture." *Mid-Stream* 38 (1999): 71–78.

Miller, James D. *The Pastoral Letters as Composite Documents*. Society for New Testatment Studies Monograph Series 93. Cambridge: Cambridge University Press, 1997.

Mitchell, Margaret M. " 'Speaking of God as He Was Able': A Response to Luke Timothy Johnson and Jerry L. Sumney." *Horizons in Biblical Theological* 21 (1999): 124–39.

Murphy-O'Connor, Jerome. *Paul: A Critical Life*. Oxford: Oxford University Press, 1997.

Nasrallah, Laura. *The Ecstasy of Folly: Prophecy and Authority in Early Christianity*. Cambridge, Mass.: Harvard University Press, 2003.

Neymeyr, U. "Episkopoi bei Clemens von Alexandrien." Studia patristica 26 (1993): 292–95.

Neyrey, Jerome H. *Paul in Other Words: A Cultural Reading of His Letters*. Louisville: Westminster John Knox, 1990.

Nida, Eugene A. *Componential Analysis of Meaning: An Introduction to Semantic Structures*. The Hague: Mouton, 1975.

———. *Exploring Semantic Structures*. International Library of General Linguistics 11. Munich: Wilhelm Fink, 1975.

Nielsen, Charles Meritt. "Polycarp, Paul, and the Scriptures." *Anglican Theological Review* 47 (1965): 199–216.

Noormann, Rolf. *Irenäus als Paulusinterpret: Zur Rezeption und Wirkung der paulinischen und deuteropaulinischen Briefe im Werk des Irenäus von Lyon.*

Wissenschaftliche Untersuchungen zum Neuen Testamentum 2. Tübingen: J. C. B. Mohr (Paul Siebeck), 1994.

Norris, Richard A. "Theology and Language in Irenaeus of Lyon." *Anglican Theological Review* 76 (1994): 285–95.

———. "The Transcendence and Freedom of God: Irenaeus, the Greek Tradition and Gnosticism." Pages 87–100 in *Early Christian Literature and the Classical Intellectual Tradition.* Edited by William R. Schoedel and Robert L. Wilken. Paris: Editions Beauchesne, 1979.

———. "Irenaeus' Use of Paul in His Polemics Against the Gnostics." Pages 79–98 in *Paul and the Legacies of Paul.* Edited by William S. Babcock. Dallas: Southern Methodist Univeristy Press, 1990.

Oberlinner, Lorenz. "Die 'Epiphaneia' des Heilswillen Gottes in Christus Jesus: Zur Grundstruktur der Christologie der Pastoralbriefe." *Zeitschrift für die neutestamentliche Wissenschaft und die Kunde der ältern Kirche* 71 (1980): 192–213.

Oden, Thomas C. *First and Second Timothy and Titus, A Bible Commentary for Teaching and Preaching.* Louisville: John Knox , 1989.

Osborn, Eric F. "The Bible and Christian Morality in Clement of Alexandria." Pages 112–30 in *The Bible in Greek Christian Antiquity.* Edited by Paul M. Blowers. Notre Dame, Ind.: University of Notre Dame Press, 1997.

———. "Clement and the Bible." Pages 121–32 in *Origeniana Sexta: Origène et la Bible.* Leuven: Leuven University Press, 1995.

———. *Justin Martyr.* Beiträge zur historischen Theologie 47. Tübingen: J. C. B. Mohr (Paul Siebeck), 1973.

———. "Reason and the Rule of Faith in the Second Century A.D." Pages 40–61 in *The Making of Orthodoxy: Essays in Honour of Henry Chadwick.* Edited by Rowan Williams. Cambridge: Cambridge University Press, 1989.

Pagels, Elaine H. *The Gnostic Paul: Gnostic Exegesis of the Pauline Letters.* Philadelphia: Fortress, 1975.

Paget, James Carleton. "Paul and the Epistle of Barnabas." *Novum Testamentum* 38 (1996): 359–81.

Patterson, L. G. "The Divine Became Human: Irenean Themes in Clement." Studia patristica 31 (1997): 497–516.

Perkins, Pheme. "Paul, Apocalypse of." Pages 203–4 in vol. 5 of *The Anchor Bible Dictionary.* Edited by David Noel Freedman. 6 vols. New York: Doubleday, 2002.

———. "Philippians: Theology for the Heavenly Politeuma." Pages 89–104 in *Pauline Theology*1. Edited by Jouette M. Bassler. Society of Biblical Literature Symposium Series 4. Minneapolis: Fortress, 1991.

Pervo, Richard I. *Luke's Story of Paul.* Minneapolis: Fortress, 1990.

———. *Profit with Delight: The Literary Genre of the Acts of the Apostles.* Philadelphia: Fortress, 1987.

Petersen, Norman R. *Rediscovering Paul: Philemon and the Sociology of Paul's Narrative World.* Philadelphia: Fortress, 1985.

Porter, Stanley E. *Paul in Acts.* Library of Pauline Studies. Peabody, Mass.: Hendrickson, 2001.

———. "What Does It Mean to Be 'Saved' by Childbirth' (1 Timothy 2:15)." *Journal for the Study of the New Testament* 49 (1993): 87–102.

Potworowski, Christophe F. "The Question of Truth (ἀλήθεια) in the Hermeneutics of Origen and Paul Ricoeur." Studia patristica 26 (1993): 308–12.

Price, Robert M. "The Evolution of the Pauline Canon." *Hervomde Teologiese Studies* 53 (1997): 36–65.

Prior, Michael. *Paul the Letter-Writer: And the Second Letter to Timothy.* Journal for the Study of the New Testament Supplement Series 23. Sheffield: JSOT Press, 1989.

Quasten Johannes. *Patrology.* 4 vols. Utrecht-Antwerp: Spectrum, 1964–1986.

Quinn, Jerome D., and William C. Wacker. *The First and Second Letters to Timothy.* The Eerdmans Critical Commentary. Grand Rapids: Eerdmans, 2000.

Rankin, David. *Tertullian and the Church.* Cambridge: Cambridge University Press, 1995.

———. "Tertullian's Use of the Pastoral Epistles in His Doctrine of Ministry." *Australian Biblical Review* 32 (1984): 18–37.

Reist, Irwin. "The Christology of Irenaeus." *Journal of the Evangelical Theological Society* 13 (1970): 241–51.

Robeck, Cecil M. "Canon, 'Regula Fidei,' and Continuing Revelation in the Early Church." Pages 65–91 in *Church, Word, and Spirit: Historical and Theological Essays in Honor of Geoffrey W. Bromiley.* Edited by James E. Bradley and Richard A. Muller. Grand Rapids: Eerdmans, 1987.

Robinson, James M. and Helmut Koester. *Trajectories through Early Christianity.* Philadelphia: Fortress, 1971.

Roetzel, Calvin. *Paul: The Man and the Myth.* Minneapolis: Fortress, 1999.

Rordorf, Willy. "Nochmals: Paulusakten und Pastoralbriefe." Pages 319–25 in *Tradition and Interpretation in the New Testament: Essays in Honor of E. Earle Ellis for His 60th Birthday.* Edited by Gerald F. Hawthorne and Otto Betz. Grand Rapids: Eerdmans, 1987.

———. "Tradition and Composition in the *Acts of Thecla*: The State of the Question," *Semeia* 38 (1986): 43–52.

Sandmel, Samuel. "Parallelomania." *Journal of Biblical Literature* 81 (1962): 1–13.

———. "Tradition and Composition in the Acts of Thecla: The State of the Question." *Semeia* 38 (1986): 43–52.

Scalise, Charles J. "Origen and the 'Sensus Literalis.'" Pages 117–29 in *Origen of Alexandria: His World and His Legacy.* Edited by Charles Kannengiesser and William L. Peterson. Notre Dame, Ind.: University of Notre Dame Press, 1988.

Schoedel, William R. *Ignatius of Antioch: A Commentary on the Letters of Ignatius.* Hermeneia. Philadelphia: Fortress, 1985.

———. "Polycarp of Smyrna and Ignatius." Pages 272–358 in *Principat.* Volume 2 of *Aufstieg und Niedergang der römischen Welt.* Edited by H. Temporini, W. Haase, and J. Vogt. Berlin and New York: de Gruyter, 1993, 27:1.

Schwartz, Daniel R. "The End of the Line: Paul in the Canonical Books of Acts." Pages 3–24 in *Paul and the Legacies of Paul.* Edited by William S. Babcock. Dallas: Southern Methodist University Press, 1990.

Segal, Alan F. *Paul the Convert: The Apostolate and Apostasy of Saul the Pharisee.* New Haven and London: Yale University Press, 1990.

Sider, Robert D. "Literary Artifice and the Figure of Paul in the Writings of Tertullian." Pages 99–120 in *Paul and the Legacies of Paul.* Edited by William S. Babcock. Dallas: Southern Methodist University Press, 1990.

Siker, Jeffrey S. *Disinheriting the Jews: Abraham in Early Christian Controversy.* Louisville: Westminster John Knox, 1991.

Smith, Jonathan Z. *Drudgery Divine: On the Comparison of Early Christianities and the Religions of Late Antiquity.* Chicago: University of Chicago Press, 1990.

Sobosan, Jeffrey G. "The Role of the Presbyter: An Introduction Into the Adversus Haereses of Saint Irenaeus." *Scottish Journal of Theology* 27 (1974): 129–46.

Standhartinger, Angela. "The Origin and Intention of the Household Code in the Letter to the Colossians." *Journal for the Study of the New Testament* 79 (2000): 117–30.

Stanton, Graham. "Other Early Christian Writings: 'Didache,' Ignatius, 'Barnabas,' Justin Martyr." Pages 174–90 in *Early Christian Thought in Its Jewish Context.* Edited by John Barclay and John Sweet. Cambridge: Cambridge University Press, 1996.

Stark, Rodney. *The Rise of Christianity.* San Francisco: HarperCollins, 1996.

Steinhauser, Kenneth B. "Authority in the Primitive Church." *Patristic and Byzantine Review* 3 (1984): 89–100.

Stendahl, Krister. "Paul Among Jews and Gentiles." Pages 1–7 in *Paul among Jews and Gentiles, and Other Essays.* Philadelphia: Fortress, 1976.

Story, Cullen I. K. "The Christianity of Ignatius of Antioch." *Evangelical Quaterly* 56 (1984): 173–82.

Stowers, Stanley K. "Social Status, Public Speaking, and Private Teaching: The Circumstance of Paul's Preaching." *Novum Testamentum* 26 (1984): 59–82.

———. "Friends and Enemies in the Politics of Heaven: Reading Theology in Philippians." Pages 105–21 in *Pauline Theology* 1. Society of Biblical Literature Symposium Series 4. Edited by Jouette M. Bassler. Minneapolis: Fortress, 1991.

Sumney, Jerry L. "Those Who 'Ignorantly Deny Him': The Opponents of Ignatius of Antioch." *Journal of Early Christian Studies* 1 (1993): 345–65.

———. "'God Our Savior': The Fundamental Operational Theological Assertion of 1 Timothy." *Horizons in Biblical Theology* 21 (1999): 105–23.

———. *'Servants of Satan,' 'False Brothers,' and Other Opponents of Paul.* Journal for the Study of the New Testament: Supplement Series 188. Sheffield: Sheffield Academic Press, 1999.

Torjesen, Karen Jo. *Hermeneutical Procedure and Theological Method in Origen's Exegesis.* Patristische Texte und Studien. Berlin: de Gruyter, 1986.

Torrance, T. F. "The Deposit of Faith." *Scottish Journal of Theology* 36 (1983): 1–28.

Towner, Philip H. *The Goal of Our Instruction: The Structure of Theology and Ethics in the Pastoral Epistles.* Journal for the Study of the New Testament Supplement Series 34. Sheffield: Sheffield Academic Press, 1989.

———. "Pauline Theology or Pauline Tradition in the Pastoral Epistles: The Question of Method." *Tyndale Bulletin* 46 (1995): 291–300.

Trakatellis, Bishop Demetrios. "God Language in Ignatius of Antioch." Pages 422–30 in *The Future of Early Christianity: Essays in Honor of Helmut Koester.* Edited by Birger A. Pearson, A. T. Kraabel, and George Nickelsburg. Minneapolis: Fortress, 1991.

Trevett, Christine. *A Study of Ingatius of Antioch in Syria and Asia.* Studies in the Bible and Early Christianity. Lewiston, N.Y.: Mellen, 1992.

Trigg, Joseph. "Origen." Pages 42–48 in vol. 5 of *The Anchor Bible Dictionary.* 6 vols. Edited by David Noel Freedman. New York: Doubleday, 2002.

Trummer, Peter. *Die Paulustradition der Pastoralbriefe.* Beiträge zur biblischen Exegese Theologie 8. Frankfurt: Peter Lang, 1978.

Tugwell, Simon. *The Apostolic Fathers.* Outstanding Christian Thinkers. Harrisburg, Pa.: Morehouse, 1989.

Vallée, Gérard. *A Study in Anti-Gnostic Polemics: Irenaeus, Hippolytus, Epiphanius.* Studies in Christianity and Judaism. Waterloo, Ont.: Wilfrid Laurier University Press, 1981.

Verner, David C. *The Household of God: The Social World of the Pastoral Epistles.* Society of Biblical Literature Dissertation Series 71. Chico, Calif.: Scholars Press, 1983.

Walton, Steve. "The State They Were In: Luke's View of the Roman Empire." Pages 1–41 in *Rome in the Bible and the Early Church.* Edited by Peter Oakes. Carlisle, UK: Paternoster, 2002.

Wehn, Beate. "'Blessed Are the Bodies of Those Who Are Virgins': Reflections on the Image of Paul in Acts of Thecla." *Journal for the Study of the New Testament* 79 (2000): 149–64.

Weinrich, William. "The Concept of the Church in Ignatius of Antioch." Pages 137–50 in *Good News in History: Essays in Honor of Bo Reicke.* Edited by L. Miller. Atlanta: Scholars Press, 1993.

Wieland, George M., *The Significance of Salvation: A Study of Salvation Language in the Pastoral Epistles.* Paternoster Biblical Monographs; Milton Keynes, U.K.: Paternoster, 2006.

Wiles, Maurice F. *The Divine Apostle: The Interpretation of St. Paul's Epistles.* Cambridge: Cambridge University Press, 1967.

———. "The Theological Legacy of St. Cyprian." *Journal of Ecclesiastical History* 14 (1963): 139–49.

Wilson, Stephen G. *Luke and the Pastoral Epistles.* London: SPCK, 1979.

Wolfe, B. Paul. "Scripture in the Pastoral Epistles: Premarcion Marcionism." *Perspectives in Religious Studies* 16 (1989): 5–16.

Woszink, J. H. "Tertullian's Principles and Method's of Exegesis." Pages 65–91 in *Early Classical Christian Literature and the Classical Intellectual Tradition.* Edited by William R. Schoedel and Robert L. Wilken. Paris: Editions Beauchesne, 1979.

Young, Frances. *The Theology of the Pastoral Letters.* New Testament Theology. Cambridge: Cambridge University Press, 1994.

# INDEX OF MODERN AUTHORS

# INDEX OF SUBJECTS

# Index of Ancient Sources